P9-ARK-196

KENNEDY'S QUEST FOR VICTORY

KENNEDY'S QUEST FOR VICTORY

American Foreign Policy, 1961–1963

EDITED BY
Thomas G. Paterson

New York   Oxford
OXFORD UNIVERSITY PRESS
1989

Oxford University Press

Oxford   New York   Toronto
Delhi   Bombay   Calcutta   Madras   Karachi
Petaling Jaya   Singapore   Hong Kong   Tokyo
Nairobi   Dar es Salaam   Cape Town

Melbourne   Auckland
and associated companies in
Berlin   Ibadan

Published by Oxford University Press, Inc.,
200 Madison Avenue, New York, New York 10016
Oxford is a registered trademark of Oxford University Press

Library of Congress Cataloging-in-Publication Data
Kennedy's quest for victory: American foreign policy, 1961–1963 /
edited by Thomas G. Paterson.
p. cm.   Bibliography: p.   Includes index.
Contents: Introduction: John F. Kennedy's quest for victory and
the global crisis / Thomas G. Paterson—The pursuit of Atlantic
community / Frank Costigliola—Defending hegemony / William S.
Borden—When push came to shove / J.L. Granatstein—Controlling
revolutions / Stephen G. Rabe—Fixation with Cuba / Thomas G.
Paterson—From even-handed to empty-handed / Douglas Little—
Clinging to containment / James Fetzer—Choosing sides in south
Asia / Robert J. McMahon—The failed search for victory / Lawrence J. Bassett and
Stephen E. Pelz—New frontiers and old priorities / Thomas J. Noer
—Passing the torch and lighting fires / Gary May.
ISBN 0-19-504585-8   ISBN 0-19-504584-X (pbk)
1. United States—Foreign relations—1961–1963. 2. Kennedy, John
F. (John Fitzgerald), 1917–1963. I. Paterson, Thomas G., 1941– .
E841.K466 1989
973.922'092'4—dc19   88-22739   CIP

9 8 7 6 5 4 3 2

Printed in the United States of America

For teachers who stimulated, tolerated, and encouraged—
Hans Heilbronner, David Long, Richard Abrams, and Armin Rappaport

Preface

In the quarter-century since John F. Kennedy's death in that chilling November of 1963, studies of the man and his presidency have proliferated. Friends, family, and assistants have dominated the writing on Kennedy and his administration through a host of biographies, memoirs, and oral history interviews. Journalists have also offered approving yet revealing portraits of the President and his times. Although scholars have long been intrigued by the Kennedy presidency, their works, until several years ago, lacked research in archival documents—the mass of memoranda, notes, minutes, telegrams, letters, reports, and the like generated by the Kennedy team as it made its decisions.

Many of the historical documents created in the early 1960s have now become available at American libraries—opened by participants themselves or through declassification under the Freedom of Information Act and under the mandatory review procedures of the presidential libraries, including the John F. Kennedy Library in Boston. Some records and personal papers for the Kennedy years remain security-classified or closed by family or individual request. Historians must do their reconstructing without all the parts. Some materials, such as those initiated by the Central Intelligence Agency, may never be released to scholars; other papers, such as Robert F. Kennedy's diaries, although researched by at least one memoirist-biographer in the 1970s, Arthur M. Schlesinger, Jr., may continue to rest in family hands, beyond the reach of historians for some time to come. Still, the history of the Kennedy years no longer needs to be left to memoirists, favored biographers, journalists, or sensationalists. As the chapters in this book demonstrate, important documentation exists to permit a searching reassessment of John F. Kennedy, his foreign policy, and his times.

Each chapter in this book addresses several questions: What were Kennedy's primary foreign policy assumptions and objectives and how did he come by them? What problems and policies did he inherit from the Eisenhower Administration? What role did domestic politics, the international system, and personality have in shaping his decisions? What tools or instruments of power did he have at his command in order to pursue his policies? How did he and his advisers go about making and implementing their decisions? How well did they meet their goals? And, finally, what were the costs and consequences of Kennedy policies—what is the Kennedy legacy?

The authors thank the staffs of the John F. Kennedy Library, Dwight D. Eisenhower Library, Lyndon B. Johnson Library, and the many other depositories cited in the endnotes. For his chapter on economic foreign policy, William Borden acknowledges the assistance of Thomas McCormick and Thomas Good. Frank Costigliola thanks Walter LaFeber, Werner Link, David A. Rosenberg, Detlef Junker, the National Endowment for the Humanities, the Lyndon B. Johnson Foundation, and the University of Rhode Island Alumni Association Faculty Development Fund for helping him prepare his chapter on the Atlantic alliance. James Fetzer appreciates the financial assistance he received from the Maritime College Foundation to complete his contribution on China. Douglas Little is grateful for grants from the National Endowment for the Humanities, the American Historical Association, and the Clark University Faculty Development Fund, which supported research for his chapter on the Middle East. Gary May acknowledges the financial assistance of the American Historical Association and the University of Delaware and, for papers and interviews, Peace Corps Volunteers Marian Haley Beil, Linda Bergthold, John Coyne, Peter Gessell, Ron Kazarian, Paul Koprowski, Lynn Linman, Mary Lou Linman, Anne Martin (pseudonym), John Rex, Carol Miller Reynolds, Robert Savage, and Martha Stonequist. For interviews, May thanks Harris Wofford and William Josephson.

For his chapter on South Asia, Robert McMahon expresses his gratitude to Melvyn Leffler, Gary Hess, and Dennis Merrill. Mc-

Mahon also appreciates financial assistance from the National Endowment for the Humanities, the Lyndon B. Johnson Foundation, and the Division for Sponsored Research at the University of Florida. Thomas Noer thanks the John F. Kennedy Foundation for a grant-in-aid to facilitate his research on Africa. Lawrence Bassett and Stephen Pelz thank the following for comments on earlier versions of their chapter on Vietnam: Dorothy Borg, Waldo Heinrichs, Michael Hunt, George Kahin, Richard Minear, and James W. Morley. Pelz also acknowledges financial support from the National Fellows Program of the Hoover Institution, the International Security Studies Program of the Woodrow Wilson International Center for Scholars, and the East Asian Institute, Columbia University. Stephen Rabe recognizes Karen O. Garner for her helpful criticisms of an earlier draft of his chapter on Latin America.

Thomas G. Paterson appreciates research support from the National Endowment for the Humanities, the Institute for the Study of World Politics, the American Philosophical Society, the Lyndon B. Johnson Foundation, and the University of Connecticut Foundation. He is also grateful to the following for suggestions or readings of drafts of his chapter on Cuba: Jules Benjamin, J. Garry Clifford, Peter H. Crooks, Raymond Garthoff, George H. Herring, Elizabeth Mahan, Rufus Miles, Stephen Streeter, Lucien Vandenbroucke, and Richard Welch. For research help, Paterson thanks Barney J. Rickman III, Laura Grant, Rodney Scudder, and the National Security Archive (Washington, D.C.).

For the index, the authors thank Alexandra L. Weir. Our editors at Oxford, Sheldon Meyer, Stephanie Sakson-Ford, and Rachel Toor, are gratefully acknowledged for their help.

The views expressed in this volume of original essays are those of the authors and do not necessarily reflect the opinions of the institutions and individuals who so generously assisted them.

Storrs, Connecticut   T.G.P.
June 1988

Contents

The Authors

Lawrence J. Bassett is a doctoral student in History at the University of Massachusetts, Amherst, where he received his Master's degree. He earned his Bachelor of Arts degree from Franklin and Marshall College. He served as an editorial assistant for Lewis Hanke's *Guide to the Study of United States History outside the U.S.* (1985).

William S. Borden is the author of *The Pacific Alliance: Japan and United States Foreign Economic Policy, 1947–1955* (1984). He received his doctorate from the University of Wisconsin, Madison, and is now Project Manager at Mathematica Policy Research, Inc., Princeton, New Jersey, where he heads a project for the United States Department of Labor to design and create the first comprehensive database on American pension and welfare benefits.

Frank Costigliola is Professor of History at the University of Rhode Island. Since receiving his doctoral degree from Cornell University, he has published *Awkward Dominion: American Political, Economic, and Cultural Relations with Europe, 1919–1933* (1984) and articles in the *Journal of American History, Business History Review,* and *Diplomatic History,* among others. He is currently at work on a history of United States relations with France since 1940.

James Fetzer is Associate Professor of History at the Maritime College of the State University of New York. He earned his doctorate from Michigan State University and has authored articles for the *Foreign Service Journal* and *The Historian* on topics in Sino-American relations.

J.L. Granatstein is Professor of History at York University in Canada. He holds a doctorate from Duke University and has written several books, including *The Politics of Survival: The Conservative Party of Canada, 1939–45* (1967), *Canadian-American Relations in Wartime* (1975, with Robert Cuff), *Canada's War: The Politics of the Mackenzie King Government, 1939–45*

(1975), *A Man of Influence: Norman A. Robertson and Canadian Statecraft, 1929–68* (1981), and *Canada 1957–1967: The Years of Uncertainty and Innovation* (1986). His articles have appeared in the *International Journal* and *International History Review*, among many others. He is writing a book on Pierre Trudeau's foreign policy from 1968 to 1984.

Douglas Little is Associate Professor of History at Clark University in Massachusetts. He received his doctorate from Cornell University. He has written a book, *Malevolent Neutrality: The United States, Great Britain, and the Origins of the Spanish Civil War* (1985), and his articles have appeared in *American Quarterly, Business History Review, Journal of Contemporary History,* and *Journal of American History*. His current research focuses on United States relations with the Middle East, 1945–1967.

Gary May is Associate Professor of History at the University of Delaware. After earning his doctorate at the University of California, Los Angeles, he published *China Scapegoat: The Diplomatic Ordeal of John Carter Vincent* (1979), winner of the Allan Nevins Prize from the Society of American Historians. Besides studying the history of the Peace Corps, he is writing a book about the William Remington case.

Robert J. McMahon is Associate Professor of History at the University of Florida. The University of Connecticut awarded him his doctorate. He is the author of *Colonialism and Cold War: The United States and the Struggle for Indonesian Independence, 1945–49* (1981) and articles in *Diplomatic History, Political Science Quarterly, Pacific Historical Review,* and *Journal of American History*. As an historian in the Office of the Historian, United States Department of State, 1977–1982, he edited several volumes in the *Foreign Relations of the United States* series. He serves on the editorial board of *Diplomatic History* and is currently writing a book on United States relations with India and Pakistan, 1947–1965.

Thomas J. Noer is Professor of History at Carthage College in Wisconsin. Since receiving his doctorate from the University of Minnesota, he has published two books: *Briton, Boer, and Yankee: The United States and South Africa, 1870–1914* (1978) and *Cold War and Black Liberation: The United States and White Rule in Africa, 1948–1968* (1985). His articles have appeared in *Diplomatic History* and the *Journal of Ethnic Studies*, among others. He is currently at work on an oral history of the Peace Corps.

Thomas G. Paterson is Professor of History at the University of Connecticut, where he has taught since receiving his doctorate from the University of California, Berkeley. He has written *Soviet-American Confrontation* (1973), *On Every Front: The Making of the Cold War* (1979), *Meeting the Communist Threat: Truman to Reagan* (1988), and *American Foreign Policy: A History* (3rd edition, 1988, with J. Garry Clifford and Kenneth J. Hagan). His edited works include *Cold War Critics* (1971) and *Major Problems in American Foreign Policy* (3rd edition, 1989). His articles have appeared in the *American Historical Review, Journal of American History,* and *Diplomatic History*, among many others. He has served as president of the Society for Historians of American Foreign Relations, sat on the editorial boards of the *Journal of American History* and *Diplomatic History,* and directed National Endowment for the Humanities Summer Seminars for College Teachers. His current research centers on the United States response to the Cuban Revolution.

Stephen E. Pelz is Professor of History at the University of Massachusetts, Amherst, where he has taught since receiving his doctorate from Harvard University. A specialist in United States relations with Asia, he has published *Race to Pearl Harbor: The Failure of the Second London Naval Conference and the Onset of World War II* (1974) and several articles, including one on the Vietnam War in the *Journal of Strategic Studies,* one on American decisions leading to the Korean War in Bruce Cumings, ed., *Child of Conflict: The Korean-American Relationship, 1943–1953* (1983), and another, "A Taxonomy for U.S. Diplomatic History," in the *Journal of Interdisciplinary History.*

Stephen G. Rabe is Professor of History at the University of Texas, Dallas. After receiving his doctorate from the University of Connecticut, he published *The Road to OPEC: United States Relations with Venezuela, 1919–1976* (1982). His second book is *Eisenhower and Latin America: The Foreign Policy of Anticommunism* (1988). *Diplomatic History, Peace and Change,* and the *Latin American Research Review,* among other journals, have published his articles. In his current research he is studying United States relations with Argentina in the Perón era.

KENNEDY'S QUEST FOR VICTORY

Introduction: John F. Kennedy's Quest for Victory and Global Crisis

THOMAS G. PATERSON

John F. Kennedy was a "statesman" who respected "excellence," wrote a pensive columnist shortly after the shocking assassination of the young President.[1] "He glittered when he lived," observed one of Kennedy's admiring aides and biographers, Arthur M. Schlesinger, Jr.[2] "It can be said of him," eulogized one editorial, "that he did not fear the weather, and did not trim his sails, but instead challenged the wind itself, to improve its direction and to cause it to blow more softly and more kindly over the world and its people."[3]

People everywhere mourned the death of John F. Kennedy. In his brief presidency, he had come to exemplify youth, energy, and innovation. People liked his self-confidence, "can-do" style, quick wit, sense of humor, and good looks. He seemed a man of great intellect who read widely, and he surrounded himself with bright assistants. "There's nothing like brains," he once remarked. "You can't beat brains."[4] They saw a cultured man who invited the eminent Robert Frost to read a new poem at the inauguration and Pablo Casals to fill the White House with music. They smiled at the proud father who played with his children, sometimes even during high-level meetings. They remarked on the attractiveness of the married couple: the poised, masculine President and his beautiful, talented wife Jacqueline Bouvier, who spoke in Spanish to a gathering of Cuban-Americans and in French to a charmed Charles de Gaulle. "I am the man who accompanied Jacqueline Kennedy to Paris," he joked.[5] Whether dueling outmatched journalists, speed-reading books and newspapers, launching a physical fitness program, or delivering one of his stirring speeches, the forty-three-year-old John F. Kennedy symbolized competitive motion. After the dull and uninspiring leadership of Dwight D. Eisenhower, people seemed eager for an idealist-activist who promised to get the United States moving again and to get the world moving toward economic progress, peace, and stability. And they applauded his achievements: Peace Corps, Alliance for Progress, space program, Arms Control and Disarmament Agency, Trade Expansion Act, Laotian settlement, Limited Test Ban Treaty, and management of the Cuban missile crisis.

Kennedy and his advisers knew that positive images mattered, that upbeat public symbols improved his chances of persuasion, permitted him to lead more effectively, and gave him power. They skillfully used televised press conferences and well-crafted speeches, and they created myths to promote the man and his record. Kennedy spent a great deal of time on "public communication—educating, persuading and mobilizing that opinion through . . . continued attention to mass media: radio, television, and the press."[6] He and his advisers were so effective that a compliant press largely reported the news as the President wanted it.[7]

After a quarter of a century, we now know that a conspicuous chasm separated appearance and reality. At the time, although much of the story was known, it was submerged under a celebratory image. Today scholars and sensationalists alike have forced us to acknowledge a much less flattering portrait of the President and his Administration—one that has called into question his character, judgment, and accomplishments.[8] "You say JFK 'moved' people," a skeptical former Secretary of State Dean Acheson once remarked. "To what end and for how long?"[9]

The demythologizing of John F. Kennedy, for example, includes evidence that he was a brazen womanizer who named the women he wanted for sex and usually got them, including Hollywood starlets and Judith Campbell Exner, mistress to crime bosses as well as to the President. His book, *Profiles in Courage* (1955), for which he took personal credit and won a Pulitzer Prize, was actually written for him by an aide and a university professor. His Administration wiretapped Martin Luther King, Jr., and others and it searched Internal Revenue Service tax records for information to discredit political foes. Kennedy had shown little courage on the issue of McCarthyism in the 1950s, refusing to condemn the behavior or views of the reckless Wisconsin senator. In the early 1960s Kennedy followed rather than led the fight for civil rights for black Americans. Central Intelligence Agency officials, believing they were following presidential instructions, tried to kill Cuba's Fidel Castro and sent sabotage teams to destroy life and property on the island. The presidential candidate who hammered the Eisenhower Administration for permitting the Soviets to gain missile superiority (the famed charge of a "missile gap") became the President who learned that the United States held overwhelming nuclear supremacy—yet he nonetheless tremendously expanded the American nuclear arsenal.

For a President who said that Americans should "never fear to negotiate,"[10] Kennedy seemed more enamored with military than with diplomatic means: defense expenditures increased 13 percent in the Kennedy years, counterinsurgency training and warfare accelerated, and United States intervention in Vietnam deepened. A study of the use of the armed forces as a political instrument has found that Kennedy used them at a greater rate than any other postwar President. His Administration recorded 39 instances (or roughly 13 per year), compared to 35 (or 4 per year) for Harry S Truman, 57 (or 7 per year) for Eisenhower, 47 (or 9 per year) for Lyndon B. Johnson, and 33 (or 5 per year) for Richard M. Nixon and Gerald R. Ford.[11] By 1963 the United States had 275 major bases in 31 nations and one and a quarter million military-related American personnel stationed abroad. One of Defense Secretary Robert McNamara's assistants, Adam Yarmolinsky, has noted that in wisely jettisoning Eisenhower's policy of massive retaliation and initiating instead "flexible response," Kennedy produced unfortunate results: "Theories of limited war and programs to widen the President's range of choices made military solutions to our problems more available and even more attractive."[12]

Given the disparity between image and reality and the inevitable reinterpretation that new documentation and distance from events stimulate, it is not surprising that ambiguity marks Kennedy scholarship. He appears as both confrontationist and conciliator, hawk and dove, decisive leader and hesitant improviser, hyperbolic politician and prudent diplomat, idealist and pragmatist, glorious hero and flawed man of dubious character. On the one hand he sponsored the Peace Corps, and on the other he attended personally to the equipment needs of the Green Berets. On the one hand he called for an appreciation of Third World nationalism, and on the other he intervened in Vietnam and Cuba to try to squash nationalist movements he found unacceptable. He said the United States respected neutralism, yet he strove to woo important neutrals, such as India, Indonesia, and Egypt, into the American Cold War camp. He preached democracy, but in Latin America he sent military aid to the forces of oppression. On the one hand he heralded Canada as a cherished ally, but on the other he became impatient with the neighbor's desire for an independent foreign policy. On the one hand he appealed for liberal trade principles, and on the other he supported many protectionist measures. He vowed to solve the balance of payments problem, yet increased defense spending abroad. He said he understood the Sino-Soviet split, but he spoke often about a monolithic Communism and rejected options to improve relations with the People's Republic of China. On the one hand he created the Arms Control and Disarmament Agency, and on the other he expanded the number of American intercontinental ballistic missiles from some 60 to more than 420. He preached diplomacy, yet in the dangerous Cuban missile crisis he initially shunted aside negotiations in favor of a surprise television address. On the one hand, seeing Eastern Europe as the "Achilles heel of the Soviet empire" and discarding John Foster Dulles's provocative and failed policy of "liberation," he strove for improved relations with Soviet Russia's neighbors, but on the other he bowed to conservative opinion, declaring a "Captive Nations Week" and signing a trade bill that denied most-favored-nation treatment to Yugoslavia.[13] He determined to negotiate a settlement of the Berlin crisis, but he resorted to militant rhetoric and an armed forces buildup. On the one hand he called for a new Atlantic community, and on the other he refused to share decision-making power with increasingly disgruntled Western European allies.

Historian C. Vann Woodward wrote in late 1963 that Kennedy "had had time to make mistakes and to learn from them, but not enough time to profit much from them. He had had time to make plans and policies, but not time to fulfill them."[14] Some have argued that, had Kennedy lived and won re-election in 1964, he would have withdrawn from Vietnam and transformed the Cold War from confrontation to peace and disarmament. "He never had the chance," Schlesinger has written.[15] Some Kennedy-watchers have emphasized that the President was evolving as a leader; that is, through education imposed by crises, Kennedy grew and began to temper his ardent Cold War anti-Communism and learn the limits of American power.[16]

"The heart of the Kennedy legend," James Reston has noted, "is what might have been."[17] We can never be sure about what Kennedy might have done, but we do know what he *did* in a period of less than three years. The scholarship, including this book, suggests not that Kennedy changed during his presidency or that he was in the process of changing, but rather that he could not and did not change to any significant degree for several reasons: because of his own deep-seated foreign policy views, his personality, prior American commitments, domestic politics, and the intractability of many foreign issues. The "might-have-beens" can only be evaluated and their viability scrutinized through close study of the record. The brevity of the Kennedy presidency should not discourage analysis. To be sure, Kennedy was no Winston S. Churchill or Franklin D. Roosevelt during times of cataclysm like the Great Depression and the Second World War. But the years 1961–1963 witnessed an unusually high number of crises, some of which seemed to court nuclear cremation, and Kennedy produced programs and policies whose durability is registered to this day. Schlesinger and others have argued, moreover, that John F. Kennedy made a difference, that he left a definite imprint on history. Historians are thus invited to assess the Kennedy legacy by studying Kennedy's successes and failures—his performance as distinct from his promise.

Several factors stand out in the search for what made John F. Kennedy's foreign policy tick and for what most influenced his diplomacy: the global crisis of his time and the decline of American hegemony; the lessons he and his generation drew from the past and the impact of this heritage upon an ambitious politician; the American counter-revolutionary tradition and endorsement of nation-building as a non-revolutionary alternative; and the President's personality and style. In all cases, Kennedy strove to win—the Cold War, the allegiance of the Third World, the space race ("If the Soviets Control Space—They Can Control Earth" read the title of one of Kennedy's articles[18]), the nuclear arms race, Southeast Asia, and more. Eisenhower too had wanted first ranking for the United States, but he seemed less of a risk-taker than his successor. Kennedy also infused the races with unusual energy, personal commitment, impatience, and a sense of immediate peril that demanded action. National Security Council staffer (and later chairman of the State Department's Policy Planning Council) Walt W. Rostow exaggerated but still captured the essence of the question when he noted that the difference between Eisenhower and Kennedy "was a shift from defensive reaction to initiative. . . ."[19] Crisis was the norm rather than the exception in the Kennedy Administration.[20] "Crisis management" became celebrated codewords of the Kennedy team, which seemed to thrive on the opportunities.

One major influence upon Kennedy's foreign policy was the fluid, unpredictable international setting that produced a host of challenges for the United States. Having dominated the postwar period with unparalleled economic and military power, the United States in the 1960s was slipping from its Olympian position.[21] European allies and Japan, with American help, had recovered from the ravages of World War II to become economic and political competitors. A chronic balance of payments problem revealed the dollar as vulnerable and signaled that America was spending beyond its means. The once mighty European empires had crumbled or were still collapsing from within and from the pressures of revolutionary nationalists. As Under Secretary of State George W. Ball later put it, President Kennedy's foreign policy necessarily "focused on problems involving the bits and pieces of disintegrating empires."[22] New nations emerged in startling succession; in 1960 alone eighteen gained independence. These Third World countries, often poor and wracked by civil strife, disturbed international stability, drew the great powers into conflict, and shifted power in the international system—removing "the old metropoles from world power roles," observed Ball.[23] Many of these new nations chose neutralism rather than Cold War partnership; they formed a non-aligned movement that bedeviled both the United States and the Soviet Union. In the Third World, too, torturous regional disputes, such as those in South Asia between Pakistan and India and in the Middle East between Israel and the Arab states, threatened greater upheaval. Even in the United States's most direct sphere of influence, Latin America, instability and the popularity of Castroism, both springing from economic stagnation and dependency, class politics, and corrupt authoritarianism, disrupted traditional relationships and threatened United States interests. The nuclear arms race persisted with new and more destructive weapons, and nuclear proliferation promised more fingers on atomic triggers. The Soviet Union, climbing out of the ashes of the Second World War, became more active on a global scale. Nikita Khrushchev's bellicose rhetoric thundered through diplomatic chambers, where many leaders concluded that the Cold War was being racheted up a notch.

Eisenhower's last year as President revealed the unrelenting tumult of global politics: Castro's Cuba accelerated its revolution, challenging the United States by signing a trade treaty with the Soviets and nationalizing more American-owned property; fraudulent elections in South Korea sparked riots against the Syngman Rhee regime, forcing America's longstanding ally to resign; China's Zhou Enlai visited India but failed to settle the simmering Sino-Indian border dispute; North Atlantic Treaty Organization (NATO) ally Turkey suffered a military coup; French President Charles de Gaulle challenged American policy on Berlin and in NATO; the U-2 incident wrecked the Paris summit meeting; the Trujillo dictatorship of the Dominican Republic tried to overthrow the democratic government of Venezuela, prompting Washington to break diplomatic relations with Santo Domingo; Eisenhower canceled a planned tour of Japan after anti-American riots; the Congo gained independence but immediately descended into bloody civil war; terrorists killed Jordan's premier; Laotian neutralists staged a successful coup, only to be driven from power a few months later; the United Nations Organization admitted seventeen new members, pointing toward greater Third World power in the international forum; in South Vietnam a military coup against America's ally Ngo Dinh Diem failed and the National Liberation Front (Vietcong) organized to battle his besieged regime; and Khrushchev gave an alarming speech in which he endorsed anti-imperialist wars of national liberation.

The world was unsettled and unsettling, America's place in it less familiar and less secure. In his inaugural address, Kennedy grimly noted the global crisis; he spoke of the "hour of maximum danger" and asked Americans "to bear the burden of a long twilight struggle."[24] In his first State of the Union message less than two weeks later, the President declared himself "staggered" by the "harsh enormity of the trials through which we must pass. . . ." The culprits behind the world's troubles, he asserted in traditional Cold War language, remained Moscow and Beijing. "We must never be lulled into believing that either power has yielded its ambitions for world domination. . . ."[25]

A second influence on Kennedy's foreign policy, as the last statement suggests, was history and the lessons he and Americans of his generation drew from the past. John F. Kennedy and his advisers were captives of an influential past. They constituted the 1940s' generation, having come to political maturity during World War II and the early years of the Cold War. Kennedy himself served during the war on a PT boat; he was elected to Congress in 1946, just a few months before the enunciation of the Truman Doctrine, the most commanding principle in the postwar era. Members of Kennedy's containment generation claimed victories in Iran, Greece, and Turkey, launched the Marshall Plan, broke the Berlin blockade, created NATO, and extended Point Four technical assistance to developing nations. But they also suffered the defeat of Jiang Jieshi (Chiang Kaishek) by Mao Zedong and his Communist revolutionaries in China and the frustrations of limited war in Korea.

When asked in 1963 whether he would reduce aid to South Vietnam, Kennedy revealed the pull of the past and his political sensitivity: he would not, he replied, because "strongly in our mind is what happened in the case of China at the end of World War II, where China was lost. . . . We don't want that."[26] He remembered how Truman and Acheson had been politically wounded by the "fall of China" and how Adlai Stevenson, the Democratic presidential candidate in 1952, had to fight the charge that the Democrats were soft on Communism. A friend of Kennedy, journalist Charles Bartlett, recalled that Kennedy worried often about the forthcoming 1964 election. "We don't have a prayer of staying in Vietnam. We don't have a prayer of prevailing there," Kennedy told Bartlett. "But I can't give up a piece of territory like that to the Communists and then get the American people to reelect me."[27]

Kennedy and his generation learned from their 1940s–1950s' experiences not only the political dangers lurking in Cold War diplomacy, but also a set of influential policy axioms: totalitarian states like Nazi Germany and Soviet Russia were inherently aggressive, and aggression fed on aggression; toughness against Communism works; a nation must negotiate from strength and avoid sellouts in negotiations (in 1949 Kennedy had blasted Roosevelt for having signed the Yalta accords); American economic health and leadership were needed to ensure worldwide political stability and prosperity; Communism was a cancer that nourished itself on economic misery; Communism was monolithic; Communism had to be met wherever it appeared to be gaining ground, at almost any cost ("creeping Communism is a greater enemy than creeping inflation," Senator Kennedy said in the late 1950s[28]); revolutions and civil wars, if not instigated by Communists, were usually exploited by them; and a powerful United States, almost alone, had to protect a threatened world from the Communist menace.

Like so many of his generation, Kennedy came to believe in the efficacy of the "domino theory" in Southeast Asia and the "zero-sum" nature of the Cold War (that a victory for "them" meant a loss for "us").[29] He thought that the containment doctrine should be applied universally because Communism, masterminded and directed from Moscow, loomed as a universal threat. An expansionist, obstructionist Soviet Union, counting on the "free world's" decay, relishing dislocation in the Third World, and utilizing client states, had to be confronted at every turn. Although Kennedy concluded that the Soviets had unlimited amibitions, he calculated that they had limited means. Vigorous American growth in all categories of national power would thus deter Moscow and give the upper hand in negotiations to the United States.[30] Kennedy and his advisers expressed confidence that through their enlightened leadership the United States could move the Cold War from stalemate to victory. National Security Affairs Adviser McGeorge Bundy once commented that "he had come to accept what he had learned from Dean Acheson—that, in the final analysis, the United States was the locomotive at the head of mankind, and the rest of the world the caboose."[31] Such references left no doubt that the engineer of the fast-moving train of the early 1960s was John F. Kennedy.

Kennedy and his advisers not only took office with considerable historical baggage; they also charged that an unimaginative and complacent Eisenhower Administration had let American power and prestige deteriorate as global crisis accelerated in the 1950s. "We have allowed a soft sentimentalism to form the atmosphere we breathe," Kennedy claimed. "Toughminded plans" had to be devised.[32] The Kennedy team craved triumphs like those over Nazism and Stalinism. "I think it's time America started moving again," proclaimed Kennedy.[33] "Our job was to deal with an automobile with weak brakes on a hill," recalled Walt W. Rostow in yet another vehicle-in-motion metaphor. "It was slowly sliding backward. If we applied enormous energy, the car would begin to move forward and in time, we would get it up to the top of the hill."[34]

In the 1960 presidential campaign Kennedy demonstrated both this mood and the tenacity of Cold War thinking. Richard M. Nixon and Kennedy actually differed little in their foreign policy views. Nixon was also a member of the containment generation, having been elected to Congress with Kennedy in 1946. Throughout the 1950s, Kennedy's Cold War mentality had been displayed again and again, as when he called for higher military expenditures than even General Eisenhower wanted. In 1956 Kennedy identified Vietnam as the "finger in the dike" of Communism.[35] In his 1960 campaign speeches, Kennedy chastised the Republicans for having lost Cuba, for losing the contest over the Third World, and for lagging behind in the missile race. "I think there is a danger that history will make a judgment that these were the days when the tide began to run out for the United States," he lectured. "These were the times when the Communist tide began to pour in."[36] On another occasion the Democratic candidate sounded like the very John Foster Dulles whose foreign policy he was excoriating: "The enemy is the Communist system itself—implacable, unceasing in its drive for world domination. For this is not a struggle for the supremacy of arms alone—it is also a struggle for supremacy between two conflicting ideologies: Freedom under God versus ruthless, godless tyranny."[37]

Such phrases cannot be dismissed simply as the common, exaggerated, throw-away rhetoric of a campaign. Such words flowed regularly from the lips of the Kennedyites. They represented the legacy of the 1940s that shaped the assumptions of Kennedy's generation. Reflecting on the foreign policy troubles of the 1960s, Clark Clifford, White House aide to Truman, Kennedy's liaison during the presidential transition, and later Secretary of Defense under Johnson, admitted, "I am a product of the Cold War. . . . I think the Truman Doctrine, the Marshall Plan, and NATO saved the free world. . . . But I think part of our problem in the early nineteen-sixties was that we were looking at Southeast Asia with the same attitudes with which we had viewed Europe in the nineteen-forties. . . . The world had changed but our thinking had not, at least not as much as it should have."[38]

With the global crisis and the historical lessons stood a third significant influence on Kennedy's foreign policy: a counter-revolutionary tradition. In the twentieth century, the United States became an imperial power with global interests. Deeming radical or revolutionary change inimical to America's global position, American leaders became unabashedly hostile to revolution and the political turmoil in the Third World. They believed that Third World disturbances threatened United States interests (trade, sources of strategic raw materials, intelligence posts, military bases, allies, votes in international organizations) and liberal political principles. The United States has opposed virtually every revolution in this century—Mexican, Russian, Chinese, Vietnamese, Cuban, Iranian, Nicaraguan. The American military has been dispatched to a host of Caribbean nations to prevent revolutions or to oust leftist governments. This counter-revolutionary thrust of American foreign policy took form *before* the Russian Revolution unleashed its dreaded Communism. In the 1950s the tradition of counter-revolution found expression in interventions in Iran, Guatemala, and Lebanon.

Under Kennedy the tradition manifested itself in the concept of nation-building. By means of modernization, Third World nations would be helped through the stormy times of economic infancy to economic and political maturity. In this process they would choose the model of capitalist development and avoid flirtations with radicalism, socialism, or Communism. They might even throw off their neutralism and align with the United States. Kennedy officials understood the force of Third World nationalism and the neutralism that emanated from it; rather than flatly opposing both, they sought to channel them toward non-Communist paths. Walt W. Rostow, who had popularized nation-building in his book *The Stages of Economic Growth: A Non-Communist Manifesto* (1960), told the 1961 graduating class of the Special Warfare School at Fort Bragg that "modern societies must be built, and we are prepared to help build them."[39] Schlesinger urged "middle class revolution" upon the President. Land reform, industrialization, tax reform, and public health and sanitation programs had to be undertaken. Without nation-building, "new Castros will infallibly arise across the continent."[40] The Alliance for Progress and the Peace Corps signaled Kennedy's determination to prevent revolution and control change.

Kennedy liked to quote Mao Zedong's statement that "guerrillas are like fish, and the people are the water in which fish swim. If the temperature of the water is right, the fish will thrive and multiply."[41] The President intended to destroy the fish by changing the temperature of the water. Because American leaders interpreted revolutionary insurgencies as threats to the United States, undermining interests and destabilizing societies such that Communists would be attracted to the scene, counter-insurgency became necessary. As Americans guided non-violent "revolution" from the top down, so would they inhibit revolution from the bottom up. Besides training native police forces, the United States elevated the American Special Forces units (Green Berets) as a spearhead for action. These gritty, tough-minded commandos would supposedly turn back rebel movements. Rostow championed a "counter-offensive" in Indochina by using "our unexploited counter-guerrilla assets." As he advised Kennedy, "we are not just saving them for the Junior Prom."[42] Kennedy's favorite general, Maxwell Taylor, considered Vietnam a "laboratory" in counter-insurgency techniques.[43] Nation-building represented the traditional if arrogant view that the American development model could be duplicated elsewhere. It was also meddlesome and interventionist, presuming that Americans must mold other societies. Schlesinger himself came to regret the Administration's fascination with counter-insurgency, for it was "a mode of warfare for which Americans were ill-adapted, which nourished an American belief in the capacity and right to intervene in foreign lands, and which was both corrupting in method and futile in effect."[44] He might have added that Kennedy officials initially embraced this type of warfare because of their deeply ingrained assumptions about the ubiquitous Communist menace and the dangers that revolutions posed to the United States.

A fourth important influence on the foreign policy of the early 1960s was Kennedy's personality and style. "It is extraordinary," Rostow wrote a friend shortly after Kennedy entered the White House, "how the character of the President's personality shapes everything around him"—and "it is the damned liveliest thing I have ever seen."[45] Secretary of State Dean Rusk remembered Kennedy as an "incandescent man. He was on fire, and he set people around him on fire."[46] Schlesinger has written that "everyone around him thought he had the Midas touch and could not lose."[47]

Kennedy admirers and detractors alike have agreed that Kennedy was driven by a desire for power, because power insured winning. Whatever the sources of this drive—his father's example and pressure,[48] "macho values and sexual drives,"[49] the combativeness induced by political ambition and athletic competition, or precarious health (he was afflicted with Addison's disease)—Kennedy personalized issues, converting them into tests of will. Two words most often uttered by the President and his associates were "tough" and "soft," and they passionately disassociated themselves from the latter. One journalist observed a "cult of toughness" in the Administration.[50] In early 1961, when he was considering going to a summit meeting with Khrushchev, Kennedy asserted, "I have to show him that we can be as tough as he is. . . . I'll have to sit down with him, and let him see who he's dealing with."[51] One presidential aide explained the invasion at the Bay of Pigs, Cuba, this way: "Nobody in the White House wanted to be soft. . . . Everybody wanted to show they were just as daring and bold as everybody else."[52]

Box scores proliferated for everything from the arms race to the space race, from the race for influence in the Third World to the number of enemy troops killed in Vietnam. "If we can successfully crack Ghana and Guinea, Mali may turn to the West," Kennedy told Rusk after learning that the first two nations had requested Peace Corps volunteers. "If so, these would be the first Communist-oriented countries to turn from Moscow to us."[53] Peace Corps Director Sargent Shriver placed a sign on his desk: "Good Guys Don't Win Ball Games."[54] Kennedy was eager to win in another category too: "Do we have a chance of beating the Russians by putting a laboratory in space, or by a trip around the moon, or by a rocket to go to the moon and back with a man? Is there any other space program which promises dramatic results in which we could win?"[55] McGeorge Bundy expressed the Administration's general frustration over having gained few decisive victories in 1961: "We are like the Harlem Globetrotters, passing forward, behind, sideways, and underneath. But nobody had made a basket yet."[56] Whether they drew their metaphors from sports or transportation, the Kennedyites always celebrated impressive motion. How upset Kennedy became at a luncheon for Texas publishers when one of them audaciously stood up and said: "Many Texans in the Southwest think that you are riding [your daughter] Caroline's tricycle, instead of being a man on horseback."[57] Friendly journalists were soon enlisted to help counter this suggestion of a weak President.

The Kennedy Administration actually cultivated and projected quite a different image—one of boldness and activism. Cocky and certain that they were the "right" people to restore America's strength, the young Kennedy officials swept into Washington as "action intellectuals," wrote Theodore H. White.[58] Schlesinger captured their mood this way: "Euphoria reigned; we thought for a moment that the world was plastic and the future unlimited."[59] When the former Harvard historian advised the President on Latin American policy, he described "the atmosphere" as "set for miracles."[60] Bustle, zeal, energy, optimism—and always toughness—became popular bywords. The Administration's programs were given names appropriate to this activist style: the "Grand Design" for Europe; the "New Africa" Policy; the "Alliance for Progress for Latin America"; and the "New Frontier" at home. The President's Inaugural Address sounded the popular theme when Kennedy declared that "the torch has been passed to a new generation." He went on: "Let every nation know that we shall pay any price, bear any burden, meet any hardship, support any friend, oppose any foe to assure the survival and the success of liberty."[61] Since those heady days, Schlesinger has come to agree with many scholars that the address contained "extravagant rhetoric" that amounted to an "overreaction" to Khrushchev's January 1961 speech that had applauded wars of national liberation.[62]

The personality and style of the President influenced not only his key foreign policy decisions but also the process by which decisions were made. Unlike Eisenhower, Kennedy had had no previous experience as an executive.[63] He thought Eisenhower's National Security Council (NSC) too encumbered by bureaucratic structure, and he shared the popular and probably accurate view that the Department of State was too cautious, too slow, and too large—a "bowl of jelly."[64] Kennedy preferred to run foreign policy in the White House "by seminar" using a small staff, many of whom were young men who lacked expertise but possessed high intelligence.[65] For example, Richard N. Goodwin, only twenty-nine years old in 1961 and recently graduated from law school, was first hired by Kennedy as a speechwriter. Goodwin knew little about Latin America when he entered the White House, yet he became one of the "experts" on the region, getting fast on-the-job training. Staffers like Goodwin participated in a system marked by informality, shifting responsibilities as issues changed, and an ad hoc approach that reflected the President's style. Their brainpower and energy were enviable, but their experience was limited—as was their knowledge of and sensitivity to foreign cultures and traditional disputes resistant to outside manipulation.

Kennedy chose Dean Rusk as his Secretary of State. A quiet, competent, and relatively unknown person, Rusk had been an Assistant Secretary of State for Far Eastern Affairs in the Truman years.[66] Presidential aide Theodore Sorensen recalled that Rusk "deferred almost too amiably to White House initiatives and interference."[67] Rusk believed in the presidential mastery of foreign policy—that "a secretary of state serves at the pleasure of the president. . . ."[68] Kennedy thought Rusk suitable not only because he would not challenge the President's desire to be his own Secretary of State but also because Rusk brought a compatible Cold War mind-set to the administration. Criticized by White House advisers as too reserved, sitting like a Buddha at meetings, Rusk has rebutted that he preferred to advise the President in private. "When people like Arthur Schlesinger were in the room I kept my mouth shut," Rusk later said with bite in reference to his constant concern over leaks.[69]

McGeorge Bundy, the forty-one-year-old Harvard dean, became Kennedy's Assistant for National Security Affairs. Like so many others who joined Kennedy's team, Bundy had served in the Second World War and in the Truman Administration. He had worked for the Marshall Plan and developed close relations with Henry L. Stimson and Dean Acheson. Self-assured and arrogant, Bundy helped the President shape a centralized decision-making system by streamlining the NSC and ensured that the President was made aware of policy options. Although Bundy had his own opinions and expressed them, his primary role was that of "synthesizer"—a "brilliant sifter, collator, and condenser of foreign policy advice."[70] He also tried to manage the sometimes haphazard way in which Kennedy conducted foreign policy. Bundy has admitted an "untidiness of management" stemming from Kennedy's distaste for orderly procedures and his habit of seeking ideas from several quarters and alternating advisers as topics shifted.[71] Loose management and lack of oversight permitted subordinates in the bureaucracy the freedom to act insubordinately. Bundy has singled out the Central Intelligence Agency as having abused its power.

Among the other New Frontiersmen who advised the President was his brother Robert. Robert F. Kennedy was the Attorney General, but he often "dabbled" in the affairs of other departments, including the State Department.[72] Valued as an effective troubleshooter by the President, Robert certainly wielded more influence than Vice President Lyndon Johnson and Dean Rusk. Like the President, Robert was action-oriented, a doer impatient with the lethargy of traditional bureaucratic channels. Appointments Secretary Kenneth O'Donnell recalled, "When we wanted to let Jack know about a problem too sensitive for one of us to mention to him, Bobby would tell him about it and bring back an answer. When Jack was in one of his inaccessible moods, Bobby could always reach him. . . ."[73] The President used "Bobby" during the Cuban missile crisis both to monitor Executive Committee meetings and to meet with the Soviet Ambassador. The Attorney General also became one of the Administration's experts on and an ardent advocate of covert actions.[74]

Other key advisers included Secretary of Defense Robert McNamara and General Maxwell Taylor, both of whom worked to reorganize the military under the new philosophy of "flexible response." Allen Dulles, his reputation besmirched by the Bay of Pigs disaster, stepped down as Director of Central Intelligence in September 1961. Kennedy replaced him with John McCone, a conservative Republican who had served as Under Secretary of the Air Force under Truman and as Chairman of the Atomic Energy Commission, 1958–1961. An ardent anti-Communist, McCone presided over a CIA enamored with covert actions, including operations to assassinate Fidel Castro. But McCone has denied that he knew about the assassination plots. A holdover from the Eisenhower Administration was C. Douglas Dillon, who had responsibilities for international finance. "I can use a few smart Republicans [like Dillon]," Kennedy remarked. "We need a Secretary of Treasury who can call a few of those people on Wall Street by their first names."[75] With the help of Schlesinger, Goodwin, and others, thirty-two-year-old Special Counsel Theodore Sorensen served as Kennedy's chief speechwriter and general sounding board.

As Schlesinger has noted, the Administration "put a premium on quick, tough, laconic, decided people. . . ."[76] One Kennedy aide told a journalist in 1962 that Kennedy's first comment is usually "What have you got?" or "What's up?" Then, "You're supposed to tell him— bang, bang, bang."[77] Kennedy had little tolerance for meetings that dealt more with ideas than with operations. The Executive Secretary of the NSC recalled that "Kennedy wouldn't sit still for briefings like Ike."[78] Although surrounded by intellectuals and books, Kennedy himself was not an intellectual but a supreme pragmatist with a quick mind. For Kennedy, Rostow has written, "ideas were tools. He picked them up easily like statistics or the names of local politicians. . . . He wanted to know how ideas could be put to work."[79] Rapping with his hand and tapping his teeth, a restless Kennedy grew impatient with people who played with ideas.[80] George Ball remembered that "when one tried to point out the long-range implications of a current problem or how it meshed or collided with other major national interests, Kennedy would often say, politely but impatiently, 'Let's not worry about five years from now, what do we do tomorrow?' "[81]

Ball, a seasoned government servant, was not as impressed as many were with the new Kennedy team's "exuberance and its confidence in the bright new plans and brilliant insights shortly to be disclosed."[82] Like others who had been around Washington for some time, Ball thought the "action intellectuals" rather impulsive and presumptuous. Adlai Stevenson, former Governor of Illinois and two-time unsuccessful Democratic candidate for President in the 1950s, also grew disenchanted. Named Ambassador to the United Nations, Stevenson became a peripheral adviser; he opposed the Bay of Pigs invasion and urged negotiations during the missile crisis. Kennedy thought Stevenson "a weeper"—that is, too idealistic.[83] Kennedy once rejected the draft of a public statement with the comment that "this would be good copy for Adlai. But it's not my style. It's too soft. My style is harder."[84] An unimpressed Stevenson told a friend that "they've got the damndest bunch of boy commandos running around . . . you ever saw."[85] Chester Bowles, second in command under Rusk before the President purged him from the State Department (Bowles too had opposed the Bay of Pigs operation), also seemed out of step with the bumptious Kennedy style. The Kennedyites, he recalled, were "full of belligerence" and "sort of looking for a chance to prove their muscle."[86] Schlesinger later agreed that the "besetting sin of the New Frontier . . . was the addiction of activism." He said in the early 1980s "that the commitment on the part of professional diplomats to restraint, slowness, and caution probably had more wisdom than we understood at the time."[87]

John F. Kennedy's foreign policy, influenced by unrelenting international friction, the lessons of the past, the United States counterrevolutionary tradition, and the President's personality and style, bequeathed a mixed legacy. The Kennedy Administration helped quiet the crisis over Laos and followed a cautious policy in the Congo; it took important steps toward trade liberalization; it enhanced America's reputation as a humanitarian nation with a generous helping hand through the Peace Corps and Alliance for Progress; it brought about a peaceful solution of the West Irian dispute between Indonesia and the Netherlands—a dangerous and complicated problem that had defied previous diplomats; it negotiated the Limited Test Ban Treaty and created the Arms Control and Disarmament Agency; it kept a commitment to defend Berlin and strengthened European defenses, and its ultimate readiness to negotiate helped soothe the Berlin crisis. And the President's personal diplomacy courted some Third World leaders.

In June 1963 President Kennedy delivered a speech at American University that seemed to mark a break with the past. He asked Americans to rexamine their hard-line anti-Soviet attitudes and their skepticism about the chances of gaining peace through negotiations.

"No government or social system is so evil that its people must be considered as lacking in virtue," he said. The United States "can seek a relaxation of tensions without relaxing our guard." He also revealed his discomfort with a strategic policy so dependent upon nuclear weapons, and urged the Soviets to join him in halting the arms race and reducing the "idle stockpiles—which can only destroy and never create. . . ." Kennedy recognized that Soviet-American differences would continue, but he appealed for an understanding of the common interests of the two giants in limiting the possibilities for war. "And if we cannot end now our differences, at least we can make the world safe for diversity."[88]

This high-minded, conciliatory speech, coming just months before his assassination and at a time when he was preparing the country and the Senate for a possible test ban treaty, has persuaded some that Kennedy was shedding his intransigent Cold Warriorism. Was he? Or, put another way, had he lived, would he have moved United States Cold War foreign policy from confrontation to conciliation, from "a strategy of annihilation" to "a strategy of peace?"[89] It seems unlikely. As the father of the containment doctrine and Kennedy's Ambassador to Yugoslavia, George F. Kennan remarked, "one speech is not enough."[90] One can, for example, contrast the American University address with two speeches that Kennedy was prepared to deliver in conservative Texas on November 22, 1963, had he not been killed. In the first, Kennedy boasted about the "status of our strength and our security" and "our successful defense of freedom" in the Congo, Berlin, Cuba, and Laos, which he attributed "not to the words we used, but to the strength we stood ready to use. . . ." The President went on to applaud his Administration's great military buildup, including the modernization and expansion of United States strategic nuclear power: a 50 percent increase in Polaris submarines; a 75 percent increase in the Minuteman purchase program; a 100 percent increase in the total number of nuclear weapons available in America's strategic alert force. He also listed advances in the development and deployment of tactical nuclear weapons—especially a 60 percent increase in tactical nuclear forces in Western Europe. Kennedy also noted improvements in combat readiness, ship construction, tactical aircraft, and airlift capabilities. Why was this remarkable peacetime swelling of the military undertaken? Because the United States—the "watchman on the walls of world freedom"—had to blunt the "ambitions of international Communism." As for Vietnam in particular, the United States "dare not weary of the task." Neither in this undelivered Dallas speech nor in another planned for Austin did Kennedy speak of negotiations.[91] Indeed, the Cold War rhetoric that Kennedy had asked Americans to temper just months earlier at American University sounded through these two speeches. The arms race that he had earlier recommended be moderated now seemed to be a matter of American triumph.

The issue of Vietnam also raises doubts about whether Kennedy would have changed had he lived. It is an appealing view: Kennedy would not have plunged the United States into the Southeast Asian morass as did Johnson and Nixon; he would have withdrawn the many military personnel he himself had sent—after his victory in the 1964 election. Numerous questions dog this view. First, the sources for it are suspect. The stories come largely from partisan followers such as Kenneth O'Donnell or Arthur M. Schlesinger, Jr., or from Senator Mike Mansfield, who was a dove on Vietnam. Kennedy probably told the Montana senator what he wanted to hear— something Kennedy was known to have done as a matter of style. "I had hundreds of talks with John F. Kennedy about Vietnam," Dean Rusk has remarked, "and never once did he say anything of this sort. . . ."[92] And what did Kennedy mean by "withdrawal?" Former State Department officer William Bundy, McGeorge's brother, has questioned whether Kennedy would have withdrawn under all circumstances.[93] Kennedy always conditioned withdrawal on the creation of a South Vietnam that could survive without the presence of an American garrison. That never occurred in Kennedy's time (or after), and his Administration's removal of Diem only accentuated South Vietnam's political instability, which in turn obstructed its ability to wage an effective war. Finally, Kennedy's advisers—Rusk, Bundy, Rostow, McNamara among them—stayed on after his death and advised Johnson into a major Americanization of the war. No evidence suggests that they would have given President Kennedy different advice. And surely he would not have fired them. Given the persistently poor prospects of victory in Vietnam, Kennedy may very well have pushed on—fearful of both the international and political consequences of failure and driven by a personality that could seldom accommodate defeat. An agonized Kennedy saw the dangers of escalating the Vietnam War and believed that the Vietnamese themselves would ultimately determine the outcome, but he escalated nonetheless.

More typical of Kennedy's foreign policy legacy than the American University address, then, were escalation in Vietnam; an arms race of massive proportion and fear, including the bomb-shelter mania that the Administration stimulated;[94] a huge increase in nuclear weapons; neglect of traditional, patient diplomacy; involvement in Third World disputes beyond America's capabilities or talents to resolve; greater factionalism in the Atlantic alliance; and a globalism of overcommitment that ensured crises and weakened the American economy. Kennedy remained attached to the core of Cold War thinking: the containment doctrine, domino theory, zero-sum game, anti-Communism. As the Sino-Soviet split widened, Kennedy clung to old assumptions of a monolithic or "international" Communism: "A dispute over how to bury the West is no grounds for Western rejoicing."[95] He exaggerated the Communist threat to the Third World, failing to appreciate the local sources that would and did deter Communist inroads.

Although Kennedy said that "there cannot be an American solution to every world problem," he and his advisers often acted as if there were—in South Asia, Africa, Latin America, and the Middle East.[96] The Kennedy team presumed that Americans had answers for others' deep-seated problems, and they sent ill-prepared Americans to places where their good intentions could not be realized. On the question of neutralism, Kennedy certainly seemed more open than Eisenhower, but he proved inconsistent. In Africa, where the United States had little influence and few positions of power, Kennedy thought neutralism might serve as a bulwark against Communism. But there and elsewhere he became intolerant of neutralists who received Soviet assistance or who criticized the United States in ways that fed the Soviet propaganda machine. In South Asia he tried to move India away from non-alignment through economic and military aid. The President also feared that some Western European nations would turn neutral. Overall, it seems fair to conclude that Kennedy wanted to defeat neutralism and bring its adherents into the American Cold War network. As for relations with allies, Kennedy proved incapable of meeting his goal of an Atlantic community, contributed to Canadian anti-Americanism, tried to nudge Israel toward peace with the Arabs but failed, and, in Africa, sided with colonials who also happened to be allies in Europe.

In the end, Kennedy revealed himself as an American traditionalist extending America's considerable global power, defending that power through hegemonic policies, protecting American interests challenged by Third World nationalists, advocating reform abroad to ensure non-radical change, thwarting revolutions, deterring Communists, attempting to uphold the credibility of the United States's deep commitments, standing with dictators in Latin America, interpreting most world events as tests between East and West, and trying to win the Cold War through both foreign aid and military superiority. Kennedy did not seek a balance of power in the international system; he sought United States supremacy. He surely had doubts about the clichés of the Cold War, but he never shed them. Despite the rhetoric of bold, new thinking, Kennedy and his advisers never fundamentally reassessed American foreign policy assumptions. Instead, they endowed them with more vigor and less patience—inviting the shortfalls and failures that dominate the diplomatic record of John F. Kennedy. Arrogance, ignorance, and impatience combined with familiar exaggerations of the Communist threat to deny Kennedy his objectives—especially the winning of the Third World. The world was not plastic, nor did Kennedy have the Midas touch. Out of such disappointment has sprung comforting myth. Out of well-researched historical scholarship emerges unpleasant reality and the need to reckon with a past that has not always matched the selfless and self-satisfying image Americans have of their foreign policy and of Kennedy as their young, fallen hero who never had a chance. Actually, he had his chance, and he failed.

1

The Pursuit of Atlantic Community: Nuclear Arms, Dollars, and Berlin

FRANK COSTIGLIOLA

Western Europeans reacted to John F. Kennedy's assassination much as Americans did.[1] At first they could not comprehend the tragedy. Then, many felt personal grief. Typical were the usually reserved north Germans of Bremen, who now expressed sorrow in overflowing memorial services, tearful condolences, and "a sea of flowers" sent to the American consulate.[2] Kennedy's death sparked mourning throughout most of the world. But especially in Western Europe people felt they had lost, as some French put it, "their own leader."[3] Some Germans remembered Kennedy as their "Super-Chancellor."[4] "The President of the United States is the President of Britain," became a common English sentiment.[5] From Paris, American Ambassador Charles E. Bohlen reported that, in contrast to recent statements that France would "go it alone," public figures "now act almost as if they had lost their own head of state."[6] Another experienced American diplomat, Ambassador to London David Bruce, informed Washington that "recognition of [Kennedy's] position as leader of the free world was, at last[,] ungrudgingly accorded him."[7]

Bohlen's and Bruce's comments on the sudden turnaround in opinion point to an irony. Kennedy's death created, if only briefly, what his policies had failed to achieve, a "New Atlantic Community" that accepted the President's leadership.[8] A further irony is that the Kennedy Administration undermined its own quest for community by refusing to share real decision-making authority with either Western

24

Europe as a whole, or with America's major allies. The Kennedy Administration talked community, but practiced hegemony.

Within the Atlantic alliance—composed of unequal states of unequal independence—the matter of how decisions were made colored all other questions. This issue of alliance governance divided Americans and Europeans, and Europeans from each other, as they confronted crises over Berlin and Cuba, questions of nuclear and economic strategy, and the issue of whether Great Britain would join the European Economic Community (Common Market). In the abstract, Americans sought partnership or community with a united Western Europe. But the Europeans remained divided. And the United States insisted on the right to make most of the decisions. These harsh realities doomed the "Atlantic Community." Relief tinged American disappointment. Washington always feared that a unified Europe—if it were truly independent—could be dangerous.

Washington's effort to supervise the allies went back to the dawn of the postwar era. In 1948–49, the United States promoted the North Atlantic Treaty Organization (NATO) to corral its allies and to head off neutralism, as well as to deter the Russians. In the early 1950s, with David Bruce as point man, Washington pushed for the European Defense Community, a European army which, through NATO, would be under United States command. This obvious reduction of sovereignty was too much for France to swallow, and in 1954 it rejected the scheme. The United States recouped somewhat by gaining tighter integration and more NATO control over the separate national armies.

By the late 1950s, managing the allies had become more problematic. American command of Western Europe's military was challenged by President Charles de Gaulle's removal of French units from NATO's integrated force. De Gaulle also questioned NATO's first premise: that the United States would retaliate against a Russian invasion of Western Europe with an atomic assault on the Soviet heartland. America's new vulnerability to nuclear-tipped missiles, dramatically underscored by Russia's launching of the *Sputnik* satellite in 1957 and rocketry advances since then, had made this a hollow promise, de Gaulle insisted. Although de Gaulle stood out as Washington's most persistent critic, other Europeans shared his doubts. The security of America's nuclear umbrella became an urgent question in 1958 and 1961 when the Russians precipitated crises over Berlin. The Soviets threatened to sign a peace treaty with their East

German satellite, ending the Western powers' occupation rights in West Berlin.

Doubts about America's nuclear credibility compounded the economic/military predicament Kennedy faced on taking office. Since the early 1950s, Washington had maintained in Europe some 400,000 military men, 500,000 dependents and service-connected personnel, and a large arsenal of conventional and nuclear weapons.[9] This fighting machine was supposed to deter an invasion by Russia or adventurism by West Germany, the latter still smarting from its division and its territorial losses after World War II. In the first postwar decade, America's huge trade surplus had easily financed this military force as well as a generous foreign aid program. Such relatively easy predominance ended in the late 1950s. The United States faced growing trade competition from Japan and from the Common Market (a customs union composed of France, West Germany, Italy, Belgium, the Netherlands, and Luxemburg). Like President Dwight D. Eisenhower in his last years in office, Kennedy confronted the dilemma that the troops in Europe undermined the nation's economic strength even as they shored up its military might. Dollars spent in Europe to maintain these forces added to the nation's balance of payments deficit. Although small compared to later times, the persistent payments deficits—averaging $2.4 billion in each of the Kennedy years—undermined confidence in the dollar. Worried foreigners exchanged their dollars for gold, and United States gold reserves sank from $21.8 billion in 1955 to $15.6 billion in 1963.[10] Attracted by Europe's rising economy and productivity, many United States corporations built new, efficient factories on that continent instead of at home, adding further to the balance of payments drain. That deficit became a symptom and a symbol of the nation's fading ability to pay for all it wanted to do in the world. Running against Eisenhower's record in the 1960 election campaign, Kennedy scored the elderly President for failing to close either the payments deficit or the alleged missile gap with Russia.

Yet the candidate suggested few changes in European policy. Like Eisenhower, Kennedy feared retreat from Berlin would destroy West Germany's confidence in America and drive that country, and perhaps all of Western Europe, into neutralism. Yet both men wanted to avoid war and admitted the necessity of some concessions in Berlin negotiations. In 1959, Kennedy argued that the Berlin crisis required beefed up military might, but no basic policy shift. He and Eisenhower shared concern over the payments deficit and gold drain, and agreed the Europeans should do more to help America. As a senator, Kennedy saw the Third World, not Western Europe, as the hottest Cold War battleground. In 1957, he stirred the wrath of the French by urging them to grant independence to rebellious Algeria.[11] In his 1960 campaign debates with Richard Nixon, Kennedy did not include Western Europe in the list of trouble spots where he faulted Republican policies.[12]

Although Western Europe figured neither as a campaign issue nor as the main Cold War battlefield, it remained of central importance. Europe's booming economy could help support America's global responsibilities, Kennedy declared in a 1959 speech. This address revealed some of the thinking which made it difficult for American leaders to redeem their rhetoric about the "Atlantic Community." "[T]he North Atlantic Alliance must be an alliance among equals," Kennedy began. He then urged a tighter grouping, able to tap Europe's new wealth for "common purpose[s]." Presuming that Washington itself could define those "common" tasks, the senator called on Europe to strengthen the underdeveloped world and the weakened dollar. He relied on the comfortable assumption—outdated by the time he became President—that "vigorous American leadership" could line up Western Europe behind the United States. Such a grouping, Americans liked to tell themselves, was a community of equals.[13]

As President, Kennedy never tackled the contradiction between American hegemony and Atlantic Community. Instead, his Administration crafted a policy, labeled the "Grand Design," to bolster the American position by making Western Europe a unified, faithful helpmate.[14] This ambitious plan included several goals: to ease Britain into the European Common Market, to increase exports by reducing trans-Atlantic tariff barriers, to persuade Europe to bear more of the burden of defense expenses, and to channel European nuclear aspirations into a Multilateral Force (MLF) under Washington's supervision. Britain's presumed "special relationship" with the United States, more special to London than to Washington, seemed the appropriate vehicle for expanded American influence in uniting Europe. A senior Kennedy adviser inadvertently exposed the contradiction in the policy by explaining it as getting Britain "to act as our lieutenant (the fashionable word is partner)."[15]

Both Americans and Europeans favored "consultation" on the issues of the Grand Design and the Cold War, but they attached different meanings to the word. The Kennedy Administration discussed issues with the allies and informed them of its thinking. This is what it meant by "consultation." If, however, some of the allies remained unpersuaded, the Americans went ahead anyway. President de Gaulle's version of "consultation" or "coordination" of policy was far different; indeed, he sought genuine sharing of decision-making. But such coordination was rare. Partly this was because of the Europeans' own internal divisiveness. Mostly it was due to the American's conviction that their power and insight gave them the right to lead. Kennedy paid even less attention to the allies' views than Eisenhower had, an American diplomat recalled.[16] De Gaulle saw this conflict over alliance governance as an instance of age-old national rivalry.

Kennedy officials saw de Gaulle's restiveness as a challenge to their creativity. "The political problem of running the present world has changed its character in this decade," asserted Walt W. Rostow, the State Department Policy Planning chief. "Look at Nasser, look at Nehru, look at de Gaulle." Their "new assertiveness . . . does not scare me," he explained, "because . . . we know, out of the way we run our own society, how one weaves together diverse interests around common purposes." Having crafted a unified nation out of different states and peoples, Americans had the "innate . . . skill," a confident Rostow claimed, to stitch together a "free world" consensus.[17] This tapestry was backed, however, by military steel. "We need to keep [the diversity] under tolerable control," Rostow asserted. For United States military forces stationed around the globe, this task of controlling the allies was "equally" important to containing the Communists. In particular, the integration of American and German troops on German soil was essential to holding Bonn "on a collective course with the U.S. and the West."[18]

David Bruce was more perceptive than Rostow about the contradiction between hegemony and community, but he was no more successful in resolving it. Bruce pointed to the "considerable anti-Americanism in Europe." He blamed the "vicious circle of European dependence and US predominance." He understood that a healthy Atlantic relationship demanded "treat[ing] a uniting Europe as an equal partner," entitled to meaningful consultation. Yet even this sophisticated diplomat expected the "equal partner" to follow America's lead and support the "Atlantic Community" tasks and policies set by the United States. He saw "dangers" if Europe "struck off on its own, seeking to play a role independent of the US." "We must have a voice and play a stabilizing role in European affairs," he emphasized.[19] Like other American officials, Bruce wanted "equal" partnership—with the United States in a superior position.

Confident of their ability to manage such a contradiction, Kennedy officials focused on the promise of the Grand Design. In a secret session of the Senate Foreign Relations Committee, Secretary of State Dean Rusk explained how the scheme could help the United States organize the world and achieve victory in the Cold War: "Western Europe, if it were really unified, and the North Atlantic Community, if we really developed the relationships that all of us have been discussing . . . , would be a nexus of special relationships reaching right around the world, with our relations with Latin America, and with the countries in the Pacific, the British with the Commonwealth, and the French with the French-speaking countries. Germany [too] is establishing some interesting relationships with selected countries." As Rusk and others saw it, the United States would be at the hub, with direct and indirect channels of influence radiating to most of the world. Such organization would isolate the Communists and, Rusk predicted, "would be reflected in growing caution on the part of the Soviet Union."[20] The so-called Communist bloc would be outclassed and reduced, as Rostow put it, to a "relatively minor power in the world."[21]

The officials who sought this Cold War victory—Kennedy, Rusk, National Security Affairs Adviser McGeorge Bundy, Rostow, Under Secretary of State George W. Ball, Secretary of Defense Robert McNamara, Assistant Secretary of Defense for International Security Affairs Paul Nitze, Assistant Secretary of State for European Affairs William R. Tyler, and the two most influential ambassadors, Bruce and Bohlen—all favored closer economic and military ties with a uniting Europe. Many were veterans of Dean Acheson's State Department of 1949–1953. Kennedy found Acheson in the early 1960s too militant toward the Soviet Union, but the President's policy on Germany and Europe derived much from the man who had been present at the creation of the Cold War. Acheson remained a consultant throughout Kennedy's presidency. Ball, Rostow, and Rusk became the Grand Design's most ardent proponents.[22] Although Kennedy and Bundy did not share their passion for the policy, they nonetheless supported it up to the summer of 1963.

The Grand Design interested Kennedy as a tactic to deal with the two dangers that scared him most, nuclear war and the balance of payments deficit.[23] JFK understood that the time of easy economic predominance had passed. "We have been very generous to Europe," he told the National Security Council (NSC), "it is now time to look out for ourselves."[24] He feared that the payments deficit complicated such self-defense by giving "the French and other countries a stick with which to beat us."[25] Indeed, during the Kennedy years, the French began to complain that America's payments deficit exported inflation and financed the takeover of foreign industry. Later, France openly assaulted America's gold reserves.[26] Kennedy believed that the United States had to close the payments deficit by expanding exports—or else face decline, like that Britain had suffered. "If we cannot keep up our export surplus, we shall not have the dollar exchange with which to meet our overseas military commitments," Kennedy warned the NSC. "We must either do a good job of selling abroad or pull back."[27]

Expecting that lower tariffs would boost trade between America and Europe, particularly United States exports, the Kennedy Administration pushed Congress to pass the Trade Expansion Act (TEA), empowering the negotiation of tariff decreases (see Chapter 2). De Gaulle and German Chancellor Konrad Adenauer worried that Americans would export "monstrous amounts" to Europe and overwhelm their industries.[28] Such fears of the TEA proved ironic since the freer trade negotiated later in the 1960s found the United States increasingly helpless against foreign competition.

Pinched by the gold drain, Washington prodded Western Europeans to buy conventional weapons from the United States, thus offsetting the cost of the American defense umbrella. Flush with funds and committed to an integrated defense with the United States, the Germans and Italians complied, but the French balked. Because Washington refused to sell items needed for the French nuclear force, Paris would not buy large amounts of conventional equipment.[29]

Like Eisenhower, Kennedy opposed the nascent French nuclear force because it aggravated the problems of nuclear proliferation and managing the alliance. The fewer nuclear powers, Kennedy officials believed, the easier it was to direct the West's nuclear forces, prevent accidental war, reach arms control, and maintain allied cohesion. In 1958, Eisenhower had renewed nuclear cooperation with the British, but had refused to include France in the entente. Embittered, de

Gaulle accelerated the French program and tested France's first atomic bomb in 1960. JFK considered and then rejected the option of nuclear assistance to France. "The finally persuasive argument" against such help, noted a Kennedy aide, "was that it would not bend General de Gaulle to our purpose but only strengthen him in his."[30] Kennedy wanted not nuclear sharing with the allies, but centralized deterrent management in Washington. He decided to reverse Eisenhower's policy by "mov[ing] away from any intimate [nuclear] partnership with the British."[31] He aimed to persuade London to trade in its independent deterrent for membership in the proposed Multilateral Force, in which the United States would have a major voice. This would set a precedent for France, perhaps after de Gaulle, to abandon its separate nuclear weapons program. The American Ambassador to NATO explained that *any* truly "independent" nuclear deterrent—British, French, or European—was "dangerous." "We simply have to be in it," he insisted."[32]

National nuclear forces appeared especially dangerous because they might stimulate West Germany to obtain its own nuclear arms. This was a recurring nightmare for Kennedy officials. "The mere prospect" of German nuclear weaponry, they worried, would wreck NATO and scare Western and Eastern Europe into the arms of Russia.[33] Most British, French, and German leaders shared Washington's fears of the nuclear genie, but they were skeptical that an American monopoly was the safest way to control it. Such doubts multiplied when McNamara and others began to explain "flexible response."

Flexible response was the Kennedy Administration's strategy to minimize the threat of nuclear war and to manage Soviet-American conflict if it occurred. It was defense analysts' latest attempt to make rational contingency plans for an inherently crazy situation—nuclear war. The Kennedy Administration backed away from Eisenhower's reliance on massive retaliation as deterrence to Soviet aggression. What if the Soviet provocation was too slight, Kennedy officials questioned, to justify such an awful response? How could nuclear weapons deal with Soviet-supported "wars of liberation"? While increasing the nuclear arsenal, the President asked the Pentagon to expand capability to fight non-nuclear wars. He urged the allies to augment their conventional forces (preferably with American-made equipment) so that the West could resist a Russian invasion without immediate resort to nuclear weapons. This would allow time for negotiation to head off Armageddon. With its emphasis on centralized crisis management, flexible response demanded that the United States direct the West's nuclear forces. For example, if Washington ever dropped a nuclear bomb on remote Siberia to signal its serious intent in a crisis, the French could jumble the message by dropping one on Leningrad.

Despite all the calculating and war gaming, nuclear security remained a gamble. One little-discussed risk involved America's many short-range nuclear weapons deployed in NATO countries, particularly West Germany. According to agreement, both Washington and the host country had to approve the firing of these weapons. This "two-key" system amounted to "just a lot of nonsense," Senator Stuart Symington, a defense expert, testified in a secret hearing. "In case of trouble," the host country's armed forces could "always knock our man in the head and fire the missile."[34] The Kennedy Administration improved security at the European missile sites. Yet the nightmare remained that one of the allies would trigger a nuclear war which the United States would have to enter.[35]

The two other main concepts in the Kennedy Administration's nuclear strategy, counterforce and mutual assured destruction (MAD), also assumed that Washington—not the allies—would initiate and direct any attack on the Soviets. Kennedy inherited from Eisenhower the counterforce doctrine and the massive nuclear superiority over Russia necessary to carry it out. The missile gap on which Kennedy had based much of his 1960 campaign turned out to be huge—but in America's favor. Counterforce strategists argued that in a crisis the United States could launch a surgical first strike, destroying almost all of Russia's nuclear forces. Then the Soviets would have to surrender or risk destruction of their cities. In the war-fighting plan which McNamara and aides drafted in 1963, 82 percent of the strategic nuclear force on constant alert was aimed at Soviet military installations. Still, even a victorious limited nuclear war meant mass death for Americans. In 1962–1963, as the Soviets built more missiles, hardened their missile sites, and deployed more nuclear submarines, McNamara grew increasingingly skeptical that a counterforce first strike could win a nuclear war. He and other Pentagon officials talked more about MAD. The MAD strategy figured deterrence as the best protection: Washington and Moscow each would maintain nuclear forces capable of enduring a first attack and then destroying the aggressor. If neither superpower could win a nuclear war, the thinking ran, neither side would start one. Despite the shift in McNamara's public statements from counterforce to MAD, most of America's nuclear arsenal continued to be aimed at Soviet military targets.

Already horrified by the prospect of nuclear war in Europe, many Europeans became frightened by these changing strategies, this thinking about the unthinkable. Densely populated nations close to the Soviet Union, the allies wanted deterrence, not vaporization. They feared that flexible response proved that the United States, now vulnerable to Soviet missiles, was backing away from its commitment to use nuclear weapons to avenge (and deter) a Russian invasion of Europe. A more convincing conventional defense meant a less credible nuclear deterrent, it seemed to Europeans. And limited war between the superpowers could mean a total war in their homelands. As to what to do if nuclear deterrence failed, the Europeans expressed uncertainty. During the Berlin crisis (discussed below), Pentagon officials invited their British, French, and German counterparts to participate in a war game. When the scenario escalated to the nuclear threshold, the Europeans refused to push the button.[36]

Like the superpowers, however, the British and French eagerly deployed what they dreaded to use. Each coveted an independent deterrent, the ability, as de Gaulle put it, to "tear off an arm" of the Soviets or to trigger a war that America would have to enter.[37] They remembered that the United States had come late into the two world wars and had opposed them at Suez in 1956. The French and the British (despite some opposition from the left wing of the Labour party) also appreciated nuclear arms as a relatively cheap way to shore up their world status after losing their empires.[38]

De Gaulle became Washington's most persistent critic on nuclear, as well as political and economic issues. Kennedy admired the general for his heroism during World War II and for letting go of the Algerian colony while heading off a French civil war.[39] The United States would have welcomed de Gaulle's restoration of French pride, power, and prestige—if France had become a loyal helpmate. Instead, an exasperated Kennedy official noted, de Gaulle's bid for European leadership "cuts directly across US interests all along the board."[40] The State Department tried to monitor the difficult general. Bohlen revealed that the American Embassy in Paris "had him taped"—that is, one of de Gaulle's advisers gave reports on de Gaulle to the Americans.[41] Yet the French leader often kept his innermost thoughts to himself. His defiance of United States hegemony won support or at least sympathy from many Europeans. De Gaulle's challenge signaled that at least some Europeans had outgrown Washington's protectorate—and gave the lie to Acheson's claim that "there are no [European] leaders unless we create some."[42]

De Gaulle's rivalry with Washington went back to World War II, when Franklin D. Roosevelt had tried to create a malleable French leader to replace the difficult general. De Gaulle concluded that France should never again allow another power to control its defense. Out of office from 1946 to 1958, the general threatened to stage a revolution or turn to the Russians if it became necessary to keep France out of the proposed European army. After coming to power, he pulled French naval units out of NATO and refused to reintegrate into NATO those army divisions then returning from the colonial war in Algeria.[43] The French Army's withdrawal from Algeria, its third setback in two decades, made it seethe with frustration. Attempted military coups and assaults on de Gaulle's life followed. The "only way" to restore the army's faith in itself and in France was by "building its faith in France's nuclear weapons future," explained de Gaulle's inspector general of the army.[44]

An independent nuclear force would also boost France's bid to become the senior partner of West Germany, which in 1954 had renounced production of nuclear weapons. "Germans are Germans," mused de Gaulle, who feared the old enemy would strike a deal with Russia unless it was tied to France and the rest of continental Western Europe.[45] When de Gaulle returned to power, he cultivated Chancellor Adenauer. Both men had a conservative, Catholic, early-twentieth-century background. Both came from the border region over which French and Germans had fought since Charlemagne's day. The modern Grand Charles appealed to Adenauer's desire to end the ancient quarrel and to the German's distrust of the Kennedy Administration. During the 1961 Berlin crisis, de Gaulle tried to out-German the Germans, opposing any concessions to the Communists.[46]

De Gaulle also tried to persuade Washington to accept Paris's preeminence over Bonn. France was the natural spokesman for Western Europe, the general asserted soon after he assumed power in 1958. France, Britain, and the United States should join to coordinate the West's global military and political strategy, with each having the major voice in its domain and a veto over the others' use of nuclear weapons. From 1958 to 1962, de Gaulle repeatedly pushed this tripartite directorate. "Eisenhower rejected it, Kennedy rejected it, and he [de Gaulle] never forgave us for it," Rusk recalled. Washington intended to set policy itself. It was not about to relinquish American predominance in Western Europe. Nor did the United States favor shutting out the other allies, particularly the Federal Republic of Germany (West Germany) and Italy.[47]

"Germany is the most important country in the world to us," Acheson emphasized to McNamara. It "is subject to be influenced by us . . . as the Soviet Union, France, and Britain are not."[48] Even though McNamara, Bundy, and Kennedy were not as Europe-oriented as were Acheson and the State Department, they understood that the alliance with Germany propped up America's global power. Germany had become the powerhouse of the Common Market and a favored investment site for United States corporations. In 1962, the United States sold goods worth $1.8 billion to West Germany and bought $1 billion worth from it, yielding a handsome trade surplus. Americans hoped to enlist global-minded German trading interests in the TEA tariff negotiations. The Federal Republic manned the large army necessary for a conventional defense of Europe, and it would be the front line in a European battle. Without Germany, "Western Europe is an eggshell," veteran adviser W. Averell Harriman told the President.[49] Finally, Germany was central to the major issues before the Western alliance: Franco-American rivalry, the Berlin crisis, British admission to the Common Market, and the Multilateral Force.

Germany had become particularly important in an area of burning concern to Kennedy, the gold drain and balance of payments deficit. The President and others insisted on Germany's help. Under Secretary Ball argued that Germany owed the United States a debt for past aid, for current military support, and for America's having opened world markets. In a personal letter to Adenauer, Kennedy detailed the American military buildup in the Berlin crisis and repeated the request for substantial balance of payments help.[50]

Finally in 1961–1962, under the Gilpatric/Strauss agreements negotiated by American and German defense officials, the Federal Republic agreed to offset through purchases of United States weapons the balance of payments cost (including spending by dependents) of maintaining American troops in Germany. In 1963 that amounted to $675 million per year. The link between German money and United States troops was quite explicit. The "Chancellor should be left in no doubt," Bundy told President Lyndon B. Johnson shortly after Kennedy's death, "that [this] performance is indispensable for our continued six division presence."[51] Analyzing America's worldwide military expenditures and receipts, a White House official informed Kennedy that "almost all of the improvement between . . . [19]62 and [19]63 lies in the increased receipts from Germany."[52]

The Kennedy Administration also urged the Federal Republic to spend more on foreign aid. Ball recalled that Kennedy and Rostow viewed Germany's payments surplus (earned from its vigorous global exports) "as a bank . . . for our grandiose Third World programs."[53] When Bonn officials worried that the trial of Nazi war criminal Adolf Eichmann and the publication of William Shirer's best-seller *The Rise and Fall of the Third Reich* would refocus world attention on the Nazi past, Rostow suggested "a generous German commitment" to Indian and Pakistani aid to buoy Germany's public image.[54] As United States ambitions in the Third World conflicted with balance of payments difficulties, Washington looked to Bonn to pay more of the bills.

Germany's importance sharpened the anxiety with which Kennedy officials viewed its future. Priding themselves as modernists, these men remained prisoners of the past. Kennedy, Bundy, Rusk, Ball, Rostow, and others saw German developments in the early 1960s through a lens shaped by the 1930s and 1940s. They remembered how Adolf Hitler had overthrown the Weimar Republic by exploiting resentment of the Versailles treaty's discrimination against Germany. They recalled Germany's sudden deals with the Soviets in 1922 and in 1939 and its lunge against Russia in 1941. As junior officials, many had worked on the postwar integration of Germany into Western Europe through the Marshall Plan and NATO.

In the early 1960s, Germany stood again as a rising nation suffering territorial grievances and discrimination, this time as the only major Western power without nuclear weapons. After World War II, Germany lost territory to Russia, Poland, and Czechoslovakia. What remained was divided into East and West Germany. The Russians' control of East Germany meant they held the key to reunification. This raised the frightening prospect of a German deal or a duel with the Soviets. Adenauer, who since 1949 had kept West Germany tied safely to the West, was about to retire. A possible successor was the popular, nationalistic defense minister from Bavaria, Franz Josef Strauss, who made plain his dissatisfaction with Germany's non-nuclear status. Unable to forget Hitler's rise to power, Americans worried that Strauss or someone like him might come to power by fanning German discontent.[55]

At the root of American anxiety stood the belief that United States policy did not satisfy—and did not intend to satisfy—Germany's deepest interests as an independent nation. Therefore the Americans (like the French) tried to contain German nationalism and to promote German leaders who accepted foreign advice. "A more nationalist German government would try independent negotiations with the Soviets," feared Acheson and other European experts.[56]

Unease about the German phoenix also swept through the public realm. In addition to *The Rise and Fall of the Third Reich,* Shirer, formerly a correspondent in Nazi Germany, wrote for *Look* magazine a gruesome tale about America's fate if Germany had won the war. A major publisher advertised another journalist's account—*The New Germany and the Old Nazis*—as a timely warning about "the Frankenstein monster" created by the United States. Such fears were aggravated when Strauss ordered a raid on the offices of the muckraking German magazine *Der Spiegel.*[57] Some wartime feeling persisted. During the Berlin crisis, J. William Fulbright, chairman of the Senate Foreign Relations Committee, found it "absurd" to risk "the United States, with 180 million people, over 2 million Germans, when they were trying to destroy us 15 years ago."[58]

Policymakers worried that these former enemies still were prone to emotional instability. Ball feared "a revival of the inter-war German psychosis."[59] Part-time adviser Henry A. Kissinger gave Kennedy an analysis which characterized the Federal Republic as "a candidate for a nervous breakdown."[60] Bohlen recalled Kennedy's fear that "Germany could again become a menace."[61] The Grand Designers concluded that Germany was a problem in the making—but they were confident they could manage it.

The 1961 Berlin crisis added urgency. The United States, Britain, and France still occupied, by right of conquest, the Western sectors of Berlin, in the heart of Communist East Germany. In support of Bonn's claim to be the only legitimate German state, the Western alliance insisted that East Germany, which called itself the German Democratic Republic (GDR), was neither German nor democratic, and certainly not a republic, but only a Soviet-occupied "Zone." In 1958, Soviet Premier Nikita Khrushchev had threatened to sign a peace treaty with the GDR. Britain, France, and the United States would then have to recognize the government of the GDR and arrange access to West Berlin with it. After long negotiations, the two superpowers had edged toward a working agreement. Then came, in 1960, the U-2 spy plane affair and the abortive Paris summit. Both sides pulled back from compromise. The crisis heated up again in February 1961 when Khrushchev, under pressure from the GDR, the Chinese, and hard-liners in his own country, announced he would sign a peace treaty with East Germany by the end of the year. At the June 1961 Vienna summit, Kennedy and Khrushchev warned each other that they had vital interests in Berlin and would not back down. Yet both left the door open to negotiation.[62]

The confrontation had deep historical roots. It was the final Soviet-American dispute stemming from the territorial spoils of World War II. The free movement of people between East and West Berlin permitted before August 13, 1961, was a remnant of Europe before its division in the Cold War. The crisis erupted over the old German capital, from whence had come the war which had brought American and Russian power into the heart of Europe.

As Kennedy came to realize, the crisis turned on two levels. The first was the emergency in East Germany imposed by the attractions of West Berlin. The GDR suffered a population exodus through the open border between East and West Berlin. The outflow surged to some 30,000 in July 1961, most of the émigrés going on to more prosperous West Germany. With more than 50 percent of the refugees under the age of twenty-five and many of them skilled workers (with training paid for by the East German state), the GDR seemed to be bleeding to death.[63] The glitter of West Berlin's prosperity and freedom, set amidst gray East Germany, made the city a unique Western showcase. The island city also served as a base for propaganda and agents sent into Eastern Europe.

On a second, more dangerous level, the crisis tested each superpower's toughness and position in Germany. Neither was about to back down, and each would negotiate only after it had demonstrated its military resolve. Yet American and Russian leaders understood that gunfire could quickly escalate to nuclear war. Both tried to escape the dilemma by beefing up their military forces—to signal serious intent, to enhance capacity for a conventional struggle, and to ease their own anxieties by taking *some* assertive step. The stakes in Berlin ran so high because they included West and East Germany, that is, each superpower's strategically and economically most important protectorate. The Soviets sought to breathe life into East Germany by stanching the refugee flow, forcing the West to grant political recognition, and, ideally from the Communist viewpoint, ending the Western presence in Berlin.

West Berlin itself was not vital to the United States. But a broad consensus of American leaders feared that if they abandoned that city—or even if they negotiated directly with East Germany to *preserve* the Western presence in Berlin—the shock would loosen the Federal Republic of Germany from its mooring in the West. Since 1949, Chancellor Adenauer had assured his people that reunification could be won through the strategy of alliance with the West and ostracism of East Germany. However, no one outside Germany really desired reunification. Indeed, Adenauer understood that his own political and cultural base in Catholic, conservative Western Germany would be undercut by reunion with traditionally Protestant, domineering Prussia—now indoctrinated with Communism.

Yet no one dared admit that the emperor had no clothes. If the GDR gained all Berlin and recognition by the West, Adenauer and others warned, the West German people would feel betrayed and turn away from the Western alliance. Then, the nightmare scenario ran, some nationalist leader would ride to power on this resentment and grab for reunification by dealing with the Russians or threatening them with war.[64] Bonn appeared to be like a domino that could be toppled from either the right or the left. America's power and credibility in Europe, and in much of the world, depended on keeping the Germans upright and facing West.

The Grand Design aimed to brace the Germans with NATO, the Multilateral Force, and the Common Market (made stronger and more open to United States influence through Great Britain's admission). This strategy followed the postwar pattern, Bruce noted to Kennedy, of using Western European unity as a "framework within which to *contain* and provide a *creative outlet* for a West Germany which might be tempted to seek reunification with East Germany through bilateral arrangements with Moscow, or otherwise prove a disruptive element in the world power balance."[65]

The French complicated this tactic of Western European unity. They agreed the Germans had to be contained—that is, kept away from both nuclear weapons and the Russians. Yet neither Paris nor Washington trusted the other. "We have to have a control ourselves," explained Georges Pompidou, who later succeeded de Gaulle. "We ourselves cannot risk that someday Washington might decide to neutralize Germany, without even asking us."[66] Rivalry also fueled differences; de Gaulle wanted Bonn's "creative outlet" to be support of France. He hoped that Paris, not Washington, would lead united Europe. The French general stood steadfastly against the Multilateral Force and British admission to the Common Market. He fed Adenauer's fears that Kennedy would reach a Berlin agreement with Khrushchev at German expense.

Indeed, during the Berlin crisis fear of war moved Kennedy toward compromise. "We shall probably come very close to the edge" of nuclear conflict, the President ruminated.[67] With massive American and Russian forces faced off in West and East Germany, JFK feared the crisis could easily explode. He and his advisers reviewed the options of conventional war, a warning nuclear shot, and limited and all-out nuclear war. A poll of American citizens showed a 57 percent to 21 percent margin believed Berlin "worth risking a total war."[68] Intrigued White House and Pentagon officials analyzed satellite photographs showing the pitiful condition of Soviet strategic forces. In the spring of 1961, the Russians had far fewer operational ICBMs than did the United States; none of their bombers or other forces had been put on alert; and their early warning system had gaping holes. A surgical first strike seemed easy, yet further analysis suggested that the few Soviet nuclear weapons likely to survive a United States attack could kill up to fifteen million Americans. In Western Europe, under the gun of harder-to-destroy Soviet short-range missiles, deaths could reach into the tens of millions.[69]

This horror brought into sharper focus the shared perspectives of the superpowers. Throughout the confrontation, there persisted the faint outline of the Russian-American alliance against Germany during the Second World War. The United States and the Soviet Union groped to adjust the delicate European balance to the revival of *two* Germanys, one far more powerful than the other, and to do this without having either superpower suffer humiliation or lose control of its portion of Germany. Americans and Russians arrived separately at the conclusion that if they lost their positions in Berlin, West Germany would be set loose on a dangerous path. If Russian pressures drove the United States out of Berlin, Rusk warned, the "chain reaction" would blow up America's alliance system.[70] Then, Kennedy worried, West Germany might go "off on a nationalistic and independent course . . . setting off another war."[71] Many observers thought the East Germans might revolt if their escape hatch to West Berlin were slammed shut. Washington viewed the GDR "as a gigantic pressure cooker, about to explode," a State Department official recalled.[72] If such a rebellion against Moscow's client government erupted, Khrushchev feared, West Germany might intervene. Kennedy's representative assured him that West Germany could not rush in because it was under United States and NATO control. Yet the Soviet leader still doubted that one could trust "the old Nazi generals."[73]

Such complaints against Bonn's militarism and revanchism had become a staple of Soviet propaganda, and American leaders routinely and publicly dismissed such charges. Privately, however, Kennedy officials showed more understanding. From talks with the Russians, Ambassador Llewellyn "Tommy" Thompson reported deep "fear [that] West Germany will eventually take action which will face them with [the] choice between world war or retreat from East Germany."[74] Rusk agreed that the Soviets "are undoubtedly genuinely worried about the rearmament of Germany."[75] The Secretary realized that they wanted to "get . . . stabilized" the post-World War II boundaries of Eastern Europe.[76] With Western backing, the Federal Republic had refused to recognize these territorial losses, hoping to win concessions in the final World War II settlement.

Throughout their confrontation, the superpowers shared an interest in the GDR's stability. "Like the Soviets, U.S. is faced with dilemma on East Germany," Rusk decided.[77] The United States sympathized with the refugees' plight and exploited the propaganda opportunity. Edward R. Murrow's United States Information Agency beamed around the world such features as "West Berlin Today—A Refugee a Minute," which "dramatized" the Soviet failure to respect "self-determination" and satisfy "human needs."[78] Although eager to embarrass the Russians, the Kennedy Administration "would not like [to] see [an East German] revolt," Rusk instructed diplomats. "We plan, therefore [to] do nothing at this time which would exacerbate situation."[79] An explosion would only demonstrate United States impotence (as in the 1953 and 1956 Eastern European revolts) and inflame the West Germans.

As the number of refugees climbed higher, the United States signaled that whatever the Communists did in East Berlin was their business. "I don't understand why the East Germans don't close their border," Fulbright suggested on nationwide television; "I think they have a right to close it."[80] Bundy charted the "helpful impact of

Senator Fulbright's remarks." So did East German chief Walter Ulbricht, who reportedly quoted Fulbright when explaining to a meeting in the Kremlin why the escape way should be plugged.[81]

Early on August 13, 1961, the East Germans began stringing barbed wire on their side of the border between East and West Berlin. Later reports suggested that the GDR guards, if challenged by Western forces, were prepared to pull back and start putting up barbed wire further inside East Berlin.[82]

Kennedy officials were privately relieved. The GDR had stopped the exodus without triggering a revolt and had not interfered with Western access to West Berlin. The barbed wire came not as a complete surprise, since analysts had expected a "Chinese wall," most probably on the East German-East Berlin border. When the news reached the President at Hyannis Port, he conferred briefly with his advisers and then announced, "I am going sailing."[83] Foy Kohler, a State Department expert on Berlin, remarked, "The East Germans have done us a favor. That refugee flow was becoming embarrassing."[84] Now the Communists would suffer embarrassment. "The whole world is watching Berlin," Vice President Lyndon Johnson reported to Kennedy.[85]

The fence cutting through Berlin—which grew from barbed wire to a high, double wall of concrete—also sliced open the pretense that Adenauer's policy of linkage with the West could deliver German reunification. The division of the old capital pushed that dream further into the future. The Wall highlighted the futility of trying to ignore the GDR out of existence. It thus marked the beginning of West Germany's slow turn toward *Ostpolitik,* that is, direct ties with East Germany and Eastern Europe. Some Kennedy officials thought this move could be useful as long as the U.S. kept an important say in Bonn's policy.[86]

In spite of its public protest, Washington accepted the Wall, which did not violate vital American interests. West Berliners and West Germans felt frightened and betrayed by the action of the East and the inaction of the West. Lord Mayor Willy Brandt led a mass demonstration of West Berliners who asked Washington to do something. Brandt sent Kennedy an angry, distraught letter. Berlin students sent JFK an umbrella, thereby comparing him to Neville Chamberlain, the 1930s appeaser.[87]

Washington was "surprised that the reaction in Berlin was so strong," Bohlen admitted in a meeting with West Berlin officials. The diplomatic troubleshooter revealed the gap between American and German perspectives when he insisted that "this was not the real Berlin crisis; that will come only when the Russians try to interfere with the rights of the Allied powers." Such remarks were cold comfort to German patriots and to those persons suddenly cut off from relatives and friends in the eastern sector of the city. Washington's interest, Bohlen stressed, was limited to the "three essential[s]" of "maintaining Allied presence, Allied access[,] and West Berlin's viability and contact with the West."[88]

If Washington wanted to maintain its presence in *West* Germany, however, it had to bolster morale there. Kennedy officials waxed confident that they could fine-tune German psychology. "The obvious gambit is for us to make vigorous noises about German reunification," a Bundy aide recommended, while encouraging "East German dissidence, not resistance."[89]

To cover the German-American rift over the Wall, Kennedy employed melodramatic symbols of solidarity, which proved ironic in view of American unease at German emotionalism. This planted the seed for West Berlin's passionate attachment to JFK. Kennedy sent to West Berlin Vice President Johnson, General Lucius Clay, the hero of the 1948–49 airlift (and a conservative Republican who, Kennedy believed, would protect his domestic flank), and a token force of 1500 American soldiers with heavy armor. Kennedy hoped these gestures would project an image of American commitment. "A brilliant stroke—*Gestalt* psychology at its best," applauded a German expert.[90] After the trip, Johnson stressed to Kennedy the importance of "public opinion in West Germany . . . in the shaping of German policy." Kennedy carefully cultivated this opinion, most successfully during his 1963 trip to Germany. "Despondency" over the Wall could become "explosive," the Vice President warned, unless the United States satisfied the Germans' hunger for emotional support.

Johnson, who tended toward the maudlin, seemed perfect in this role. He made a passionate speech to the huge crowds of West Berliners who, at Brandt's urging, turned out to greet him. Their "smiles and tears of relief . . . [their] exalted mood . . . approached frenzy," LBJ reported. He too became caught up in the hyper-charged atmosphere. An old woman handed Johnson a bouquet of flowers allegedly picked before fleeing from East Berlin. "As I looked up," he later reported to Kennedy, "I saw the ruins of a building that had been wrecked by our bombers in the war, and here was a German woman kissing my hand in gratitude."[91]

Although the Wall sparked high sentiment, it lowered the pressure on East Germany. Shutting the escape valve, Khrushchev thought, would force young East Germans to build up their own country. As he later remarked, the Wall "restored order and discipline in the East Germans' lives (and Germans have always appreciated discipline)."[92] Meanwhile, Khrushchev underscored Soviet determination by deferring the release of servicemen to the reserves and by resuming nuclear testing. This latter step broke the informal test ban begun in 1958.[93] Having secured their stake in East Germany and demonstrated their toughness with military preparations, the Russians stood ready to negotiate.

Kennedy was not sure how to avoid humiliation or a holocaust over Berlin. Acheson, the President's most militant adviser, stressed the need to show resolve with a large military buildup, a declaration of national emergency, and a possible armed probe on the Autobahn link to West Berlin. So-called soft-liners such as Bohlen, Adlai Stevenson, and Arthur M. Schlesinger, Jr., wanted immediate negotiations. In between these two views stood Rusk, who, sensitive to French and German opposition to compromise, thought the "soft-liners" too eager to negotiate. Along with McNamara, however, Rusk judged Acheson too belligerent.

Spurred by fear of war, an underlying consensus developed by late July 1961. Kennedy officials agreed on some increase in the military budget and force levels, to show toughness and to improve the capacity to stop a Soviet attack with conventional forces before having to go nuclear. And most thought the United States could make some concessions by considering how to guarantee the security of West Berlin within the context of a more stable East Germany. Even Acheson, two weeks before the Wall, advocated that the United States first build up the military, then negotiate a formula including some "indirect" recognition of the GDR, "discouragement of movements of population," trade agreements, and "assurances on the Oder-Neisse boundary" (which meant recognition of German territorial losses to Poland).[94]

On July 25, Kennedy expressed this consensus in a grave speech to the nation. He described the crisis as a "great testing . . . of Western will and courage." At risk, he explained, stood "the morale and security of Western Germany . . . the unity of Western Europe, and . . . the faith of the entire free world."[95] Unwilling to take the irrevocable step of declaring a national emergency, Kennedy nonetheless tripled draft calls, called up reserves, and asked Congress to add $3.25 billion to the defense budget. In the next months, armed forces strength rose by 300,000 men, with 40,000 going to Europe. While boosting conventional forces, the President spread the word through his brother and others that "we will use nuclear weapons" to defend West Berlin.[96] JFK urged Americans to be prepared to protect themselves in a nuclear war, spawning a boom in fall-out shelters. He balanced this militancy with a call for negotiations.

At first, tensions rose. An angry Khrushchev called Kennedy's speech a preliminary declaration of war on the Soviet Union.[97] Local incidents flared easily in the divided city, where the GDR police shot those attempting escape and where the Americans still exercised the right, going back to 1945, to travel freely to East Berlin in official vehicles. (The Russians enjoyed the same prerogative in West Berlin.) In response to the GDR's pinching of American rights, General Lucius Clay ordered tanks up to the border with East Berlin. The Soviets then lined up their tanks to face the Americans. Clay, not Kennedy, initiated this confrontation. But it came in the context of JFK's blunt warning to Moscow a few days earlier that the United States *knew* that Russia had only a few intercontinental missiles. In fact, a Pentagon official explained in a speech intended for the Kremlin's ear, Washington's second strike capability—the American nuclear weapons that would survive a Russian attack—amounted to more than Moscow could launch in its first assault. Perhaps this information was on Khrushchev's mind when he ordered Soviet armor in Berlin to back off, explaining that such a tank battle would have been "absurd."[98] In early 1962, the Russians harassed Allied civilian planes in the air corridors by dropping tin-foil chaff to interfere with radar. Washington overruled Clay's plan to send fighter escorts with the commercial planes. Each superpower tested the other, but neither wanted the hypertension of the city—"Berlinitis" one State Department official called it—to start a war or to block negotiations.[99]

By late August 1961, with the Wall up and the military buildup underway, Kennedy, like Khrushchev, stood ready to talk. JFK became impatient with foot-dragging by the State Department and by the French and Germans. The allies "must come along or stay behind," Kennedy told Rusk. "[W]e cannot accept a veto from any other power."[100] German apprehension about superpower negotiations was understandable, because Kennedy and Bundy barely paid lip service to reunification. "We can and should shift substantially toward acceptance of the GDR, the Oder-Neisse line, a non-aggression pact, and even the idea of two peace treaties," Bundy concluded.[101] Khrushchev "has thrown out quite a few assurances and hints here and there," Kennedy told Rusk. "Examine . . . [them] for pegs on which to hang our position."[102] One such hint came from the Soviet embassy official who assured Schlesinger, "We honestly wish to keep things as they are in West Berlin within the new context" of recognizing the GDR.[103] In late August, a CIA source in Eastern Europe reported that Khrushchev had decided to back away from his threat to sign a peace treaty with the GDR by the end of 1961.[104]

Both sides sought compromise, but no explicit accord emerged from the Soviet-American talks, which began in September 1961 and continued on and off throughout the Kennedy Administration. Pressure eased in October 1961 when Khrushchev publicly withdrew the year-end deadline. He and Kennedy initiated a personal correspondence. A tentative deal traded Russian guarantee of Western access to Berlin for an American guarantee against German access to nuclear weapons. Basically, the superpowers agreed to defuse the crisis and postpone a final settlement. The confrontation passed with the American position in West Berlin largely intact. Khrushchev had won only his minimal goal, greater stability in the GDR. Perhaps he backed away from signing the peace treaty with the GDR after sober calculation of America's nuclear superiority, just as fear of nuclear devastation pushed Kennedy to seek negotiations. Even this modest détente worried Adenauer, who tried to sabotage the talks. In April 1962, the Bonn government leaked Washington's suggestion to have an international commission—rather than the Russians or the East Germans—oversee Western access to Berlin. A few weeks later Adenauer criticized this proposal at a press conference and predicted the failure of the superpower negotiations.[105]

Adenauer's dissatisfaction with Washington grew. The Chancellor emphasized the "blow" to German-American friendship from the Wall and questioned United States nuclear credibility. De Gaulle encouraged such doubts, predicting that just as they had accepted the Wall, so too would the Americans consent to permanent division.[106] The proud French leader thought the United States "should stay out of [the] affairs of Europe," reported the American ambassador.[107]

Stung, Kennedy threatened that if the United States were ever excluded from Europe's diplomacy, it would withdraw its defense of the continent.[108] Disillusion with the United States helped sour de Gaulle and Adenauer on admitting Britain to the Common Market. Britain would "always be too intimately tied up with the Americans," de Gaulle bluntly told Prime Minister Harold Macmillan. The Anglo-American linkage was dangerous because "America wants to make Europe into a number of satellite states."[109]

The Kennedy Administration's preference for running the alliance out of Washington was starkly revealed during the Cuban missile crisis (see Chapter 5). As America faced the Soviet Union over Cuba, Europe faced annihilation without representation. Britain was America's closest ally. Kennedy telephoned Macmillan daily and found him a useful sounding board. But as one of the Prime Minister's colleagues remembered: "We were kept fully informed—more fully informed than anybody else. But we were not really consulted about the actual decisions."[110] Excluded from the decision-making, the allies were reduced to "protectorate nations," observed Raymond Aron, a pro-American French commentator.[111]

Acheson reminded Kennedy that since the United States was not going to consult with de Gaulle, it should at least inform him "in an impressive way." Perhaps thinking that Acheson was as impressive as anyone and that his hard-line stance in the crisis more suited the mood in Paris than in Washington, Kennedy asked the elder statesman to go to France. De Gaulle greeted Acheson with the premier question: "In order to get our roles clear . . . , have [you] come . . . to inform me of some decision taken by your President—or have you come to consult me about a decision which he should take[?]" When Acheson replied, "I have come to inform you," de Gaulle dropped the issue. Argument was useless and undignified. The general, however, added this incident to his list of black marks against the Americans. De Gaulle agreed with Acheson that Khrushchev probably was bluffing and would withdraw the missiles. But whatever happened, he declared, "France will support [Kennedy] in every way in this crisis." The general did not expect to have to make good on this promise, but it fit his image of France as an ally independent but loyal in wartime. Moreover, he was setting a precedent for American loyalty in a European crisis. Almost as an afterthought, Washington officials cabled Acheson to go on to Bonn, where Adenauer "was pretty excited."[112]

After the Cuban missile crisis, Administration officials pointed, with some justification, to the problem of security leaks if the allies had been consulted before Kennedy's late October decision to impose the "quarantine" against Cuba. That was only a partial explanation, however, since Kennedy also failed to consult the allies after his decision. Later, at a secret Senate hearing, Rusk related the Administration's fear that making the Cuban crisis a NATO affair would have increased the chance that Russia would have moved on Berlin. Further, "we could not be sure *in advance* what the response of our NATO allies would be." Kennedy officials did not want an exchange of opinion. Rather than ask the Europeans whether they "agree[d]" with American actions," Rusk explained, it was "simpler" and "easier" to ask: "Do you in this situation of danger support the United States?"[113]

Even de Gaulle answered "yes," but French and German resentment over American unilateral decision-making worked against British admission to the Common Market. By late 1962, these negotiations had become bogged down over London's desire to enter Europe while still keeping its preferential trade agreements with the Commonwealth. Washington shared French opposition to the Commonwealth trade ties which, if adopted by Europe, could hurt United States and South American exports. Kennedy officials also worried that, once in the European Economic Community, London's traditional opposition to European political unity would work to weaken the institution, thus limiting its ability to contain West Germany. Yet, if strong and united, the Common Market could turn against America. Undaunted by these problems, the Kennedy Administration did "a lot of arm twisting in Europe," London's chief negotiator observed, to have Britain enter on American terms—that is, with a minimum of Commonwealth preferences and without the power to weaken the grouping.[114] "The one thing that the European governments have been unanimous on," Rusk observed, "is that the United States should stay out of these Common Market negotiations. But nevertheless we continue to insist upon our own basic interests."[115] Through the admission of global-trading Britain, the Grand Designers hoped to head off European—particularly French—tendencies toward "inward-looking and restrictionist" commercial policies. A larger, outward-looking Common Market would offer an improved market for American products and a safe outlet for German expansion.[116] The French concluded from all of this that admitting Britain to the Common Market would be admitting America's Trojan horse.

De Gaulle's indignation over American pushiness became aggravated when Macmillan spurned nuclear liaison with France in favor of continued marriage with the United States. In 1960, in return for an atomic submarine base in Scotland, Eisenhower had promised to develop and sell to the British the aircraft-borne Skybolt missile. This agreement appeared a relatively inexpensive way for London to maintain a modern, independent deterrent. Of course, the deal made Britain more dependent on America. In late 1962, however, Skybolt's poor test performance prompted McNamara to scrap it in favor of the submarine-borne Polaris missile. "We knew of course the arrangements with Britain," a senior Kennedy official later recalled, "but they didn't influence us."[117] The more ardent among the Grand Designers saw in this technological setback an opportunity to close out Britain's independent deterrent.

When Macmillan met with de Gaulle on December 14, 1962, the general suggested development of a Franco-British missile to replace Skybolt. Macmillan deflected this proposal, aware that Washington had warned sternly against such an "unholy alliance."[118] The British Prime Minister stressed instead Britain's eagerness to join the Common Market. Britain and France remained at loggerheads. A few days later, Macmillan flew to Nassau to meet Kennedy; there he pressed for the sale of Polaris missiles to Britain. Macmillan warned that his nation would not surrender its autonomous force: "Britain has had a great history and is not about to give up now."[119] Kennedy was torn between his desire to phase out Britain's nuclear independence (hopefully a precedent for post-de Gaulle France) and the need to support the pro-American Macmillan, who warned of a storm of anti-American opinion if he returned home empty-handed. The President relented. Hoping to mollify de Gaulle, JFK offered to sell Polaris missiles to France too. Yet, as one of Kennedy's advisers warned, the offer would be read as "insulting," because France had neither the warheads nor the submarines required for the Polaris missile.[120]

Nassau deepened de Gaulle's anger and conviction that Britain remained an American satellite. On January 14, 1963, the imperious French leader poked a gaping hole in the Grand Design by vetoing Britain's admission to the Common Market. London's dependence on America and its ties with the Commonwealth made it an unfit partner in an independent Europe, the general charged. Once in the Common Market, Britain would tip the grouping toward close cooperation with the Americans, de Gaulle feared. London would probably find support among the many West Germans who also had Atlantic leanings. This would doom de Gaulle's dream of harnessing German power to French leadership of Europe. De Gaulle also rejected the Polaris offer. Mocking McNamara's effort to centralize the West's nuclear deterrent in Washington, he observed that "in strategy . . . as in economics, monopoly . . . appears to him who holds it as the best possible system."[121] The Cuban crisis had demonstrated that America, without consulting its allies, might initiate nuclear war to protect *its* interests. No one could say whether the United States would risk the same for Europe. While rebuffing the British and Americans, de Gaulle snuggled closer to the West Germans. Despite warnings from Washington and from more Atlantic-minded officials such as Foreign Minister Gerhard Schroeder and Economics Minister Ludwig Erhard, Adenauer signed a friendship treaty with France a week after the general's bombshell.[122]

The Kennedy Administration was shaken. The President became "extremely concerned" over intelligence reports (later shown to be false) of a Franco-Russian deal to shut the United States out of Europe. Officials feared the strong-willed general might shape the Common Market into an autarchic bloc, closing out American business through discriminatory tariffs and investment policies. The nation's "world leadership" appeared to be under attack.[123]

"What kind of a deal [could] de Gaulle make with the Russians which would be acceptable to the Germans?" JFK wondered.[124] Germany was the first prize in this sharpened competition with de Gaulle. To win it, Kennedy and Bundy gave free rein to the Europeanists. "Any discussion we have on . . . Germany," Kennedy instructed, "should include Dean Acheson."[125] This old war-horse was furious at "the whole Gaullist, anti-American plot," growling that the Germans "need to know again the feel of [our] contempt."[126] Kennedy ordered Bruce to review postwar policy toward Europe.

The Kennedy Administration followed Bruce's recommendation of making it "absolutely clear to Adenauer, his government, and parliament that the stability of U.S.-German relations requires unambiguous commitment, in words and deeds to: 1. NATO; 2. the multilateral force—rather than to national or Franco-German nuclear programs; and 3. British accession to the Common Market."[127] Since Adenauer had already signed the treaty with de Gaulle, the Kennedy Administration "put a lot of pressure" on Bonn, Ball recalled, to get

the German parliament to attach to the treaty a resolution reaffirming the primacy of Atlantic relations.[128] In addition, Acheson and
John J. McCloy, both 1940s godfathers of the Federal Republic, lobbied German leaders. McCloy warned that de Gaulle's "power play"
could lead to American isolation and "a special arrangement between
Paris and Moscow" at Bonn's expense.[129]

While laying down the stick, the Kennedy Administration held out
a funny-looking carrot, the Multilateral Force. Conceived in the Eisenhower years, the MLF was supposed to consist of a fleet of surface
ships, manned by a mix of NATO nationalities and armed with nuclear missiles. From the American perspective, the MLF would head
off nuclear proliferation by giving Germany and other allies more
participation in the West's deterrent apparatus.[130] Tighter military
integration through the MLF would help compensate for de Gaulle's
veto of enhanced economic integration through the Common Market. Kennedy appreciated the MLF as a device to "increase our influence in Europe and provide a way to guide NATO." By deploying the
force, he sought to "weaken de Gaulle's control of the [Common
Market] Six."[131]

Typically, Kennedy officials tried to sell the MLF to Europe as a
means toward a more equal Atlantic Community—although they
themselves valued it as a sophisticated instrument to refurbish American hegemony. Inviting the allies to help mold the MLF concept, JFK
sent Livingston Merchant, an experienced diplomat, on a tour of
NATO capitals. Germany and Italy, the nations most interested in
the MLF, quickly learned that two crucial aspects had already been
determined. The Kennedy Administration decided against equipping
the MLF with nuclear-powered submarines because too many members of Congress had voiced opposition. Nor would it give up the
American veto on firing the MLF's missiles. Europeans decried this
"multifarce" of a "second-class weapons system" still under Washington's control.[132] Merchant and the other salesmen fretted about their
sinking "image" of openness even while they busied themselves to
"mold" European opinion.[133] The episode demonstrated that American officials were unwilling to share real control over the nuclear
deterrent, yet they feared what the Germans might do on their own.
So they proposed a nuclear force for the allies—but refused to give
the allies the right to fire it without Washington's approval. The MLF
amounted to a psychological device for Germans to *feel* as if they too
had a finger on the nuclear button.

The British, the smaller NATO allies, and the United States Congress remained cool toward the scheme. The Soviets denounced it as a step toward a German nuclear force. The French understood it as an attempt to contain their independent deterrent. Atlantic-minded Germans such as Schroeder and Erhard, Adenauer's heir-apparent, favored the MLF. Merchant recognized Germany's "hidden hopes" to gain more control over the MLF in the future. But he was willing to take this "calculated risk in order to prevent the Germans [from] turning down a more dangerous path."[134] That "more dangerous path" was an independent German nuclear force or a joint one with France.

By June 1963, however, new calculations made the MLF less attractive. On May 16, the German parliament ratified the Franco-German treaty with a preamble reaffirming Bonn's Atlantic ties. The MLF now seemed less urgent. Administration officials noted that the proposal alienated many French leaders, including some otherwise pro-American ones. It had also become clear that the intelligence rumors of a Franco-Russian deal were false. De Gaulle had no Russian card to play. But Kennedy did have such a card, the prospect of a limited nuclear test ban treaty with the Soviets. This "is now a factor of real importance," Bundy emphasized. In an era of budding détente, the United States should not appear "as the nuclear rearmers of Germany." JFK accepted Bundy's advice to stop pushing so hard and to let the Europeans press for the MLF if they wanted it.[135]

This decision marked another milestone in America's slow shift away from the Europe-oriented policy of the 1940s and 1950s. "What made things interesting to Kennedy," Bundy recalled, was the "prospect that you *could* do something or that you *must* do something."[136] With the Grand Design stalled and the Berlin crisis eased, Western Europe fit neither category. Kennedy focused instead on the promise of a nuclear test ban treaty and the precariousness of South Vietnam (see Chapter 9). After mid-1963, coordination with the allies seemed even less important or necessary. The United States avoided consultation on South Vietnam because "we wanted to . . . do it ourselves, and didn't want anybody else to tell us how," a State Department official recalled.[137] A month before his death, JFK considered pulling some American military forces out of Europe. The withdrawal affected Europe's security, yet the President ordered that the matter "not be discussed . . . with our allies until [after] a decision has been made." Then, officials should "consult" the Europeans and "proceed

with our intended actions." At the same meeting, Kennedy approved
a speech in which Rusk promised the Germans "intimate . . . consul-
t[ation]."[138] More candidly, Bundy confided that "if we thought we
could get a major settlement" with Russia, "we would not be deterred
from bilateral discussion."[139]

Although the Kennedy Administration shifted attention away from
Europe, the management of the allies, particularly France, continued
to absorb its energies. The established nuclear powers—the United
States, the Soviet Union, and Britain—negotiated the Limited Test
Ban Treaty of July 1963, intending that, once signed by most of the
world's nations, the accord would slow nuclear proliferation. With
just a nascent force, de Gaulle adamantly refused to participate. The
treaty permitted only underground tests—more expensive and more
difficult to monitor than atmospheric explosions. Americans hoped
that other nations would hesitate to go nuclear if they had to pay the
huge costs and face negative world public opinion. "The central problem," Rusk remarked, "is France."[140] Despite Kennedy's personal
plea and offer to share technology on underground testing, de Gaulle
refused to compromise independence by signing the pact. This
holdout made it harder to crack down on the nations whose nuclear
potential was most feared—the People's Republic of China (see Chapter 7) and, to a lesser extent, West Germany. To the question of
whether Russia would join in "coercive action against China," Rusk
replied: "If we got everybody but China to sign . . . we could . . .
take some action along this line."[141]

In 1963, de Gaulle further undermined efforts to isolate China by
publicly criticizing American intervention in South Vietnam and by
formally recognizing the Communist Chinese government the following year. By the end of the Kennedy Administration, "Franco-
American relations . . . had really deteriorated," recalled the French
foreign minister.[142]

Yet, he added, JFK "was certainly very popular" in France.[143]
Thus this story of the fissured Atlantic alliance returns to the initial
irony. Even as the Kennedy Administration failed to shape Europe's
development and stimulated anti-Americanism, many Europeans admired the charismatic President. How did this happen? Kennedy
promoted his popularity as a foreign policy tool, most notably during his triumphant June 1963 trip to Europe. The President "talked
over the heads of government to the hearts of people," recalled a
top adviser.[144] Kennedy used his vaunted charm to counter de

Gaulle's thesis of an undependable America and the need for an independent Europe. JFK's youthful good looks, his elegant, multilingual wife, his wit, intellect, and reputation as a connoisseur of the fine arts all appealed to Europeans. Many admired his triumph over anti-Catholic prejudice and his stand (though belated) for racial integration. The carefully planned trip advertised these presidential assets, adviser Theodore Sorensen explained, with "all the old Kennedy campaign techniques including advance men, motorcades, outdoor rallies, local humor and maximum television coverage."[145]

The President's most dramatic moments came in Germany (he had not been invited to France). At Frankfurt, JFK ringingly denied any intention to dominate Europe and affirmed that "the United States will risk its cities to defend yours because we need your freedom to protect ours." Then on June 26, he gave a now famous speech in West Berlin, with a reported 60 percent of the city's residents in attendance. Carefully uttering words still ringing in German ears a quarter-century later, Kennedy declared: "All free men, wherever they may live, are citizens of Berlin. . . . I take pride in the words 'Ich bin ein Berliner.' "[146] The crowd roared approval. A cool man adept at arousing the feelings of others, JFK later remarked that he had found the mass response "exciting but also disturbing." He felt that if he had said, "March to the Wall—tear it down," the Berliners would have obeyed. His speech had "unlocked [the Germans'] irrationality and repressed hysteria," Kennedy concluded.[147]

JFK's politics of emotion touched the general public; he persuaded millions of Europeans that he counted himself one of them and that the United States was their trusted protector. His approval rating among West Germans climbed from 76 percent before the visit to 83 percent afterward.[148] His competitor appreciated the performance. Himself planning a visit to Germany, de Gaulle wanted it "to be 'something of a show' similar to President Kennedy's trip."[149] Leaving Berlin, JFK told Sorensen: "We'll never have another day like this one as long as we live."[150]

In Kennedy's short life he cultivated an almost legendary image; in death that legend in Europe and elsewhere assumed heroic proportions. No doubt the circumstances of his death led Europeans to sentimentalize about a lost prince. Yet the outpouring of feeling also reflected the fact that Kennedy had established himself as Europe's leader too. He was "the most European of your presidents," recalled Antonio Gambino after the assassination. JFK's "style and personality"—"more than his policies"—gave him the advantage over de Gaulle, the Italian concluded.[151] The Cuban missile crisis brought home to Europeans that the President of the United States, not the Prime Ministers or Chancellors, made the basic decisions of life and nuclear death for Europe. "We have been shown," a Member of Parliament wrote after the crisis, that "the President of the U.S. is far more important to us than . . . any Briton, even the Prime Minister."[152] Despite its slippage, America remained the predominant force in Western Europe. On a policy level in Paris, London, and Bonn, this hegemony spawned resentment, resistance, and dependence. On an emotional level, mediated through Kennedy's attractive style and tragic death, it created a community of shared fate.

The Atlantic Community was gone in a flash. No President after Kennedy captured Europe's imagination. America's relative power declined further, but not its will to dominate the alliance. Inheriting the problems of German frustration and French intransigence, Lyndon Johnson heeded the Grand Designers' advice and revived the MLF proposal. By late 1964, domestic and foreign opposition to the MLF had grown so great that Johnson finally dropped the troubled project. This decision crippled Chancellor Erhard, who had staked his government's prestige on the scheme.[153] But Johnson no longer cared much. Bitter conflict with France had stalemated European unification. Next to the new main event in Southeast Asia, Europe appeared as a jumble of sideshows.

The Vietnam War further undermined Atlantic partnership. It tore apart whatever consensus had existed in the United States and across the Atlantic. Europeans, who had idolized the United States as the hero of World War II and the Marshall Plan and as their defense against the Red Army, now grew repulsed by pictures of American atrocities in Vietnam.[154] Stung by the allies' refusal to send troops to Southeast Asia, Washington pressed more heavy-handedly for balance of payments help.

Even as they differed on Southeast Asia, the superpowers kept their *modus vivendi* in Berlin. In 1971, this led to the Quadripartite Agreement, which established West Berlin's status as a quasi-free city legally separate from the Federal Republic, but with secure access to the West and with close economic and social ties to West Germany. The Americans, British, and French maintained their troops and ultimate authority in the city.[155] The GDR won the West's recognition as

Bonn continued on the path left open by the Berlin Wall—increased ties with the East. Washington waxed nervous that *Ostpolitik* could lead to a German deal with Russia. After Kennedy, Germans found it difficult to conceal their contempt for what they saw as Washington's blunders in Vietnam, in relations with the Soviets, and in defense of the dollar. De Gaulle's policy of French independence outlasted the general. Despite economic summits and nuclear weapons planning and coordination, the basic interests of Europe and America grew further apart.[156] The Grand Design lay in shambles by late 1963. Kennedy had failed to build the Atlantic alliance into an Atlantic Community. His successors failed to try.

2

Defending Hegemony:
American Foreign Economic Policy

WILLIAM S. BORDEN

On October 20, 1960, shortly before John F. Kennedy's presidential election triumph, the London gold price reached $40 per ounce. The basis for the United States-controlled Bretton Woods international economic system had long been the fixed gold price of $35 per ounce, and the United States was pledged to maintain that figure. Speculators bid the gold price to $40 in anticipation of the continuing weakness of the dollar due to a puzzling yet persistent deficit in the overall United States balance of payments. Republican candidate Richard Nixon charged that Kennedy's recent rise in the electoral polls had stimulated speculators to attack the value of the dollar, because they feared that as President, Kennedy would maintain an expansionist (i.e., loose) monetary policy, increasing the United States budget deficit and eventually forcing the devaluation of the dollar against gold. Kennedy responded in amusement to Nixon's accusation, telling a campaign rally: "Mr. Nixon, if you are listening, I did not do it, I promise you."[1] Thereafter, however, Kennedy could not afford to be amused by the United States balance of payments deficit, because the thorny issue haunted his presidency—and that of his successors as well.

In the 1940s the United States had created the Bretton Woods international economic system, named for the New Hampshire hotel where the initial agreements among the key capitalist powers were forged. Bretton Woods established the gold-dollar exchange rate system which valued all currencies against the dollar and fixed the price

57

of gold at $35 per ounce. After the war, additional rules were established to govern international economic conduct and prevent the economic hostilities which had led to the Great Depression and indirectly to war between the capitalist powers in the 1930s and 1940s. American leaders blamed the depression on the proliferation of neo-mercantile policies during the 1930s and sought to achieve a multilateral world trading system with as few barriers to trade and capital movements as could be achieved. In simplest terms, multilateral policies sought to reduce or eliminate barriers to trade and capital flows between nations, whereas neo-mercantile policies sought to erect barriers to give advantages to domestic industries over foreign industries. Neo-mercantile tactics included a multitude of tariff devices, quotas, subsidies, and bilateral barter arrangements with fixed prices and regional trade blocs.

Two institutions performed the key functions of regulating both international trade and payments in the postwar economic system. The International Monetary Fund (IMF) loaned money to nations which had a negative balance of payments because they spent more for foreign goods and services than they earned from sales to foreigners. The IMF enforced deflationary policies on debtor nations (high interest rates and balanced budgets), reducing their domestic purchasing power and causing their imports to fall and their exports to rise. If these deflationary policies failed, the IMF forced the debtor nation to devalue its currency—that is, to reduce the value of a unit of its currency in relation to a unit of other nations' currencies—to make the debtor's exports less expensive and its imports more expensive. The other key institution, the General Agreements on Trade and Tariffs (GATT), was both a body of rules to govern world trade barriers (tariffs and import quotas). The IMF and GATT enforced multilateralism by restricting the ability of governments to use tariff and non-tariff trade barriers, export subsidies, capital and exchange controls, competitive currency devaluations, the expropriation or nationalization of foreign capital, and bilateral deals for guaranteed markets and sources of raw materials.

After World War II the United States ran a huge trade surplus with the rest of the world, because foreigners had great demand for American goods and Americans had much less demand for foreign goods. To help balance their trade, foreign nations devalued their currencies against the dollar, making American goods more expensive and their goods less expensive in world markets. The high value of the dollar increased the wealth and power of the United States, because Americans could buy increasingly more foreign goods and industries with the same number of dollars. Although speculators could trade gold on the open market, the United States owned the bulk of the world's gold supply, and was thus able to control gold's market value of $35. A devaluation of the dollar would raise the price of gold above $35 per ounce—which is what the speculators were predicting once the United States had become a debtor nation. The fundamental goal of American foreign economic policy after 1945 had been to achieve full convertibility of currencies. (A nation's currency is convertible when it allows its citizens to exchange it freely for other currencies in order to purchase foreign goods and services without restriction.) Making other currencies freely convertible into dollars was critical to maintaining high American export levels.

To allow their currencies to be freely convertible into dollars, foreign nations required ample monetary reserves to cover payments deficits (when their imports exceeded their exports). Because Europe and the world lacked the initial monetary reserves to allow free currency convertibility, however, the United States in the 1940s and 1950s consciously provided dollars to the world in the form of foreign aid and vast foreign military expenditures. The dollar became the accepted medium of exchange for global trade and thus a "reserve currency." This increasing supply of dollars was then held by foreign central banks as monetary reserves, which eventually grew to the point at which European nations made their currencies convertible by 1960. Even though foreign nations now had ample monetary reserves, United States military expenditures abroad continued to cause a deficit in the balance of payments, leading to a glut of dollars in European banks. Because foreign central banks commonly held the dollars in the form of monetary reserves and did not normally cash them in for American gold, the United States did not have to balance its trade but could instead run a constant deficit and simply print more paper dollars to ship abroad to pay for foreign goods and industries. The system worked as long as foreign governments agreed to hold the increasing glut of dollars and not redeem them for gold, which would deplete the American gold supply and eventually lead to a decline in the value of the dollar. From 1950 to 1960 the American gold supply fell from $22 billion to its prewar level of $17 billion. As the following table indicates, the United States continued to maintain a large balance of trade surplus, which was offset by large overseas

United States Balance of Payments, Annual Averages in Billions of Dollars[2]

	1951–1956	1958–1961
Current Account	+1.8	+2.1
Merchandise trade	+2.7	+3.6
Earnings on investments	+1.7	+2.4
Military expenditures	−2.2	−2.8
Other services/transfers	−0.4	−1.0
Long Term Capital Account	−3.2	−4.7
Private long-term capital	−0.9	−2.2
Govt. Grants/Credits	−2.3	−2.5
Balance on Basic Accounts	−1.4	−2.6
Short Term Capital and Unrecorded Transactions	+0.2	−0.8
Overall Deficit	−1.2	−3.4

government expenditures and the export of dollars (capital exports) to purchase foreign companies.

When relative equilibrium in trade among the core powers was achieved in 1958–1960, three significant trends emerged to produce decay in the structure of United States hegemony. First, investors of American capital, too timid to invest heavily abroad after the war despite Washington's pleas to help offset the American payments surplus with Europe and Japan (the "dollar gap"), now increased their foreign investment dramatically. By the late 1950s, the United States was investing abroad $2 to 3 billion more than foreigners were investing in the United States. Emboldened by the advent of currency convertibility and political stability, and encouraged by the subsiding postwar domestic investment boom (which reduced profits on domestic investment), American capital sought higher profits in the more dynamic European economy. Second, American foreign military and economic aid expenditures, which had played a key role in creating the multilateral world which Kennedy inherited, did not decrease in response to the balance of payments deficit. Instead, they remained high, as what Kennedy critic David Calleo has called the "imperial burden" of American hegemony (military spending and foreign aid) became irreversible.[3] Finally, European nations and Japan created modern and efficient industries and perfected export marketing techniques to try to catch up to and surpass American production and trade.

Kennedy took command of the greatest economic power in the

history of the world at the height of its hegemonic rule. The United States held conspicuous economic superiority over the other core capitalist powers from 1945 until 1958, but since that time has been gradually relinquishing that power. Kennedy was the first President to confront the decline and attempted in vain to reverse it. Relative economic power has been shared by an ever-evolving group of nations since modern capitalism was born in the sixteenth century. Great Britain dominated the economic world-system for most of the nineteenth and early twentieth centuries, gradually declining as the United States, Germany and its continental neighbors, and Japan increased their productive capacities. These nations have constituted the core of the capitalist world-system; they include the key industrial and financial centers of world trade and dominate world trade and production.[4]

The position of the United States in the international economy in 1961 reflected the gradual resolution of the overriding paradox of the postwar world economy. The very economic superiority of the United States was the root cause of the frailty and imbalance of the international economic system. The cure was the outflow of dollars in the form of government expenditures in the 1950s.[5] By 1961, on one hand, the United States was beginning to lose its economic superiority; on the other hand, the Bretton Woods system, based on the supremacy of the dollar, was at last healthy because Europe and Japan had recovered and made their currencies convertible.

After World War II, the United States bureaucracy had reflected in microcosm the rivalry and cooperation of the relationships among the core economies. During the period of extreme disequilibrium between 1945 and 1955, the Economic Cooperation Administration (which oversaw the Marshall Plan) and its successor, the Mutual Security Agency, were charged with aiding European revival to ameliorate the dollar gap, nurture Bretton Woods, and preserve American export markets. In the postwar period it seemed appropriate for the State Department to handle foreign trade policy, because the United States sought to make short-term economic concessions to achieve political goals (building core cooperation) and long-term economic goals (sustaining American exports). The increasing threat to American market domination led to a shift in emphasis in American foreign economic policy. With the return of equilibrium (relatively balanced trade among the core economies), the Department of Commerce sought to regain control of trade policy from the State Department, because the new American goal was to achieve a quid pro quo in trade negotiations, for which the Commerce Department was better suited to protecting American corporate interests.[6]

At the moment that the edifice of the postwar world system was in place, the first loud crack, heralding the oncoming structural collapse, reverberated around the world in the form of the London Gold Crisis, the concrete symptom of the decline of American hegemony. Because foreign investment would benefit the balance of payments in the long term, from a structural perspective it was the continuation of the vast overseas military expenditures that created the payments deficit which weakened the dollar and threatened Bretton Woods. As a pre-inaugural report on foreign economic policy advised Kennedy: "We have not reached a crisis. We have reached a turning point in our world economic position, one that calls for fresh analysis and determined action."[7]

Determined action, of course, was the battle cry of the Kennedy Administration; however, fresh analysis, in view of the consensus of economists and government officials on multilateralism, became virtually impossible. Under Secretary of State for Economic Affairs George Ball posed the key question at one policy meeting, asking whether it was in the interests of the United States to lower trade barriers.[8] The ensuing discussion, however, was predictably sterile. The executive branch contained no powerful advocates of neo-mercantilism. The economists viewed neo-mercantile thought as the equivalent of original sin, and Kennedy's most influential advisers— Ball, former Secretary of State Dean Acheson, and others—had a global, systemic perspective and viewed particular local interests as impediments to the virtuous evolution of an efficient single world market system. There really was no internal debate. This is not to imply that in the complex international economy there was a neo-mercantile alternative that Kennedy should have or could have easily pursued, and which would have prevented the decline of American hegemony. First, the American decline was relative to the rise of the core powers. Second, although the traditional American industrial sector was hurt by the transfer of technology and lack of neo-mercantile protection, strong American economic sectors (especially finance and high technology) benefited greatly from multilateral conditions. Third, neo-mercantilism *was* pursued by Europe, Japan, and the United States for some weak economic sectors, but with mixed results.

President Kennedy's advisers have uniformly praised him for his keen interest in international economics—sparked by Nixon's challenge and the continuing balance of payments crisis—as well as his growing mastery of the technical language and mechanics of international economics.[9] Kennedy became obsessed with the balance of payments crisis after the gold crisis. Everywhere he turned to implement his policies—especially military intervention abroad and stimulation of the domestic economy by lowering interest rates—he met its influence. His advisers told him again and again that the balance of payments deficit would be severely exacerbated by one proposed policy or another. Walter Heller, Chairman of the Council of Economic Advisers, called this policy straitjacket the "cruel dilemma" of economic policy.[10]

Kennedy understood how important American economic power was to domestic prosperity and to his foreign policy of renewing American power both economically and militarily. He sensed that the balance of payments crisis and the threat to the supremacy of the dollar signaled the impending decline of American hegemony. The deficit threatened the overall United States position in the world, aide Walt W. Rostow recalled advising him. "I wanted to leave one thought in his mind before the inaugural. We will not be able to sustain in the 1960's a world position without solving the balance of payments problem." Rostow grasped the profound nature of the problem. He counseled Kennedy that it was not just a matter of controlled expenditures or increased exports, but of two fundamental aspects of the domestic economy: wage discipline and the modernization of the American industrial plant. This problem, then, was as complicated as any Kennedy would encounter. Rostow recalled: "I think he really feared we might be in a secular decline like the British."[11] George Ball has suggested that Kennedy's "brooding concern" over the payments problem was due to his father's oft-stated emphasis on the value of gold and his sense of vulnerability to business and Republican charges that Democrats were inept at economic policy.[12]

Indeed, Kennedy seemed more obsessed with the problem than were his own economic advisers. Rostow recalled that "above all he felt impaled on our balance of payments deficit. . . . It humiliated him" when General Charles de Gaulle of France obstructed Kennedy's policies and threatened to deplete the American gold reserve: "He hated de Gaulle's having a whip hand over him—getting our protection free; hurting us whenever he could; and piling up a gold surplus at our expense, via our NATO outlays in France. This sense of weakness in dealing with a nation we were protecting, violated something personal in the President. . . . He would come back to it time and time again—the image of de Gaulle sitting there sassing him from his little pile of gold."[13] Yet, as economist Harry G. Johnson noted, the United States had a "rather facile tendency" to attribute to de Gaulle European opposition to American policies. European attitudes on the whole, however, were "radically at variance with the Anglo-Saxon attitude" toward multilateralism, preferential trading arrangements, and the political nature of competition in international trade.[14] Thus, as David Calleo quipped: "If de Gaulle did not exist he probably would have to be invented" by the many Europeans who agreed with his taking a stand against American hegemony.[15]

As with all Presidents, Kennedy was not the originator of foreign economic policy, but rather the judge who weighed and chose among the opinions of economists, bankers, industrialists, and other experts. The basic debate turned on the relative benefits of multilateral policies or neo-mercantile policies to the various economic sectors of the United States. Kennedy was not a doctrinaire free trader. He was well aware of the perils of the uncontrolled movement of capital and goods for economic regions. As a congressman and senator, he had defended the Massachusetts textile industry, voting, for example, to recommit the Trade Agreements Extension Act in 1949 to fend off lower textile tariffs.[16] As President, however, Kennedy had to put the national and gobal interests of the multinational corporations, banks, and investment houses first. These dominant groups in the sophisticated area of foreign economic affairs supported multilateralism to protect American exports and capital investment from the restrictive actions of foreign governments.

Kennedy was thus both concerned with the loss of American economic superiority and skeptical about the assurances of his advisers that multilateralism would save the dollar. However, he could not reverse the multilateral tide without rebuffing his entire presidential heritage dating to Wilson. He would have to turn his back on the still-powerful architects of multilateralism—Dean Acheson and his peers, and the corporate policy-making bodies, especially the Committee for Economic Development, the Council on Foreign Relations, the National Planning Association, and the National Foreign Trade Council. Kennedy would also have to throw the dogma of multilateralism in the face of an economics profession whose doctrine was based on free trade and international economic efficiency, as well as defy the strongest segments of industry, agriculture, and finance. Thus, in practical terms, an opportunity for a decisive "turning point" in policy seemed unlikely. In short, there was neither sufficient urgency (Bretton Woods did not collapse for another decade) nor support for a drastic shift in American policy. Yet, in historical perspective, Kennedy was elected in the midst of a profound turning point: the dramatic decline of American economic dominance began during his tenure, and he set the pattern of aggressively resisting that decline.

Five major issues dominated the Kennedy Administration's foreign economic policy: core financial cooperation to strengthen the dollar artificially; the Trade Expansion Act and the Kennedy Round of trade negotiations; trade in agricultural products with Europe; the global military expansion of the United States, which hastened the demise of American economic hegemony; and the effort to limit trade between Japan and European nations and the Soviet bloc. These issues are analyzed in turn in the remainder of this chapter.

The most urgent of these five issues was the weakness of the dollar. After Nixon's charge that Kennedy's election would hurt the dollar, the Democratic candidate assembled his advisers. They assured him that the problem was largely psychological. If speculators thought that the devaluation of the dollar against gold was probable or even possible, they would naturally seek to sell dollars and buy gold to reap speculative profits as gold became more valuable and the dollar less valuable. If they became convinced that devaluation would not occur, they would halt their attacks on the dollar. Thus reassured, Kennedy on October 31, 1960, gave a major campaign address on the balance of payments crisis: he pledged that he would never devalue the dollar.[17] He also vowed to end the deficit within three years. Council of Economic Advisers Chairman Walter Heller later told Kennedy that New York bankers and Europeans were to blame for the dollar's weakness. He advised Kennedy that the bankers were portraying Uncle Sam as "weakened by living beyond his means, thrown upon the mercy of currency speculators and bankers, begging for patience and credit from friends he so recently saved, admonished from all sides to mend his loose and profligate ways."[18] Kennedy's Halloween campaign address foretold his Administration's approach to correct the payments deficit: increase "burden sharing" with the allies by demanding that Europeans pay more of the costs of maintaining the vast American military presence overseas; limit domestic price increases (by increasing productivity and curbing inflation), which were hurting export expansion and attracting imports; end foreign limits on the flow of capital to the United States; and change interest rate policies to keep short-term rates high in an effort to stem the flow of capital to Europe and keep long-term rates low, thus encouraging domestic investment (a policy tagged the "twist"). The basic economic strategy of the Kennedy Administration, heavily influenced by the Keynesian Heller, was to achieve rapid, non-inflationary domestic growth, which would lower unit production costs, making American exports more competitive and easing the dollar crisis. [19]

Kennedy's decision to foreclose the option of devaluation resulted in a consistent building of pressure on the value of the dollar, much like a pressure cooker but without any controlled release of the pressure. The erosion in the American balance of payments which began in 1958 led to ever-growing dollar holdings by foreign nations. European central banks had accumulated their massive dollar holdings under great American political influence not to cash dollars in for gold. Heller said the key was to convince foreigners "to accept and hold our IOU's instead of gold" (to foreigners, paper dollars are IOUs from Americans). [20] To Kennedy, devaluation would violate repeated American pledges and reduce the value of the European holdings by billions of dollars. The massive loss in the value of their dollars would be the European bankers' "reward" for supporting the value of the dollar. "This growth in foreign dollar holdings placed upon the United States a special responsibility," Kennedy told Congress in February 1961. [21] The consequences of devaluation grew ever more severe the longer the decision to devalue was postponed. Kennedy's successors maintained his defensive policies, until by 1971 the pressure had built to a point at which the lid blew off. The Bretton Woods exchange rate system then collapsed, along with the value of the dollar and the Eurodollar reserves.

The debate on international monetary reform sparked by the American deficit focused on the benefits and burdens of the reserve currency status of the dollar. The capitalist world-system was entering a new era of equilibrium, and the managers of the system were groping for rules under which modern capitalism would be able to function during a persistent American payments deficit and thus a weak dollar. Robert Roosa, the clever and energetic Under Secretary of the Treasury for International Monetary Affairs, carefully engineered a system providing for close cooperation among the world's central banks to support the dollar. In order to maintain the price, he persuaded the Europeans to neutralize the speculative attacks by purchasing dollars when speculators were selling. This stockpiling of dollars would keep the system afloat artificially until American policy-makers could achieve a permanent cure.[22]

France under de Gaulle fiercely protected the independence of continental Europe from American influence. The Gaullists and their financial mentor, Jacques Rueff, charged that the reserve currency status of the dollar violated all natural economic laws. It allowed the United States to run a permanent deficit and buy up European industry with paper IOUs that might never be redeemed. The French solution was to apply to the United States the same rules which disciplined the actions of other nations—in essence saving the United States from itself.[23] Kennedy, however, would not consent to IMF-style discipline (balanced federal budgets or tight credit), which would violate his growth policy. Ball, Roosa, and much of the American economic intelligentsia responded to the French by claiming that, far from taking advantage of an artifically strong dollar to buy up European industry at bargain prices, the United States was unselfishly bearing the "burden" of reserve currency status. They argued that the United States balance of payments deficit was necessary to increase world liquidity (the amount of money in circulation and available to finance international trade deals). They correctly noted that the deficits created by American military expenditures abroad had fueled the world trade boom of the 1950s.[24] Yale political scientist Robert Triffin set the focus for the international debate by calling for multilateralization of the reserve currency function. He proposed using a "market basket" of currencies to underlay a new form of international currency with the purpose of increasing liquidity—ultimately realized as IMF Special Drawing Rights in the late 1960s. "Triffin's Paradox" held that the American deficit was the key to world growth; that simply balancing American payments would deprive the rest of the world of the outward flow of dollars on which it relied to finance investment and trade. Triffin was a maverick from the prevailing American perspective. He advocated the sharing of economic power with Europe and Japan by reducing the dollar to one of several key currencies and resting ultimate authority in an international agency (the IMF) rather than in the American Treasury.[25]

It was not coincidental that the Triffin Plan emerged at the very time that the United States had transformed from a creditor into a debtor nation. The plan was a warmed-over version of Lord Keynes's vision of a postwar international monetary system designed to assist debtor nations, rather than to rely primarily on the IMF discipline. Keynes sought a more generous version of the IMF which would lend funds to cover payments deficits without the onerous recessionary policies that the IMF imposed on debtors. The Germans, who enjoyed huge trade surpluses, became the chief advocates of discipline for debtors in the 1960s. Nor is it mysterious that American officials began claiming in the 1960s that surplus countries were responsible for reducing their surpluses, after having ridiculed European assertions in the late 1940s that the huge dollar gap was an American problem and the solution was not Europe's responsibility.[26]

In the debate about the reserve currency status of the dollar, "nationalist" Americans supported the existing reserve currency status of the dollar; the monetary reformists supported Triffin's idea to share the reserve currency status; and the Eurocentric Gaullists supported a return to a gold standard to reduce the Anglo-Saxon control over Europe, exercised through both the dollar standard and the American/ British-dominated IMF. The debate proved inconclusive during the early 1960s. The Administration itself was divided, with Roosa and Treasury Secretary C. Douglass Dillon defending Bretton Woods and the supremacy of the dollar and the State Department advocating the multilateralization of the reserve currency function. Kennedy sided with Dillon at a key White House meeting, thus blocking reform, but he also expressed sympathy for Triffin's ideas.[27]

Roosa became the lynchpin in core financial cooperation. Because he initially believed that the deficit problem was temporary, he saw no need to sacrifice the rule of the dollar and rush into untried schemes to multilateralize the reserve currency function. He never failed, however, to insist that the dollar's reserve currency status burdened the United States. Although Europe increasingly supported the dollar, it also began to chip away at the American domination of the world financial system, demanding limits on American autonomy, much as the United States had used its postwar leverage to limit European autonomy. By July 1962, however, Roosa began to view the American deficit as structural and long-term. Eventually, both he and Dillon became advocates of international monetary reform.[28]

The Kennedy Administration attempted to have the best of two worlds. On the one hand, the Administration sought to maintain freedom from the IMF discipline it imposed on others, thus enabling Washington to pursue growth policies. At the same time, the Administration tried to persuade foreign governments to share the burden of reserve currency status by supporting the value of the dollar themselves. By the end of the Kennedy Administration, it was clear that Roosa's policies had worked to maintain the dollar's value in the short term, but that the payments deficit would persist because of continuing military expenditures and declining American competitiveness.

The second major foreign economic policy issue, the Trade Expansion Act of 1962 (TEA), represented the culmination of Wilsonian multilateralism and ranked as one of the greatest legislative accomplishments of Kennedy's presidency. The act was designed to replace the Roosevelt-era Reciprocal Trade Agreements Act (RTA), by which Congress had restricted executive authority to negotiate tariff reductions. Under the provisions of the proposed TEA, Congress would authorize the President to negotiate tariff reductions of up to 50 percent on most goods and up to 100 percent on goods for which 80 percent of world trade was between Europe and the United States.[29] The Administration first had to decide whether to attempt to obtain sweeping trade liberalization authority embodied in the TEA from the traditionally cautious and nationalistic Congress as early as 1962, when the current two-year extension of the RTA would expire. Kennedy appointed Philadelphia Republican Howard Petersen as his Special Assistant to formulate a new trade policy. The other key actors in the TEA development included: Under Secretary of State Ball; Secretary of Commerce and North Carolina businessman Luther Hodges; former Secretary of State under Eisenhower and free trade crusader Christian Herter (whom Kennedy appointed as his Special Representative for Trade Negotiation); and key congressional leaders who supported trade liberalization, especially two powerful House committee chairmen, Democrats Hale Boggs and Wilbur Mills. All except Ball urged pushing for the passage of liberalized trade legislation in 1962, and Ball was one of the most vehement supporters of the legislation after his more ambitious plan was shelved. Indeed, Ball's globalist views—especially increased trade with the Soviet bloc—made him unpopular in Congress. Kennedy appointed Hodges—a mainstream politician who had strong relations with Congress—to head the TEA legislative effort.[30] Kennedy remained an active participant in the TEA process because he viewed the legislation and the increased exports he hoped would result to be the keys to domestic growth, curing the balance of payments deficit, and cementing the alliance with Western Europe.

The TEA represented a strategic, political, and economic effort to strengthen the Western alliance with Europe and Japan on American terms, to attack head-on the impending Common External Tariff (CXT) of the European Economic Community (EEC), popularly known as the Common Market, and to render powerless the internal opponents of multilateralism by limiting congressional input into foreign economic policy. Kennedy wanted an "open Europe" versus a "closed Europe" to minimize the "trade diversion effects" of the CXT. The CXT created free trade among European nations but kept a tariff on non-European goods. It threatened to alter trade patterns by increasing intra-European trade, thus reducing American exports to Europe. If the CXT were kept low, less trade would be diverted, and the chances would be better that EEC would develop into a more open regional economy. Americans feared that, if a high CXT were allowed to exist for a period of time, weak industrial sectors would develop behind the protective wall, and insurmountable political pressure would grow in Europe to protect them. This protection would allow Europe to broaden its product mix by enabling nascent industries to grow, sheltered from foreign competition, and to capture potential American markets.[31]

Kennedy's strategy sought to improve access to European markets and to rely on continued American manufacturing superiority to generate an even greater trade surplus. As Administration spokesmen warned Congress, unless the TEA passed, the United States would not be able to increase its trade surplus enough to maintain its global military network.[32]

George Ball, however, described Petersen's TEA approach as an inadequate improvement. Describing the majority approach as "too little, too soon" and condemning the existing international trade mechanisms as "bankrupt," Ball wanted to go beyond a reduction of trade barriers and establish a supranational authority to manage the world economy directly—without interference from national legislatures. He suggested empowering the Organization for Economic Cooperation and Development (OECD), the institutionalization of core cooperation, with authority to settle potentially divisive trade problems.[33] The OECD seemed the logical governing body of the economic world-system, as power gradually evolved from a national to a supranational basis. This evolution reflected the growth of multinational banks and corporations and truly global markets. Kennedy's other advisers represented a nationalist consensus on bargaining down the EEC's Common External Tariff to help American exports, while minimizing damage by imports. They adopted the conventional approach to trade negotiations: bargaining for national advantage among competitive entities. Ball, representing the multinational financial sector in New York, which had a more global perspective than the more locally oriented manufacturing sector, believed that the primary task in 1962 was not to maximize the wealth of the United States through conventional bargaining with rivals.

Ball understood that perpetuating the framework of nationalist bargaining for competitive advantage would unleash trade conflicts among the core powers, leading to distasteful economic regionalism and neo-mercantilist trade barriers. He also knew that national entities could never achieve consensus on such systemic trade problems as the absorption into core markets of goods manufactured in peripheral economies and the widespread discrimination in agricultural trade. Knowing that Congress would not be prepared to shift control of American policies to a supranational institution in 1962, Ball advised waiting until 1963 to seek new trade legislation. Ball's radical proposal rallied little support. Kennedy decided to present the TEA to Congress in 1962.[34] Competitive approaches to core relations were thus institutionalized with the rise of the EEC, and the Kennedy Administration failed to realize its ambition of Atlantic unity on American terms.

The Administration's brilliantly orchestrated campaign for TEA passage included pacifying potent opposition such as the textile industry and then mounting a powerful public relations effort. Ironically, Kennedy made Ball, the most vociferous opponent of neo-mercantilism, responsible for negotiating an international agreement to protect American textiles from foreign competition. Ball engineered the Long-Term Textile Agreement, consummated on September 30, 1962, which established a cartel-like cementing of world market shares and allowed new entrants the opportunity to increase their market shares gradually so as to assure the textile interests of the core economies guaranteed, if potentially decreasing, markets. Ball settled for this compromise, which he acknowledged "made a mockery" of free trade principles.[35]

Ball made no effort to conceal his utter disgust for the greedy

textile magnates who were protecting their profit margins and ineffi-
ciency against the virtuous evolution of the world system, which dictated that the core powers concede labor-intensive production to the
peripheral areas. His comments dramatically reveal the sharp psychological schism between the weak capitalist sectors and the global
capitalists who applauded the social Darwinian effects of the destruction and rebirth of productive forces: "For my private and secret
gratification, I appeared before each textile group dressed in a
British-made suit, a British-made shirt, shoes made for me in Hong
Kong, and a French necktie. . . . I heard an industry representative
say, 'that's the slyest bastard I've seen in years. We certainly have to
watch him.' I found such praise heartwarming." Ball believed it was
the responsibility of the textile manufacturers to move their production to the low-wage periphery; they should stop "wasting" the 1.3
percent of American labor resources devoted to textile production
and redirect those resources to advanced, high-profit production
lines.[36]

The textile agreement also forced Europe, at American insistence,
to accept larger shares of Asian textiles. This effort represented the
longstanding desire to shift production from the European to the
American textile industry and the textile industries of the American
client states on the Pacific Rim.[37] The agreement illustrates as well
the political battle for markets among the core economies which
raged within the common strategy of increasing world markets.

The packaging of the TEA for congressional consumption was remi-
niscent of the Truman Administration's selling of policies to Congress. State Department consultant Eugene Rostow recommended
selling it on the standard grounds of anti-Communism—the rationale
developed in the 1940s. Anti-Communism was the only appeal that
could overcome congressional economic nationalism; as Rostow
noted, the "fear of imports will be almost insuperable." State Department veteran Edwin Martin, Assistant Secretary for Economic Affairs, warned, however, that an anti-Communist sales pitch "only
works for military expenditures." Ball's approach suggested the optimistic tone that the Administration would use to obtain congressional
approval: "[We cannot] arouse all the forces of restrictionism. We
must say that this is what we need to raise the standard of living of
every American, keep industry at home, and prevent capital exports."[38] The upbeat approach led to rhetorical excesses extolling the
benefits of the TEA to the American economy. These excesses expe-

dited congressional approval but later weakened the American bargaining position in reciprocal trade negotiations with the Europeans. European negotiators used the inflated advantages to the United States of tariff cuts as developed during the TEA hearings to bargain down American tariffs. The hyperbolic rhetoric also unrealistically inflated domestic expectations.[39]

In early December 1961, Kennedy launched the TEA public relations campaign, telling the National Association of Manufacturers that exports were good for business and the balance of payments, and assuring the AFL-CIO that they were good for employment. When Kennedy formally announced the TEA legislation in January 1962, he asserted that the TEA would bestow benefits on every state, every segment of the economy, and every aspect of American foreign political and economic policy.[40]

Testimony at the TEA hearings and the blitz of Administration speeches featured sermons on how American productivity would be improved by foreign competition. They appealed to the innate American sense of exceptionalism, boasting—with a mixture of salesmanship and true belief—of American superiority. Kennedy claimed that "once artificial restraints are removed, a vast array of American goods, produced by American know-how with American efficiency, can compete with any goods in any spot in the world."[41] Hodges echoed that the TEA was "based on the conviction that American producers, as they have time and again demonstrated, can enter world markets, compete soundly, and prevail."[42] He cited the example of the apparant American repulsion of the threat of small car imports to the American auto industry in 1961: "We showed after a very late start on the part of our automobile manufacturers that we could compete and the imports of automobiles from other countries are coming down rather than going up and I think will continue to come down."[43] Imports of Japanese transistor radios were heralded as a stimulus to the American electronics industry, which would respond to and triumph over the competition.[44]

The congressional debate on the TEA featured over four weeks of hearings in the spring of 1962 by the House Ways and Means Committee. The many impassioned witnesses from the supporting and opposing camps represented a massive slice of American economic interests. TEA proponents came armed with impressive evidence to support the Administration's claim that export growth was more beneficial to American prosperity than was protection from imports. The distinguished Brookings Institution economist Walter Salant had published a key analysis in 1961 which showed that the United States would lose only 63,000 jobs for each increase of $1 billion in imports, but would gain far more from an increase in exports by the same amount.[45] Kennedy's advisers assured him that the bold TEA clause to allow zero tariffs on industrial goods trade would generate a 10 percent increase in American exports and a smaller increase in imports so as not to threaten American employment levels.[46] A separate Brookings study of the balance of payments, commissioned by the Council of Economic Advisers in 1962, predicted "steady improvement over the coming years in the competitive position of American products." Its optimism was based on the assumption that American inflation rates would continue to be lower than European rates, which would outweigh the increasing competition from Japan.[47]

Backers of multilateral policies were far more powerful than the weak sectors of the American economy, such as textiles and other labor-intensive industries, which bitterly opposed further trade liberalization. American heavy and high technology industries were still strong, and were interested in good relations with Europe to expand their markets and investment avenues. American agriculture, in particular, depended greatly on European markets and had everything to lose if negotiations to minimize the Common External Tariff on agricultural products failed. In addition, the American financial sector was always the greatest force behind multilateral policies which guaranteed the most freedom to global capital. Even large segments of organized labor, riding the crest of the postwar American boom and impressed by arguments and evidence that millions of jobs depended on exports, gave qualified support to the TEA.[48]

By far the most aggressive American industrial sector—at the opposite end of the scale from the textile sector—was the aluminum industry. Aluminum represented a sector in which the United States still enjoyed global economic supremacy. As steel, automobiles, and consumer goods were beginning to feel the pressure of European and Japanese competition, the aluminum industry was in a position to capture the European market, giving it a position of global dominance which would ensure large profits for decades. From the European perspective, free trade through the absence of tariffs was highly desirable when European companies could compete with the United States (as was the case with German industry—hence the strong impetus provided by Germany to maintain an open Europe against the regionalist leanings of the French). But because Europe lagged behind the United States in aluminum production, it was in Europe's interest to use the Common External Tariff to shelter and nurture an incipient European aluminum capacity at first and then relax the barriers when European industry could compete. When the Commerce Department sought to arouse business support for the TEA and exports, it was the aluminum industry that demanded strong American action against the CXT, which would unfairly deprive them of global supremacy.[49]

The major political opposition to the TEA came from those conservative Republicans who represented the nationalist elements of the manufacturing sector. They despised taxes and aid to foreign competitors and feared imports from low-wage countries. They attacked the Achilles heel of the TEA case, the argument that the combination of much higher American wages and lower tariffs would not incite a damaging import deluge. They expressed the basic impulse of local American manufacturing: enforce free trade on other nations but protect all weak American manufacturing sectors from competition.[50] Although the Administration dismissed the wage-related fears of the opposition during the TEA debate in Congress, the President's Advisory Committee on Labor Management Policy reported on October 4, 1962, that wages should be controlled to stimulate exports.[51]

Business opposition to the TEA naturally encompassed those weak economic sectors engaged in low-wage, labor-intensive production, and which supported neo-mercantilist policies. The glass, tile, plywood, bicycle, clock, scissors, glove, shoe, and millinery products industries all claimed that American tariffs were already dangerously low.[52] The TEA opponents were "shocked" at the "reprehensible" government-sponsored "drum beat of propaganda" for the TEA which had reached "fantastic proportions."[53] The Tile Council of America said that the bill "coldbloodedly contemplates the disruption and destruction of domestic industry. . . . It might be better to retitle the bill the 'Domestic Industry Destruction Act of 1962.'"[54] For opponents, "whether the United States [could] absorb such an increased volume of Japanese imports without serious dislocation in the domestic economy [was] open to question."[55] They predicted that "drastic reduction such as requested by the President on goods having a high labor content will result in a flooding of merchandise which will seriously jeopardize many important American industries" and turn many areas into "ghost towns."[56]

The voices of TEA opponents were prophetic, but also the last cries of a simpler era; they were fearful of the implications of a truly global economy for some Americans and regions and skeptical of the grandiose and overtly manipulative promises of the Administration. They maintained that the "myth" of American productive superiority "[had] been exploded," that the United States had lost its technological edge and that the "worst [was] yet to come."[57] Republican Congressman Bruce Alger of Texas asked presciently: "Suppose you are wrong and we can't compete because of the wage rate . . . and we find out too late to our sorrow that we could not compete?"[58] Pittsburgh Congressman John Dent declared, ". . . I am protecting the jobs of the people in my district from being eliminated by conditions over which they have no control. . . . If that makes me a protectionist, I am one."[59] The machine tool lobby noted the distortions in the Administration's case on various issues—in particular, that the United States needed more investment to compete because "our plant equipment is obsolete, but that when it comes to H.R. 9900 [the TEA] somehow it is our superlative production efficiency, automation and sophisticated plant equipment that will translate our 3–1 disadvantage in labor costs into a unit cost equivalence."[60]

TEA proponents naturally viewed opponents as inferior and expendable. Hodges described TEA opponents as "smaller, and less sophisticated, and less progressive industries."[61] One study, commissioned by a global trading firm, said that the "industries most anxious for protection today are declining and outside the main stream of industrial development. While their voices may be powerful, their interests are often not vital to their nation's prosperity in the long pull."[62]

Ball and Petersen were disappointed that even industries which profited heavily from exports were reluctant to give up tariff protection at home in return for better access to foreign markets. Ball commented that "the spirit of defeatism in business circles is disturbing. They feel they can't resist the wage-price spiral, and want to build a protective wall. We must try to educate them that the biggest restraint on the wage-price spiral is a liberal trade policy. The President must play a part in the process of restoring self-confidence, educating, hammering home the lesson."[63] Ball's frustration derived from the cautious nature of the manufacturers, who were happy to increase foreign markets but reluctant to compete in unprotected American markets. Petersen was disappointed in the reactions of forty trade groups that the Department of Commerce had called in to discuss the TEA. He remarked that American companies were not strong seekers of export opportunities and that Commerce "heard mostly about protection, not the desire for export opportunities."[64]

Ball also expressed disappointment that the companies with strong positions in world markets and which one would expect to clamor for export opportunities "are capital exporters instead, and consequently don't care about foreign tariffs."[65] Ball meant that these companies preferred to build plants overseas rather than to export. This was another twist in the balance of payments problem. The overall world share of manufacturing production of the United States fell from 70 percent in 1950 to 50 percent in 1960, but the production share of companies based in the United States remained 60 percent. American industry moving overseas thus hurt the balance of payments because it reduced American exports. One of Kennedy's hopes was to obtain reduced European tariffs, which would encourage American industry to increase its exports and provide an incentive not to relocate plants behind the protective wall of the CXT. This strategy would increase exports, cut the outflow of investment capital, and stimulate the domestic plant modernization essential to long-range competitiveness.

The combination of the well-executed legislative strategy and the optimism about continuing American economic superiority led on June 28 to a surprising 298–125 House vote to pass the TEA. The Senate passed the measure 78–8 on September 19, with only Democrat Strom Thurmond joining seven arch-conservative Republicans in opposition.[66] Passage paved the way for the "Kennedy Round" of GATT tariff negotiations, which began in May 1963 with an acrimonious clash between the EEC and the United States and lasted until 1967. The Kennedy Round was the sixth round of international tariff negotiations since GATT began in 1949. The Europeans held firm to their demands that the United States at least partially dismantle its protective devices, such as the American Selling Price (ASP) scheme of import controls and the Buy American Act. The ASP paralleled Europe's agricultural variable level system in that it keyed import duties to domestic price levels. Europeans also became outraged at United States Tariff Commission rulings against European carpet and glass products and refused to discuss lowering tariffs on chemical products until the ASP was abolished.[67]

Europeans, however, were also eager to reach a free trade compromise with the United States. At the heart of EEC policy was the grand compromise between Germany and France, whereby the agricultural French agreed to a successful Kennedy Round of industrial tariff cuts in return for the industrial Germans' agreement to support the Common Agricultural Policy (CAP) of the Common Market.[68]

The results of the TEA and the Kennedy Round were mixed in almost every sense.[69] Industrial tariffs were cut 35 percent, much less than the Administration had hoped. Indeed, Kennedy had been greatly educated about international economic competition, especially the European intransigence on agricultural trade. Just before his death, he told Agriculture Secretary Orville Freeman that "he was coming to the opinion that the whole Kennedy Round had been oversold; that he was not at all sure that it was in our own national interest."[70] Liberalized trade was achieved, but the open American market invited a flood of damaging imports. Finally, the progress on industrial products was offset by the bitter disappointment suffered by the United States in agricultural negotiations.

The third key challenge of Kennedy's foreign economic policy was the preservation of vital American agricultural exports to Europe. Under the CAP, the Common Market instituted a variable levy system whereby a flexible tariff was applied to agricultural imports. This floating tariff ensured that import prices were always higher than the prices for domestically produced agricultural goods. Critics have aptly labeled as naïve Kennedy's strategy to use agricultural exports to Europe to increase the trade surplus to pay for his foreign military expenditures.[71] The CAP foiled his strategy and led to the sharpest trade conflict among the core powers since World War II. The struggle over the CAP symbolized Washington's effort to use its considerable political power to maintain American economic hegemony. The United States had enjoyed huge postwar European agricultural markets, but European agriculture, aided by new technology, had recovered. With the rise in European agricultural prices inherent under the CAP and its subsequent stimulus to European production, Freeman warned Kennedy against "the consequences of runaway agricultural production in Western Europe on the future unity of the free world."[72]

The political economy of agriculture in the postwar world-system dictated that trade in farm goods between non-tropical nations would decline relative to total production and consumption. Relative self-sufficiency in non-tropical agricultural products became an obsession in Europe and Japan, because ruling parties relied on political support from rural constituencies.

The considerable political clout of American agriculture lay behind the demand that American negotiators not approve any deal on industrial trade with Europe until American agricultural exports to Europe were protected from the potentially damaging cut in agricultural exports under the CAP.[73] In the worst case, American agriculture was more than willing to lower American tariffs on manufactured goods to enable foreigners to "continue to take this awesome farm surplus off our hands."[74] Near the end of the Dillon Round of GATT tariff reduction negotiations in 1961, Freeman had to beg Kennedy to ignore the howls of protestation from the State Department and send Freeman's aid Charles Murphy to Europe to represent American agriculture at the negotiations.[75] Murphy's presence prevented the State and Commerce departments from trading away American agriculture's access to Europe in return for European industrial concessions. American threats to retaliate intensified as Europe held firm to the variable levy system concept of the CAP.[76]

The battle began in earnest when, on July 30, 1962, after months of delicate compromises among the European nations, the Common Market finally imposed the CAP variable levies. Frozen chicken carcasses, more of a manufactured product than a classical agricultural product, triggered the dispute. The American poultry industry had revolutionized the mass production of frozen chickens and created a huge market in Europe, especially in Germany, by importing the birds at low prices. These inexpensive imports stimulated German poultry consumption to triple within a few years. Europeans could produce such goods themselves, however, given the new technology. And the EEC doubled the tariff on frozen poultry in retaliation for American tariff commission rulings that had invoked punitive tariffs on European carpet and glass.[77]

Freeman quickly urged Kennedy to put "vigorous coordinated pressure" on the EEC to preserve the "historical markets" of American agriculture in Europe. Europeans maintained that the Common Market and CAP made the old patterns of trade irrelevant. The Agriculture Secretary advised the President that "all of agriculture is watching carefully, hence it is timely now to dramatize your interest and your willingness to act personally". During the poultry crisis Kennedy intervened personally with Germany Chancellor Konrad Adenauer. Freeman himself used "rough" tactics when browbeating the Europeans on the CAP, despite strong criticism from the State Department.[78] The EEC, however, resisted even entering into agricultural negotiations, claiming that internal European conflicts, especially over crucial grain price levels, precluded bargaining with the United States.[79]

On May 30, on the eve of the greatest free trade negotiations ever launched, the EEC raised the poultry tariff again and set off the great "chicken war." Special Trade Representative Christian Herter took personally the slap in the face that the Common Market delivered by brazenly raising duties unilaterally. He advised Kennedy to retaliate.[80] The President petitioned GATT for permission to invoke $46 million in damages; the EEC claimed that the proper amount was $19 million. GATT eventually ruled, in early 1964, that President Lyndon B. Johnson could invoke $26 million of punitive tariffs on European products.[81] The perceived European intransigence during the chicken war was a huge blow to the Kennedy Administration and the hopes raised by the TEA, and cast a pall over the Kennedy Round of negotiations.[82]

By late 1963, the Agriculture Department, frustrated by European agriculture's leverage, abandoned its free trade strategy toward dealing with the EEC in favor of a policy of managed trade. American agriculture now sought "quantitative access assurances," or "low duty quotas," on a fixed amount of imports to guarantee the "historic market share" of agricultural exporters despite the CAP.[83] This policy shift marked a significant admission by a key American economic sector that, as envisioned by postwar American leaders, multilateralism had failed, and it revealed the priority of market share over economic principles.

The failure of the American strategy to hold its agricultural markets in Europe was the most disappointing aspect of Kennedy's foreign economic policy. Ever since Kennedy's death the United States has been trying in vain to defeat the CAP, which has led to ever-increasing European production.

The fourth major theme of Kennedy's foreign economic policy was the significant impact that American military spending overseas had on the balance of payments deficit. International economic conditions had changed drastically since the United States first began pumping dollars into foreign treasuries in the form of vast foreign military expenditures for troop support, supplies, and weapons. This drain on the Treasury caused as much consternation in the Kennedy Administration as did the variable levy system. Kennedy repeatedly pledged to press America's allies to "share the burden" and thus relieve the balance of payments problem. He instructed the State and Defense departments to make the Europeans pay up.[84] Europe and Japan did not share the American view, as Roosa explained: "Many countries today object to our balance of payments deficit on the grounds that we are financing an aid and military effort which they could not afford or would not willingly undertake by foisting on them dollar deposits which they have no need to hold."[85] As Acheson's protégé, Defense Department Deputy Paul Nitze, pointed out in 1959: "Initial overseas military arrangements were designed to minimize the economic drain on others and thus maximized the dollar drain of the U.S."[86] Deputy Secretary of Defense Roswell Gilpatrick advised Congress, "We in the Defense Department . . . are extremely conscious of the fact that we are, in effect, creating the balance of payments problem of this country. . . . For many years we stressed buying United States military supplies overseas to help their economy. Now the shoe is on the other foot."[87] Indeed, the United States now sought to sell arms to help its trade balance.

Republican policy adviser Henry A. Kissinger insightfully perceived in the early 1960s what would later frustrate American leaders for decades: European and Japanese governments would not readily agree to finance the American troops on their soil. He wrote that Europe would play only a "token" role in the global American military network, and then only "to obtain a veto over United States actions." He noted that Americans tended to treat their NATO allies "paternalistically" and to think that "by definition" the interests of the allies "cannot diverge" from American interests.[88] In December 1960 President Eisenhower had sent Treasury Secretary Robert Anderson to Bonn to seek $650 million from Germany to support American troops. Anderson held the minority view at that time that the American balance of payments deficit was structural, not temporary, and when the Germans refused, Anderson left Bonn in a huff and threatened to reduce American troops. The pro-European majority in the State and Defense departments severely criticized Anderson for humiliating the United States and threatening the delicate NATO alliance.[89] The presence of large numbers of American forces in Europe under NATO constituted the heart of American military hegemony. The Administration agreed early on that a sharp reduction in American military expenditures abroad was an unwelcome "drastic step."[90] If the balance of payments drain was to be stopped without reducing foreign troop levels, Kennedy had no choice but to get Europe and Japan to make support payments.

The Kennedy Administration set out immediately, with Acheson as the chief communicator, to rectify Anderson's error in the eyes of the Europeans. When he journeyed to Paris to meet with de Gaulle in early 1961, Acheson "corrected the impression given last December" that the "presence of American forces in Europe might depend upon our Balance of Payments situation. The present administration has no such idea."[91] Both Treasury Secretary Dillon and Defense Secretary McNamara were nonetheless very committed to foreign military savings.[92] Reflecting the consensus on foreign military savings as projected by the Defense Department, a Brookings study on the balance of payments issue used as an operating assumption a $400 million annual decrease in those expenditures by 1968.[93]

In the fall of 1961 Gilpatrick and German Foreign Minister Franz Josef Strauss concluded the first military "offset" agreement. Germany agreed to purchase American weapons and military training worth about $700 million per year to "offset" the net American dollar drain caused by military expenditures in Germany. The agreement was renewed in 1963 and 1965, but in 1966 the Germans balked at continuing, and another diplomatic flap developed as the Americans again threatened sharp troop reductions.[94] Not only were the savings in foreign exchange considerable, but the constant political pressure on Europe to compensate the United States for military expenditures also made it politically awkward for Europeans to cash in their bloated dollar reserves for gold. The Administration then turned to France to obtain payments for troop support. But the French refused, citing American obstruction of French atomic weapons plans.[95]

Much like the struggle with Europe over the CAP, the American effort to obtain support payments from its allies to compensate for American military expenditures abroad continued into the late 1980s, and these expenditures continued to contribute significantly to American deficits.

The fifth foreign economic policy question, and a disconcerting symbol of the decline of American hegemony, was the increasingly independent attitude of European governments toward trade with the Soviet bloc. Under fierce domestic pressure to increase trade with the East and thus increase profits, European governments took increasingly lenient views on trade and resisted the corresponding American pressure to maintain a unified core policy. Ever since the onset of the Korean War, American policy, dictated by the Battle Act, had imposed restrictions on allied trade with the Soviets. The European tendency to export what were considered by the Americans to be "strategic" items to the Soviet Union destroyed the fragile consensus in the United States on supporting the trade restrictions. Corporations were willing to forgo increased sales, until they began to see their European competitors grabbing up lucrative markets in the East. This trend armed the American companies with a new moral attack: foreigners were making "real suckers" of Americans.[96]

In a sequence of events which vividly revealed the nature of the rivalry among the core capitalist powers, the United States attempted to enforce its restrictions on European and Japanese companies that sold high technology and strategic goods to the Soviets. The American government was deathly afraid that the Soviets and Europeans would combine their considerable resources to further Eurasian prosperity and strengthen European neutrality. If the Soviets could transport their gas and oil cheaply to Europe in return for European products, both areas would prosper immensely, and the United States would lose to the Soviet Union tremendous leverage over Europe. Moreover, the American oil giants, reaping monopoly profits from their control of Mideast oil reserves, were complaining to the government about price competition from Soviet oil sales to the West.[97] In an almost Keystone Cops routine, the Kennedy Administration exerted pressure on national governments in Germany, Italy, Great Britain, and Japan to forbid their corporations from selling large diameter pipe to the Soviets (for oil and gas pipelines) in late 1962 and the spring of 1963. First, against fierce domestic protest, the German government relented and banned the sale by a German corporation. Quickly, however, a company in Britain struck a deal with the Soviets to provide the pipe. Washington, knowing that the German government would be subjected to intense domestic ridicule for hurting a German company and allowing a British rival to get the business, had to exert even more pressure on the British government to halt the transactions. At that point, Italian, Japanese, and Swedish firms offered their products to the Soviets.[98] The State Department scurried around to suppress the latest offer, with limited success. But to succeed, the United States used enormous political capital, enraged foreign business interests, and embarrassed foreign governments by forcing them to concede to American pressure in an ultimately vain attempt to preserve American oil markets and limit European automony.[99]

In conclusion, in the Kennedy years, American policy sought to defend the reserve currency status of the dollar and Bretton Woods. Kennedy's pledge not to devalue the dollar was the key to defending the status of the dollar, but it also bound his successors to this defensive strategy, and brought the entire system down with the dollar in 1971 and 1972 when the American deficits reached what at that time seemed gigantic proportions. Critics look back at Kennedy's defensive and hegemonic strategy as a root cause of the long-term decline of American industrial supremacy. They charge that, had Kennedy been more flexible and allowed the dollar to decline from its lofty postwar perch, the collapse of American manufacturing trade in the face of European and Japanese competitiveness would not have been as devastating.[100] At the heart of the relative decline of the United States as an economic power were the ill effects of vast American military spending, both on the balance of payments and on domestic capital investment. With the Vietnam War—the logical culmination of Kennedy's aggressive foreign policy—the hemorrhage of dollars accelerated. Under Kennedy, the United States chose to have both guns and butter, yet it had lost the ability to pay for its global military domination. Gains in American productivity, the only way to preserve the market share of American industry without devaluation, declined in the 1960s. In consequence, the United States balance of trade dropped from a $5 billion annual surplus in the early and mid-1960s to a $2 billion deficit in 1971.

It is ironic that the United States grew to break more and more of the rules of Bretton Woods in order to save these same rules. Bretton Woods was designed to promote the free flow of capital, but the United States, in order to save Bretton Woods, placed controls on private capital exports. The United States refused to submit to IMF discipline and continued to behave as a surplus nation, spending billions abroad that it could not afford, especially during the Vietnam War. To keep domestic harmony, the government also imposed "voluntary" export restraints on various trading partners. The presumed "voluntarism" of the offending exporter made these quotas legitimate under the GATT rules, but quotas they remained.

With the return to genuine economic rivalry among the core capitalist powers in the late 1950s, the twin forces of rivalry and cooperation assumed their natural balance. From 1945 to 1960, the forces of rivalry had been suppressed by the extreme disequilibrium in the world economy. The manifestations of the forces of intra-core cooperation during the Kennedy Administration were: the efforts of Roosa to unify the core central bankers in the cause of preserving Bretton Woods and the rule of the dollar from the avaricious financial community, and the TEA and the Kennedy Round, in which Europe, Japan, and the United States hammered out acceptable positions of trade cooperation. The manifestations of core rivalry were the flip sides of the same events: the unwillingness of Europe and Japan to subsidize the American military machine overtly (although the Americans got them to do so against their will by shipping printing-press IOUs in the form of paper dollars abroad to cover payments deficits); the unwillingness of Europe and Japan to refrain from trade with the Soviets; the resistance of the pro-European (i.e., Gaullist) financial interests to Roosa's propping up of the dollar versus gold; and the infighting over neo-mercantilist interests—agriculture (especially poultry), chemicals, textiles, oil, coal, and others—during the Kennedy Round.

What emerged after Kennedy's death was thus a hybrid world system, still based largely on the dollar and the might of the United States, but now fragmented increasingly into regional economic blocs, centered around the Soviet Union, the EEC, North America, Japan, and China. Relatively free trade in advanced industrial products coexisted with increasingly managed trade in less advanced products, where the means of production were easily obtained and where national governments sought to protect domestic producers. American officials issued lofty statements about the sanctity of free trade, followed by an endless series of exceptions to protect particular interests, such as agriculture, oil, textiles, and other industries. Europeans and Japanese were even more forthright in pursuing neo-mercantile strategies to placate domestic interests and provide economic security, which some Administration officials feared in 1962. By the 1970s, for example, Europe had created a trading bloc with Africa through the Lome Convention. The fierce competition for market advantage intensified and shaped core diplomacy.[101] Thus, Kennedy's claim that the "Marxist predictions of 'capitalist' empires warring over markets and stifling competition would be shattered for all time" proved premature.[102]

Kennedy did not realize his ambition to cure the balance of payments deficit and enhance American economic superiority. He launched an aggressive but ultimately futile defense of American economic hegemony.

3

When Push Came to Shove: Canada and the United States

J.L. GRANATSTEIN

"I never realized they resented us as much as they do." After serving as the United States chair of the International Joint Commission that adjudicated Canadian-American boundary questions, Teno Roncalio thought that he had learned something about Canadians in the early 1960s. "I didn't realize that they felt we were a monstrous, mammoth obliteration of their own identity and of their own arts and . . . culture."[1] That was a slight overstatement of the reality, perhaps, but Roncalio captured the essence of the Canadian mood that prevailed during the presidency of John F. Kennedy.

Beginning in the mid-1950s, Canadians, as so often in their past, had begun to be concerned once more with the impact that the United States was having on them and their country. Canada's historic defense relationship with Great Britain had largely disappeared in the postwar years, replaced by ever-tightening links with the Pentagon. This process toward military cooperation with the United States had commenced with the creation of the Permanent Joint Board on Defense in 1940 and had then proceeded without check through a variety of agreements and arrangements to the creation of the North American Air Defense (NORAD) Command in 1957 and the Defense Production Sharing Agreement of 1959. Particularly shattering to national pride was the cancellation in 1959 of the Canadian-designed CF-105 Arrow supersonic fighter,[2] a victim of spiraling costs. Instead of building the Arrow, the Canadian government purchased American-produced Bomarc surface-to-air missiles, intended to carry atomic warheads, and in 1961 struck a complicated deal with the United States for American Voodoo interceptors, capable of carrying MB-1 nuclear missiles. Canadian forces on duty with the North Atlantic Treaty Organization (NATO) in Europe also used American-designed equipment and assumed roles that required nuclear weapons. To many, Canadian military independence seemed to be disappearing, and the close connections with the United States disturbed all who anguished over John Foster Dulles's alarmist Cold War rhetoric and policies, massive retaliation, and military expansionists in the Pentagon.[3]

The American economic presence in Canada had become equally worrisome and pervasive. The Royal Commission on Canada's Economic Prospects reported in 1957 that the massive American investment that had fueled Canada's postwar boom had also resulted in American ownership of huge percentages of the oil and gas (73 percent in 1955), manufacturing (42 percent), and mining and smelting (55 percent) sectors of the economy. At the same time, Canada's trade was overwhelmingly linked to the United States. In 1955, 60 percent of Canada's exports went south while 73 percent of its imports came from the United States. The apparent loss of economic independence involved in such reliance on one country for foreign investment and trade alarmed nationalists in all political parties, in the universities, and in the trade unions.[4]

Cultural influence from the south had become more pervasive still. American movies held total dominance in the profitable Canadian market, leaving only documentaries, produced by the government's National Film Board, to Canadian talent. *Saturday Evening Post, Life, Time,* and *Reader's Digest* claimed hundreds of thousands of Canadian readers, far more than the struggling Canadian periodicals. And the American television networks, reaching the large Canadian markets from Burlington, Buffalo, Fargo, and Seattle, brought American news, views, and sitcoms to audiences that seemed eager for something other than the often staid television programming provided by the government-owned Canadian Broadcasting Corporation. The question of national identity and cultural independence was much the same in all areas of the arts, and not even the creation in 1957 of the Canada Council, a government effort to spark creativity and foster excellence in the arts and sciences, seemed to hold out much hope for a reversal of the longstanding trends in this area of Canadian life.[5]

Canada's identity, it seemed to many, was in jeopardy. That was one of the reasons commentators offered for the stunning, narrow electoral victory of John G. Diefenbaker, the leader of the Progressive Conservative party, in the general elections of June 1957.[6] Diefenbaker, a sixty-one-year-old Saskatchewan populist with a messianic gaze and pulpit-style oratory who had been a Member of Parliament since 1940 and had won his party's leadership in December 1956 after previous rebuffs in 1942 and 1948, had played on the theme of Canadian nationalism in his campaign. That powerful theme, implicitly (and sometimes explicitly) connoting anti-Americanism, had proved very useful in toppling Prime Minister Louis St. Laurent, the leader of the entrenched Liberal party which had held power continuously since 1935. In 1958, after a successful session of Parliament that had seen Diefenbaker mesmerize the country with his vigor and implementation of progressive change, the Conservatives crushed Lester Pearson, the Liberals' new leader, almost wiped out the democratic socialists of the Cooperative Commonwealth Federation, and captured the largest parliamentary majority to that time. Political pundits soon wrote expansively of the Conservative century, and Diefenbaker acquired an almost mythic stature within his own party.[7]

But by the time of the presidential elections in November 1960, the bloom had fallen from the Tory rose. The Canadian economy had begun a serious recession in 1958 and unemployment was rising almost as fast as the government's deficits. Diefenbaker himself repeatedly maintained that all was well, but stories of his indecisiveness became widespread. Some cabinet ministers grew increasingly disturbed by this trait, especially in the area of the government's budget, where disputes had become embittered among the Minister of Finance, a tight-fisted and orthodox thinker, and a substantial number of ministers who hoped to spend the country out of recession.[8]

The Prime Minister's indecision was also especially evident in the area of defense, where the Secretary of State for External Affairs, Howard Green, a Vancouver Member of Parliament, had become engaged in a Cabinet and interdepartmental struggle with the Minister of National Defence, the blunt and straightforward Colonel Douglas Harkness of Calgary. The Diefenbaker government had signed the NORAD agreement with the United States in its first month in office. Harkness assumed that the Bomarc missiles the government had purchased to meet Canada's commitments to NORAD would be equipped with their nuclear warheads as soon as the two installations in Canada were complete and negotiations with the United States for a "two-key" system of control were concluded. Similarly, Harkness expected the Honest John surface-to-surface missiles with the Canadian brigade group in Europe to receive their nuclear payloads, and he wanted the Royal Canadian Air Force's CF-104 aircraft on NATO "strike-reconnaisance" duties to get their nuclear armament, too. Why, after all, had Diefenbaker's government signed the agreements, purchased the weapons and accepted the roles if it did not intend to take the nuclear warheads?[9]

But Green opposed the arming of the Canadian forces with nuclear arms. A well-meaning and sincere man who had not traveled to Europe since his service in France during the Great War, Green had become convinced that Canada must play its fullest possible part in pressing the great powers toward nuclear disarmament and halting the spread of nuclear weapons. The world was in peril, he believed— a reasonable perception, to be sure, and one that had been urged upon him by his extraordinarily able and experienced under secretary, Norman Robertson.[10] And if disarmament had become a priority,[11] one avidly sought by peace groups across Canada, then how could Canada convincingly encourage the Americans and Russians toward sanity if its troops and airmen were armed with nuclear weapons? "We were advocating in the United Nations that there should be control of the spread of nuclear weapons," Green said many years later, " . . . and then to turn around and take them ourselves just made us look foolish."[12]

The two ministers and their departments became locked in a struggle for the soul and mind of John Diefenbaker—a confused mind and a troubled soul. Leery of the Canadian military, the Prime Minister grew angry that the Chairman of the Chief of Staffs Committee in 1957, General Charles Foulkes, had hustled him into accepting the NORAD agreement to honor commitments made to the American Chiefs of Staff. "We stampeded the incoming government . . . ," Foulkes later admitted.[13] Diefenbaker became understandably appalled at the costs and destructiveness of modern weaponry, and he had been badly burned politically when A.V. Roe Ltd., the manufacturer of the CF-105, had shut down the production line and laid off fourteen thousand workers the very instant the government announced the aircraft's cancellation. Diefenbaker was also acutely sensitive to the hundreds of letters he received from Canadians who called for peace and disarmament; almost none demanded bigger and better defenses. On the other hand, Diefenbaker believed in the reality of the Soviet threat. He had agreed to purchase the nuclear equipment, and, as he had told the House of Commons on February 20, 1959, the day the decision to scrap the Arrow and purchase the Bomarc had been announced: "The full potential of these defensive weapons is achieved only when they are armed with nuclear warheads."[14] President Dwight D. Eisenhower, whom the Canadian Prime Minister held in high regard, was obviously and necessarily concerned with the defense of the North American continent and the strategic deterrent, the task the Bomarcs were designed to meet. No Canadian prime minister would lightly pick a fight with Washington on such a sensitive topic as the defense of the continental heartland.[15]

Still, Diefenbaker was torn. Green urged disarmament upon him while Harkness counseled the conclusion of agreements with the United States so that warheads could be readied for use just as soon as the Bomarcs, Honest Johns, and CF-104s became operational. With some time before that eventuality arose, the Prime Minister told an Ottawa audience in November 1960 that Canada would make no decision on nuclear weapons so long as progress toward disarmament continued.[16] That heartened Green and his Department of External Affairs; Norman Robertson told his minister that "it would seem reasonable . . . to hold to the view that a decision to acquire weapons at this time is premature."[17]

Eisenhower had seemed content to allow Canada to move at its own pace toward the nuclear decision, but his successor, John F. Kennedy, proved less patient. Diefenbaker, born in 1895, was much older than the young and vigorous President and slightly alarmed by the militant rhetoric that sometimes seemed to mark his speeches. During the American presidential campaign, in fact, the Prime Minister had told Arnold Heeney, his Ambassador in Washington, of his "distaste for Kennedy." The Democratic candidate was courageously rash and predisposed to a policy of action and Diefenbaker had a much more "favourable opinion of Nixon."[18] Worse, Kennedy had failed to respond to a telegram of congratulations after his election victory. But when Diefenbaker, accompanied by Green, flew to Washington on February 20 for his first meeting with the American leader, a meeting hastily arranged at the beginning of February by Heeney at the Prime Minister's request, his attitude apparently changed. The meeting had been "excellent," he remarked to Heeney. In fact, "it could not have been better."[19] And Livingston Merchant, the American Ambassador in Ottawa, agreed: "I had the feeling that Mr. Diefenbaker and President Kennedy got along extremely well together. . . . " At Merchant's first meeting with Diefenbaker after his return to Ottawa, the Prime Minister "referred with admiration to the President and expressed his satisfaction with the personal relationship which he felt had been established. . . . "[20]

Whether Kennedy shared this view remains uncertain. His briefing papers, prepared in the Department of State, noted that, while Diefenbaker was "not believed to have any basic prejudice against the United States," he had "appeared . . . to seek on occasion to assert Canadian independence by seizing opportunities for Canada to adopt policies which deviate somewhat from those of the United States. . . . " The briefing notes described the Canadian government as marked by "general indecisiveness" on economic matters and noted it had "contributed substantially" to the growing debate in defense policy "by indecisiveness and failure to take the initiative by developing a clear and concise policy and rallying public support. This situation," the brief said darkly, "has promoted an undesirable introspection in Canada regarding the country's present and future defense role, particularly with reference to the United States."[21]

As might have been expected, the defense question dominated the discussion between the Prime Minister and the President. Diefenbaker, as he reported to his Cabinet, had told Kennedy that, so long as serious disarmament negotiations continued, "Canada did not propose to determine whether or not to accept nuclear weapons for the Bomarc base or for the Canadian interceptors; but that, if such weapons were accepted by Canada, this country would require joint custody and joint control, and use would be determined in the same manner as on U.S. bases." But Canada would decide quickly on the acquisition of the warheads if war should occur, Diefenbaker added, stating that he did not want a mere policy of "bird-watching" for his country. Kennedy asked if "the same sort of 'two key'. arrangement as the United Kingdom had would be satisfactory" and Diefenbaker said it would. Such a system would see two officers, one American and one Canadian, simultaneously arming the weapon. In short, both countries had to agree on the use of nuclear weapons before they could be launched. Kennedy could not have been entirely pleased with that exposition of the Canadian position, leaning, as it so obviously did, toward the views of Secretary of State for External Affairs Howard Green. Those views had been conveyed forcefully to Diefenbaker on the trip to Washington.

Another topic left Diefenbaker, a prickly protector of Canadian

sovereignty, uncomfortable. The two men had discussed an applica-
tion by Imperial Oil of Canada, a subsidiary of Standard Oil of New
Jersey, to provide bunker oil to Canadian ships under charter to carry
Canadian wheat to China. Kennedy had pointed out that Standard's
American directors could be liable for prosecution under American
law if they allowed Imperial to provide the fuel because of the United
States embargo on trade with the People's Republic. Diefenbaker
bristled: Canada would never accept such a restriction. What, he
asked, would the American reaction be if the shoe was on the other
foot? Believing that Beijing was deeply hostile toward Washington,
Kennedy argued that to permit this breach in the economic wall around
Communist China could throw open the door to possibilities dangerous to United States security. Then he asked an aide to fetch a memorandum on the subject for him. This statement, "far from helpful,"
Diefenbaker said, simply re-stated American law. Kennedy then replied that, if Canada applied to the United States government for an
exemption for this specific transaction, it would be granted. But again
Diefenbaker demurred. He could not concede the right of the United
States to apply its laws extraterritorially, nor did he wish his government to become a participant in a private commercial arrangement.
After further discussion, Kennedy finally conceded that Imperial
could supply the bunker fuel in the expectation that the United States
government would not bring pressure to bear on Standard Oil.[22]

Diefenbaker had won a small victory, but Kennedy's apparent inability to recognize the importance of the issue to Canadian sovereignty
must have been disturbing to him. For Kennedy, the Prime Minister's
attitude throughout the one-day visit confirmed the remarks in the
State Department briefing paper that the Diefenbaker government has
"tended to attach less weight than we have to the need for ostensible
military strength . . . [and] has more readily accepted as sincere Communist protestations of good faith. . . . "[23] Canadian-American relations, despite the cordiality of the Diefenbaker-Kennedy talks, remained troubled.

When Kennedy, battered the month before by the failure at the
Bay of Pigs, came to Ottawa in May 1961 for a full state visit, he was
armed with yet another blunt briefing paper, this one prepared by the
Central Intelligence Agency. Diefenbaker showed "disappointing indecisiveness on important issues, such as the defense program, as well
as a lack of political courage and undue sensitivity to public opinion,"
it read.[24] The tensions between the two countries inevitably became

exacerbated despite the popular acclaim the youthful President and his attractive wife received from a fawning Canadian people. Troubles sprang up everywhere. First, Kennedy hurt his back turning the sod at a tree planting at the Governor-General's residence. Then, Diefenbaker, whose confidence in the President had been shaken by the Bay of Pigs fiasco, seemed even more negative on the nuclear weapons issue than he had been in February. As External Affairs informed its delegation in Geneva, "Prime Minister said that in view of public opinion in Canada, it would be impossible politically at moment for Canada to accept nuclear weapons." Nor would Canada accept Voodoo aircraft from the United States so long as arming them with nuclear missiles was required.[25] Kennedy also angered his host by urging Canada in his address to Parliament to join the Organization of American States, a prospect that had long alarmed many Canadians who had no desire to be whipped into line like the Latins on world issues and never more so than in the light of strained Cuban-American relations.

But the key incident occurred after one private meeting in Ottawa. Diefenbaker found a memorandum left behind in the folds of a couch. On it Walt W. Rostow, the President's deputy adviser on national security questions, had listed points like membership in the O.A.S. and a decision on nuclear weapons on which Kennedy should "push" the Prime Minister.[26] Diefenbaker fumed at the document's tone, and, contrary to protocol, did not return it to its authors. "The P.M.," an appalled Arnold Heeney recorded in his diary later, "said he had not so far made use of this paper but 'when the proper time came,' he would not hesitate to do so. . . ."[27]

The rancor of May had replaced the good relations of February 1961. From admiring the President, Diefenbaker had come to see him as rash and aggressive, not one who would pay attention either to Canadian national sensitivities or to the *amour propre* of the older Prime Minister. The stubborn Diefenbaker was not about to let Kennedy or his aides "push" Canada into anything.

On the other hand, when Berlin again became a flash point in the summer of 1961, Diefenbaker and his Cabinet were firm in supporting the Kennedy Administration's stance against the Soviet Union. The Canadian government in August decided on a major buildup of the country's armed forces (from 120,000 to 135,000 men) and the dispatch of an additional 1100 soldiers to Europe to strengthen the forces assigned to NATO. In addition (and partly as a measure to ease unemployment), the government decided to recruit 100,000 men in Canada for training in civil defense duties.[28] And in Vietnam, Canadian representatives on the International Control Commission tried hard to get their Indian and Polish co-commissioners to recognize and condemn the intrusions from the North, at the same time as the Canadians tried to close their eyes to American and South Vietnamese violations of the 1954 Geneva accords. Howard Green told Parliament that the United States could not be singled out for blame in Vietnam. "There have been troops infiltrating from North Vietnam," he stated, "and *I am certain* that the Communists have been at the root of most of the trouble in South Vietnam. . . . Any action the United States has taken has been in a measure of defence against Communist action."[29] In keeping with that view, Canadian officers and diplomats on the ICC shared information with the Americans in Saigon and Washington, as they had done before Kennedy took power and as they would continue to do under his successor.[30]

But it was a quite different matter to support United States policy toward Fidel Castro's Cuba. Canadian and American officials had exchanged sharp opinions before Kennedy took office, particularly at a summer 1960 meeting of the Canada-United States Ministerial Committee on Joint Defense at Montebello, Quebec. The Americans had indicated that they were moving toward economic sanctions as a way of bringing home to the Cuban people the costs of supporting Castro. As one senior Canadian wrote afterwards, they hoped "to avoid the use of armed forces." Howard Green was horrified, telling the meeting that "this was a grave and disturbing communication with very serious implications for Canada," adding, as the Canadian record put it, that "he was very doubtful of the wisdom of attempting to deal with the Cuban situation by external economic pressure. . . . "[31] In the Canadian view, such measures would surely force Havana into an ever-tighter embrace with Moscow. Whatever the government in power, Ottawa was almost always less hawkish than Washington.

That posture disturbed the Kennedy Admnistration, tougher and probably less aware of the limitations of American power than was its predecessor. Ambassador Heeney discovered this when he sat beside Dean Rusk, the Secretary of State, at the Gridiron dinner in Washington on March 11, 1961.[32] Rusk told his old friend of new measures to curb trade with Castro. American subsidiaries in Canada would be exempted from the new regulations, but, the Secretary said, "he hoped that we would agree to prevent shipment of mill & refining parts & I think vehicle replacements." Heeney replied that "this move would not be well received in Canada. . . . We doubted the wisdom of such action for the purpose for which it was intended—to prevent Cuba going completely Communist." Rusk, Heeney noted,

> got quite hot in his response. The U.S. were simply not going to have a Communist base established in Cuba . . . and would do whatever had to be done to prevent it including if necessary sending in troops. This was primarily a matter of the Monroe Doctrine for protection of the hemisphere. Further U.S. policy was not going to be altered because Canada didn't like it.[33]

Such ardent American attitudes soon manifested themselves in the disaster at the Bay of Pigs. In the fall of 1962, the Administration's fixation with Cuba—and the extraordinarily risky gamble of Soviet Premier Khrushchev in placing missiles on the island—would bring the world close to the brink of general war and profoundly embitter Canadian-American relations in the process.

The Diefenbaker government was *in extremis* by the fall of 1962. The great majority of 1958 had been wiped out in the election of June 18, 1962, when a disenchanted Canadian people gave Diefenbacker's Progressive Conservatives 116 seats in a House of Commons of 265, enough for only the most tenuous minority government. Worse yet, a pre-election run on the dollar had threatened Canada's economy while a post-election austerity program jeopardized what remained of the government's popularity, and the balance of power in the new Parliament rested in the hands of the Social Credit Party, a group with only the haziest grasp on economic reality. Diefenbaker, moreover, continued to temporize on the nuclear question. He had also been forced by the economic crisis to slap temporary tariff surcharges on American exports to Canada. However necessary they were, the import-reducing duties seemed like scant thanks for Washington's ready assistance in propping up the shaky Canadian dollar.[34]

Such was the setting on October 21 when two Canadian intelligence specialists who had been at a meeting in Washington returned to Ottawa with the first word of impending crisis. The next day, Assistant Secretary of State Livingston Merchant, a popular former Ambassador to Canada, flew to Ottawa to brief Diefenbaker and deliver a letter from Kennedy. As the President wrote to the Prime Minister, "we are now in possession of clear evidence . . . that the Soviets have secretly installed offensive nuclear weapons in Cuba and that some of them may already be operational."[35] Merchant showed Diefenbaker photographs of the installations, explained forthcoming American actions, and read Kennedy's speech, to be delivered on television two hours later to announce the imposition of a blockade around Cuba. Some questions arose, but, as Defence Minister Harkness later wrote, "the Prime Minister stated that in the event of a missile attack on the United States from Cuba, Canada would live up to its responsibilities under the NATO and NORAD agreements."[36]

No one doubted Canada's response in time of war. The question now was what Canada would do in the immediate crisis. As soon as Kennedy's television broadcast ended, the NORAD Command went to Defense Condition (DEFCON) 3, the middle of the five alert statuses. The Canadian contribution to NORAD was expected to follow suit within a few hours at most,[37] but when Harkness asked the Prime Minister for the necessary authority, he found Diefenbaker "loath," arguing that "it should be a Cabinet decision." The next morning, October 23, Harkness explained to his ministerial colleagues the reasons why an alert had become necessary. "I believe all the cabinet would have agreed to this," Harkness said, almost certainly underestimating the resentment of many of his colleagues at Kennedy's late notice of his blockade to Canada, "but the Prime Minister argued against it on the ground that an alert would unduly alarm the people, that we should wait and see what happened etc. He and I finally came to fairly hot words, but he refused to agree. . . . " The Cabinet agreed only to consider the matter once more, after the reactions of other countries and especially Britain had been ascertained. When Harkness returned to the Department of National Defence, however, he ordered on his own the Chiefs of Staff to put an alert into effect "in as quiet and unobtrusive a way as possible." That made the Canadian forces as ready as they could be, given the unarmed nature of much of their weaponry, but it did not "reassure the United States and our other allies . . . that we were prepared to fight," or so Harness noted.[38] Not until October 24 did Diefenbaker finally agree to authorize the NORAD forces alert, and then he acted only because NORAD headquarters in Colorado Springs had moved to DEFCON 2 and because Harkness shouted at him until he agreed to act.[39]

What lay behind Diefenbaker's extraordinary immobility? Part was unquestionably his congenital inability to make difficult decisions. Part was his dislike for the brash young President and his conviction that Kennedy's Cuban policy was dangerously unsound. Part was his resentment that, in his view, the United States had not met its obligation under the NORAD agreement to consult Canada.⁴⁰ And part also was his call, announced in the House of Commons on October 22, for a United Nations-sponsored mission to Cuba to give the peoples of the world "a full and complete understanding of what is taking place in Cuba." That idea had emerged from the Department of External Affairs essentially as a way to cool the crisis or, as some suggested, to secure Diefenbaker's ultimate support for the American demand for the withdrawal of the Soviet missiles when their existence could be confirmed.⁴¹ Whatever its motive, the proposal for a United Nations role landed as an immediate dud in Washington, for it implied that the government of Canada did not believe Kennedy or the evidence in the reconnaissance photographs.

If the Americans became angry, so too did Canadian public opinion, which overwhelmingly supported American actions during the crisis. As important, several of Diefenbaker's Cabinet colleagues, their faith in "The Chief" already shaken by the 1962 election results and Diefenbaker's indecisiveness on a plethora of issues, had their worries reinforced mightily.⁴²

These doubts about Diefenbacker's judgment mattered because his government was clearly faltering, about to be laid low by the festering nuclear arms controversy with the United States. Through 1961 and 1962, negotiations with Washington on the Bomarcs, Honest Johns, CF-104s, and Voodoos had proceeded at a glacial pace. Diefenbaker at times sounded determined to move ahead on the question and at others determined only to go slow.⁴³ But after the Cuban missile crisis, Harkness demanded that negotiations be concluded without delay. The ministers decided on October 30, 1962, to take the "nuclear ammunition" for the Honest Johns and CF-104s in NATO on the same terms as other alliance members had accepted, although no announcement was made because Diefenbaker vowed to delay informing the public until the whole nuclear package was resolved. For the Bomarcs and Voodoos in Canada, Harkness wrote, "we were to try to get an agreement under which the nuclear warheads, or essential parts of them, would be held in the United States, but could be put on the weapons in Canada in a matter of minutes or hours."⁴⁴ The Cabinet named a committee of three ministers to negotiate this arrangement with the Americans, and it did not take long before Harkness, at least, convinced himself of the essential impracticality of the scheme. What if there were a heavy fog or a snowstorm (the Bomarc bases were in northern Canada, after all) on the day of a crisis and the aircraft with the missing parts could not get to Canada? Howard Green, also on the negotiation committee, typically did not see this as an obstacle, and the Americans quickly became convinced that there was little prospect for any agreement with Diefenbaker.[45] Again, matters had stalled.

But events intervened. On January 3, 1963, General Lauris Norstad, the retiring NATO Supreme Commander and a United States Air Force officer, told an Ottawa press conference that Canada had committed itself to accept a nuclear role in Europe[46]—a question that Diefenbaker had fuzzified enough to have created doubts. Then on January 12, Lester Pearson, the leader of the Liberal party, reversed his and his party's position and announced that Canada "should end at once its evasion of responsibility by discharging the commitments it has already accepted. . . . It can only do this by accepting nuclear warheads. . . . "[47]

For the next three weeks, turmoil rocked the Cabinet and the country. Harkness fought the issue daily in Cabinet while Diefenbaker, now certain that he should oppose the Liberals on the defense issue by delaying the nuclear decision still further, resisted. Finally, on January 25, Diefenbaker delivered an equivocal address to the House of Commons and the nation. He revealed the secret negotiations with the United States over the "missing part" approach, but then he cast doubt on the utility of a nuclear role for Canada.[48]

Diefenbaker's speech infuriated the United States government. At 6:15 p.m. on January 30, the Department of State issued a press release. The document detailed the weapons Canada had purchased, noted the inconclusive nature of the negotiations, corrected some of Diefenbaker's errors in his House address, and then noted with devastating force that "the Canadian Government has not as yet proposed any arrangement sufficiently practical to contribute effectively to North American defense."[49] The Americans had called the Prime Minister a liar, and Dean Rusk, briefing the media the next day, removed none of the sting: " . . . we regret it if our statement was phrased in any way to give offense. The need for this statement, however, arose not of our making but because of statements which were made in the defense debate in Ottawa. . . . "[50]

Theodore Sorensen, White House aide, later noted that the President "did not like and did not respect Diefenbaker, and had no desire to see him continue in office,"[51] a comment that could be read to mean that Kennedy intended the press release to hurt Diefenbaker politically. McGeorge Bundy, however, told the Canadian Ambassador that Kennedy had known nothing about the statement in advance.[52] Washington's new ambassador in Ottawa, Walton Butterworth, reported his unsurprising view that no apology was needed, a comment that was entirely predictable because his embassy had drafted the release. It was "very useful" and "will be highly beneficial in advancing U.S. interests by introducing realism into a government which had made anti-Americanism and indecision practically its entire stock in trade." Butterworth also referred to Canada's "neurotic" political leadership.[53] According to the ambassador, the release had been sent from the embassy to the State Department where it was reviewed by George McGhee, George Ball, and Secretary Rusk; then it had gone to the White House where Bundy gave it his approval.[54] Weeping crocodile tears, Bundy soon took the blame (or credit) himself: it was "a case of stupidity and the stupidity was mine."[55]

Stupid or deliberate, the press release finished the Diefenbaker government. Within days Harkness and two other ministers resigned and the government, defeated on a vote of no-confidence in the House of Commons, had to call an election. Cabals of rebels and clutches of loyalists, Cabinet revolts and caucus battles soon rocked Ottawa. Diefenbacker hung on to the prime ministership, however, and led his party into the election. But virtually every observer was pronouncing the Conservative century at its end.[56]

The Canadian electorate, however much it may have distrusted Diefenbaker, was still sorely torn. No one, whatever his or her political coloration, tolerated the American intervention into Canadian politics, and noisy statements of anti-Americanism abounded. The nuclear issue continued to trouble many, and Diefenbaker, conveniently forgetting that he had purchased the weapons, now denounced nuclear warheads with fervor. His new stance was greatly aided by the badly timed release of secret congressional testimony by Secretary of Defense Robert McNamara that suggested the Bomarcs in Canada were useful only because they might draw Soviet fire toward Canada.[57] In this atmosphere, many Canadians believed the story, leaked during the campaign, that Butterworth had written Liberal leader Pearson with assurances of American support.[58] The letter was actually forged, but it reinforced the Conservatives' anti-Americanism. In these circumstances, the Liberals won by only a small margin. Pearson won 129 seats while Diefenbaker held 95, many more than anyone had expected. The balance of power remained with the anti-nuclear New Democratic Party and the divided Social Crediters.

Pearson's victory produced great sighs of relief in the American embassy in Ottawa (and in the Department of External Affairs and its posts abroad). Ambassador Butterworth, his strategy vindicated, wrote to Walter Lippmann, the distinguished columnist, that the outcome of the election had turned on fundamental questions. "That is why the facing up to them was so very serious and why the Pearson victory in the April 8 election was so significant." Canada's place in world affairs and particularly its relations with the United States had been the key issue. He added confidently that "at any rate, the outcome holds salutary lessons which will not be overlooked by future aspirants to political office in Canada."[59]

If Butterworth expected relations between Canada and the United States to be smooth now that Diefenbaker had been disposed of, he was mistaken. The Liberal government had pledged to honor the nuclear commitments made to the United States, but it was a nationalist government nonetheless, committed to reducing the Canadian economy's dependence on foreign, and especially American, investment. The new Minister of Finance, Walter Gordon, had been the chair of the 1956 Royal Commission on Canada's Economic Prospects, which had pointed to foreign investment as a major problem, and he was also an old friend of Lester Pearson, the architect of his leadership convention victory in 1957, and the man who had organized the Liberal party for its election victory in 1963. When Walter Gordon spoke, in other words, Mike Pearson listened.

Pearson himself was no anti-American. A phenomenally successful diplomat since the late 1920s, he had served in Ottawa, London, and Washington, and in 1944 he had become Canada's first Ambassador to the United States. In 1948 he had entered politics at the top, becoming Secretary of State for External Affairs in the St. Laurent government. He won the Nobel Peace Prize in 1957 for his role in creating the United Nations Emergency Force, which allowed Britain and France to extricate themselves from their incompetently managed war against Egypt, and he had become the public's very embodiment of enlightened Canadianism—a man of great personal charm who combined the reserved attitudes of the British and the open friendliness of Americans into something uniquely Canadian.

The new Prime Minister and the President met at Hyannis Port on Cape Cod for an extraordinarily cordial two-day discussion within three weeks of the change of government in Canada.[60] Kennedy had already sent a genuinely warm message to Pearson saying that the "early establishment of close relations between your administration and ours is a matter of great importance to me."[61] But the serious problems between the two countries could not be resolved by good intentions alone.

The nuclear question, however, *could* be settled. Pearson told the President that "he was sorry that the previous Canadian Government had undertaken nuclear commitments," but in the circumstances his government "was prepared to stand or fall in Parliament on its intention to conclude the bilateral agreement" with Washington for the acquisition of the warheads. The House of Commons on May 20 narrowly accepted the Pearson government's decision to arm the Bomarcs, CF-104s, and Honest Johns. That festering issue was effectively concluded.

But the seeds of future difficulty were sown when the two talked about American investment, apparently a subject on which Kennedy had not been briefed.[62] His government, Pearson said, "did not wish to discourage the inflow of United States capital, but nonetheless it had to be recognized that the effect of United States investment in Canada constituted a political problem." The Prime Minister added that "it was the intention of the Government to take steps not to penalize United States interests but to encourage Canadians to invest more in Canadian companies." Kennedy asked how Pearson intended to proceed and was told

> that there were means of encouraging Canadian control by informal methods, e.g., by persuading United States companies of the importance of putting Canadians in management positions and also by resisting any tendency to make United States regulations and laws apply to Canadian companies in Canada. The Government also intended to establish a Canadian development corporation, one purpose of which would be to help Canadians to buy into industrial companies in such a way as not to invite legitimate United States criticism.

The Canadian note on the meeting added that "the president listened attentively but did not comment."[63] Once Ottawa's proposals were on the table, however, that silence would be broken.

The Pearson government's plans to control foreign investment formed a critical part of Walter Gordon's hurriedly prepared budget—the Liberals had campaigned with the promise that they would deliver "Sixty Days of Decision" so the budget, delivered on June 14, had to come within that two-month time frame—and it drew instant and devastating criticism at home and abroad. The central points were a 30 percent takeover tax on sales of shares in Canadian companies to non-residents and a reduction in the withholding tax on dividends paid to non-residents by 5 percent for companies that were at least one-quarter Canadian-owned and an increase of 5 percent for companies with a lower proportion of domestic control. Companies with more than 25 percent Canadian ownership also received benefits in calculating their depreciation allowance.[64]

Gordon might have expected criticism. The Governor of the Bank of Canada had warned that the withholding tax could produce "massive attempts at liquidation" of foreign investment, but Gordon had gone ahead nonetheless.[65] Canadian businessmen, directly hooked into the continental economy, were furious, and the talk in the clubs of Toronto and Montreal, to say nothing of the business pages of the newspapers, became poisonous. By June 19, Gordon had withdrawn the takeover tax, and the next day, the battered minister offered his resignation to Pearson. The gesture was not accepted.

The Kennedy Administration was similarly agitated, the retreat of June 19 notwithstanding. Part of the anger arose because Pearson had not informed Kennedy of the extent or nature of the discriminatory actions.[66] As Assistant Secretary of State Griffith Johnson told the Canadian Chargé in Washington:

> Frankly these features had come as a real surprise. While Prime Minister Pearson had indicated at Hyannisport that consideration was being given to some measures regarding investment, we were not under the impression that any measures were contemplated which would affect United States investment so directly.[67]

American resentment surfaced strongly the next month when the Kennedy Administration proposed that restrictive measures be applied to Canadian and other foreign borrowing in the United States—measures designed to grapple with the emerging American balance of payments deficit. There was some pleasure on the American side as the Canadians scrambled to deal with a policy that threatened to choke their economy. With a straight face, for example, the Under Secretary of State offered the Canadian Ambassador

[his] categoric assurance that there was no element of retaliation or discrimination in the development of these measures. Rather they were the consequence of the need to meet an urgent situation.

The Under Secretary also observed that the United States had shown much restraint in reacting to the Canadian budget measures. . . . In addition, United States assistance to the Canadian government during the 1962 balance of payments crisis was mentioned.[68]

On July 21, after Canadian appeals for an exemption, a deal was struck.[69] The Kennedy Administration had demonstrated very effectively that Canada—and its Minister of Finance—needed the United States. And none in Canada failed to draw the appropriate lesson. The Assistant Deputy Minister of Finance, for example, told a meeting of Canadian and American officials that "Canadians [were] seriously disturbed by this reminder of dependence on U.S.A."[70]

Pressure within the Liberal party for Canada to create a nationalistic economic policy did not disappear after the July humiliation. Similarly, the widespread Canadian desire for a foreign and defense policy that was not dragged behind Washington's chariot wheels also persisted. But it proved much easier to move in those directions after Kennedy, both very popular in Canada and tough in his actions toward it, was assassinated. Indeed, just before November 22, McGeorge Bundy had sent a memorandum to key Cabinet members and others noting that "all aspects of Canadian-American relations are of intense interest and concern to the President himself." For that reason, "the President desires that the White House be fully informed of all significant negotiations or plans for negotiation with the Government of Canada. . . ."[71] The Bostonian's charm had only lightly masked his interest in and his toughness toward his North American ally, and John Diefenbaker, no less than Walter Gordon, had reason to remember clashes with the President.

Did Kennedy leave a lasting imprint on Canadian-American relations? For the United States, his legacy was likely a realization that Canada could be a difficult, hesitant partner, but one that could be made to do the "right" thing. For Canada, Kennedy was the first President in the postwar era to use American muscle to achieve his ends, and that left a lingering caution, a certainty that the United States could not be pushed too far. But that caution should not be overstated. Pearson essayed economic nationalist gestures, and his successor, Pierre Trudeau, at various points reduced Canadian defenses, set up an agency to screen foreign investment, and implemented a strongly nationalist oil policy. Canadian nationalism, in other words, survived the clash between Kennedy and Diefenbaker intact and alive. Indeed, the clash probably induced a greater sense of nationalism in Canadians. Yet the defense and economic aims of Kennedy's America have not been truly checked by this nationalism. In the 1980s, American investment was more dominant in Canada than it had been a quarter century before, Canada's trade had become even more concentrated on the market to the south, and the two countries' defenses had become, if anything, even more closely integrated. The Americans, as one Canadian politician of the 1960s put it with unintended meaning, are Canadians' best friends whether they like it or not.

4

Controlling Revolutions: Latin America, the Alliance for Progress, and Cold War Anti-Communism

STEPHEN G. RABE

The White House ceremony was impressive and unusual. The new President, John F. Kennedy, and his wife, Jacqueline Bouvier Kennedy, hosted an elegant reception in the Rcd, Blue, and Green rooms for 250 people, including the diplomatic corps of the Latin American republics, United States congressional leaders, and their spouses. At the appointed time, the guests then moved to the East Room, where they sat themselves on gilt-edged chairs arranged in semicircles on both sides of the rostrum. The President soon addressed them. The speech, which lasted only twenty minutes, was simultaneously broadcast by the Voice of America in English, Spanish, French, and Portuguese, the languages of the Western Hemisphere. The President thrilled his attentive audience, telling them what they had been waiting nearly two decades to hear: the United States would join in "a vast cooperative effort, unparalleled in magnitude and nobility of purpose, to satisfy the basic needs of the Latin American people for homes, work and land, health and schools—*techo, trabajo y tierra, salud y escuela.*" Called the Alliance for Progress—Alianza para el Progreso—the new program represented a Marshall Plan for Latin America.

In his stirring speech of March 13, 1961, the President outlined a ten-point program to transform the Americas during the 1960s—"the decade of development." The United States pledged to support long-range economic planning, economic integration and common markets, and solutions to commodity market problems. Scientific and technical cooperation would be expanded and cultural relations strengthened. The United States also intended to rush emergency shipments of food to Latin America and cooperate with Latin Americans to curb unproductive military spending. As a down payment to his good intentions, the President promised to ask Congress to appropriate immediately $500 million to begin a campaign to eradicate illiteracy, hunger, and disease in the hemisphere. But the Alliance for Progress, the President vowed, meant more than economic aid. Political freedom and social reform must accompany material progress. Archaic tax and land-tenure structures had to be dismantled and self-serving tyrants cast aside. North and South Americans had "to demonstrate to the entire world that man's unsatisfied aspiration for economic progress and social justice can best be achieved by free men working within a framework of democratic institutions."[1]

The Kennedy Administration soon gave substance to these words. It quickly secured from Congress the requested $500 million to initiate the war against poverty in Latin America and an additional $100 million to help Chile recover from a recent, destructive earthquake. It also established a "Seasonal Marketing Fund" for the purpose of stabilizing the price of coffee, Latin America's chief export; the United States, as well, joined an international study group to find permanent solutions to the world oversupply of coffee.[2] And the Kennedy Administration hastily assembled economic rescue packages for hard-pressed nations such as Bolivia, sending it $60 million in loans and grants.[3]

The true measure of the Administration's commitment to Latin America came at an inter-American conference held in August 1961 at Punta del Este, a seaside resort in Uruguay. Speaking for the President, Secretary of the Treasury C. Douglas Dillon assured Latin American delegates that they could expect more than $20 billion in public and private capital over the next ten years from the United States, international lending authorities, charitable foundations, and private United States investors. With this influx of foreign money and an additional $80 billion from internal investment, he predicted, Latin American nations could expect to achieve a real economic growth rate of 2.5 percent a year, approximately double the rate of economic growth during the late 1950s. Dillon also predicted that, by 1970, all Latin American children would achieve literacy by the time they reached the age of 12.[4] Other Administration officials surpassed Dillon's optimism. Presidential adviser Adolf Berle boldly prophesied that the United States would raise the living standard of every Latin American by at least 50 percent.⁵

The Kennedy Administration and its successor, the Lyndon B. Johnson Administration, made good on most promises of economic aid for Latin America. In 1962, for example, the United States assigned over $1 billion to Latin America through the Social Progress Trust Fund, Food for Peace, Export-Import Bank, and Agency for International Development. During the decade, Latin America received over $18 billion in public and private assistance, including over $10 billion from United States public agencies. North American capitalists supplemented such public assistance with over $3 billion in new direct investments and reinvested earnings.⁶ The United States also funded new trade groups such as the Central American Common Market and signed an international coffee agreement that regulated the market by fixing import and export quotas.⁷

The Kennedy Administration decided to embark on a campaign to underwrite change and development in Latin America, because United States officials feared that the region seemed vulnerable to radical social revolution. In the late 1950s, a series of crises had rocked inter-American relations. In mid-1958, angry South Americans hounded Vice President Richard Nixon during his tour of the continent, with a howling mob nearly killing him in Caracas, Venezuela. These protestors claimed that the United States had supported tyrants like Marcos Pérez Jiménez (1952–1958) of Venezuela and ignored Latin America's pressing socioeconomic needs. The next year, violent anti-United States demonstrations erupted in Panama. Guerrillas who espoused a variety of leftist doctrines also began to operate in the mountains of Colombia and Venezuela. And, in what would prove to be most momentous of changes, Fidel Castro overthrew the pro-American dictator of Cuba, Fulgencio Batista, and turned the Cuban Revolution into a bitterly anti-American movement.⁸ Many foreign-policy analysts blamed this hemisphcric turmoil on the machinations of the "international communist conspiracy" directed by the Soviet Union. Latin America had become, in the views of the two task forces that sketched out the Alliance for Progress, "an active Cold War theatre of attack on the United States." The ultimate goal of the Communists in Latin America, claimed Adolf Berle, the chairman of both task forces, was "to enslave the agricultural and industrial masses, as the Soviet Union and Chinese have done, and hold them in slavery for an indefinite period."⁹ The Communist threat was augmented by the "revolution of rising expectations." With dramatic improvements in communication and transportation, the Latin American poor had begun to understand that their dismal lot in life was not preordained. As Under Secretary of State George Ball put it, "The winds of change are blowing over the continent. Millions of people have come to know that a better life is possible and they are determined to secure it." The task for the United States, then, was to channel those legitimate aspirations away from communism and toward peaceful change, so as to achieve, in Douglas Dillon's description, "a controlled revolution."[10]

In building progressive, socially just, anti-Communist societies, the United States would have to avoid the mistakes of the immediate past. It could no longer support dictators who professed to be zealous anti-Communists. Such strong-arm leaders created "Batista-like" conditions, leaving frustrated Latin Americans susceptible to the appeal of communism. Berle told Kennedy that the United States could no longer purchase short-term security by allying itself with dictators like Rafael Trujillo of the Dominican Republic, François "Papa Doc" Duvalier of Haiti, the Somoza family of Nicaragua, and General Alfredo Stroessner of Paraguay. As Berle warned, "The present struggle will not be won, and can be lost, by opportunist support of transitory powerholders or forces whose objectives are basically hostile to the peoples they dominate." Instead, the United States needed to assist democratic, progressive groups and thereby gain "a political instrument with which to fight the 'Cold War' on the streets, outside the limitations of formal diplomacy."[11]

The context for a Marshall Plan for Latin America was the Cold War. Task Force reports emphasized that Latin Americans had to become convinced that Washington's policy was not based narrowly on expanding United States investments in the region but on protecting the hemisphere from international communism. Nonetheless, North Americans had substantial material interests, which would be jeopardized by "workers and peasants' revolutions" in Latin America.[12] In 1960, North Americans owned over $8 billion in direct investments in Latin America, representing 25 percent of United States direct investments in the world. The bulk of this investment was at work extracting strategically vital raw materials such as Venezuelan oil and Chilean copper. Trade with Latin America also ranked high, amounting to 20 percent of the international trade of the United States.[13] Castro had demonstrated, however, how quickly the United

States could lose its dominant economic position in Latin America. Within two years after taking power, his revolutionary government had expropriated the nearly $1 billion in United States direct investments in Cuba.

In securing United States interests in the hemisphere, Kennedy and his advisers were building upon the initiatives of Dwight D. Eisenhower. The Eisenhower Administration had similarly feared unrest in Latin America. In the aftermath of the Nixon trip and Castro's triumph, Eisenhower officials concluded that Latin America had become a critical Cold War battleground. The United States, national security advisers warned, had to forgo "the easy luxury of being simply anti-Communist" and respond "dynamically and creatively to our age of revolution." As such, between 1958 and January 1961, President Eisenhower established a regional lending agency, the Inter-American Development Bank, and asked Congress to authorize funds for a Social Progress Trust Fund to alleviate poverty, ignorance, and disease in Latin America. The Eisenhower Administration conspicuously began to spurn dictators, breaking relations in August 1960, for example, with Trujillo, and to support reformers, like Rómulo Betancourt of Venezuela, who favored "rising living standards and a more equitable distribution of national income within the general framework of a free enterprise system and through peaceful evolutionary means rather than violent."[14] These actions led President Eisenhower and his brother, Dr. Milton Eisenhower, to claim in their memoirs that they had founded the Alliance for Progress—all President Kennedy added to the program was an "appealing title."[15]

Kennedy admirers have dismissed the Eisenhowers' paternity claim. Only the Kennedy Administration had designed a comprehensive reform package; the Eisenhower Administration had neither pledged to transfer $20 billion to Latin America nor set economic growth targets for the region.[16] But although the Eisenhower Administration had been clearly less ambitious than the Kennedy government in its approach to Latin America, its new policies arose from the same source—a fear of the political and social consequences of the Cuban Revolution. The United States had to contain and control the revolutionary ferment. As Eisenhower's National Security Council saw it, the failure "to align and keep Latin America on our side" would call into question the international leadership and even security of the United States.[17]

Whatever the resolution of the debate over the origins of the Alliance for Progress, the reform program ultimately failed to transform Latin American societies. As during the late 1950s, Latin American economies performed poorly during "the decade of development," registering an unimpressive annual growth rate of 1.5 percent during the 1960s. The number of unemployed Latin Americans actually rose from 18 million to 25 million, and agricultural production per person declined. And the Alliance made imperceptible progress in achieving its objectives of adding five years to life expectancy, halving the infant morality rate, eliminating adult illiteracy, and providing access to six years of primary education for every school-age child. At the end of the decade, more than one-half of the population of the region continued to live on an annual per capita income of $120.[18] But only part of the failure is found in economic statistics. The Alliance aimed at creating socially just, democratic countries. Latin American societies remained, however, grossly inequitable. The wealthy 10 percent in countries such as Argentina and Brazil continued to retain ownership of vast plantations and *haciendas* and command more than 40 percent of their nations' income. These class-ridden societies also remained politically unstable. During the 1960s, sixteen extraconstitutional changes of government shook Latin America. During the Kennedy years alone, military men overthrew six popularly elected Latin American presidents.[19]

Although few observers have disputed these dismal results of the Alliance, the question of why the Alliance "lost its way" remains sharply controversial. Analysts have focused on either the character of Latin American societies or the reorientation of Alliance programs by President Kennedy's successors. The "New Frontiersmen" undoubtedly overestimated their ability to foster change, and they underestimated the daunting nature of Latin America's socioeconomic problems. Teodoro Moscoso, the administrator of Alliance programs, typified that naïve optimism, when, in 1962, he boldly declared that "within a decade the direction and results of centuries of Latin American history are to be changed."[20] In a short ten years, Moscoso expected to end privilege, abolish illiteracy, impart scientific training and technical expertise, and create political stability. Yet, he was speaking of a region where illiteracy rates were as high as 90 percent, life expectancy was as low as 35 years, and as many as 11 percent of infants died. Moreover, the poorest of Latin Americans tended to be those of Amerindian and African heritage, people who had endured centuries of discrimination.

United States officials also did not anticipate problems engendered by the population explosion. With an annual growth rate of 3 percent, Latin America's population of 195 million was expected to double within 25 years. Gains in economic growth could be undercut by declines in infant mortality. To be sure, the Kennedy Administration played down population control, because it did not want to anger Roman Catholics at home or abroad. But its position, as voiced by Secretary Dillon, was that "in Latin America the question of population control is not as serious as it may be in other areas of the world because there are substantial resources, substantial land, substantial availability for a growing, expanding population."[21] In fact, population expansion became an obstacle to economic growth. Alliance programs helped cut the percentage of Latin American children not attending school from 52 to 43 percent. But, because of population growth, the number of children not attending school actually increased during the 1960s.[22]

Administration officials also proved too sanguine about the readiness of Latin Americans to reform their societies. In early 1961, presidential adviser Arthur M. Schlesinger, Jr., assured Kennedy that Latin America was "set for miracles." Between 1956 and 1960, ten Latin American dictators had fallen from power. They had been replaced by men such as Betancourt, Arturo Frondizi of Argentina, and Alberto Lleras Camargo of Colombia, all of whom came from the burgeoning new urban middle classes, perhaps 25 percent of Latin America's population. These leaders and their constituents presumably wanted to "modernize" their societies through a "middle-class revolution." Prominent United States social scientists, such as presidential adviser Walt W. Rostow, author of the influential book *The Stages of Economic Growth* (1960), predicted that these middle-class revolutionaries would foster industrialization and economic growth and the concomitant features of a modern technical society, such as constitutional government, bureaucratic efficiency and honesty, and social mobility. All they needed was outside assistance to reach the "take-off" stage of economic growth.[23] But the middle-class or "middle-sector" groups turned out to be faint-hearted revolutionaries, more concerned with individual than with national goals. In Costa Rica and Venezuela, middle-sector political groups succeeded in enshrining constitutional practices. But in other countries, such as Argentina (whose constitutional government was overthrown in 1968 and 1972), Brazil (1964), and Chile (1973), they welcomed the overthrow of elected governments and the restoration of military rule, because they feared both the radicalism of peasants and workers and the loss of their own privileges.[24]

Kennedy and his advisers talked about Latin America so confidently because they drew lessons from history. The United States had rebuilt Western Europe and Japan in the immediate postwar years. Now it was time to start the United States and the world moving once again—to replay the successes of the 1940s. As Thomas Mann, a veteran State Department officer widely known for his hardboiled, skeptical outlook, noted, the Kennedy Administration worked under an "illusion of omnipotence." The United States had reconstructed Europe; therefore, "it's going to work in Latin America." In the postwar world, the United States was "on the crest of a wave and nobody, literally nobody on the Hill or anywhere else ever questioned our ability to do anything." Mann, who became the chief administrator for the Alliance for Progress during the Johnson presidency, confessed that, in 1960–1961, he shared that optimism.[25]

But Latin America was not Europe. Western European countries had been devastated by war, but they had financial and technical expertise, institutionalized political parties, skillful politicians, strong national identities, and, except for Germany, a democratic tradition. The United States had helped to rebuild countries whose social fabrics, political traditions, and economic institutions were notably similar to those of North Americans. On the other hand, the Iberian and Amerindian political heritage, characterized by planned economies, strong central governments, and the organization of society into corporate groups, was virtually non-existent in the United States.[26] In his last speech on Latin America, President Kennedy conceded that the Alliance for Progress could not be compared to the Marshall Plan, for "then we helped to rebuild a shattered economy whose human and social foundation remained. Today we are trying to create a basic new foundation, capable of reshaping the centuries-old societies and economies of half a hemisphere." Yet Kennedy assured his audience that idealism, energy, and optimism would bridge the vast cultural gap and bring about the "modernization" of Latin America.[27]

Fervent supporters of President Kennedy believe that with time he would have overcome these cultural differences and obstacles to change. Schlesinger, the President's most influential biographer, has asserted that "the Alliance was never really tried. It lasted about a thousand days, not a sufficient test, and thereafter only the name remained." President Johnson and advisers like Mann, claim Kennedy's admirers, removed the program's political and social components, the "heart" of the Alliance for Progress, turning it into a bilateral economic aid program.[28] As demonstrated in the so-called Mann Doctrine of 1964, United States officials began to see advantages in military rule for Latin America, reasoning privately that the military could provide the political stability and administrative competence necessary for economic growth. Moreover, as the Kennedy people concerned about Latin America—Schlesinger, Moscoso, Robert F. Kennedy—left government, the Johnson Administration began to solicit advice from North American businessmen such as David Rockefeller, who argued that social reform must await the economic growth created by private initiative. The Alliance thereafter, in Schlesinger's words, was "put into the service of American business."[29] Kennedy adherents have also recalled that, by the end of the decade, decent democrats like President Eduardo Frei of Chile (1964–1970) were decrying the loss of the "fundamental" part of the Alliance, "a revolutionary approach to the need for reform."[30]

Predictably, former Johnson Administration officials have dismissed these allegations, labeling them "Camelot myth-making." Arguing that the Alliance had begun to show results in the late 1960s, with, for example, a modest gain in 1968 in the economic growth rate, they have shifted blame to the Nixon Administration, accusing *it* of ignoring Latin America.[31] How the Alliance for Progress fared after 22 November 1963 is a significant question. But an equally important question is this: Did the Kennedy Administration doggedly pursue the goals for the hemisphere that it enumerated in 1961? Did President Kennedy, as his memorialists claim, consistently place United States support behind democracy, economic progress, and social change in Latin America?

Kennedy Administration officials have contended that the President based United States policy in Latin America on the "clear, consistent, moral, democratic principles" that Berle recommended in his task force report.[32] For example, Kennedy refused to resume diplomatic relations with Trujillo, who was assassinated by Dominican dissidents in May 1961; dispatched in November 1961 a naval flotilla to Dominican waters to block the restoration of Trujillo family rule; and successfully prodded Dominicans into holding an open presidential election.[33] The President also personally identified with constitutional governments, making goodwill trips to Venezuela, Colombia, Mexico, and Costa Rica. In Washington, he hosted the democratic leader of Venezuela, Rómulo Betancourt, and informed the hemisphere that Betancourt represented "all that we admire in a political leader."[34] And, in July 1962, after the military overthrew the government of President Manuel Prado in Peru, Kennedy broke diplomatic relations, suspended United States economic aid, and demanded a return to constitutionalism. Peru's new military rulers succumbed to this intense pressure and scheduled a presidential election for mid-1963.[35]

President Kennedy did not, however, always stoutly oppose military coups, or *golpes de estados*. His Administration virtually ignored the mid-1962 overthrow of President Frondizi in Argentina, acquiesced in *golpes* in early 1963 in Ecuador and Guatemala, and only mildly protested the removal in late 1963 of constitutional rulers in Honduras and the Dominican Republic. In part, the President became less interventionist because he thought he was handicapped by the unenthusiastic response his Peruvian policy had received throughout the hemisphere. Influential countries, such as Mexico, declined to rupture relations with Peru, arguing that such actions constituted an unacceptable intervention in the internal affairs of a neighbor. Constitutional leaders, moreover, were not always competent. President Julio Carlos Arosemena of Ecuador had a serious drinking problem; he was inebriated, for example, when he called on Kennedy at the White House.[36] The President had now come to wonder what more the United States could do to establish a stable, sound democracy in the Dominican Republic, where tyranny and corruption had a long, tenacious history. The ousted president, Juan Bosch, later noted that Kennedy "did all that could be done to help the Dominican Republic."[37]

In reviewing the Administration's record on military *golpes,* presidential adviser Theodore Sorensen concluded that the Administration pursued a policy that had "no discernible pattern."[38] But, in fact, the Administration's recognition policy carried underlying themes. The Administration calculated the internal Communist threat and the Latin American government's attitude toward Cuba in determining its stance toward military *golpes*. The Kennedy Administration lashed out at the annulment of elections by the Peruvian military not just because one of Washington's favorite middle-class revolutionaries, Víctor Haya de la Torre, had been denied victory, but also because officials judged Peruvian officers ultranationalistic and soft on communism.[39] In deposing President Frondizi, the Argentine military removed a Latin American leader who believed that the United States was obsessed with Castro and who opposed excluding Cuba from the inter-American community. Argentina's new military rulers, however, denounced Castro and thus quickly won a new economic assistance package from the United States.[40] And by seizing power and cancelling elections, the Guatemalan military forestalled the return to power of Juan José Arévalo, the former president, political leftist, and colleague of Jacobo Arbenz, the Guatemalan president that the United States had helped topple in 1954.[41] Indeed, Latin American military officers surmised that, if they pursued an anti-Communist line, the Kennedy Administration would not isolate them. The United States briefly suspended relations with Honduras in October 1963, after Colonel Oswaldo López Arellano, an arch-conservative, seized power. But a confident López correctly predicted to Ambassador Charles Burrows that United States aid would return in six months. Ambassador Burrows ruefully admitted that the colonel implicitly understood the parameters of Washington's policy.[42]

In October 1963, Assistant Secretary of State Edwin M. Martin made explicit for the rest of hemisphere the Kennedy Administration's "policy regarding military governments in Latin America." The United States had concluded that the Alliance's goal of development, within the framework of democracy, was not attainable in the near future in every country, because "in most of Latin America there is so little experience with the benefits of political legitimacy." The United States would continue to oppose the overthrow of constitutional governments, but it would use force only against "intervention from outside the hemisphere by the international Communist conspiracy." In any case, it was beyond the power of the United States, Martin argued, to "create effective democracy" or to keep "a man in office by use of economic pressure or even military force, when his own people are not willing to fight to defend him."[43] Some officials, such as Arthur Schlesinger, Jr., disapproved the statement, believing that it tacitly assured military insurgents that they need not fear the wrath of the United States. President Kennedy read a draft of the statement, however, before it was sent to United States diplomatic posts in Latin America and then published. The President, Sorensen later wrote, had come to recognize "that the military often represented more competence in administration and more sympathy with the U.S. than any other group in the country." Martin added that Kennedy considered the military an anti-Communist force and that Latin America needed a certain degree of authority to prevent the instability and disorder that provided opportunities for Communists.[44]

The Administration's brief that there were limits to United States power in Latin America was unassailable. But the Administration frequently undermined its public commitment to democracy and constitutionalism. In closed congressional testimony, Secretary of State Dean Rusk accurately depicted the Duvalier regime as "a disgrace to this hemisphere." Yet, because he wanted to buy Haiti's vote to exclude Cuba from the inter-American community, Rusk approved economic aid for Haiti, including money for an airport. State Department officials fully realized that Duvalier would divert these funds to projects that would enhance his own power and prestige.[45]

Although the Administration found that it could work with despots, it rejected the idea of working with popularly elected left-wing parties. Fearing that Chilean groups of the Popular Action Front (FRAP) led by Socialist Salvador Allende would win the presidential election scheduled for 1964, the Administration embarked upon a sustained campaign to bolster Allende's opponents in the Radical and Christian Democratic parties. State Department officers had grown displeased with the pace of socioeconomic change in Chile under the conservative government of President Jorge Alessandri (1958–1964). But, at the direction of President Kennedy, in 1962 the department approved a $120 million emergency loan for Alessandri and promised $350 million more over the next five years. As a National Security Council memorandum noted, "We are not prepared to risk a Socialist or FRAP victory, for fear of nationalization of U.S. investments, the consequence of that action, and the probable Communist influence in a Socialist (or FRAP) government." Between 1962 and 1964, the Central Intelligence Agency (CIA) supplemented that public assistance by directly interfering in the Chilean political process, funneling over $4 million to moderate and conservative political candidates and to student, labor, and media groups opposed to Allende. The agency also used "black propaganda" and "disinformation" in an attempt to turn the Socialists and Chilean Communists against one another. The CIA proudly, albeit secretly, claimed that it was responsible for Christian Democrat Eduardo Frei's smashing electoral victory in 1964.[46]

The Kennedy Administration further compromised democracy in Latin America by enhancing the role of the military and internal security forces in Latin American life. Upon taking office, the Administration redirected inter-American military cooperation toward internal security and counterinsurgency. During the Eisenhower years, the United States had granted Latin America over $400 million worth of jet airplanes, ships, and heavy weapons for hemispheric defense. The new Administration discounted external threats, claiming that "the principal threat faced in Latin America is Communist subversion and indirect attack." Castro could be counted on to spread his revolution through guerrilla warfare in such countries as Venezuela. In early January 1961, moreover, Premier Nikita Khrushchev had boasted that the Soviet Union would back "wars of national liberation." Khrushchev underscored that boast during his meeting with Kennedy in Vienna in May 1961, when he "voiced Soviet intent to support 'popular' movements against 'rotten and anti-popular regimes.' " Elsewhere in his talks with Kennedy, Khrushchev "expressed his belief that there were a number of governments in Latin America which opposed the interests of the people."[47]

Whether the Soviet Union planned to assist directly guerrilla movements in Latin American remains, however, uncertain. In closed congressional testimony, Rusk conceded that Khrushchev had not, in his talks with Kennedy, specifically named a country in Latin America that the Soviets would support. In a 1963 study, the CIA Office of National Estimate predicted that Moscow would concentrate on traditional diplomatic and economic overtures in Latin America.[48] In any case, violence in the region had indigenous roots. Colombia had been beset by turmoil since 1948, with fighting between Liberals and Conservatives, the country's historic political rivals. A 1965 CIA study pointed out that in Venezuela, although radicals there accepted outside aid, they "ran their own shows" and were a "home-grown revolutionary organization."[49]

Despite the lack of hard evidence, President Kennedy directed a vigorous United States response to the perceived Soviet threat. He approved approximately $77 million a year in military aid to Latin America, a 50 percent increase over the average annual aid given during the 1950s. In a series of national security action memoranda, the President also ordered his subordinates to develop new courses on riot control, psychological warfare, and counterguerrilla operations at military schools in the United States and Panama, to establish an inter-American police academy to train Latin Americans in mob control and counterinsurgency, and to fund "civic action" programs in which Latin American military units would contribute to the economic infrastructure by building roads and bridges. The President also accepted the advice of his brother, the attorney general, and sent Federal Bureau of Investigation teams to Latin America "to determine whether all necessary steps are being taken by the internal police to deal with Communist infiltration." The President insisted that this feature of his Latin American policy be assigned the highest priority. The Agency for International Development's new Office of Public Safety, which oversaw police training programs, was given a separate budgetary line "so it would not be cut with economic development projects." The new police program was expected to grow rapidly, and any equipment requested by Latin American police would be delivered expeditiously in order "to deny the police assistance field to the Communist bloc."[50]

United States officials followed the President's orders. In 1962, the United States paid for the training of 9,000 Latin American military personnel, most of whom took the new counterinsurgency courses. Police training teams trooped to major urban areas in Latin America, and Latin American police officials traveled to the United States for three to six months of "indoctrination and training." More United States technicians worked in Office of Public Safety projects in Latin American than worked in health and sanitation programs. The Administration judged this allocation of resources a good investment, for, as one study pointed out, "the total cost of a 225 man riot control company, fully equipped with personnel carriers, tear gas, batons, hand arms, and a tank car for spraying crowds with indelible dye comes to only $58,000."[51]

By fostering these new programs, the Kennedy Administration increased the coercive abilities of Latin American armed forces and violated Kennedy's pledge, in his Alliance for Progress speech, to reduce military expenditures in the region. Officials justified these programs on national security grounds and by claiming that internal security programs strengthened democratic institutions. Secretary of Defense Robert McNamara testified that "the exposure of the military officers of those nations to our schools acquaints them with democratic philosophies, democratic ways of thinking, which they, in turn, take back to their nations." McNamara also waxed enthusiastic about civic action programs, discovering in them "an indispensable means of establishing a link between army and populace." With "well disciplined and well trained Latin American armed forces led by United States trained and oriented leaders of moderate views," Latin America would achieve the internal stability necessary "to economic and social development and to the success of the Alliance for Progress."[52]

Such rationales drew challenges from both within Washington and throughout Latin America. In September 1961, for example, Under Secretary of State Chester Bowles wrote to President Kennedy, protesting the new emphasis on counterinsurgency, doubting it inculcated democracy, and predicting that "we are creating armed forces capable of seizing power. . . . "[53] Bowles proved to be right. A confidential Defense Department survey, conducted in 1964–1965, found no empirical evidence to support the contention that military aid promoted democracy or economic progress.[54] Indeed, military officers who carried out the *golpes* in Argentina and Peru had been trained in the United States, and the Peruvians spearheaded their attack with United States tanks. In the Dominican Republic, United States-trained police helped overthrow Juan Bosch and then hunted down Bosch's partisans.[55] United States ambassadors in Latin America also questioned the benefits of military aid. Military officers in Honduras and El Salvador misused civic action funds, building fraudulent projects and using the money for their own personal and political gain. Ambassador to El Salvador Murat Williams recalled that he was "appalled" by the importance and size of the United States military and police missions in the tiny country and the infiltration of student and university groups by Defense Department intelligence agents. The United States had undercut the Alliance by identifying itself with the establishment and status quo in El Salvador. As Ambassador Williams saw it, the effect of military aid was not to "improve its [El Salvador's] position as a republic," but to "make it stronger from a security standpoint."[56]

Although not willing to acknowledge it publicly, the Kennedy Administration used military aid to preserve access and influence with the arbiters of Latin American political life, the military establishment. In Brazil, for example, the Administration was uncertain about the political loyalties of President João Goulart (1961–1964), a political leftist and vocal nationalist. Policymakers believed that Brazilian Communists were trying to infiltrate the Goulart government, but they could not decide whether Goulart was unaware of the danger, did not care, or was actually encouraging the Communists. The Administration also became angry over Brazil's refusal to break relations with Cuba, despite direct appeals from President Kennedy and

Ambassador Lincoln Gordon.[57] Unable to convince Goulart to denounce domestic Communists or Castro, the Administration prepared for his overthrow. A special task force on Brazil speculated that Goulart would be "requested" or "urged" by the Brazilian military to withdraw from the presidency. To facilitate "the most favorable possible succession," the task force recommended in October 1963 that the United States continue to cultivate friendly relations and strengthen the "basically democratic and pro-United States orientation of the military."[58] This policy came to fruition six months later during the Johnson Administration, when the Brazilian military overthrew Goulart and then broke relations with Cuba and crushed domestic radicals.[59]

As with the questions of recognition policy, constitutionalism, and military aid, the Kennedy Administration's position on social reform became dominated by Cold War concerns. President Kennedy wanted to help build humane, socially just nations in Latin America. He growled against bureaucratic delays and constantly prodded United States agencies to find ways to distribute funds more rapidly. While touring Costa Rica, for example, the President noticed an unoccupied hospital and ordered aides to find funds to help staff the facility. He listened sympathetically to the economic plans of Latin American officials and, over the objections of State Department officials, he often approved special aid packages for them, such as a $10 million loan for Panama.[60] And he called for the redistribution of power and wealth. While in Mexico City, in mid-1962, he praised the Mexican Revolution and "the largest and most impressive land reform program in the entire history of the hemisphere." He vowed that "the peaceful revolution of the Americas will not be complete" until *campesinos* owned the land they worked.[61]

The President and his aides, however, obviously made compromises and never fulfilled the promise of their lofty rhetoric. Far-reaching reform portended social instability that might threaten United States investments. In the critical area of agrarian reform, for example, the Kennedy Administration pursued only mild measures. It declined to make land redistribution a condition of aid. By comparison, it frequently tied economic aid packages to the demand that Latin American countries stabilize their currencies and liberalize exchange practices. Although sound monetary practices were desirable, such measures also had the effect of protecting United States investments in Latin America. The Administration, as well, ruled out financing expropriations of land and actually opposed agrarian reform laws. In Honduras, the Administration pressed President Ramón Villeda Morales to rescind his agrarian reform law of 1962. The Honduran law, which Villeda Morales believed addressed the goals of the Alliance program, confiscated fallow land, including the holdings of Standard Fruit and United Fruit, both United States-owned companies. In retaliation, United Fruit halted its planting program. After speaking with President Kennedy and United Fruit representatives, Villeda Morales agreed to change the law.[62]

In Brazil, also, the Kennedy Administration reneged on its commitment to long-range development and social change. The Administration had pledged to underwrite a concerted effort to develop the Brazilian Northeast, a nine-state region where one-third of Brazil's population lived. The region had the lowest average per capita income in Latin America. In 1962, President Kennedy met with Celso Furtado, a Brazilian economist and director of the regional development agency (SUDENE), and heartily pledged United States support. Brazilian-American cooperation, however, quickly broke down. Furtado and his associates, including the central government of President Goulart, believed that the region was in a "pre-revolutionary" situation, not because of Communist agitators, "a small minority," but because of widespread poverty, illiteracy, hopelessness, and hunger. What was needed was to integrate the regional economy into the national one, produce more food, build roads and power stations, and attack antiquated land tenure patterns. In Furtado's opinion, it would be better to invest in those sectors that promised long-term economic growth and development than to siphon off money on expensive show projects, thinly spread over a vast region.[63] The Kennedy Administration, on the other hand, viewed the region as an international security problem. It wanted projects that would have immediate effects and undercut the appeal of agrarian radicals. Because it distrusted Goulart, moreover, the Administration bypassed SUDENE and worked through anti-Communist state governors, many of whom represented traditional oligarchic interests. With United States money, these governors could proudly claim they had built new schools and health centers. But, because Brazil still lacked enough doctors and teachers, most of these facilities remained unoccupied. As one social scientist who carefully reviewed the United States effort in the Northeast concluded, the Kennedy Administration failed to meet Brazil's basic needs for change and modernization because it feared short-term conflict and disorder.

As such, "the United States chose a policy in the Northeast of cooperation with regional elites and justified the policy in terms of a communis-
tic threat." The United States had "contributed to the retention of
power by the traditional oligarchy" and "destroyed" a Brazilian program to modernize the political structure of the Northeast.[64]

The course of United States reform policies in Honduras and Brazil
pointed to a tension between the Administration's talk of middle-
class revolution and its search for anti-Communist stability. As Assistant Secretary Martin noted to Schlesinger in 1963, the Alliance for
Progress contained "major flaws." Its "laudable social goals" encouraged political instability, yet their achievement demanded an 80 percent private investment "which cannot be attracted amid political
instability."[65] President Kennedy recognized the problem, noting,
near the end of his administration, that the United States would have
to learn to live in a "dangerous, untidy world."[66] But little in the
President's action's or his Administration's policies indicated that the
United States was prepared to identify with progressive social revolutions. The Administration and the President, Bowles concluded,
never "had the real courage to face up to the implications" of the
principles of the Alliance for Progress.[67]

That the Alliance for Progress was a Cold War policy was never a
subject of dispute. But, in Schlesinger's words, "answering Castro
was a byproduct, not the purpose, of the Alliance." What presumably distinguished the Latin American policy of John F. Kennedy
was the belief that the key to stability and anti-communism was
democracy, economic growth and development, and social change.
The Alliance for Progress, as one observer put it, was "enlightened
anti-communism."[68] An examination of the course of inter-American relations between 1961 and 1963 points, however, to the need to
separate the President's words from his decisions and his Administration's deeds. Through its recognition policy, internal security initiatives, and military and economic aid programs, the Administration
demonstrably bolstered regimes and groups that were undemocratic,
conservative, and frequently repressive. The short-term security that
anti-Communist elites could provide was purchased at the expense
of long-term political and social democracy.

5

Fixation with Cuba: The Bay of Pigs, Missile Crisis, and Covert War Against Castro

THOMAS G. PATERSON

"My God," muttered Richard Helms of the Central Intelligence Agency, "these Kennedys keep the pressure on about Castro."[1] Another CIA officer heard it straight from the Kennedy brothers: "Get off your ass about Cuba."[2] About a year after John F. Kennedy's inauguration, a member of Congress applauded "the way you are gradually strangling Castro and Communism in Cuba."[3] In 1963 the President still sought to "dig Castro out of there."[4] Defense Secretary Robert McNamara remembered that "we were hysterical about Castro at the time of the Bay of Pigs and thereafter."[5] As someone said, Cuba was one of the four-letter words of the 1960s.

President Kennedy spent as much or more time on Cuba as on any other foreign policy problem. Cuba stood at the center of his Administration's admitted greatest failure, the Bay of Pigs, and its alleged greatest success, the missile crisis. A multitude of government agencies enlisted in the crusade against revolutionary Cuba: the Commerce Department administered trade restrictions; the State Department labored to rally the Organization of American States and North Atlantic Treaty Organization allies against Cuba; the Federal Bureau of Investigation spied on pro- and anti-Castro groups; the Immigration and Naturalization Service, Coast Guard, and Department of Health, Education, and Welfare handled the steady flow of exiles from the turbulent island; and the CIA launched covert operations designed to topple the Cuban government and to assassinate its leader Fidel Castro. Contrary to some Kennedy memoirists and schol-

ho have claimed that Kennedy was often trapped by a bureau-
acy he could not control and distracted by other time-consuming
issues, the President was knowledgeable, engaged, and influential on
matters Cuban.[6]

Why did President Kennedy and his chief advisers indulge such a
fixation with Cuba and direct so many United States resources to an
unrelenting campaign to monitor, harass, isolate, and ultimately destroy Havana's radical regime? One answer springs from a candid
remark by Robert F. Kennedy. Looking back at the early 1960s, he
wondered "if we did not pay a very great price for being more energetic than wise about a lot of things, especially Cuba."[7] The Kennedys' famed eagerness for action became exaggerated in the case of
Cuba. They always wanted to get moving on Cuba, and Castro dared
them to try. Some Europeans thought that "we kept slapping at Castro because he'd had the effrontery to thumb his nose at us," recalled
one American diplomat.[8] The popular, intelligent, but erratic Cuban
leader, whose *barbudos* (bearded ones) came down from the Sierra
Maestra Mountains in January 1959 to overthrow the United States
ally Fulgencio Batista, hurled harsh words at Washington and defi-
antly challenged the Kennedy model of evolutionary, capitalist development so evident in the Alliance for Progress. As charismatic figures
charting new frontiers, the President and *Jefe Máximo* often personalized the Cuban-American contest. Kennedy harbored a "deep feeling
against Castro," and the Cuban thought the American "an intelligent
and able leader of American imperialism," and, after the Bay of Pigs
invasion, he branded him a new Hitler.[9] To Kennedy's great annoyance, Castro could not be wheedled or beaten.

Kennedy's ardent war against *Fidelismo* may also have stemmed
from his feeling that Castro had double-crossed him. As a senator,
Kennedy had initially joined many Americans in welcoming the Cuban Revolution as a decided advancement over the "oppressive" Batista dictatorship. Linking Castro to the legacy of Bolívar, Kennedy
urged a "patient attitude" toward the new government, which he did
not see as Communist.[10] Denying repeatedly that he was a Communist, Castro had in fact proclaimed his allegiance to democracy and
private property. But in the process of legitimizing his revolution and
resisting United States pressure, Castro turned more and more radical. Americans grew impatient with the regime's highly charged anti-
Yankeeism, postponement of elections, jailing of critics, and nationalization of property. The Cuban police state system reminded many of

Hitler's and Stalin's dreaded totalitarianism. The President rejected the idea that intense United States hostility to the Cuban Revolution may have contributed to Castro's tightening political grip and flirtation with the Soviet Union. Nor did Kennedy and other Americans wish to acknowledge the measurable benefits of the revolution—improvements in education, medical care, and housing, and the elimination of the island's infamous corruption that once had been the American Mafia's domain. Instead, Kennedy officials concluded that Cuba's was a "betrayed revolution."[11]

Richard N. Goodwin, the young White House and State Department official with responsibilities for Latin America, provided another explanation for the Kennedy fixation with Cuba. He remarked that "the entire history of the Cold War, its positions and assumptions, converged upon the 'problem of Cuba.' "[12] Indeed, the Cold War dominated international politics, and in the zero-sum accounting of the time, a loss for "us" meant a gain for "them." As Cuban-American relations steadily deteriorated, Cuban-Soviet relations gradually improved. Not only did Americans come to believe that a once-loyal ally had jilted them for the tawdry embrace of the Soviets; they also grew alarmed that Castro sneered at the Monroe Doctrine by inviting the Soviet military to the island. When Castro, in late 1961, declared himself a Marxist-Leninist, Americans who had long denounced him as a Communist then felt vindicated. American leaders began to speak of Cuban membership in the "Sino-Soviet bloc," thus providing Communists with a "spearhead" to penetrate the Western Hemisphere.[13] From the moment of victory, Castro had called for Cuban-style revolutions throughout Latin America, and Havana had sent agents and arms to other nations to kindle radical fires. Castro's revolutionary mission happened to coincide with Nikita Khrushchev's alarming statement that the Soviet Union supported wars of national liberation worldwide. It mattered little to Americans that the two appeals appeared independently or that Havana and Moscow differed markedly over the best method for promoting revolutionary change—the Soviets insisted on utilizing Communist parties within political systems, whereas the Cubans espoused peoples' rebellions. Cuba came to represent the Cold War in the United States's backyard, and, as such, one senator explained, it became a "target for our national frustration and annoyance with Moscow and the whole Communist conspiracy."[14]

In addition to the Kennedy style and the Cold War, American politics influenced the Administration's Cuba policy. In the 1960 presidential campaign, Kennedy had seized the Cuban issue to counter Richard Nixon's charge that the inexperienced Democratic candidate would abandon Quemoy and Matsu to Communism and prove no match for the hard-nosed Khrushchev. "In 1952 the Republicans ran on a program of rolling back the Iron Curtain in Eastern Europe," Kennedy jabbed. "Today the Iron Curtain is 90 miles off the coast of the United States."[15] Privately he asked, "How would *we* have saved Cuba if we had [had] the power"? but he nonetheless valued the political payback from his attack. "What the hell," he informed his aides, "they never told us how they would have saved China [in 1949]."[16] He did recommend a controversial method to reclaim Cuba for the American system. Apparently unaware that President Dwight D. Eisenhower had initiated a clandestine CIA program to train Cuban exiles for an invasion of the island, candidate Kennedy bluntly called for just such a project.

After exploiting the Cuban issue, Kennedy, upon becoming President, could not easily have retreated. Partisan politics kept his gaze fixed on the defiant leader in the Caribbean. Hardly a press conference went by without an insistent question about Cuba. Republicans and Democracts alike peppered the White House with demands for action against Castroism. The vocal, burgeoning Cuban exile community in Florida never let the issue rest. Businessmen protested that the Cuban government nationalized American-owned property worth a billion dollars, and they grew apprehensive that the practice would become attractive in the hemisphere. The outgoing Treasury Secretary told Kennedy that "large amounts of capital now planned for investment in Latin America" were being held back, because investors were "waiting to see whether the United States can cope" with Castro's Cuba.[17] George Meany, the cantankerous head of the AFL-CIO, decried the communization of the Cuban labor federation.[18] The Joint Chiefs of Staff advised the President to invade Cuba.[19] Everyone seemed eager to know when Kennedy would knock Castro off his perch, and many expected the President to act before the next election.

Overarching all explanations for Kennedy's obsession with Cuba is a major phenomenon of twentieth-century world history: the steady erosion of the authority of imperial powers, which had built systems of dependent, client, and colonial governments. The strong currents of decolonization, anti-imperialism, revolutionary nationalism, and social revolution, sometimes in combination, undermined the instruments the imperial nations had used to maintain control and order. In the 1950s France was driven from Indochina, and Great Britain's position in the Middle East receded dramatically after the Suez crisis, to cite two prominent examples.

The Cuban Revolution exemplified this process of breaking up and breaking away. American leaders reacted so hostilely to this revolution not simply because Castro and his 26th of July Movement taunted them or because domestic politics and the Cold War swayed them, but because Cuba, as symbol and reality, challenged United States hegemony in Latin America. The specter of "another Cuba" haunted President Kennedy, not just because it would hurt him politically, but because "the game would be up through a good deal of Latin America."[20] Americans refused to accept a revolution that not only targeted Batista and their island assets but also the Monroe Doctrine and the United States's claim to political, economic, and military leadership in the hemsiphere. "The revolution became anti-imperialism and freedom, the overthrow of the monoculture-militarist-dictatorship-dependence structure," remembered Carlos Franqui, a *Fidelista* who later went into exile.[21] Given this fundamental conflict, a breakdown in Cuban-American relations was inevitable: Cuba sought independence and radical social change which would necessarily come at the expense of the United States, and the latter, not unexpectedly, defended its interests against revolutionary nationalism. As Castro put it, "the United States *had* to fight his revolution."[22] Khrushchev, in pondering the American campaign against Cuba, once asked: "Why should an elephant be afraid of a mouse?"[23] The Soviet leader, who certainly knew his own nation's imperial record in suppressing its neighbors when they became too independent-minded, surely knew that the answer to his question could be found in the American fear that the Cuban Revolution would become contagious and further diminish United States hegemony in the Western Hemisphere.

After the United States helped expel Spain from Cuba in 1898 and imposed the Platt Amendment on the island in 1903, Americans gained influence through military interventions, occupations, threats, economic penetration, and political manipulation. By 1959 Americans dominated Cuba's oil, telephone, mining, and electric industries and produced more than a third of its sugar. That year, too, the United States bought 74 percent of Cuba's exports and supplied 65 percent of the island's imports.[24] Because the United States had such tremendous economic favors to dispense (especially a quota system that guaranteed Cuba sugar sales in the American market), Washington wielded political influence in Havana. The United States also stationed a military mission in Cuba and sent arms to Batista's forces. The CIA infiltrated political groups and helped Batista organize an anti-Communist police unit.

After having underestimated Castro's 26th of July Movement and the depth of the nation's unrest, the Eisenhower Administration tried to manipulate Cuba once again on the very eve of Castro's victory. With the President's blessing and CIA instructions, William D. Pawley, owner of Cuban lands and former Ambassador to Brazil, traveled to Havana to press Batista to resign in favor of a military junta in order to prevent the 26th of July Movement's imminent triumph. The Cuban President balked at this exercise of "Plattism," and Pawley's mission aborted.[25] Even after this setback, the United States's continued sense of its strength in Cuba appeared in a CIA report that concluded that "no sane man undertaking to govern and reform Cuba would have chosen to pick a fight with the US." Because Castro did not honor traditional United States power in his nation, he must have possessed a "psychotic personality."[26] Americans, unable or unwilling to acknowledge that the Cuban Revolution tapped deep nationalistic feelings and that their own interventionism and island interests made the United States a primary target, preferred to depict Fidel Castro as a crazed *guerrillero* whose temporarily frenzied people would toss him out when their rationality returned.

The Eisenhower Administration bequeathed to its successor an unproductive tit-for-tat process of confrontation with Cuba and a legacy of failure.[27] In 1959–1960, with Ambassador Philip Bonsal thinking that Castro suffered "mental unbalance at times" and Eisenhower concluding that the Cuban leader "begins to look like a madman," Havana and Washington traded punch for punch.[28] In November 1959 the President decided to encourage anti-Castro groups within Cuba to "check" or "replace" the revolutionary regime, and thus end an anti-Americanism that was "having serious adverse effects on the United States position in Latin America and corresponding advantages for international Communism."[29] In March of the next year Eisenhower ordered the CIA to train Cuban exiles for an invasion of their homeland—this shortly after Cuba signed a trade treaty with the Soviet Union. The CIA, as well, hatched assassination plots against Castro and staged hit-and-run attacks along the Cuban coast. As Cuba undertook land reform that struck at American interests and nationalized

American-owned industries, the United States suspended Cuba's sugar quota and forbade American exports to the island, drastically cutting a once-flourishing commerce. On January 3, 1961, fearing an invasion and certain that the American embassy was a "nest of spies" aligned with counter-revolutionaries who were burning cane fields and sabotaging buildings, Castro heatedly demanded that the embassy staff be reduced to the small size of the Cuban delegation in Washington.[30] The United States promptly broke diplomatic relations with Cuba.

Eisenhower failed to topple Castro, but American pressure accelerated the radicalization of the revolution and helped open the door to the Soviets. Moscow bought sugar, supplied technicians, armed the militia, and offered generous trade terms. Although the revolution's radicalization was probably inevitable, it was not inexorable that Cuba would end up in the Soviet camp. Hostile United States policies ensured that outcome. Revolutionary Cuba needed outside assistance to survive. "Russia came to Castro's rescue," Bonsal has concluded, "only after the United States had taken steps designed to overthrow him."[31]

Kennedy's foreign policy troubles have sometimes been explained as inheritances from Eisenhower that shackled the new President with problems not of his own making. To be sure, Kennedy inherited the Cuban problem from Eisenhower. But he did not simply continue his predecessor's anti-Castro policies. Kennedy greatly exaggerated the Cuban threat, attributing to Castro a capability to export revolution that the Cuban leader never had and lavishing on him an attention he did not deserve. Castro was "an affront to our pride" and a "mischief maker," Walter Lippmann wisely wrote, but he was not a "mortal threat" to the United States.[32] And because of his obsession with Cuba, Kennedy significantly increased the pressures against the upstart island. He thus helped generate major crises, including the October 1962 missile crisis. Kennedy inherited the Cuban problem—and he made it worse.

The new President actually made his first important policy choice on Cuba before he entered the White House. On the day Cuban-American relations were severed, Secretary of State Christian Herter telephoned Secretary-designate Dean Rusk and asked for Kennedy's reaction. Rusk talked with Kennedy and reported that the President-elect "would not associate himself with the Administration stand, i.e., he would not take a position for or against it at the present time. . . ."³³ By saying nothing, Kennedy accepted a decision that reduced his own options for dealing with Cuba. The United States lost an embassy which had served as a first-hand listening post; now Washington would have to rely upon a fast diminishing number of CIA informants and deep-cover agents or upon often exaggerated information from exiles. Most important, with economic coercion having failed to bring down Castro and diplomacy now impeded, the rupture in relations elevated covert action—especially an invasion by Cuban exiles—as one of the few means left to resolve the contest with Cuba.

The questions of whether and under what conditions to approve an exile expedition dominated the President's discussion of Cuba in his first few months in office.³⁴ Although Kennedy always reserved the authority to cancel the operation right up to the moment of departure, his choices, made after much deliberation, pointed in one direction: Go. National security adviser McGeorge Bundy later said that the President "really was looking for ways to make it work . . . and allowed himself to be persuaded it would work and the risks were acceptable."³⁵ Not simply a prisoner of events or of the Eisenhower legacy, Kennedy associated so closely with the covert operation that it became identified as *his*. He listened to but rejected the counsel of doubting advisers, and he never revealed moral or legal qualms about violently overthrowing a sovereign government. He never requested a contingency plan to disband the exile brigade. In questioning aides, the President worried most about which methods would deliver success and whether the guiding hand of the United States could be concealed. Kennedy sought deniability of an American role, but never the demise of the project.

On March 11, Kennedy's chief advisers gathered in a critical National Security Council (NSC) meeting. CIA Director Allen Dulles and Deputy Director for Plans Richard Bissell explained plans for an invasion at the town of Trinidad, on Cuba's southern coast near the Escambray Mountains, where CIA-backed rebels were already operating. The President criticized the plan as too much like a spectacular World War II amphibious landing. He asked for something quieter, and he instructed planners that no American forces were to be used. Dulles advised that the mission had to go forward, because "we have a disposal problem." Great embarrassment would beset Washington if the exile brigade, training in Guatemala, were to disband and its members return to the United States to bellow their anger. Kennedy requested "new proposals"; he ordered the CIA to force bickering exile groups to unite behind one leader; he directed Arthur M. Schlesinger, Jr., the Harvard historian-turned-White House assistant, to draft a White Paper to justify an invasion; and he asked the State Department to gain OAS backing for strong anti-Castro measures.[36]

Officials moved fast. The CIA devised a plan for dawn landings in the area of Bahía de Cochinos (Bay of Pigs). The existence of an air strip at the town of Playa Girón, the surrounding Zapata swamps with few access roads, and the region's sparse population made this an appealing entry site. In a Miami motel, a CIA operative bluntly forced exiles to form the Cuban Revolutionary Council under José Miró Cardona, a former foe of Batista and a onetime member of Castro's government. Schlesinger quickly produced a White Paper. Issued on April 3, this propagandistic justification for anti-Castroism condemned the Cuban radical for betraying his revolutionary promises, delivering his island to the "Sino-Soviet bloc," and attempting to subvert Latin American governments.[37] After several high-level meetings and Dulles's assurance that the prospects for Operation Zapata were even greater than they had been for the successful CIA plot in 1954 against Guatemala, Kennedy set April 17 as D-Day.

The Bay of Pigs plan began to unravel from the start. As the brigade's old, slow freighters, obtained from the United Fruit Company, plowed their way to Cuba, B-26 airplanes took to the skies from Nicaragua. On April 15, D-Day minus 2, the brigade pilots destroyed several parked planes of Castro's meager air force. That same day, as part of a pre-invasion ploy, a lone, artificially damaged B-26 flew directly to Miami, where its pilot claimed that he had defected from the Cuban military and had just bombed his country's airfields. But the cover story soon cracked. Snooping journalists noticed that the nose cone of the B-26 was metal; Cuban planes had plastic noses. They observed too that the aircraft's guns had not been fired. The American hand was being exposed. The President, still insistent upon hiding American complicity, decided to cancel a second D-Day air strike against the remnants of the Cuban air force. CIA officials protested, because they believed the invasion force could not succeed unless Castro's few planes were knocked out. After conferring with Secretary Rusk, Kennedy stuck with his decision.

Shortly after midnight on April 17, more than 1400 commandos motored in small boats to the beaches at Bahía de Cochinos. The invaders immediately tangled with Castro's militia. Some commandos never made it, because their boats broke apart on razor-sharp coral reefs. In the air, Castro's marauding airplanes shot down two brigade B-26s and, in the water, sank ships carrying essential communications equipment and ammunition. Fighting ferociously, the brigade nonetheless failed to establish a beachhead. Would Washington try to salvage the mission? Kennedy turned down CIA appeals to dispatch planes from the nearby USS *Essex,* but he did permit some jets to provide air cover for a new B-26 attack from Nicaragua. Manned this time by American CIA pilots, the B-26s arrived an hour after the jets had come and gone. Cuban aircraft downed the B-26s, killing four Americans. With Castro's boasting that the *mercenarios* had been foiled, the final toll was grim: 114 of the exile brigade dead and 1,189 captured. A pall settled over the While House.

"How could I have been so stupid, to let them go ahead?" Kennedy asked an assistant.[38] Stupid or not, Kennedy knew the answers to his own question. First, he dearly sought to oust Castro and score a victory in the Cold War. Second, his personality and style encouraged action. Always driven to win, Kennedy believed "that his disapproval of the plan would be a show of weakness inconsistent with his general stance."[39] One foreign policy observer explained "how the President got such bad advice from such good advisers":

> The decision on which they were asked to advise was presented as a choice between action and inaction. . . . None of the President's advisers wants it said of him by his colleagues . . . that he . . . loses his nerve when the going gets hot. The Harvard intellectuals are especially vulnerable, the more so from being new on the scene. They are conscious of the fact that the tough-minded military suspect them of being soft-headed. They have to show that they are he-men too, that they can act as well as lecture.[40]

Third, fear of nasty political repercussions influenced the President. Told to disband, brigade members might have refused to give up their arms or even have mutineed. In any case, Republicans would have scorned a weak-kneed Administration.[41] Kennedy approved the operation, finally, because he felt a sense of urgency. CIA analysts advised that time was on Castro's side. Delay would permit the Soviets to strengthen the Cuban military, perhaps with MIG fighters, and the rainy season was about to begin, making military maneuver difficult. The Guatemalan president, facing awkward questions about Cuban trainees in his country, was also beseeching Washington to move the exiles out by late April.[42]

Failures in intelligence, operations, decision-making, and judgment doomed the Bay of Pigs undertaking. Arrogant CIA architects knew too little and assumed too much about Cuba, particularly about the landing site. Although Bissell and Dulles have staunchly denied that they ever told the President that the invasion would ignite an island-wide rebellion against the Castro regime and thus ensure the ascendency of Miró's provisional government, Kennedy decision-makers nonetheless believed that the invasion would stimulate a popular revolt against an unpopular government. But the CIA did not coordinate the invasion with the anti-Castro underground in Cuba, because the agency feared leaks and the likely infiltration of opposition groups by Castro's security forces. No rebellion erupted.[43] Kennedy and his advisers also assumed that, should the brigade prove incapable of taking territory, it could melt into the mountains and become a guerrilla army. But, because the invasion site had been shifted, the mountains now lay some 80 miles away, with impassable swamps between. Neither Kennedy nor CIA advisers had explored this problem. The guerrilla option, which, like the belief in a rebellion, probably led Kennedy to suppress doubts about the operation, was actually impossible.

CIA planners failed in other ways. If they overestimated Cuban discontent with Castro, they underestimated the effectiveness of his military. They anticipated that he would crack; in fact, he expertly led his forces at the Bay of Pigs, where he had vacationed. CIA analysts had failed to detect the coral reefs. CIA-issued equipment malfunctioned; crucial communications gear was concentrated in one ship that sunk; paratroopers did not drop far enough inland to cut off causeways.[44] Another operational failure remained a tightly held secret. The CIA had been attempting since 1960 to kill Fidel Castro, even employing Mafia thugs for the task. The CIA activated assassination plots in March and April. It seems likely that assassination was part of the general Bay of Pigs plan. Bissell has admitted that he was hopeful "that Castro would be dead before the landing."[45]

The most controversial operational question remains the cancelled second D-Day air strike. Post-crisis critics have complained that the President lost his nerve and made a decision that condemned the expedition to disaster.[46] Castro and Bissell have agreed that Cuban air supremacy was important to Cuba's triumph.[47] But was it decisive? A pre-emptive strike on D-Day against the Cuban air force would not have delivered victory to the invaders. After the first air attack, Castro had dispersed his planes; the brigade's B-26s would have encountered considerable difficulty in locating and destroying them. And, even if a D-Day assault had disabled all of Castro's planes, then what? *La brigada*'s 1400 men would have had to face Castro's army of 25,000 and the nation's 200,000 militia. The commandos most likely would not have survived the overwhelming power of the Cuban military.

A flawed decision-making system also contributed to failure. Bissell and Dulles were too emotionally committed to the project to see the shortcomings in their handiwork. CIA planners were less than candid with the President, for fear that he would terminate the project. Operation Zapata was even kept a secret from many other CIA professionals responsible for intelligence analysis. Had they been asked to assess the chances for national rebellion, for example, they probably would have reported negatively, pointing out Castro's continued popular appeal.[48] CIA officials also contributed to the President's thinking that American participation could be hidden and plausibly denied. But how could Kennedy ever have thought that secrecy was possible? Wishful thinking provides the best answer.[49] "Trying to mount an operation of this magnitude from the United States," a CIA official wrote later, "is about as covert as walking nude across Times Square without attracting attention."[50] Nonetheless, until his decision to cancel the second strike, Kennedy clung to the fiction of deniability.

The Joint Chiefs of Staff and Secretary of State also failed as advisers. Although the generals and admirals had serious reservations, they always evaluated the operation favorably. Sworn to secrecy, they did not seek close staff analysis of the CIA plan. Not "cut in" until the later stages of planning, they hesitated to "pound the desk," because the operation was "not our show."[51] Nor did Dean Rusk provide rigorous scrutiny or press his case against the invasion. A "good soldier" who went along with the apparent consensus, he seemed to believe that he sould preside over debate rather than influence it. Rusk later regretted his restraint:

> As a colonel of infantry [in the Second World War], I knew that this brigade didn't have the chance of a "snowball in hell." But I wasn't a colonel of infantry; I was sitting there in a very special cubicle. I failed President Kennedy by not insisting that he ask a question that he did not ask. He should have turned to our Joints Chiefs of Staff and said to them: "Now gentlemen, I may want to do this with U.S. forces, so you tell me what you would need. . . ." By the time the Joint Chiefs had come in with

their sustained and prolonged bombing, their several divisions, a massive fleet, and their big air force, it would have become obvious to the President that that little brigade didn't have a chance at all.[52]

One wonders, of course, why Kennedy himself did not think to ask the question. Rusk also kept departmental intelligence and Cuban specialists in the dark.[53]

Kennedy encountered a good deal of dissenting opinion and he rejected it. Schlesinger, for example, wrote several memoranda to the President, arguing that time was actually not on Castro's side and that the Cuban leader, at least for the moment, remained popular.[54] The skeptics included Richard Goodwin, John Kenneth Galbraith, Charles E. Bohlen, Chester Bowles, and Adlai Stevenson. In making his decision, Kennedy also bypassed Congress, further ensuring that he received limited advice. Only Senator J. William Fulbright, Foreign Relations Committee chairman, was let into the inner circle, and, at that, only once. Picking up rumors of a forthcoming invasion of Cuba, Fulbright sent the President a memorandum that strongly disapproved invasion—it was "of a piece with the hypocrisy and cynicism for which the United States is constantly denouncing the Soviet Union . . . ," he wrote. Kennedy thereupon invited the Arkansas senator to attend an April 4 meeting. Fulbright spoke forthrightly to the assembled top-level advisers, chiding them for exaggerating the Cuban threat. As he had told the President earlier, the Castro regime "is a thorn in the flesh; but it is not a dagger in the heart."[55] No one in the room agreed with Fulbright.

"Mr. President, it could have been worse," remarked a Stevenson assistant. How? "It might have succeeded."[56] Had all gone well with the chain reaction of beachhead, rebellion, and Castro's death or departure, the victory would only have "exchanged a Castro pesthouse for a post-Castro asylum."[57] Tainted as an American stooge, the head of the new government would have struggled to win public favor. Well-armed Castroites, including Fidel's brother Raúl and Che Guevara, would probably have initiated a protracted guerrilla war against the American-created regime. The Soviets might have helped these rebel forces, and volunteers from around the world might have swelled the resistance—like the Spanish Civil War of the 1930s, Schlesinger had warned. The United States would have had to save its puppet government through military aid, advisers, and maybe even troops. To have sustained a successful Bay of Pigs invasion, then, the

Kennedy Administration probably would have had to undertake a prolonged and expensive occupation of the island.[58]

As it was, defeat did not chasten the Administration. While a secret presidential panel investigated the disaster, Kennedy and his advisers huddled. At the April 20 Cabinet meeting, Bowles found his colleagues "almost savage." Robert Kennedy became especially agitated, and "there was an almost frantic reaction for an action program which people would grab onto."[59] With Republicans belittling the President—Eisenhower said the story ought to be titled "Profile in Timidity and Indecision" and Nixon allowed that Kennedy should have known that "when you commit maximum U.S. prestige you have to commit maximum U.S. power to back it up," Kennedy was not sympathetic to Bowles's call for patience and caution.[60] The Under Secretary was "yellow-bellied," press secretary Pierre Salinger snorted, and "we're going to get him." White House aide Harris Wofford shot back: "Why don't you get those who got us into this mess?"[61] Kennedy pushed Bowles out of the State Department later in the year.

On April 20 the beleaguered President spoke out. "Let the record show," he boomed, "that our restraint is not inexhaustible." Indeed, the United States intended to defend the Monroe Doctrine and carry on a "relentless" struggle with Communism in "every corner of the globe." In familiar words, Kennedy declared that "the complacent, the self-indulgent, the soft societies are about to be swept away with the debris of history. Only the strong . . . can possibly survive."[62] That day, too, Kennedy ordered American military advisers in Laos to put on their uniforms to show United States resolution in the face of defeat. "A new urgency" was injected into "Kennedy's concern for counterinsurgency . . . ," recalled General Maxwell Taylor, who headed the post-crisis inquiry.[63] Although Kennedy privately claimed that the Cuban failure deterred him from military intervention in Laos, the record of the April 22 NSC meeting demonstrates that the President chose an activist policy of confrontation with the "Communist world."[64] Such a posture was more in line with the advice a Bundy aide offered Robert Kennedy during the Bay of Pigs crisis. When the Attorney General growled that Moscow would now judge America weak, Walt W. Rostow commented that "we would have ample opportunity to prove we were not paper tigers in Berlin, Southeast Asia, and elsewhere."[65] This thinking also resembled the recommendations of the Taylor Study Group, which on June 13 reported secretly to the President that "we are in a life and death struggle which we may be losing," so henceforth all of the nation's Cold War resources had to be mobilized.[66]

Robert Kennedy told counterinsurgency specialist Colonel Edward Lansdale that the Bay of Pigs "insult needed to be redressed rather quickly."[67] But that redressing faced some heady obstacles. The anti-Castro underground lay shattered. Cuban security forces, before and after the landing, rounded up, jailed, killed, or converted thousands of anti-regime subversives, most of whom were surprised because the CIA had not forewarned them about D-Day. In the United States the Cuban Revolutionary Council splintered, as the demoralized and angry Cuban community descended once again into fierce factionalism. Castro triumphantly exploited patriotic nationalism to strengthen his regime.[68] Instead of driving the Soviets out of Cuba, the botched Bay of Pigs operation drew Havana and Moscow closer together. Understandably fearing another invasion, perhaps with American troops, Castro sought Soviet military assistance. The Soviets shipped small arms, machine guns, howitzers, armored personnel carriers, patrol boats, tanks, surface-to-air missiles, and, ultimately, nuclear missiles that could reach into the United States itself.[69]

Persuaded that "there can be no long-term living with Castro as a neighbor," Kennedy officials launched a multi-track program of covert, economic, diplomatic, and propagandistic elements.[70] Encouraged by the White House, the CIA created a huge operations station in Miami called JMWAVE to recruit and organize Cuban exiles. In Washington, Robert Kennedy became a ramrod for action. At a November 4 White House meeting, the Attorney General made his pitch: "stir things up on the island with espionage, sabotage, general disorder . . . ."[71] The President himself asked Colonel Lansdale to direct Operation Mongoose—"to use our available assets . . . to help Cuba overthrow the Communist regime."[72]

Operation Mongoose and JMWAVE, although failing to unseat Castro, punished Cubans. CIA-handled saboteurs burned cane fields and blew up factories and oil storage tanks. In a December 1961 raid, for example, a seven-man team blasted a railroad bridge, derailed an approaching train, and torched a sugar warehouse. Myriad exile groups, from Alpha 66 to the Revolutionary Student Directorate, left the Florida Keys to stage hit-and-run attacks along Cuba's coast. CIA agents contaminated goods leaving European ports for Cuba, and they bribed European manufacturers to produce faulty equipment for

Cuba—as when a German industrialist shipped off-center ball bearings. British-made Leland buses were sabotaged too.[73] These spoiling operations compelled the Castro government to divert scarce resources from economic and social programs to coastal defense and internal surveillance. They also pushed Cuba toward greater dependence upon the Soviet Union.

The CIA devised new plots to kill Castro. Poisonous cigars, pills, and needles were directed Castro's way, but to no avail. Did the Kennedys know about these death schemes? Robert Kennedy learned about them in mid-1962, and his biographer claims that the Attorney General ordered an end to assassination projects. John Kennedy said at the time that in general he disapproved of the killing of foreign leaders.[74] The President apparently never directly ordered the assassination of Castro—at least no trail of documents leads to the Kennedy White House. But, of course, the word "assassination" was never uttered in the presence of the President or committed to paper, so that he could be protected by the principle of plausible deniability. What was always mentioned was the need to remove Castro. "And if killing him was one of the things that was to be done in this connection," assassination was attempted because "we felt we were acting within the guidelines." So bespoke Bissell's replacement, Richard Helms.[75] President Kennedy may or may not have known about the assassination plots, but he did set the general guidelines.

Intensified economic coercion joined assassination and sabotage as methods to undermine the Castro government. American officials did not expect the economic denial program alone to force Castro's fall. But they did seek to inhibit the island's economic development, thereby decelerating socialization, spurring Cuban discontent, and diminishing Cuba's appeal as a model for Latin America. In February 1962 Kennedy further tightened the economic screws by banning most imports of Cuban products (especially tobacco). *El bloqueo,* as the Cubans called the embargo, hurt. Cuba was forced to pay higher freight costs, enlarge its foreign debt, and suffer innumerable factory shut-downs due to the lack of spare parts once bought in the United States. Cuba's economic woes also stemmed from the flight of technicians and managers, a decline in tourism, high worker absenteeism, the drying up of foreign capital investment, hastily conceived policies to diversify the economy, and suffocating government controls. The overall effect on Cuba of American economic measures was not what Washington intended: greater political centralization, more state management, closer ties to the Soviet Union. By 1962, 82 percent of Cuba's exports flowed to Communist countries, and 85 percent of its imports came from them. As with military defense, so with the economy: the Soviet Union became Cuba's lifeline.[76]

The Kennedy Administration also lobbied the OAS to isolate Cuba. Eisenhower had grown frustrated with the regional organization's refusal to "do something about Castro."[77] Secretary Herter explained in March 1960 why the OAS hesitated: "Our own latest National Intelligence Estimate does not find Cuba to be under Communist control or domination, and we lack all of the hard evidence which would be required to convince skeptical Latin American Governments and the public opinion behind them."[78] But after Castro declared himself a Marxist-Leninist in late 1961, the United States managed to obtain the votes to oust Cuba from the OAS, even though Mexico voted "nay" and Argentina, Bolivia, Brazil, Chile, and Ecuador abstained.[79] The expulsion registered loudly in Havana, which interpreted it as "political preparation for an invasion."[80] By the spring of 1962, moreover, fifteen Latin American states had answered Washington's call to break relations with Cuba.

Diplomatic contact between Cubans and Americans also virtually ceased, with two exceptions. When in May 1961 Castro offered to trade the Bay of Pigs prisoners for American farm tractors, the White House encouraged a private committee of distinguished Americans to negotiate with Cuba. But the Tractors-for-Freedom Committee could not reach terms and disbanded. Then New York lawyer James B. Donovan, working closely with Washington officials, gained Castro's trust and bargained directly with him in Havana. In December 1962, in exchange for food and medicine, Castro released the brigade members. In a celebration at Miami's Orange Bowl, Kennedy received their flag. "I can assure you," an emotional President told the huge crowd, "that this flag will be returned to this brigade in a free Havana."[81]

Another encounter took place during the August 1961 Punta del Este conference that drafted the Alliance for Progress charter. Che Guevara initiated contact with Richard Goodwin by sending a box of Cuba's finest cigars to the White House assistant. "Since to write to an enemy is difficult, I limit myself to extending my hand," read an attached note.[82] At a farewell party, the two men held an intense conversation. Che first thanked Goodwin for the Bay of Pigs—it had helped the regime solidify its power. Goodwin remarked that the

Cubans could repay the favor by attacking the American naval base at Guantánamo. In a frank yet reasonable manner Che asked for a *modus vivendi* with Washington and urged talks on trade, compensation for nationalized property, and Guantánamo. Cuba would even be willing to discuss its ties with the Soviets and Cuban activities in the hemisphere. Goodwin carried the promising August 17 overture to Kennedy, who, smoking one of Che's cigars, listened to his aide's appeal for further exploration of the "below ground dialogue" with the Cubans. The President rejected the suggestion: it came too soon after the humiliating Bay of Pigs, would likely disturb some Latin American governments, and would legitimize a Marxist government.[83] Che's important initiative died that abruptly—at JFK's desk.

By the spring of 1962 Cuba was losing on several fronts in its contest with the United States: diplomatic isolation in the hemisphere, ouster from the OAS, economic embargo, CIA assistance to anti-Castro rebels in Cuba, exile raids and sabotage, assassination plots, Operation Mongoose, and the successful launching of the anti-Cuban Alliance for Progress. After the American failure at the Bay of Pigs and in the face of the studied American effort to cripple the Cuban Revolution, "were we right or wrong to fear direct invasion" next? Fidel Castro later asked.[84] Although Kennedy had actually ruled out invasion as a method to overthrow Castro, in large part because Latin American opinion would have been so negative and American casualties would have been so staggering, Castro could only think the worst in 1962. After all, some Washington politicians were shouting for invasion and Kennedy officials spoke frankly about getting rid of Castro.

It may be plausibly argued that, had there been no exile expedition, no destructive covert activities, and no economic and diplomatic boycott—had there been no concerted United States vendetta to quash the Cuban Revolution—there would not have been an October missile crisis. The principal source for that frightening crisis lay in Kennedy's unvarnished hostility toward Cuba and in Castro's understandable apprehension that United States invasion was inevitable.

The origins of the missile crisis, then, derived largely from United States-Cuban tensions. To stress only the global dimension of Soviet-American competition, as is commonly done, is like saying that a basketball game can be played without a court. Cuba was the court. To slight the local or regional sources of the conflict is to miss a central point: Nikita Khrushchev would never have had the opportunity to begin his dangerous missile game if Kennedy had not been attempting to expunge Castro and his revolution from the hemisphere. This interpretation does not dismiss but incorporates the view, predominant in the scholarly literature, that the emplacement of nuclear missiles in Cuba served the Soviet strategic goal of catching up in the nuclear arms race.[85] This interpretation emphasizes that both Cuba and the Soviet Union calculated that their interests would be served by putting medium and intermediate-range rockets on the island. Havana hoped to gain deterrent power to thwart an expected American invasion, and Moscow hoped to enhance its deterrent power in the Cold War and save a new ally.[86] From Castro's perspective, the United States would not start a local, conventional war out of fear that it would then have to risk a nuclear war.[87] "We'd carried out the Bay of Pigs operation, never intending to use American military force—but the Kremlin didn't know that," Defense Secretary Robert McNamara recalled. "We were running covert operations against Castro" and "people in the Pentagon were even talking about a first strike [nuclear policy]. . . . So the Soviets may well have believed we were seeking Castro's overthrow *plus* a first strike capability. This may have led them to do what they did in Cuba."[88]

Cuba's eagerness for Soviet military assistance is well documented in the contemporary record. Castro and other Cuban officials made repeated, consistent, and compelling statements that their nation faced an American onslaught. "Cuba took measures to defend its security against a systematic policy of hostility and aggression," Castro privately explained to United Nations Secretary General U Thant during the October crisis.[89]

Contemporary, secret, now declassified United States documents reveal that American decisionmakers knew that the Cuban-Soviet military linkage, which included the June 1962 agreement on nuclear missiles, grew from Cuba's fear of invasion. They did not say so publicly, of course, for such would have acknowledged their own responsibility for generating the fear. In September 1962, CIA analysts concluded that "the main purpose of the present military build-up in Cuba is to strengthen the Communist regime there against what the Cubans and Soviets conceive to be a danger that the US may attempt by one means or another to overthrow it."[90] In early October the Department of State cabled its diplomatic posts that Castro feared an American invasion and that "the available evidence suggests strongly that this crash build-up of military and economic assistance did not represent a Soviet initiative but rather a response to insistent demands from Castro for help."[91] Early in the crisis, a CIA office issued a secret report that noted Cuba's numerous "invasion scares" in the summer of 1962. But the Cubans "felt progressively more secure as the work [Soviet installation of military equipment] advanced."[92] Finally, to cite yet another example, a post-crisis State Department study indicated that when Soviet "military equipment began arriving in volume in late summer 1962 the US government realized that these chronic [invasion] fears played a part in Castro's motives."[93]

Why did the Cubans and Soviets decide upon medium (MRBM) and intermediate (IRBM) missiles, with ranges of 1,020 and 2,200 nautical miles respectively, instead of upon a military pact, non-nuclear, conventional forces, or weapons that could satisfy American tolerance for "defensive" assistance? Perhaps the Cubans were confused about the types of missiles they would receive.[94] During the 1958 Middle East crisis, when American troops landed in Lebanon, Khrushchev and Gamal Abdul Nasser discussed "rockets" and "missiles" for Egypt. Nasser betrayed considerable ignorance about the details of these weapons—as perhaps Castro did later.[95] The Cubans may not have paid much attention to missile type, because to them more powerful weapons simply meant more deterrence. Or they may have assumed that impressive surface-to-surface missiles (42 MRBMs arrived; the IRBMs never arrived) were necessary for true deterrence against an aggressive United States. One thinks here of a similar American assumption at the end of the Second World War that the fanatical Japanese would surrender only under threat of annihilation from the atomic bomb.

On October 14 an American U-2 plane photographed missile sites in Cuba, thus providing the first "hard" evidence, as distinct from the "soft" reports of exiles, that the island was becoming a nuclear base. "He can't do that to me!" snapped Kennedy when he saw the pictures on the 16th.[96] He had warned the Soviets that the United States would not suffer "offensive" weapons in Cuba, although the warnings had come after the Cuban-Soviet decision of early summer.[97] The President convened his top advisers shortly before noon on October 16. His first questions focused on the firing readiness of the missiles and the probability that they carried nuclear warheads. The tentative answers were negative, although he was advised that the missiles could become operational in a brief time. Discussion of military options (invasion? air strike?) dominated this first meeting. Kennedy's immediate preference became clear: "We're certainly going . . . to take out these . . . missiles." McGeorge Bundy urged consideration not only of military plans but of a "political track" or diplomacy. But Kennedy showed little interest in negotiations. When McNamara mentioned that diplomacy might precede military action, the President immediately switched the discussion to another question: How long would it take to get air strikes organized? Conspicuously absent from this first meeting was a serious probing of Soviet and Cuban motivation.[98]

At a second meeting on the 16th, Rusk argued against the surprise air strike that General Maxwell Taylor had bluntly advocated. The Secretary of State recommended instead "a direct message to Castro." At the close of Rusk's remarks, Kennedy immediately asked: "Can we get a little idea about what the military thing *is*?" Bundy then posed a question now central to the history of the missile crisis: "How gravely does this change the strategic balance?" McNamara, for one, thought "not at all," but Taylor disputed him. Kennedy himself was uncertain, but he did complain that the missile emplacement in Cuba "makes them look like they're co-equal with us." And, added Treasury Secretary C. Douglas Dillon, who obviously knew the President's competitive personality, the presence of the missiles made it appear that "we're scared of the Cubans."

Then the rambling discussion turned to Khrushchev's motivation. The Russian leader had been cautious on Berlin, Kennedy said. "It's just as if we suddenly began to put a major number of MRBMs in Turkey," the President went on. "Now that'd be goddam dangerous. . . ." Bundy jumped in: "Well, we *did*, Mr. President." Not liking the sound of a double standard, Kennedy lamely answered, "Yeah, but that was five years ago."[99] Actually, the American Jupiter missiles in Turkey, under a 1959 agreement with Ankara, were put into launch position in mid-1961—during the Kennedy Administration—and not turned over to Turkish forces until October 22, 1962, the very day Kennedy informed Moscow that it must withdraw its SS-4 missiles from Cuba.[100]

For the next several days, Kennedy's group of advisers, named the Executive Committee or Ex Comm, met frequently in tight secrecy. Taylor later summarized policy options: "talk them out," "squeeze them out," or "shoot them out."[101] In exhausting sessions marked by frank disagreement and changing minds, Ex Comm members weighed the advantages and disadvantages of invasion, bombing, quarantine, and diplomacy.[102] The President gradually moved with a majority of Ex Comm advisers toward a quarantine or blockade of Cuba: incoming ships would be stopped and inspected for military cargo. McNamara persistently argued this alternative against the generals, Dillon, CIA Director John McCone, and Dean Acheson, all of whom urged an air strike. When queried if an air strike would knock out all of the known missiles, Taylor replied: "The best we can offer you is to destroy 90%. . . ." In other words, some missiles in Cuba would remain in place for firing against the United States. Robert Kennedy also worrried that the Soviets might react unpredictably with military force, "which could be so serious as to lead to general nuclear war." In any case, the Attorney General insisted, there would be no "Pearl Harbor type of attack" on *his* brother's record.[103]

By October 22 the President had made two decisions. The chief decision was to quarantine Cuba to prevent further military shipments and to impress the Soviets with American resolve to force the missiles out. If the Soviets balked, other, more drastic, measures would be undertaken. The second decision was to inform the Soviets of United States policy through a television address rather than through diplomatic channels. Ex Comm advisers have dubiously argued that a surprise public speech was necessary to rally world opinion behind United States policy and to prevent Khrushchev himself from issuing a "blustering ultimatum."[104] At least two Ex Comm participants recommended that negotiations be tried first. Former Ambassador to the Soviet Union Charles Bohlen advised that Moscow would have to retaliate against the United States after its technicians were killed by American bombs. A stern letter to Khrushchev should be "tested" as a method to gain withdrawal of the missiles. "I don't see the urgency of military action," Bohlen told the President.[105] And a grim Ambassador to the United Nations Adlai Stevenson appealed to an unreceptive Kennedy: "the existence of nuclear missile bases anywhere is negotiable before we start anything."[106] Going into the crisis, Kennedy refused to negotiate with either Khrushchev or Castro.

Kennedy's evening television speech on October 22 sounded familiar themes in American diplomatic history. He recalled the special United States relationship with the Western Hemisphere, and he reminded Americans that 1930s lessons taught them to resist aggression and surrender. The President lectured the Soviets to reverse their "deliberately provocative" decision by dismantling their "strategic" missiles in Cuba, and he announced the Caribbean quarantine as an "initial" step. The United States Information Agency beamed his words around the world in thirty-seven languages, including Spanish for Cuba itself. For the Cubans Kennedy had an oft-heard message: Castro and his clique had become "puppets" of an "international conspiracy."[107]

The missile crisis became an international war of nerves. More than sixty American ships went on patrol to enforce the blockade. The Strategic Air Command went on nuclear alert, moving upward to Defense Condition (DEFCON) 2 for the first time ever (the next level is deployment for combat). B-52 bombers, loaded with nuclear weapons, stood ready, while men and equipment moved to the southeastern United States to prepare for an invasion (thousands of road maps of Cuba were distributed).[108] American diplomats hastened to inform NATO allies; two African nations agreed to deny landing rights for Soviet aircraft, so that the Soviets would have trouble resupplying their military on the island; the OAS voted to endorse United States policy; and the United Nations Security Council debated. Strangely, the Soviets did not mobilize or redeploy their huge military, nor did they take measures to make their strategic forces less vulnerable.[109] The Soviets also refrained from testing the quarantine: their ships turned around and went home. But what next? On the 26th, Kennedy and some Ex Comm members, thinking that the Soviets were stalling, soured on the quarantine. Sentiment for military action strengthened.[110]

Kennedy also approved a State Department message to Brazil that invited its ambassador in Havana to talk with Castro about the "great jeopardy" in which the Soviet missiles had placed his government. Indeed, the Cubans could expect to suffer "desperate hand-to-mouth existence" under an expanded American quarantine. But, if the missiles and Soviet military personnel departed, "many changes in the relations between Cuba and the OAS countries, including the US, could flow." For the first time in the Kennedy presidency, as nuclear war threatened, Washington was suggesting an accommodation of Cuban-American differences. This overture, however, may have represented no more than a ploy to divide Moscow and Havana, for the President himself "doubted that it would do any good . . . ."[111]

The "first real blink" in the crisis came in the afternoon of the 26th. A Soviet embassy officer, Aleksander Fomin, called ABC correspondent John Scali and asked for a meeting. They talked in a Washington restaurant, where Scali was surprised to hear Fomin urge him to carry a message to the television journalist's high-level friends in the State Department: the Soviet Union would withdraw the missiles if the United States would promise not to invade Cuba. Scali scurried to Rusk, who sent the unusual emissary back to Fomin with the reply that American leaders were interested in discussing the proposal.[112] In the meantime, a private Khrushchev letter arrived with the same offer, as well as with a pointed reminder for Kennedy: the missiles were in Cuba only because the United States had been threatening the island.[113]

But the next morning another letter came. Khrushchev now upped the stakes: he would trade the missiles in Cuba for the American missiles in Turkey. An angry Kennedy felt boxed, because "we are now in the position of risking war in Cuba and in Berlin over missiles in Turkey which are of little military value."[114] Indeed, the President in early 1961 had expressed doubts about the military efficacy of the Jupiters in Turkey and had later directed the Defense Department to prepare a study for phasing them out. But he had not ordered their removal.[115] Now they seemed to stand in the way of settling the October crisis, for Kennedy hesitated to accept a swap—first, because he did not want to appear to be giving up anything in the face of Soviet provocation; second, because he knew the proud Turks would be upset with the appearance of being "traded off in order to appease an enemy";[116] and third, because acceptance of a missile trade would lend credence to charges that the United States all along had been applying a double standard. Kennedy told his Ex Comm advisers that Khrushchev's offer caused "embarrassment," for most people would think it "a very fair trade." Indeed, Moscow had played "a very good card."[117] Some of Kennedy's advisers had explored the issue days before Khrushchev's second letter. Stevenson had recommended a horse trade, and Ambassador W. Averell Harriman counseled that America's "ring of bases" around the Soviet Union had proven "counter-productive." The way out of the crisis, Harriman said, was to let Khrushchev save face through an agreement to withdraw the Jupiters. Such a bargain would also permit Khrushchev to gain politically on his tough-minded military and "swing" toward improved relations with the United States.[118]

This discussion raises another question: What if the Soviets and Cubans had *announced* in the summer of 1962 that they were deploying a limited number of missiles—the same number as Americans had stationed in Turkey (and Italy)? Would the United States have been able to compel reversal of a publicly announced decision and prevent emplacement without having to abandon the Jupiters in Turkey in a negotiated deal? Some Ex Comm advisers later suggested that, in such a case, Washington might not even have sought to force withdrawal of the SS-4s from Cuba.[119] Many people abroad, including some European allies, would have asked if the USSR had any less right than the United States to practice deterrence. Moscow no doubt calculated differently—that Washington would attempt to halt shipments of missiles—and thus tried to sneak them in.

In the afternoon of the 27th more bad news rocked the White House. An American U-2 plane overflew the eastern part of the Soviet Union, probably because equipment malfunctioned. Soviet fighters scrambled to intercept it, and American jets from Alaska took flight to rescue the errant aircraft. Although the spy plane flew home without having sparked a dog fight, Moscow might have read the incident as provocative. Worse still, a U-2 was shot down over Cuba by a surface-to-air missile (SAM). *Cubans,* after having fought Soviet soldiers for control of the SAM sites, may have brought down the U-2.[120] American decisionmakers assumed at the time that the Soviets manned the SAM batteries; thus the shoot-down constituted a dangerous escalation. A distressed McNamara now thought "invasion had become almost inevitable."[121] But Kennedy hesitated to retaliate, surely scared about taking a step in the direction of nuclear war. Upon brother Robert's advice, the President decided to ignore Khrushchev's second letter and answer the first. And he dispatched the Attorney General to deliver an ultimatum to Soviet Ambassador Anatoly Dobrynin: start pulling out the missiles within forty-eight hours or "we would remove them."[122] After Dobrynin asked about the Jupiters in Turkey, Robert Kennedy presented an important American concession: they would be dismantled if the problem in Cuba were resolved. As the President had said in an Ex Comm meeting, "we can't very well invade Cuba with all its toil . . . when we could have gotten them out by making a deal on the same missiles in Turkey."[123] But, should the Soviets leak word of a "deal," Robert Kennedy told the Soviet ambassador, the United States would disavow the offer.[124] Just in case this unusual style of diplomacy failed, the President ordered the calling up of Air Force reservists. In the last Ex Comm meeting on the 27th, McNamara reminded his colleagues that the United States had to have two contingencies ready if a diplomatic settlement could not be reached: a response to expected Soviet action in Europe and a government to take power in Cuba after an American invasion. Someone remarked: "Suppose we make Bobby mayor of Havana."[125]

On October 28, faced with an ultimatum, a concession, and the possibility that the Cubans would shoot down another U-2 and precipitate a Soviet-American conflagration, Khrushchev retreated. An agreement, although not written, was struck: the Soviet Union agreed to dismantle the MRBMs under United Nations supervision and the United States pledged not to invade Cuba. "Everyone knew who were hawks and who were doves," Bundy told Ex Comm that morning, but "today was the doves' day."[126] A wary President cautioned his gleeful advisers that "this is not a time for gloating," for problems remained: implementing supervision, pressing the Soviets to remove their IL-28 bombers from the island too, and watching for Soviet mischief elsewhere.[127] But the crisis had passed—just when the nuclear giants seemed at the brink. Although an embittered Castro thwarted a United Nations inspection system, American reconnaisance planes monitored the departure of the SS-4s. The IL-28 bombers were also crated and shipped back to the Soviet Union.[128] In April 1963 the Jupiter missiles came down in Turkey. Castro remained skeptical of the no-invasion pledge. As he once remarked to U Thant, it was difficult for Cubans to believe a simple American "promise not to commit a crime."[129]

John F. Kennedy's handling of the Cuban missile crisis has received high grades as a success story and model for crisis management. But it was a near miss. "We were in luck," Ambassador John Kenneth Galbraith ruminated, "but success in a lottery is no argument for lotteries."[130] Many close calls threatened to send the crisis to greater levels of danger. Besides the two U-2 incidents, there was the serious possibility that a "crackpot" exile group would attempt to assassinate Castro or raid the island.[131] As well, Operation Mongoose sabotage teams were inside Cuba during the crisis and could not be reached by their CIA handlers. What if this "half-assed operation," Robert Kennedy worried, ignited trouble?[132] One of these teams actually did blow up a Cuban factory on November 8.[133] To cite another mishap: not until October 27 did Administration officials think to inform the Soviets that the quarantine line was an arc measured at 500 nautical miles from Cape Maisi, Cuba.[134] What if a Soviet captain inadvertently piloted his ship into the blockade zone? And, when the commander of the Strategic Air Command issued DEFCON 2 alert instructions, he did so in the clear, instead of in code, because he wanted to impress the Soviets.[135] Alerts serve to prepare American forces for war, but they also carry the danger of escalation, because movement to a high category might be read by an adversary as American planning for a first strike. Under such circumstances, the adversary might be tempted to strike first. Finally, the Navy's anti-submarine warfare activities carried the potential of escalating the crisis. Soviet submarines prowled near the quarantine line, and, following standing orders, Navy ships forced several of them to surface. In one case, a Navy commander exercised the high-risk option of dropping a depth charge on a Soviet submarine.[136] As in so many of these examples, decisionmakers in Washington actually lost some control of the crisis to personnel at the operational level.

Ex Comm members represented considerable intellectual talent and experience, and the policy they urged upon the President ultimately forced the Soviets to back down. But a mythology of grandeur, illusion of control, and embellishment of performance have obscured the history of the committee. The group never functioned independently of the President. In an example of "promotional leadership," Kennedy picked his advisers, directed them to drive the missiles out, and used his brother as a "policeman" at meetings.[137] Ex Comm debated alternatives under "intense strain," often in a "state of anxiety and emotional exhaustion."[138] Apparently two advisers suffered such stress that they became passive and unable to perform their responsibilities.[139] An assistant to Adlai Stevenson recalled that he had had to become an Ex Comm "back-up" for the ambassador because, "while he could speak clearly, his memory wasn't very clear. . . ." Asked if failing health produced this condition, Vice Admiral Charles Wellborn answered that the "emotional state and nervous tension that was involved in it [missile crisis] had this effect." Stevenson was feeling "pretty frightened."[140] So apparently was Dean Rusk. Robert Kennedy remembered that the Secretary of State "frequently could not attend our meetings," because "he had a virtually complete breakdown mentally and physically."[141] We cannot determine how stress affected the advice Ex Comm gave Kennedy, but at least we know that the crisis managers struggled against time, sleep, exhaustion, and themselves, and they did not always think clearheadedly at a time when the stakes were very high. Had Stevenson and Rusk, both of whom recommended diplomacy and compromise, been steadier, the option of negotiations *at the start* might have received a better hearing and the world might have been spared the grueling confrontation.

Contemporaries and scholars have debated Kennedy's shunning of formal, private negotiations and traditional, diplomatic channels and his opting instead for a public showdown through a surprise television speech. It does not appear that he acted this way because he thought the Soviets would protract talks until the missiles had become fully operational—even before his television address he knew that many of the missiles were ready to fire, and Ex Comm worked under the assumption that the SS-4s were armed with nuclear warheads.[142] Nor did Kennedy initially stiff-arm negotiations in order to score a foreign policy victory just before the November congressional elections. Politics does not explain his decisions; indeed, the most popular political position most likely would have been an air strike and invasion to rid the island of both the missiles and Castro.[143] Did Kennedy initially reject diplomacy because the Soviet missiles intolerably altered the strategic balance? Kennedy seems to have leaned toward McNamara's argument that the missiles in Cuba did not make a difference, given the fact that the Soviets already possessed enough capability to inflict unacceptable damage on some American cities.

President Kennedy eschewed diplomatic talks before October 22 because his strong Cold War views, drawing of lessons from the past, and personal hostility toward Castro's Cuba recommended confrontation. His conspicuous style of boldness, toughness, and craving for victory also influenced him, and he resented that Khrushchev had tried to trick him by stating that no offensive weapons would be placed in Cuba and then clandestinely sending them. Kennedy had warned Moscow not to station such weapons on the island; if he did not force the Soviets to back down, he worried, his personal credibility would have been undermined. And, even if the missiles did not markedly change the strategic balance, the new missiles in Cuba gave the appearance of doing so. One Ex Comm member remarked that the question is "psychological," and Kennedy agreed that the matter was as much "political" as "military."[144] Kennedy acted so boldly, too, because the Soviet missile deployment challenged the Monroe Doctrine and United States hegemony in Latin America. Finally, with other tests in Berlin and Southeast Asia looming, the United States believed it had to make emphatic its determination to stand firm in the Cold War. Remember, Rusk has said, "aggression feeds upon success."[145]

President Kennedy helped precipitate the missile crisis by harassing Cuba through his multi-track program. Then he reacted to the crisis by suspending diplomacy in favor of public confrontation. In the end, he frightened himself. In order to postpone doomsday, or at least to prevent a high-casualty invasion of Cuba, he moderated the American response and compromised. Khrushchev withdrew his mistake, while gaining what Ambassador Llewellyn Thompson thought was the "important thing" for the Soviet leader: being able to say, "I saved Cuba. I stopped an invasion."[146]

Kennedy may have missed an opportunity to negotiate a more comprehensive settlement. He and Ex Comm gave little attention to a proposal that Brazil had offered in the United Nations to denuclearize Latin America. This proposal also sought to guarantee the territorial integrity of each nation in the region. Harriman recommended that the United States accept the Brazilian plan, but enlarge it: the United States and the Soviet Union would agree not to place nuclear weapons in any nation in the world other than in nuclear powers. Thus Great Britain could hold American missiles, but Turkey and Italy could not. Nor could Soviet missiles be deployed in Cuba or Eastern Europe. Looking beyond the crisis, Harriman presented his scheme "as a first and important step towards disarmament," but Kennedy officials only briefly discussed the question of denuclearization.[147] Perhaps there could have been another aspect of a far-reaching agreement: the United States would turn Guantánamo over to Cuba in exchange for a Cuban pledge to end the Soviets' military presence on the island. In short, under this provisions, both American and Soviet militaries would leave Cuba, Latin America would become off-limits to nuclear weapons, Cuba's territorial integrity would be guaranteed, and Moscow and Washington would make a modest nod toward arms control.[148] Would the Cubans have accepted such a deal? Given his extreme anger with Moscow after the Soviets disengaged the missiles, Castro may well have grasped an opportunity to begin a process toward improved relations with Washington.[149] Such a bargain, of course, would have required Cuban-American discussions. Yet Kennedy never seemed open to such talks. Why? Because they would have legitimized the Castro-Communist government and signified a Cold War defeat.

In the end, Castro remained in power, the Soviets continued to garrison troops on the island and subsidize the Cuban economy, the United States persisted in its campaign of harassment, and new Soviet-American contests over Cuba erupted (1970 and 1979). The Soviets, exposed as nuclear inferiors, vowed to catch up in the arms race. At the same time, perhaps the "jagged edges" of Kennedy's Cold Warriorism were smoothed.[150] In the aftermath of the missile crisis, Moscow and Washington installed a teletype "hot line" to facilitate communication. The nuclear war scare during the missile crisis also nudged the superpowers to conclude the longstanding talks on a test ban treaty. Negotiated by Harriman in Moscow, the Limited Test Ban Treaty, signed on July 25, 1963, was limited, not comprehensive (it banned only tests in the atmosphere, outer space, and beneath the surface of the oceans). Although some analysts have trumpeted the treaty as a major accomplishment because it started the superpowers on a path toward arms control, the agreement did not prevent a plethora of underground nuclear detonations or slow the cascading arms race. It nonetheless stands as one of just a few successes in the diplomatic record of the Kennedy Administration.[151]

After the missile crisis, Cubans complained, Kennedy played a "double game." The President showed some interest in accommodation at the same time that he reinvigorated anti-Cuban programs.[152] The Administration created a new State Department office, the Coordinator of Cuban Affairs, and put more economic pressure on the island, including an unsuccessful attempt to block a United Nations-funded crop diversification project.[153] Washington intended by early 1963 to "tighten the noose" around Cuba.[154]

Operation Mongoose had been put on hold during the October crisis, but raids by exiles, some of them no doubt perpetrated with CIA collaboration, and most of them monitored but not stopped by American authorities, remained a menace.[155] In March 1963, after an exile "action group" attacked a Soviet ship in Cuban waters, Kennedy speculated that such freelance raids no longer served a "useful purpose." They seemed to strengthen the "Russian position in Cuba and the Communist control of Cuba and justify repressive measures within Cuba. . . ."[156] He knew too that some Cuban exiles had developed links with right-wing political groups in the United States—in essence the exiles had also become a threat to his Administration.[157] The President ordered restrictions on unauthorized exile activities, because they had failed to deliver "any real blow at Castro."[158] Republicans and Cuban exile leaders denounced the decision.[159] Raiding parties still managed to slip out of the Florida Keys to sabotage and kill in Cuba, and the Administration itself, to mollify the more than 500 anti-Castro groups, may have "backed away" from enforcing its own restrictions.[160]

After the missile crisis, Castro had sought better relations with Washington, and he made gestures toward détente. He sent home thousands of Soviet military personnel and released some political prisoners, including a few Americans. He remarked in an April 1963 interview with ABC Television's Lisa Howard that the prisoner release could mark a beginning toward rapprochement.[161] But then the mercurial *Jefe Máximo* departed for a four-week trip to the Soviet Union, where he patched up relations with Khrushchev and won promises of more foreign aid.[162] Washington stirred against Moscow's "grandiose" reception of Castro, the latter's "vehemence" in denouncing the United States, his "tone of defiance rather than conciliation," and the refurbished Soviet-Cuban alliance.[163] Soon Robert Kennedy asked the CIA to "develop a list of possible actions which might be undertaken against Cuba."[164] In mid-June the NSC approved a new sabotage program. The CIA quickly cranked up new dirty tricks and revitalized its assassination option by making contact with a traitorous Cuban official, Rolando Cubela Secades. Code-named AM/LASH, he plotted with the CIA to kill Fidel Castro. In Florida, American officials intercepted and arrested saboteurs heading for Cuba, but they seldom prosecuted and usually released them. Alpha 66 and Commando L raiders hit oil facilities, sugar mills, and industrial plants.[165]

In the fall of 1963 Cuba continued to seek an accommodation. Through contact with a member of Stevenson's United Nations staff, William Attwood, the Cuban government signaled once again its interest in improving relations. The President authorized an eager Attwood to work up an agenda with the Cubans.[166] In late October, when Kennedy met with the French journalist Jean Daniel, the President spoke in both hard-line and conciliatory tones about Cuba. Aware that Daniel was journeying to Havana to interview Castro, Kennedy asked the reporter to return for another White House discussion. Castro later claimed that Daniel carried a "private message" from Kennedy, who asked about the prospects for a Cuban-American dialogue.[167] Yet, on November 18, Kennedy sounded less the conciliator and more the warrior. In a tough-minded speech, he reiterated the familiar charges against Castro's "small band of conspirators."[168]

The President, reported Bundy, sought to "encourage anti-Castro elements within Cuba to revolt" and to "indicate that we would not permit another Cuba in the hemisphere."[169]

In Havana, meanwhile, Daniel and Castro met. On November 22, while discussing chances for Cuban-American détente, the news of the assassination in Dallas arrived. "Es una mala noticia" ("This is bad news"), the stunned Cuban mumbled repeatedly.[170] What would become of his overture? he wondered. In Washington, the new Lyndon B. Johnson Administration decided in fact to put the "tenuous" and "marginal" contacts "on ice."[171] Castro also worried that he would be held personally responsible for Kennedy's death, because the alleged assassin Lee Harvey Oswald had professed to be pro-Castro (he may actually have been leading a covert life as an anti-Castro agitator). Some Americans did blame the Cuban regime. Several official investigations have concluded that Cuban officials played no part in the assassination, but conspiracy theories persist. One theory actually points an accusing finger at disgruntled anti-Castro Cuban exiles in the United States.[172]

At the time of his death, Kennedy's Cuba policy was moving in opposite directions—probing for talks but sustaining multi-track pressures. "How can you figure him out?" Castro had asked in late October 1963.[173] On the very day that Kennedy died, AM/LASH rendezvoused with CIA agents in Paris, where he received a ball-point pen rigged with a poisonous hyperdermic needle intended to produce Castro's instant death.[174] But AM/LASH was but one obstacle to improved Cuban-American relations. For Kennedy and Castro to have reached détente, each would have had to suppress his strong ideological biases. Would Castro have risked a cooling of his close relationship with the Soviet Union and Cuban Communists at a time when Washington still worked for his ouster, some Americans yelped constantly for a United States invasion, and the next presidential election might send a conservative Republican to the White House? Would Castro have been willing to sever his lifeline? Would Castro have abandoned his bonds with Latin American revolutionaries in order to win a lifting of American economic sanctions?

From the Kennedy 1960s to the Reagan 1980s United States policy has consistently demanded two Cuban concessions: an end to support for revolutions in the hemisphere and an end to the Soviet military presence on the island. Havana has just as consistently refused to budge on either point before seeing United States concessions: abolition of the economic embargo and American respect for Cuban sovereignty. As for Kennedy, could he have quieted the Cuban exile community, disciplined the CIA, and persuaded hard-line State Department officials? Would he have been willing to withstand the political backlash from his dealing with "Communist Cuba"? More important, did he want to improve relations with Cuba? Would he have shelved his intense, sometimes personal, three-year war against Cuba and disbanded the myriad spoiling operations? Would he ever have accepted the legitimacy of a radical revolution in the United States sphere of influence? It does not seem likely that either Kennedy, had he lived, or Castro could have overcome the roadblocks that they and their national interests had erected.

The Cuban-American confrontation was and is a question of the Cold War, domestic American politics, and personalities. But it has been primarily a question of faltering United States hegemony in the hemisphere. Kennedy struggled to preserve that hegemony. In the end, he failed—he did not achieve his well-defined and ardently pursued goals for Cuba. His Administration bequeathed to successors an impressive fixation both resistant to diplomatic opportunity and attractive to political demagoguery.

6

From Even-Handed to Empty-Handed: Seeking Order in the Middle East

DOUGLAS LITTLE

"Peace in the Middle East is not one step nearer reality today than it was 8 years ago," John F. Kennedy declared in August 1960. "Russia's position is more entrenched. The Arab states are more divided and restless." And United States relations with "all Middle Eastern nations" had deteriorated, "primarily because neither Israel nor the Arabs knew exactly what to expect from us." Now only a "presidential initiative for peace" could reverse these adverse trends, and only new leadership—"impartial but firm, deliberate but bold"—could make such an initiative work.[1]

Kennedy's sense of urgency about the Arab-Israeli conflict stemmed less from the electoral calculations of a cunning presidential contender than from the grave misgivings of an apprentice statesman who had monitored American interests in the Middle East for more than a decade. To be sure, JFK's well-publicized support for Israel's right to exist had won him many friends within the American Jewish community during the 1950s. Yet privately he also expressed concern about preserving Western access to Mideast oil, not so much for the United States itself, which was still largely self-sufficient, but for its European allies, who obtained three-quarters of their petroleum from the Moslem world. Moreover, as the focus of both the Cold War and the 1960 presidential campaign shifted from Europe to the Third World, the Democratic nominee insisted he would be more effective than his Republican rival in combating recent Soviet inroads among anti-Western radicals in Egypt and Iraq.

During his short time as President, Kennedy struggled to transform his campaign rhetoric into diplomatic reality. He launched what he himself termed an "even-handed" policy, balancing special concern for Israeli security with greater toleration of Arab nationalism. While Kennedy worked to strengthen the bonds between the United States and Israel, he also sought to improve relations with Egypt's Gamel Abdul Nasser, a leading Third World neutralist who had received nearly $600 million in Soviet military aid since 1955. By the summer of 1962, JFK seemed on the verge of achieving a comprehensive Middle East settlement that would end Arab-Israeli bloodshed, shore up wobbly Western interests, and isolate the Kremlin from a volatile region that contained most of the world's oil.

Yet the President's even-handed solution to the Mideast puzzle proved difficult to sustain because he was unable to enlist the support of several key players. In particular, both Jordan's King Hussein and Saudi Arabia's Crown Prince Faisal worried that closer United States ties with Egypt meant that Washington now regarded Nasserism as "the wave of the future" which would sweep away their own more traditional regimes. Although Kennedy sought to allay these fears by reaffirming American friendship for Arab conservatives, his Middle Eastern policies began to unravel in late 1962 after a palace revolt in remote Yemen evolved into a proxy war pitting Nasser's United Arab Republic (U.A.R.) against Saudi Arabia and Jordan. Increasingly apprehensive that an Egyptian victory in Yemen might jeopardize American access to Saudi oil or, even worse, dethrone King Hussein and encircle Israel with aggressively hostile Arab states, JFK distanced himself from Nasser during 1963 and moved closer to Riyadh and Tel Aviv. By the time Kennedy left for Dallas, then, Washington was on a collision course with radical Arab nationalism that would culminate in the 1967 Six Day War.

JFK's views on the Middle East had taken shape long before he entered the White House. Sharing neither his father Joseph's affinity for appeasement during the 1930s nor his thinly veiled anti-Semitism, young Jack Kennedy became an early advocate of a Jewish national home in Palestine, that "unhappy land under alien rule" he had first visited in 1939.[2] Shortly after entering Congress in 1947, JFK publicly endorsed the creation of "a strong and secure Jewish Palestine," and he welcomed President Harry Truman's decision to recognize Israel a year later.[3] A return visit to Tel Aviv in 1951 persuaded Kennedy that "Israel is the bright light now shining in the Middle East," and after his election to the Senate he became a leading proponent of greater United States support for the Zionist experiment, which he likened to the opening of the American frontier a century earlier.⁴ "It is time," Senator Kennedy declared in late 1956, "that all the nations of the world, in the Middle East and elsewhere, realized that Israel is here to stay."⁵

Yet by the late 1950s, Kennedy also believed that President Dwight Eisenhower had badly mishandled another new Mideast reality, the wave of Arab nationalism unharnessed by the decline of British influence and swelled by the establishment of a Jewish state in Palestine. The Eisenhower Administration had initially distanced itself from both Britain and Israel in an attempt to lure Egypt and like-minded Arab states into the Western camp. But Nasser's decision to purchase arms from Czechoslovakia in 1955 and Washington's cancellation of its offer to help Cairo finance the Aswan Dam a year later dashed any hopes for better American relations with Egypt and triggered the November 1956 Suez Crisis. Although the White House forced British, French, and Israeli troops to withdraw from Egyptian territory in short order, it also worked to isolate Nasser by securing congressional approval for military intervention to support his conservative Arab rivals such as Lebanon's Camille Chamoun and by authorizing the Central Intelligence Agency (CIA) to undertake covert action against his increasingly pro-Soviet friends in Syria.⁶

Kennedy realized Moscow was wooing left-wing regimes from Cairo to Damascus with economic aid and military hardware, but he refused to write the radical Arabs off as mere Soviet stooges. Instead, he argued that the United States could, by emphasizing its own anti-colonial heritage and by expanding its developmental assistance programs, reverse the Kremlin's recent gains in the Arab world. As early as the Suez Crisis, Kennedy had condemned Anglo-French military intervention, insisted that Israel must return the Sinai to Egypt, and portrayed Nasser's seizure of the canal as merely the latest symptom of "the revolt in the Middle East against Western colonialism."⁷ Nine months later he made headlines by calling for Algerian independence and criticizing the Eisenhower Administration for its "head-in-the-sand" approach to Arab nationalism.⁸ Not surprisingly, by July 1958 JFK was privately suggesting that American interests in the Middle East would be better served by "doing business with Nasser" than by sending the marines into Lebanon.⁹ In February 1959 he bluntly told a group of American Zionists that "it is sheer delusion to underestimate the cutting force of Arab nationalism" and that, like it or not, the Palestinian refugee problem "is a matter on which the books cannot be closed."[10]

As his bid for the presidency accelerated later that year, Kennedy grew more strident in his criticism of Eisenhower's policies and more specific about his own proposals. Both the Baghdad Pact and the Eisenhower Doctrine had failed, he charged in November, because American officials had dealt with the Middle East for too long "almost exclusively in the context of the East-West struggle" and had "underestimated the force of nationalism" in the Arab world. "The mistaken attitudes of the past," he concluded, "must all be junked—for the sake of the Arabs and for our own sake as well."[11] JFK spelled out just how he proposed to remedy those mistakes when he addressed the Zionists of America in August 1960. "The Middle East needs water, not war; tractors, not tanks; bread, not bombs." The next President must move quickly to avert an Arab-Israeli arms race by encouraging "every experiment in cooperation, from the development of a river, to the reconsideration of the Arab refugee problem, to the crowning mercy of the final reconciliation that can be brought only by a true peace settlement." If elected, Kennedy promised "to waste no time in taking this initiative."[12]

The new President's commitment to an even-handed approach toward the Middle East was clear from the way he organized his Administration. Well aware that the Jewish vote had been critical to his narrow victory over Richard Nixon, Kennedy included in his cabinet two staunch supporters of Israel, Abraham Ribicoff and Arthur Goldberg, both of whom advocated closer ties between Washington and Tel Aviv.[13] Kennedy also named Myer Feldman, a top campaign aide and key liaison with the Jewish community, as special counsel and informal White House "assistant desk officer" for Israel.[14] In addition, JFK relied on Vice President Lyndon Johnson, a longtime friend of the Jewish state, to maintain contacts with like-minded senatorial colleagues such as Hubert Humphrey and with lobbying groups such as the American Israel Public Affairs Committee (AIPAC).[15]

Yet this pro-Israeli influence was counterbalanced by the more pro-Arab outlook of Kennedy's State Department and National Security Council staff. Secretary of State Dean Rusk, whose own commitment to a "balanced approach to Near Eastern problems" dated from his efforts in 1948 to resolve the Palestine imbroglio short of war, surrounded himself with kindred spirits such as Assistant Secretary

Phillips Talbot, a University of Chicago Orientalist and longtime advocate of better United States relations with Egypt, India, and other non-aligned nations.[16] John Badeau, the former head of the American University in Cairo, became the new ambassador to Egypt. He too believed closer ties with Arab radicals like Nasser would open the door to a lasting Middle East peace.[17] Although national security adviser McGeorge Bundy had little Middle Eastern expertise, Robert Komer, one of his top aides, had spent nearly a decade at the CIA's Office of National Estimates, where he had developed views of the Arab world which paralleled those of Rusk, Talbot, and Badeau.[18]

Before the first spring was out, the Kennedy Administration had taken important steps to signal its new approach to Arab nationalism. The most immediate problem JFK faced in the Moslem world was in Algeria, where Front de Liberation Nationale (FLN) guerrillas waged a savage war for independence from France with the Kremlin's blessing. Convinced that Paris was playing into Moscow's hands by refusing to dismantle its North African empire, Kennedy implored French officials as early as March 1961 to "free some of the anti-communist leaders of the FLN" imprisoned in France and urged President Charles de Gaulle repeatedly during the following year to withdraw from Algeria gracefully. And once the French recognized Algerian independence in July 1962, JFK "worked hard" to befriend Ahmed Ben Bella, the new regime's president, who responded by making the White House the initial stop on his first major overseas trip later that same year.[19]

Kennedy was well aware, however, that the key to better long-term relations with the Arab world lay not in Algiers but rather in Cairo, where personal diplomacy and economic assistance might persuade Nasser to concentrate on fostering Egyptian development rather than on stirring up trouble for his neighbors or flirting with Moscow. Nasser's roller-coaster relationship with the Soviets, who had agreed to finance the Aswan Dam and to replenish his arsenal in the wake of the Suez Crisis, had begun to sour as early as 1959, after he charged the Egyptian communist party with plotting a coup and forced it underground. By the early 1960s, Soviet premier Nikita Khrushchev was less interested in the Middle East than in Latin America and Africa, while Nasser was hinting that Cairo would welcome warmer relations with Washington.[20] To be sure, Nasser's bitter denunciation of Kennedy's intervention in the Congo and Cuba during the spring of 1961 suggested that achieving such a thaw would be no easy task. The new President, however, discounted these rhetorical barbs and instead assured Nasser privately of his own desire for closer ties with the U.A.R. "Look, we intend to pursue a reasonably balanced policy in the area," JFK told Komer in May. "We want to work with the Middle East countries so they control their own destinies."[21]

Despite his neutralist bluster, Nasser seemed as eager for a rapprochement as Kennedy. U.A.R. ambassador Mustapha Kamel, for example, made several visits to the State Department and the White House that spring, and each time he "suggested putting the Arab-Israeli issue 'in the refrigerator.' " After Ambassador Badeau arrived in Cairo in July, moreover, Nasser himself admitted there was no point in "starting every conversation with an argument about Palestine" and agreed to "put this in the icebox and devote ourselves to points of mutual interest."[22] By summer's end, Radio Cairo had toned down its anti-Israeli and anti-imperialist broadcasts, while Egyptian and American policymakers had begun to discuss a variety of bilateral issues ranging from nuclear technology to surplus wheat. Pleased by these favorable trends, Nasser assured Kennedy in August that "reaching an Arab-American understanding is an important aim of ours, worthy of all efforts" and vowed "never [to] despair in our attempts to reach it."[23]

Syria's secession from the U.A.R. in September amidst rumors of CIA involvement nearly sidetracked such an understanding. Badeau, however, assured Nasser that his fears of "US exploitation of the UAR breakup" were unfounded. More to the point, Kennedy delayed recognition of the new regime in Damascus long enough to demonstrate American goodwill and to encourage Nasser to "turn a little inward" and "get him more interested in Egyptian development and less interested in fomenting revolutions."[24] JFK seemed to have succeeded on both counts, for by early autumn the State Department reported that Nasser had begun "the rebuilding of his political stature with a thorough housecleaning and concentration on reform in Egypt." It was "highly unlikely," then, that he would launch "a major drive at his enemies in the other Arab countries" or that he would "embark on a course that would lead to large-scale hostilities" with Israel.[25]

Surplus wheat available under the auspices of Public Law 480 (PL-480) seemed the most likely American instrument to steer Nasser's energies inward. The U.A.R. had been receiving small amounts of food aid on an annual basis since the late 1950s, but Egyptian leaders believed a multi-year PL-480 agreement would make economic planning easier. Such key officials as State Department policy planning chief Walt W. Rostow were sympathetic, not least because they hoped American wheat might dampen Nasser's appetite for more radical agrarian reforms, including collectivization. Rostow met several times with Ambassador Kamel in late 1961 and reached a tentative agreement on a wide-ranging aid program whose first step would be a three-year $500 million PL-480 package.[26]

Other Americans, however, questioned this proposal. William Gaud, the Middle Eastern coordinator for the Agency for International Development (AID), for example, called long-term economic assistance for Egypt "dead wrong" and warned that Nasser's recent musings about "Arab Socialism" might herald a rapprochement with Khrushchev.[27] The State Department, however, insisted on the multi-year approach. "Our objective," Rusk told Kennedy in January 1962, "would be to encourage orderly economic development in the United Arab Republic with beneficial consequences for Near East area stability, and to provide significant Western alternatives to UAR economic, and possible political, dependence on the Soviet bloc."[28]

Before making a final decision, however, JFK sent a pair of personal emissaries to Egypt. Chester Bowles, Kennedy's newly appointed ambassador-at-large to the Third World, visited Cairo in late February and came away convinced that "the leaders of the UAR are pragmatists searching for techniques that will enable them to expand their economy rapidly and to maintain their political grip." Although Bowles did not believe surplus wheat alone would guarantee Egyptian recognition of Israel's right to exist or prevent Cairo from patching up its quarrel with Moscow, he did cable JFK that "if Nasser can gradually be led to forsake the microphone for the bulldozer, he may assume a key role in bringing the Middle East peacefully into our modern world."[29] Edward S. Mason, a Harvard economist who visited Egypt a month later, confirmed that Nasser seemed truly committed to improving the lot of the landless poor and that the proposed PL-480 assistance would probably prevent more radical solutions. "The spread of Nasser's influence in the Middle East is certainly not the best of all possible worlds so far as the US is concerned," Mason admitted, "but it is presumably better than the spread of communism."[30]

JFK apparently agreed, for on June 30 he signed a three-year PL-480 agreement. This marked the high point of American relations with Egypt during the New Frontier. "Nasser appreciated Kennedy's efforts to treat him as an equal and as an important world leader," Ambassador Kamel recalled years later, "just as he resented Eisenhower and Dulles's efforts to treat him like some sort of pawn in the big chess game with the Russians."[31] And JFK was very gratified when Nasser reaffirmed his earlier promise "to keep our differences within limits" by placing the potentially disruptive Arab-Israeli dispute "in the icebox."[32] Tel Aviv worried, of course, that Cairo's kitchen contained other, more dangerous appliances, but Washington remained convinced that "encourag[ing] Nasser [to] devote major energy towards solving Egypt's internal problems . . . would inevitably reduce pressure on Israel."[33]

The Kennedy Administration, however, also took much more direct steps to relieve Israel's anxieties. Israeli Prime Minister David Ben Gurion had made no secret of his desire for American weapons to offset Soviet arms sales to Nasser during the late 1950s, but he had made little headway in Eisenhower's Washington. Hopeful that JFK would prove more receptive than his predecessor, Ben Gurion arranged a meeting at New York City's Waldorf Astoria on May 30, 1961. Kennedy began by stressing "the tragic plight of the Arab refugees," and Ben Gurion "reluctantly agreed" to cooperate with the United Nations in finding a solution. The conversation then turned to military affairs, with Ben Gurion specifically asking for American HAWK surface-to-air missiles to remedy "Israel's desperate deficiency in advanced anti-aircraft weapons." According to Israeli Chargé d'Affaires Mordechai Gazit, the President "indicated some sympathy for the HAWK request and said he would look into it."[34]

The Kennedy Administration spent over a year reviewing Israel's request, but signs along the way foreshadowed a favorable outcome. In the fall of 1961, for example, Washington sold Tel Aviv $18 million worth of early warning equipment "to reduce Israel's vulnerability to surprise attack" and shortly thereafter licensed the sale of additional war materiel ranging from transport planes to spare parts.[35] And when Shimon Peres, the Israeli deputy minister of defense, visited Washington in May 1962 to renew the HAWK request, Pentagon and White House officials agreed the Israelis had "a valid military basis for their concern and for their selection of the Hawk as an item of key importance in their military posture."[36] Yet, although Kennedy himself pledged "full support" for "Israel's integrity and independence" in a private letter to Ben Gurion a month later, Washington delayed action on Peres's request and tried to link the HAWK sale to a broader Middle East settlement.[37]

Having won Ben Gurion's grudging pledge at the Waldorf to cooperate fully with the United Nations Palestine Conciliation Commission, Kennedy had quietly arranged for Secretary General Dag Hammarskjold to ask Dr. Joseph Johnson, the head of the Carnegie Endowment, to develop a refugee resettlement plan. Sporadic clashes between Palestinian guerrillas and Israeli troops during late 1961 and a series of bloody border skirmishes with Syria early in the new year left few American officials optimistic about the chances for success, but after months of shuttle diplomacy Johnson unveiled a tentative plan in July 1962. All Palestinians would be permitted to choose freely between returning to Israel or resettling in neighboring Arab states and would be compensated for lost properties and relocation costs.[38] Johnson became convinced, as did top State Department officials, that, if sufficient funds were made available, fewer than 10 percent of the 1.2 million refugees would elect to settle in Israel. Ben Gurion and Foreign Minister Golda Meir, however, disagreed, arguing that the return of even 100,000 Palestinians would create a "fifth column" in Israel and that they could accept no more than 20,000 refugees, a figure Arab leaders such as Jordan's King Hussein found unacceptably low.[39]

With Johnson's mission at a standstill and with the level of violence along the Israeli-Syrian frontier escalating ominously, the Kennedy Administration attempted to arrange a "quid pro quo" with Tel Aviv. Desultory talks with Israeli diplomats in New York and Washington in June and July had left little doubt at the State Department that the only way to break the impasse on the Palestinian question was to link it to military aid for Israel.[40] "The deal would have to be . . . Hawks, subject to progress on an Israeli-UAR arms limitation," Talbot wrote Feldman on August 9, "in exchange for . . . Ben Gurion's pledge of cooperation in Johnson's plan."[41] Feldman agreed. "The only chance the plan has for success," he wrote Kennedy the next day, "is to accompany it with notice to Ben Gurion that we will guarantee the security of Israel and provide Hawk missiles."[42] That there were desirable domestic side effects made the arms deal all the more attractive. The HAWK decision should be made not merely with the upcoming fall congressional campaign in mind, Robert Komer pointed out on August 13, but also with an eye on the "optimum political impact before the 1964 US elections."[43]

When JFK met with his top Middle Eastern advisers the next morning, the agenda listed two interrelated questions. "Should we back the Johnson Plan?" And, "should we sell HAWKs to Israel?" Several participants recalled that Kennedy questioned whether either the Arabs or the Israelis would accept the Johnson Plan. Nevertheless, with Nasser apparently still willing to keep the Palestinian dispute on ice in exchange for American economic aid, the HAWKs just might induce the Israelis to be more forthcoming on the refugee issue. No one present remembers the upcoming elections specifically entering into JFK's calculus, but it was the sort of domestic political bonus that could not have escaped his notice. In any case, the President decided to go forward with both the Johnson Plan and the HAWK sale and secretly sent Feldman to Israel and the State Department's Robert Strong to Egypt to break the news.[44]

Four days later Feldman arrived in Tel Aviv with a letter from Kennedy which tactfully linked "Israel's requests for a security guarantee and for the Hawk missile . . . to the mission of Dr. Joseph E. Johnson."[45] Feldman assured Ben Gurion and Meir on August 19 that the missiles were theirs for the asking, but he also made it clear that the White House was eager for Israeli cooperation on the refugee question. Israeli leaders were delighted to have the HAWKs, but were unwilling to endorse the Johnson Plan without explicit assurances from Nasser that the U.A.R. and other Arab states would absorb most of the refugees. The State Department advised Feldman that "these tentative aspects of Israel's acquiescence" were "inconsistent with the Johnson Plan and unacceptable to us," but after a marathon session on August 21 he reported the Israelis remained "skeptical about acceptance of plan by Arabs and insistent upon some evidence of their good faith." To be sure, Meir had hinted that Tel Aviv might be willing at least "to let the plan begin," provided "there was no objection" from Cairo, but Feldman was not optimistic and recommended that "we not commit ourselves to support of the Johnson Plan until we get Arab reaction."[46]

The State Department, however, regarded Israel's reservations as "essentially diversionary" and decided to force the issue by seeking Nasser's approval. "Although Israel's leaders are understandably hesitant to state carte blanche acquiescence in implementation of Johnson Plan," Rusk advised Strong and Badeau in Cairo on August 22, "they have apparently not repeat not found in plan sufficient hazards to Israel to justify its immediate rejection." He instructed the pair to inform Nasser about the impending HAWK sale, stressing its "purely defensive character," and to seek his support in resolving the refugee problem.[47] The Strong-Badeau meeting with the Egyptian leader two days later went better than anyone had anticipated. Grateful to have been notified of the HAWK sale in advance, Nasser expressed less concern about its impact on the Egyptian-Israeli military balance than about its likely "political repercussions" elsewhere in the Arab world. And as for the Johnson Plan, if the Egyptian leader declined to offer a blanket endorsement, neither did he raise any objections.[48] Kennedy was "surprised" by the "mild reaction" in Cairo, Feldman recalled long afterward, and "thought that his relationship to Nasser was pretty good."[49] Indeed, by early September JFK's even-handed policies seemed to have broken the Arab-Israeli impasse over the refugee dilemma and cleared the way for regional arms limitation talks as well.[50]

Before the month was out, however, these grandiose expectations lay in ruins. The first troubles surfaced in New York City, after Johnson unveiled his plan at the United Nations in mid-September. Despite the State Department's belief that Tel Aviv's objections were merely cosmetic, the Israeli delegation "raised absolute hell," charging that Johnson had approved over sixty changes to make the original plan more attractive to the Arabs. Years later Johnson acknowledged certain modifications regarding repatriation procedures, but he insisted the revised proposal "used language that I still think is very fair."[51] Israeli officials and American Jewish leaders could not have disagreed more. "The faster you disengage from this plan the better," Myer Feldman warned JFK from New York following a stormy September 20 meeting with Golda Meir. "Otherwise, . . . there will be a violent eruption both domestically and in our relations with Israel."[52] Meir personally dispelled any remaining doubts about Tel Aviv's position a week later when she bluntly informed first Rusk and then Ambassador to the United Nations Adlai Stevenson of "Israel's opposition to the Johnson Plan."[53]

To make matters worse, news of the impending sale of HAWK missiles to Israel leaked out in late September, touching off just the sort of angry negativism among Arab conservatives that Nasser had predicted a month earlier. The "strongest adverse reaction" came from Libya, where American diplomats feared that "the sale of weapons to Israel . . . could serve as catalyst to bring together vocal Libyan Arab nationalists" in an "anti-US" campaign that would "seriously undermine" Washington's friendship with King Idris.[54] Jordan's King Hussein was less vocal in his criticism, but he made no secret that he expected Kennedy to provide him with weapons comparable to the HAWKs in the near future.[55] And while public reaction in Riyadh was "relatively limited," high-ranking Saudi officials complained privately that the "US move represents departure from previous US arms policy and that it reflects strong US bias in favor of Israel."[56] Even in Lebanon, long the most pro-American of the Arab states, critics charged that the HAWK sale would tilt the regional military balance toward Israel and poison United States relations with the Moslem world.[57]

American diplomats in Amman and Riyadh warned that the protests would have been even louder had not the Jordanians and Saudis been preoccupied with ominous developments in Yemen, where Colonel Abdullah Sallal had overthrown young Imam Mohammed Al-Badr in a republican coup d'état on September 26. The coup came as no surprise in Washington, where Al-Badr was regarded as "a weakling" whose inability to defuse "reformist discontent" had produced "severe internal disturbances."[58] But Faisal and Hussein believed that Sallal's revolt foreshadowed similar fates for their own dynasties and secretly began to funnel aid to Al-Badr's royalist guerrillas in the highlands north of Sana'a, the Yemeni capital. Sallal, a self-styled Nasserite, responded by seeking aid from Egypt, which in early October dispatched the first units of what would soon become an expeditionary force of 70,000 troops in Yemen. Nasser's intervention only heightened Saudi and Jordanian fears and confirmed what the Kennedy Administration had suspected all along, that without political modernization and economic development, traditional regimes throughout the Moslem world would be engulfed by revolutionary upheavals.[59]

Indeed, the first Mideast crisis Kennedy had faced had come not in Egypt or Israel but in Iran, where bloody riots in May 1961 nearly toppled the Shah. Kennedy moved quickly, asking Robert Komer and the State Department's Armin Meyer to head up a special Iranian task force.[60] "The idea was that Iran's demise was about to take place," Meyer recalled years later, "that it was about to go down the drain, and we just had to take some dramatic drastic steps."[61] The task force recommended sweeping changes in Teheran, including extensive land reform, a thorough bureaucratic housecleaning, and the appointment of Ali Amini, a pro-American technocrat, as prime minister. According to Komer, Kennedy "warmly endorsed" these recommendations and "must have written the Shah a dozen times" offering United States help in "developing an internal consensus" and "modernizing the country."[62] During the next year and a half, Vice President Johnson and Ambassador Bowles each visited Iran at JFK's request, and both confirmed that political and socio-economic reforms were, in Bowles's words, "absolutely basic to the long-range stability of the country," a point the President himself took pains to make during a White House meeting with the Shah in April 1962. Before the year was out, Komer and other top aides could take pride that by combining "psychological massage" with $90 million in developmental aid, the Kennedy Administration had steered Iran toward "a white revolution instead of a red one."[63]

Iran provided only an early glimpse of Kennedy's broader strategy of using moderate reform to inoculate conservative regimes throughout the region against revolutionary change. In Libya, where the Pentagon had long maintained an important air base at Wheelus Field and where Occidental Petroleum had recently won an enormous oil concession, the Kennedy Administration pressed King Idris to establish the "sound political structure" necessary to ensure the "orderly development" of his country and warned that the fate of the Sanussi dynasty hinged on its own ability "to better the social and economic welfare of the Libyan people."[64] A thousand miles to the east in Jordan, the White House likewise engaged in what Ambassador William Macomber later called "a race against time" to persuade King Hussein to accept badly needed reforms before he was swept aside by a rising tide of Arab nationalism. Hussein proved more willing than Idris to cooperate, partly because of JFK's personal rapport with the "Brave Young King," but mainly because the United States wooed the Jordanians with an average of $50 million per year, five times the amount of economic aid received by Libya, in an effort "to make the odds as favorable as possible not only for their survival—but for their progress."[65]

The stakes were highest, however, in Saudi Arabia, where for eighteen months King Saud and Crown Prince Faisal had ignored repeated American calls for reform. Relations between Washington and Riyadh had cooled noticeably in early 1961, after Faisal refused to renew the Pentagon's lease on the Dhahran airbase and Kennedy froze American technical assistance to the House of Saud at a paltry $14 million per year.[66] The Yemeni revolution threatened to chill the relationship still further, for when Faisal arrived at the White House in October 1962 for a long-scheduled visit, he complained that the American rapprochement with Egypt was encouraging Nasser to step up his radical campaign against the Saudis and other traditional regimes in the Arab world. JFK denied that closer ties between Washington and Cairo explained Riyadh's woes and suggested that, if the House of Saud wished to escape Al-Badr's fate in Yemen, it must move "toward orderly transition from an autocratic monarchy to a more progressive government responsive to the country's social-economic needs."[67] Faisal apparently heeded this advice, for less than a month later he unveiled a ten-point reform plan to abolish slavery, lift the dynastic monopoly on government employment, and divert more oil revenues into economic development.[68]

Faisal's reforms would come to little, however, if Washington could not prevent the deepening crisis in Yemen from spilling across the Saudi frontier and undermining the royal government in Riyadh. As early as October 17, Rusk had sent the President a disengagement plan calling for recognition of Sallal's Yemen Arab Republic (Y.A.R.), the cessation of all Saudi assistance for Al-Badr's guerrillas, and the withdrawal of the Egyptian expeditionary force.[69] But such nagging problems in a remote corner of the Middle East paled before the grave superpower confrontation then unfolding in the Caribbean, and it would be mid-November before policymakers could turn their attention once again from Cuba to Yemen. By that time, vocal opposition to American recognition of the Y.A.R. had arisen not only from the beleaguered Saudis and Jordanians but also from the British, who blamed Nasser's meddling in Yemen for the growing unrest next door in their Aden protectorate.[70]

The Kennedy Administration nevertheless remained persuaded that speedy recognition of the Y.A.R. followed by Saudi and Egyptian withdrawal from their proxy war was the only way Washington could sustain its rapprochement with Cairo without poisoning its friendship with Riyadh. Nasser pledged his support for Kennedy's plan in late November, but Faisal and Hussein balked, as did British Prime Minister Harold Macmillan, who feared that "the Americans will risk paying the price (recognition) without effecting the purchase (Egyptian disengagement)."[71] The State Department and NSC staff, however, downplayed this mounting chorus of dissent and emphasized the potential gains among Arab nationalists and Third World neutralists. On December 19, 1962, Kennedy authorized recognition of the Y.A.R., explaining shortly afterward that "we must keep our ties to Nasser and other neutralists even if we do not like many things they do, because, if we lose them the balance of power could swing against us."[72]

The President discovered the costs of maintaining those ties in January 1963, when American relations with Saudi Arabia sank to a new low. Refusing to accept Washington's call for disengagement from Yemen, Faisal had instead stepped up his clandestine support for Al-Badr's guerrillas, prompting Nasser to launch retaliatory air raids against royalist base camps just inside Saudi Arabia. By February 1963, persistent rumors circulated that a Nasserite military coup was in the offing in Riyadh and that, even if the House of Saud survived, it might retaliate against Aramco, the American consortium which controlled the Dhahran oil fields.[73]

A worried JFK met with his Middle Eastern experts on February 25 to reassess his policy in Yemen. If the Saudis could be persuaded to disengage from the proxy war, the onus would be on the Egyptians to follow suit or risk alienating the United States. To this end, Kennedy agreed that, if Faisal promised to suspend all aid to the Yemeni royalists, the United States would station "a token air defense squadron with associated ground environment in western Saudi Arabia to deter UAR air operations."[74] Ellsworth Bunker, who had recently succeeded Bowles as Kennedy's Third World troubleshooter, persuaded Faisal to accept the proposal in mid-March. A month later eight F-100 fighter-bombers and an undetermined number of Green Berets arrived at Dhahran as part of Operation Hard Surface to train Saudi officers in aerial combat and counter-insurgency.[75]

Although Hard Surface stabilized relations with Riyadh, the operation drove Washington and Cairo farther apart. Bunker got Nasser to accept the disengagement plan in principle in early April, but he refused to withdraw his expeditionary force because Saudi covert aid continued to flow to Al-Badr, albeit at reduced levels. High over the Saudi-Yemeni frontier, then, Egyptian MIGs and American F-100s began a deadly game of cat and mouse that the White House feared "could escalate into a nice little Middle East conflict involving the United States directly."[76] And by month's end, American officials had good reason to worry that such a conflict would remain neither nice nor little for very long, because King Hussein, Nasser's other Arab rival, was locked in a deadly struggle with Palestinian radicals bent on establishing a Nasserite regime in Jordan. Were Hussein's foes to succeed, Israel would certainly seize the West Bank, and a general Mideast war would surely follow.

That Israel remained extremely sensitive about the "constant shadow of Nasser's ambitions" was obvious as early as December 1962, when Golda Meir met with Kennedy at Palm Beach, Florida. Tel Aviv had no choice but to reject the Johnson refugee plan, HAWKs or no HAWKs, Meir explained, because in recent months the U.A.R. had intervened in Yemen, stepped up its radical propaganda in Jordan, and added new Soviet TU-16 fighter-bombers to its arsenal. "We know that Israel faces enormous security problems," Kennedy replied, "but we do too." Dodging the refugee issue would only make matters worse. Likening Washington's "special relationship" with Tel Aviv to that with London, JFK said it was "quite clear that in case of an invasion the United States would come to the support of Israel," but that the Israelis must remember that "our relationship is a two-way street." Zeroing in on the ill-fated Johnson Plan, whose demise ensured that the refugee dispute would "run on and blow up," Kennedy finally managed to get Meir to agree that fresh efforts to resolve the Palestinian dilemma "were worth a try."[77]

Within weeks, however, unexpected developments in the Arab world pushed the Johnson Plan farther into the background. In January 1963 Palestinian refugees in Jordan rioted to protest Hussein's relatively moderate stance on Israel. A month later pro-Nasser officers seized power in Baghdad, and in early March Ba'athist radicals staged a coup in Damascus and called for a pan-Arab union of Egypt, Iraq, and Syria.[78] As Israeli fears of encirclement mounted, Shimon Peres returned to Washington seeking "augmentation of military hardware" and assurances that an Arab attack on Israel "would be met by immediate U.S. military intervention." The American rapprochement with Egypt had backfired, Peres told State Department officials on April 2, creating serious problems for "truer friends" such as Israel. "Here, Jordan is the key."[79] He spelled out just what he meant during a White House visit the next day. "Kennedy was interested to know what would be Israel's position in the event of 'unexpected developments' in Jordan which might put an end to Hussein's rule," Peres recalled in his memoirs. "I said that . . . Israel had already made it clear that she would not stand by idly." JFK confessed he too was "very worried about the future of Jordan" and promised to deliver the HAWKs as soon as possible, but he declined to issue a formal guarantee for the security of Israel because such action might prompt the Soviets to make similar pledges to their Arab friends and fuel a superpower confrontation in the Middle East.[80]

Two weeks later Egypt, Syria, and Iraq issued a joint communique calling for "the liberation of Palestine," while Jordan was rocked by a fresh round of pro-Nasser disturbances. The Arab-Israeli showdown Washington had long sought to avoid seemed imminent. In an effort to downplay the urgency of the crisis, Secretary Rusk reminded Israeli officials on April 25 that "centrifugal tendencies" among the Arabs themselves made an all-out assault on Israel unlikely. He also emphasized that "we have let it be known in Cairo that we are very much interested in the independence of Jordan."[81] The next day, however, JFK received a disturbing cable from Ben Gurion, who stressed that the "situation in Mideast assumes gravity without parallel" and implied that Israel was on the verge of launching a preemptive strike on the West Bank. "Hawk is appreciated," Ben Gurion said, "but GOI regrets that in light [of] new offensive weapons being prepared by Israel's neighbors, Hawk alone is not deterrent." Only a joint Soviet-American pledge to guarantee the "territorial integrity and security of all Mideast states" could avert hostilities.[82]

Kennedy held an emergency meeting with top officials from the State Department, the Pentagon, and his NSC staff on Saturday morning, April 27, to weigh his options. Having labored for two years to reduce Russian influence in the region, everyone agreed Ben Gurion's proposed Soviet-American security guarantee was out of the question. On the other hand, a unilateral U.S. pledge to defend Israel was certain to poison relations with the Arab world. Display of support for embattled King Hussein emerged as the most attractive option, for, if successful, it would forestall an Israeli attack on the West Bank and reassure conservatives in Amman and Riyadh without necessarily driving Nasser and the radicals toward the Kremlin. A few hours later JFK ordered the Sixth Fleet to steam into the eastern Mediterranean with a "military survey mission" on board "prepared to move to Jordan immediately upon the request of Ambassador Macomber."[83] Aided by this show of force, Hussein was able to reassert his authority in short order. But Macomber and other officials remained convinced that if the Jordanian crisis had taken a turn for the worse, Kennedy would not have hesitated to airlift the marines into Amman.[84]

Having allayed immediate Israeli concerns about Jordan by moving the Sixth Fleet, JFK soon faced renewed pressure from Israel and its American friends to issue a formal security guarantee. Kennedy wrote Ben Gurion on May 4 to reiterate what he had told Meir at Palm Beach about America's "special relationship" with Israel, while Myer Feldman privately assured AIPAC leaders the following afternoon that Washington would come to Tel Aviv's aid in the event of an "unprovoked attack on its territory."[85] When reporters asked about Feldman's remarks three days later, JFK replied that the United Nations must still be Israel's first line of defense, but that "in the event of aggression or preparation for aggression, whether direct or indirect," the United States would "adopt other courses of action on our own to prevent or put a stop to such aggression."[86]

American policymakers remained reluctant to spell out publicly the implications of Kennedy's remarks. "The reality is that the United States stands firmly beside Israel," Acting Secretary of State W. Averell Harriman told B'nai B'rith officials on May 8. "Israel knows this, the Arabs know it, and Nasser knows it." But "if we were to be more specific in our assurances to Israel, the Arabs might well go to the Soviets," something Washington believed "would vastly increase the dangers of the Middle East situation."[87] Yet the Kennedy Administration also realized that, even in the absence of a formal American guarantee for Israel, the Middle East stood at a dangerous crossroads. "The chief short term risk," Komer remarked in early May, "seemed to be a change in Jordan which might bring Nasser into a more threatening position." Even graver possibilities loomed as well, including the escalation of the bloody stalemate in Yemen into a full-scale Saudi-Egyptian war or, worst of all, a decision by Israel to combat U.A.R. encirclement by accelerating production of weapons-grade nuclear fuel at its Dimona reactor.[88]

Faced with such dire prospects, Washington undertook another effort to secure Cairo's support for a comprehensive Mideast settlement. As early as April 18, JFK had assured Nasser that the United States intended to continue its "fair-minded and even-handed" policy, provided Egypt reciprocated by helping reduce "the risks—and costs—inherent in the arms spiral in the Middle East."[89] A month later Kennedy approved a secret State Department plan designed to "allay Israel's concerns for its security" and to reaffirm "continued evenhandedness in overall U.S. policy in the area." A presidential emissary would first obtain assurances that Egypt would not acquire sophisticated weaponry such as West German ground-to-ground missiles and then secure a pledge from Israel neither to initiate "cross-border military action" nor to develop nuclear weapons. The ultimate objective was "arms limitation associated with security assurances to be offered both parties," but "if no progress [was] discernible in six months (by February 1964) through fault of UAR," Washington would "revert to unilateral discussions with Israel for a security guarantee."[90] John J. McCloy, JFK's special coordinator for disarmament, required far less than six months, however, to reach a dead end in Cairo. Indeed, McCloy's three days of talks with Nasser in late June revealed that Egypt was more determined than ever to obtain missiles of its own in the wake of Israel's acquisition of the HAWKs. McCloy returned to Washington in early July without even bothering to visit Tel Aviv.[91]

By the summer of 1963, then, President Kennedy's even-handed approach toward the Middle East was failing. The American rapprochement with Egypt was strained almost to the breaking point by the nagging conflict in Yemen and the failure of the McCloy mission; the need for oil had triumphed over the commitment to reform in Washington's relationship with Riyadh; and a formal security guarantee, not the resettlement of Palestinian refugees, had become the central feature of the Israeli-American dialogue. Kennedy's efforts to secure a lasting peace that would retard Soviet influence in the Mideast had backfired, largely because he had overestimated his own ability to reach an accommodation with Nasser, miscalculated the level of anxiety such an accommodation would create in Faisal and Hussein, and underestimated how shrewdly Ben Gurion would manipulate the resulting intra-Arab friction to Israel's advantage.

With the approach of autumn, the Kennedy Administration began to adjust its Middle East policies to these new realities. Levi Eshkol, who succeeded Ben Gurion as Israel's prime minister on June 16, was determined to obtain the formal American security guarantee that had eluded his predecessor. To this end, Israel temporarily suspended retaliatory raids against its Arab neighbors, promised to participate in arms limitation talks, and agreed to permit the United States to inspect its Dimona reactor.[92] Favorably impressed by these conciliatory actions, the State Department in mid-September privately assured Israeli officials in Washington that "the United States had a moral and political commitment to both the integrity and well being of Israel" and would "come to Israel's assistance if Israel were the victim of aggression." By early October, Israel's cooperativeness and mounting congressional criticism of American aid for an increasingly uncooperative U.A.R. finally prompted Kennedy to send Eshkol a letter reiterating his earlier informal commitments to Tel Aviv. According to Mordechai Gazit, an Israeli diplomat who was then in a position to know, JFK at last confirmed formally what he had implied to Meir ten months earlier, "namely that the United States would militarily assist Israel in case of attack."[93]

The realignment of Kennedy's Middle East policies was accelerated three days later by the adoption of a revised disengagement plan for Yemen. The plan apparently provided more explicit American guarantees for the security of Saudi Arabia, paralleling those recently given to Israel, in exchange for Faisal's promise not to step up his residual aid for Al-Badr's royalists, and linked continued United States economic assistance for the U.A.R. to the expeditious withdrawal of Egyptian troops from Yemen. The Saudis were willing to cooperate, provided that U.A.R. disengagement commenced at once, but Nasser, more determined than ever to rebuild his prestige among Arab nationalists, refused to make the first move.[94] Thoroughly frustrated by the deadlock in Yemen, Kennedy, in his last letter to Nasser, left little doubt whom he held responsible. "I think it fair to say that the Saudis are carrying out their end of the bargain," he wrote on October 19. "On the other hand, . . . we cannot blink at the fact, which is becoming public knowledge, that the United Arab Republic is not carrying out a compact . . . underwritten by the United States as a friend of both parties." Furthermore, Kennedy hinted, domestic criticism was growing and might soon force major changes in his policy toward Egypt.[95]

What the President meant became obvious three weeks later when the Senate passed the Gruening Amendment to the 1964 foreign aid bill. This provision outlawed PL-480 assistance to any nation "engaging in or preparing for aggressive military efforts" against the United States or its allies. "While amendment specifies no country," Rusk noted in a November 8, 1963, circular telegram, congressional debate had focused on "UAR role in Yemen and Algeria, UAR intentions re Palestine problem, and alleged State Department 'pro-Nasser policy.' " In this case, a strange alliance of oil industry lobbyists and pro-Israeli interest groups had joined forces against Nasser, who simultaneously threatened the security of the House of Saud and the sons of David.[96]

In the days just before his death, then, Kennedy privately acknowledged that his even-handed approach to the Middle East had come up empty-handed and that he must realign his policies accordingly. Because the Mideast had seemed less explosive than Africa, Latin America, or Southeast Asia, in early 1961 JFK had been relatively optimistic that he could achieve a comprehensive settlement in the Arab-Israeli conflict and prevent revolutionary nationalism from opening the door to greater Soviet influence in the Moslem world. By the summer of 1962, Kennedy's optimism seemed well-founded. Nasser had agreed to keep Palestine "in the ice box" in exchange for a three-year $500 million PL-480 package, Israel appeared willing at least to consider Joseph Johnson's plan for the resettlement of Palestinian refugees after receiving the HAWKs, and traditional regimes from Teheran to Benghazi showed grudging signs of long-overdue reforms symbolized by the Shah's White Revolution.

But before the year was out, a revolutionary upheaval in far-off Yemen short-circuited JFK's policies and demonstrated just how difficult it would be to sustain an even-handed approach. Although Nasser honored his pledge to keep the Arab-Israeli dispute on ice, he could not resist using the Yemeni crisis to turn up the heat in his cold war against such leading Arab rivals as Faisal and Hussein. And when Egyptian MIGs bombed Saudi territory and Nasserite mobs nearly toppled the Jordanian monarchy, cries for American help echoed from Riyadh to Amman. Nasser's intervention in Yemen also lent credence to Israeli charges that he could not be trusted and strengthened Tel Aviv's case for a formal American security guarantee. By November 22, 1963, then, Kennedy's policies had crystallized around a de facto alliance with Israel and Saudi Arabia designed to isolate Nasser and the Arab radicals and ensure continued Western access to Mideast oil.

In the short run this shift allowed JFK to distance himself from what had become a diplomatic fiasco in Cairo, but the long-term dangers implicit in his tilt toward Tel Aviv and Riyadh became obvious before the decade ended. As prospects for better relations with the United States faded, Nasser took Palestine out of the icebox, placed it on the front burner, and lit the fuse that would ignite the 1967 Six Day War, in whose disastrous aftermath leaders from Baghdad to Benghazi pondered the Arab predicament. Some leaders such as Nasser and Syria's Hafez al-Assad turned to the Soviets for military aid and political support; others such as Faisal and Libya's Muammar Qaddafi parlayed growing American dependence on Mideast oil into a potent lever; and a few such as Lebanon's Imam Musa al-Sadr preached a return to the fundamentals of Islam. Although Kennedy did not live to see it, the collapse of his even-handed Middle Eastern policies helped launch America toward its rendezvous with the Organization of Petroleum Exporting Countries, the Palestine Liberation Organization, and Iran's Ayatollah Khomeini fifteen years later.

Nevertheless, Kennedy came closer than any other American President to solving the bloody riddle that has bedeviled the Middle East for more than a generation. Unlike Harry Truman and Lyndon Johnson, whose unconditional support for Israel helped sour American relations with the Arabs, Kennedy linked Washington's security assistance for Tel Aviv to Israeli cooperation in resolving the Palestinian refugee problem. Unlike Dwight Eisenhower and Ronald Reagan, whose confusion of Third World nationalism with communist subversion helped persuade some Moslems to seek Soviet backing, Kennedy regarded Arab radicals like Nasser as pragmatic neutralists more interested in economic development than revolutionary ideology and wooed them with American aid. And unlike Richard Nixon and Jimmy Carter, whose reliance on autocratic Middle East proxies like the Shah's Iran and Anwar Sadat's Egypt ironically discredited the very regimes they sought to uphold, Kennedy pressed Arab conservatives like Faisal and Hussein to implement the broad reforms necessary to prevent violent revolutions.

Sadly, the war in Yemen reignited smoldering inter-Arab and Arab-Israeli frictions at just the moment Kennedy's even-handed approach had begun to produce real progress toward peace and stability, dooming his three-pronged search for order in the Middle East while it was still in its infancy. That Kennedy could, however briefly, induce Tel Aviv to be more flexible on the refugee question, convince Cairo to place its dispute with Israel in the icebox, persuade Riyadh to make better use of its oil revenues, and still come up empty-handed foreshadowed how difficult it would be to reach a comprehensive Mideast settlement in the years ahead.

7

Clinging to Containment: China Policy

JAMES FETZER

The foreign policy discussion took place off the coast of Hyannis Port on President John F. Kennedy's boat, in August 1961. Kennedy and his advisers talked in the stern while Jacqueline Kennedy stayed forward. When the discussion got around to China, President Kennedy called out, "Jackie, we need the Bloody Marys now." The drinks were not ordered out of a sense of celebration. They were intended instead to help the discussants pass through a difficult subject—China. The President and his aides recognized that American policy toward the People's Republic of China (PRC) was not exemplifying the themes which supposedly characterized the Kennedy Administration. Dynamism and innovation were the watchwords of the New Frontiersmen. The restraints of the past, however, were tethering China policy. The perspectives and fears of Kennedy and his advisers were also producing the same effect. Brilliant achievements did not seem to be on the horizon as the President contemplated what to do about China. Small wonder, then, that drinks seemed in order.[1]

John Kennedy inherited a China policy quite hostile toward the People's Republic. In the wake of the 1949 Communist victory in the Chinese civil war, the Truman Administration refused to recognize the new regime. Truman decided instead to protect the losers in the civil war. The United States started to defend Jiang Jieshi's government on Taiwan and to provide military assistance to his Nationalist regime. The Truman Administration also brought economic relations with the People's Republic to a halt and began a campaign to keep

Mao Zedong's China out of the United Nations. The Chinese intervention in the Korean War and the reality of Americans and Chinese locked in combat indicated to most Americans that Truman's policy was correct. The desire to contain Communist China, which propelled the Truman policy, also dominated the Eisenhower Administration. President Dwight D. Eisenhower continued the major features of his predecessor's policy. The most significant addition to policy placed aid to Jiang's regime and the containment of the People's Republic on a more formal footing. A joint resolution of Congress and a mutual defense treaty codified the American commitment to the Nationalist government on Taiwan. The formation of the Southeast Asia Treaty Organization (SEATO) was intended to counter the alleged aggressive designs of the PRC.[2]

The Kennedy Administration chose to maintain the essential characteristics of this inherited policy. The Administration sought to contain the People's Republic of China on several fronts. First, it tried to prevent Chinese expansion into additional areas of Asia; China's support for wars of national liberation had to be curbed. Second, the Kennedy Administration continued to practice the diplomatic containment which sought to keep China isolated from the society of nation states. In addition, President Kennedy worried a great deal about containing China's nuclear development. American support for Jiang Jieshi also continued under Kennedy's direction. Kennedy and some of his advisers were inclined to try some new tactics toward China which might help to achieve these various containment objectives. This desire for greater flexibility, however, confronted countervailing forces, such as the pressure of domestic politics, which made new initiatives in China policy difficult. In outline, then, the Kennedy Administration's policy toward the PRC featured the attempt to contain China, a determination to support Jiang Jieshi, the inclination to attain greater tactical flexibility, and an inability to surmount obstacles standing in the way of new approaches to the People's Republic.

The perceived need to contain China was connected directly to the view that China posed a threat. Nowhere was this view of a dangerous China stronger than in the mind of John Kennedy. Kennedy came to the presidency with this attitude. Early in his congressional career, Kennedy joined those who claimed that the Communist victory in China meant that the United States had somehow "lost" China. The incompetence of the Truman Administration, the young congressman claimed, had left the United States the task of preventing "the onrushing tide of Communism from engulfing all of Asia."[3] Throughout the 1950s, Kennedy did not stray far from the basic Cold War framework which viewed China as a Communist aggressor which had chosen the "totalitarian road."[4]

During the 1950s, Kennedy did suggest occasionally that American policy toward China was too inflexible. He contended in a 1957 article that United States policy was "probably too rigid" and ran the risk of missing opportunities to improve relations with China.[5] Kennedy's attraction to greater flexibility also appeared in the 1960 campaign against Richard M. Nixon. Kennedy suggested in one of the early debates with Nixon that the American commitment to Taiwan should not extend to a dangerous defense of Quemoy and Matsu, the two offshore islands which Eisenhower earlier had chosen to defend. Nixon responded that abandoning Quemoy and Matsu would amount to appeasement of Communist aggression. In the face of this challenge to his anti-Communist credentials, Kennedy began to retreat on his Quemoy and Matsu stand. As the campaign progressed, Kennedy became quite vague on the question.[6] This unwillingness to stand by positions which might be politically risky would be characteristic of Kennedy's China policy.

Once installed as President, Kennedy left no doubt that he continued to view China as a serious threat. In his first State of the Union message he referred to the menace of Chinese Communist expansion.[7] By October 1961, Kennedy remained convinced that the People's Republic was an enemy. "We have not seen any evidence as yet," Kennedy observed, "that the Chinese Communists wish to live in comity with us."[8] President Kennedy saw Mao's regime as a disrupter of world peace and international order. He believed that China was in a "Stalinist" phase of development. Chinese aggression, therefore, was at a point comparable to that of the Soviet Union in the 1940s. This meant that the Chinese Communists were determined to seek out and seize opportunities to expand Chinese influence and control. Chinese aggression might take the form of sponsorship of wars of national liberation or more overt acts of expansion. Whatever the form, the Chinese needed to be taught that aggression did not pay. If the United States did not act to contain this expansionist tendency, Kennedy reasoned, the Chinese in time would "move out into a dominant position in all of Asia."[9]

Almost all of Kennedy's advisers believed that the PRC was a serious threat that had to be contained. There were gradations of opinion about how this should be done. People such as Robert Komer on the White House staff, Adlai Stevenson at the United Nations, and Chester Bowles in the State Department contended that the United States needed to be more flexible in dealing with China. This desire for flexibility, however, seldom reached the point of either seeking major revisions in policy or criticizing the dominant view of China as a threat. For example, Kennedy in 1961 directly asked Ambassador Stevenson if he favored China's entrance into the United Nations. Stevenson replied that he did not.[10] Chester Bowles, who favored a more flexible policy, also saw fit to inform Kennedy that the People's Republic was "a paramount threat to all the nations on its periphery."[11] The common belief in the Kennedy Administration that China was a menace was more of a governing factor in policy than were the tactical differences which existed among Kennedy's advisers.

It is a mistake to believe that there were key advisers in the Administration who somehow kept Kennedy from making changes in policy. This charge, for example, has been made about Secretary of State Dean Rusk and the Far Eastern Bureau of the State Department.[12] In Rusk's case, the Secretary of State certainly viewed the People's Republic with animosity. He saw little hope for a rapprochement with China.[13] At the same time, Rusk exhibited tactical flexibility. He sponsored a proposal that gave the appearance of American approval of China's entrance into the United Nations. Rusk also took the lead in an effort to restrain Jiang Jieshi's dangerous adverturism. The Secretary was also disposed to take his lead from the President. He was not the type of Secretary of State who was inclined to initiate a crusade.[14] In addition, the idea that key advisers could deter the President from making changes ignores the foreign policy apparatus which Kennedy constructed. The collegial style and ad hoc task forces of the Administration were designed to reserve decision-making for the President.[15] Whatever the system's faults, it was not a system in which a cabal of advisers could easily block a presidential desire to change policy.

Kennedy and his advisers saw the threat of Chinese expansion in Southeast Asia in particular. The President believed that China viewed the area as promising for expansion. Moreover, Kennedy unequivocally embraced the domino theory, which held that Communist gains in any one area of Southeast Asia would have dire consequences for the entire region.[16] He also assumed that North Vietnamese gains in the Vietnam struggle would significantly expand China's influence. There is no reason to believe that the President ever seriously examined this assumption. He seemed content with the position put forth in the State Department that, while Russia and China allowed Hanoi considerable freedom of action, "Moscow and Peiping probably would have overriding influence over any major decision critically affecting the situation in South Vietnam."[17]

President Kennedy also worried deeply about the day when China would acquire a nuclear capability. According to one of the President's aides, Kennedy "always regarded the Chicom nuclear explosion as likely to be historically the most significant and worst event of the 1960s."[18] The President spoke out on this subject with a definite sense of dread. He believed this development represented the confluence of two volatile elements: China's possession of nuclear weapons would come at a time when the Chinese Communists were in an expansionist phase. Kennedy feared this combination would produce the most dangerous times since World War II.[19]

The Kennedy Administration's view of China was also conditioned by the deepening Sino-Soviet dispute. The dispute began in the late 1950s, and was taking a turn for the worse at the time Kennedy was elected. The intelligence analyses provided to Administration officials made it quite clear that the quarrel between the two Communist powers was genuine. As early as April 1961, a Central Intelligence Agency special task force on Sino-Soviet relations concluded that the rupture between Russia and China was deep and would not be easily healed.[20] Over the course of the next year, other intelligence estimates seconded this interpretation of Sino-Soviet differences.[21] Not everyone in the Kennedy Administration at first embraced the idea that the split was an international fact of life. In July 1961, Dean Rusk was still referring in congressional testimony to the "alleged split between Peiping and Moscow."[22] Rusk, as well as some high-ranking military officers, remained fond of referring to the continuing existence of a "Sino-Soviet bloc."[23] By 1962, however, even the most stubborn of disbelievers came around to the view that the Soviet Union and China were deeply divided.[24]

American estimates of the dispute emphasized that a central element in the split was China's insistence that the Soviet Union adopt a more aggressive posture against United States imperialism. This meant that China appeared as the less cautious and more dangerous of the two Communist countries. American analysts believed, moreover, that China was under pressure to demonstrate its approach was the best to achieve Communist gains. As the split widened, then, China might well become more threatening.[25]

The steady stream of invective coming from the Chinese also reinforced the American view that China represented a threat. Beijing regularly pilloried the United States and President Kennedy as the agents of imperialist aggression in the world. In the wake of the Bay of Pigs invasion of Cuba, Mao declared that "the Kennedy Administration can only be even worse and not better than the Eisenhower Administration." The Chinese Communist's public comments also made it clear that as long as the United States supported the Nationalist government on Taiwan there was little chance of an improvement in Chinese-American relations.[26] These public statements constituted only part of the communications between the People's Republic and Washington. Private and more quiet contacts also existed. Perhaps, as some have suggested, the harsh Chinese Communist comments about the United States were part of an attempt to create a "foreign devil" in order to distract the attention of the Chinese people from the serious economic failures in their country in the early 1960s.[27] Whatever the reason, the extreme rhetoric persuaded many Americans that China was in fact an enemy of the United States.

Although most Kennedy Administration officials viewed China as a serious threat, this did not mean they thought Chinese foreign policy was in the hands of maniacal leaders hell-bent on aggression regardless of the cost. Implicit in President Kennedy's view of China as being in a Stalinist phase of development was the idea that China might evolve out of this aggressive phase. American intelligence estimates consistently noted that Chinese actions were a good deal more cautious than the warlike oratory emanating from Beijing. The intelligence evaluations also made the point that the Chinese leadership was not inclined to take risks when confronted by superior power.[28] American officials were also well aware that Beijing was confronting serious domestic difficulties in the form of food shortages and other economic failures which were byproducts of Mao's failed Great Leap Forward. A China faced with such problems was unlikely to undertake massive foreign policy adventrues.[29]

Because American analysts believed the Chinese capable of graduated and varied reactions to circumstances, the possibility existed that China's leaders might be influenced by more subtle and flexible American actions. This possibility was a major reason why some

Kennedy Administration advisers sought to broaden United States responses to China. President Kennedy himself was so inclined. This did not mean the President wanted to alter American policy in a radical fashion. As Kennedy told Chairman Nikita Khrushchev in Vienna, there were not going to be major changes in American policy, and the United States would remain committed to Taiwan.[30] Instead, the primary purpose in exploring new initiatives was to find alternative methods to contain China. If American flexibility also produced an improvement in Sino-American relations, so much the better.

A prerequisite for taking new steps was an alignment of publicly stated policy with the actual intentions of the Kennedy Administration. In 1961, the public China policy persisted in paying lip service to the existence of one China as represented by the Nationalist government of Jiang Jieshi. This public policy tended to treat the government of the People's Republic as the illegitimate pretender to Chinese political power. In fact, most officials of the Kennedy Administration, as had also been the case in the Eisenhower Administration, desired to implement a two-China policy. The assumption under Kennedy was that the Communist regime in China was not about to disintegrate or disappear. The Administration recognized that Mao's regime had to be dealt with as a fact of life. The United States, therefore, maintained diplomatic contact with the People's Republic through a Warsaw, Poland, connection. The Kennedy Administration also resisted Jiang Jieshi's desire to launch an attack on the mainland designed to topple the Beijing regime. These and other developments were indications that the Kennedy Administration was prepared to treat the Chinese Communist regime as a permanent entity. Yet, the Administration also remained committed to the defense of Taiwan. In some important respects, then, the United States followed a two-China policy. To give greater reign to this policy, the Administration publicly had to endorse the idea of two Chinas. Such an endorsement, carrying with it the belief that the Beijing regime was a permanent fixture, would clear the way for Kennedy to broaden American policy toward China. Serious obstacles, however, stood in the way.

American domestic politics hindered new measures toward China. The Kennedy Administration came to power less than ten years after McCarthyism had raised great havoc over the question of who had "lost" China to the Communists. President Kennedy shied away from policies which might have touched off a similar surge of political insanity. His electoral victory in 1960 had been narrow, and, there-fore, his political standing was not all that secure. An active lobbying group remained ready to pounce upon the Administration if it devi-ated from the orthodoxy that only Jiang Jieshi represented China. The Committee of One Million, founded in 1953, sought to marshall public and congressional opposition against any formal recognition of the People's Republic. Marvin Liebman, the Committee's secretary and chief strategist, was successful in gaining bipartisan support. The Committee's congressional membership, for example, featured Re-publicans and Democrats from various points on the political spec-trum. Congress left no doubt where it stood. A Senate resolution opposing both China's admission to the United Nations and the diplo-matic recognition of the People's Republic passed the Senate in July 1961 by a vote of 76 to 0. The same resolution was approved in the House of Representatives by a vote of 395 to 0.[31] Finally, President Kennedy himself viewed China as a threat. He was not inclined to take serious political risks at home in order to introduce new flexibil-ity toward an enemy. Given these factors, considerations of new initiatives toward China would have to be made very cautiously.

This sense of caution was evident in the early days of the Kennedy Administration. Inquiries about selling United States fuel to ships chartered by the People's Republic, for example, were met with the response that such requests would be denied. Fear of public criticism controlled this decision.[32] Chester Bowles, nominated to be Under Secretary of State, had for some time advocated breaking new ground in Sino-American relations. Worried that Bowles's confirmation hear-ings might become a forum for raising alarm, Kennedy asked Bowles to play down disagreements Bowles had with existing China policy.[33] In addition, Kennedy and his advisers continued to make public state-ments which rejected the notion of two Chinas and assigned the role of pariah to the People's Republic.[34]

China's representation in the United Nations was one area in which the Administration did consider introducing flexibility into American policy toward China. For some time, Washington had sought an an-nual suspension of any consideration of the PRC's entrance into the United Nations. The result of this tactic was to keep the question of China's entrance off the agenda. As early as February 1961, Secretary Rusk informed the Senate Foreign Relations Committee in executive session that this way of excluding China was wearing thin with other nations, and a new approach had to be found.[35] White House staff members speculated that the United States might suffer a humiliating diplomatic defeat in the near future if it did not alter this obstructionist tactic. These discussions took place against a background of Jiang Jieshi's unequivocal declaration that his government would never accept a two-China formula in the United Nations.[36]

By the end of May 1961, the State Department had prepared a proposal outlining a "successor states" solution to the problem. This approach called for the General Assembly to recognize that two governments held authority in "China." In recognizing this state of affairs, the General Assembly would affirm the continuing membership of the Nationalists, but also provide for the concurrent membership of the People's Republic. This proposal clearly embraced the two Chinas idea.[37]

High-level discussions about the "successor states" idea revealed the Kennedy Administration's caution. The proposal was not primarily designed to move the People's Republic into the United Nations. Instead, the "successor states" approach was intended to keep the Taiwan government in the international organization. The plan assumed that if Taiwan remained in the United Nations, then the Chinese Communists would refuse to enter and, thereby, shift to themselves the onus for their exclusion. Even with this purpose in mind, Kennedy recognized a political risk in extending any legitimacy to the Communist regime. The President thought that the "successor states" idea made a good deal of sense, but he decided to delay a public endorsement. Careful soundings had to be taken with people such as Henry Luce, the prominent publisher and ardent supporter of Jiang Jieshi. The President also asked if other countries might be willing to take the lead in putting forth the proposal. In sum, Kennedy gave the "successor states" plan a highly qualified backing. His hesitancy was dictated by what he saw as the "political dynamite locked up in this issue."[38]

The "successor states" approach soon ran into considerable difficulty. Administration officials found that other nations were not eager to promote it. American allies deemed the plan a good idea, but none was "aching to get out in front."[39] The Nationalist government also threw up obstacles. Not only was Jiang's government unalterably opposed to any two-China proposal; the Nationalists' stand on Outer Mongolia's entrance into the United Nations jeopardized Taiwan's seat in the international organization. As a permanent member of the Security Council, Taiwan was threatening to veto Outer Mongolia's admission. The Mongolian People's Republic in the 1960s was politically and economically oriented toward the Soviet Union. As recently as the early twentieth century, Outer Mongolia had been under Chinese control. Although the Nationalist government had subsequently recognized the independence of Outer Mongolia, Jiang resurrected the claim that the area was part of China and, therefore, should not be admitted to the United Nations. Because Outer Mongolia's entrance had become linked to Mauritania's, the effect of a Nationalist Chinese veto of Outer Mongolia would be to turn African states against Taiwan's position in the United Nations. The Kennedy Administration faced difficulty in getting the Nationalists to refrain from committing what amounted to political suicide in the United Nations. Securing Jiang's agreement to the "successor states" approach seemed remote.[40]

The accumulating difficulties surrounding the "successor states" measure meant that by the end of July the idea was virtually shelved. Washington then shifted to a new tactic: having the United Nations designate China's entrance an "important question." All "important questions" required a two-thirds' vote for approval, and the PRC could not rally that many votes. This tactic did not mean American recognition of the legitimacy of the Beijing regime. Rather, Kennedy's sensitivity to the political riskiness of the China issue and the Nationalist government's intransigence dictated the move to this position.[41] Ambassador Adlai Stevenson was instructed to pursue the "important question" tactic in order to keep "Communist China out and Nationalist China in the United Nations." The now defunct "successor states" approach was only mentioned in Stevenson's instructions as a prospective subject which might be taken up by a newly created United Nations membership committee.[42]

The Administration still confronted the problem of persuading the Nationalists to refrain from casting a veto against Outer Mongolia's membership in the United Nations. Kennedy had decided the United States would not extend diplomatic recognition to Outer Mongolia. He made this decision after Jiang's congressional supporters, fearing that the recognition of the Communist Mongolian regime might be preliminary to the recognition of China, had mounted considerable protest. Kennedy saw no reason, however, for the United States to try to keep Outer Mongolia out of the United Nations. The President and his advisers were convinced it was insane for the Nationalists to try to block Outer Mongolia's entrance.[43] Jiang's government, nevertheless, seemed intent on casting a veto. More than one impatient

message passed from Washington to Taipei on this testy subject.[44]
Finally, Kennedy decided to make a deal with Jiang. He decided to
assuage Jiang's fears by pledging that the United States would exercise its veto to block Communist China's admission if the General
Assembly should vote to oust Taiwan and admit the People's Republic. The United States also agreed not to vote for Outer Mongolia's
entrance into the United Nations in exchange for Jiang's promise not
to veto that admission.[45] Jiang honored the bargain and Outer Mongolia was finally voted into the United Nations with the United States
and the Nationalists abstaining. The Kennedy Administration also
persuaded the General Assembly to declare by a vote of 61 to 34 that
the question of China's entrance into the United Nations was an
"important question."[46]

The Kennedy Administration's unwillingness to stake out a position
at odds with the Nationalist Chinese also helped shape the American
response to Chinese Communist diplomatic overtures in the summer
of 1961. These feelers came at the ambassadorial level in Warsaw. The
Polish capital had served since the Quemoy-Matsu crisis of 1958 as a
regular channel of communication between the United States and the
People's Republic. The Warsaw talks had not produced any breakthrough but did serve as a useful means of direct communication.
Wang Bingnan, the Chinese representative in Warsaw, informed
American Ambassador Jacob Beam in the early days of the Kennedy
Administration that the Chinese government was waiting with a "great
sense of anticipation" for the United States to unveil some new initiatives. Beam responded with a detailed plan for the exchange of journalists and the hint of possible American wheat shipments to relieve
Chinese shortages.[47] In late June, Wang invited Beam for an unusual,
informal discussion over coffee. Wang indicated that the Chinese genuinely hoped the ongoing multilateral talks at Geneva would achieve a
neutral Laos. Wang also said that, if the United States would end its
ties with Taiwan, Beijing would make a peaceful settlement with
Jiang.[48]

Washington was not inclined to interpret favorably Wang's comments. The State Department concluded that the private assurances
about Laos were designed to make the harsh public terms of the Communists more palatable. As for Sino-American relations in general,
the Americans suspected the Chinese were simply trying to drive a
wedge between Washington and Taipei.[49] Beam was nevertheless instructed to inform Wang that the United States desired to identify

areas of possible cooperation. The Chinese coldly received the United States response; they claimed Kennedy really did not desire to improve relations. Sino-American relations would not improve as long as the United States remained tied to Taiwan, Wang insisted.[50] Because of the impasse over Taiwan, nothing came of these discussions.

The events of 1961 notwithstanding, there were limits to the Kennedy Administration's support for Jiang, as became evident in the first half of 1962 when tensions reappeared in the Taiwan Straits. Jiang's threats to launch major actions against the Chinese mainland were met with Washington's strong disapproval. In voicing its disapproval, the Kennedy Administration also demonstrated its allegiance to a two-China policy.

By the beginning of 1962, the Nationalists were tempted to try to exploit the serious economic difficulties on the mainland. Jiang's New Year's Day message, for example, asserted that Taiwan was preparing a major offensive and stood ready to assist mainland uprisings against the Communists should such occur. The declaration implied that the United States could be expected to support such Nationalist military operations on the mainland. The Kennedy Administration was not opposed to assisting Jiang's harrassment of the Communist regime. CIA proprietaries such as Air America and Civil Air Transport supported Nationalist raids on the mainland.[51] The Kennedy Administration, however, was not prepared to allow Jiang to draw the United States into a war with China.

Secretary Rusk quickly informed Jiang that any major Nationalist adventure on the mainland required American concurrence, and such approval had certainly not been given to a Nationalist invasion. Taipei was also informed that bellicose statements against the mainland did not help the Nationalist government's international reputation.[52] Despite United States warnings, Jiang persisted in suggesting that an internationally supported invasion of the mainland was forthcoming. W. Averell Harriman, Assistant Secretary of State for Far Eastern Affairs, soon made a special stop in Taipei in March and urged restraint upon the Nationalists. Harriman once again reminded Jiang that he did not have United States consent for major military operations against the People's Republic. The Kennedy Administration was worried enough about the effects of Jiang's posturing to use the Warsaw channel to assure the Chinese Communists that Washington was not urging Jiang to invade the mainland.[53]

It was not surprising that Taipei's bellicosity produced a reaction in

China. Chinese forces began to concentrate on the coast opposite Taiwan. American officials initially read this military activity as defensive.[54] By June 1962, however, the buildup in Fujian grew to worrisome proportions. The President told a news conference that the United States would take very seriously any Chinese Communist move against Taiwan or Quemoy and Matsu. A similar message was sent through the Warsaw channel.[55] Harriman also told Soviet Ambassador Anatoly Dobrynin that the United States would not stand idly by if the People's Republic took aggressive action. At the same time, Harriman emphasized that the United States "had no intentions under existing circumstances of giving Chiang encouragement or support for an attack on the mainland."[56] The Kennedy Administration strove to persuade all concerned parties that it intended to maintain the status quo in the Taiwan Straits. No thanks to Jiang, the crisis shortly passed on these terms. Two Chinas remained a fact of life in East Asia.

While attending to the trouble in the Taiwan Straits, Kennedy officials also discussed the revision of American economic policy toward China. The United States began to enact trade sanctions against the People's Republic as early as 1949. After the Chinese entrance into the Korean War, the Truman Administration banned all American economic relations with China. The total embargo against China had continued after the end of the Korean conflict. The United States had also attempted, with mixed results, to convince its allies to refrain from economic contact with the People's Republic.[57] The Kennedy Administration began to consider the desirability of revising the embargo policy by allowing American food shipments to China.

The idea of providing food to China was raised early in the Kennedy Administration, especially by Under Secretary Bowles. In the context of serious food shortages in China, Bowles argued, American shipments of food to China might actually moderate Chinese Communist behavior or put the United States in a better position to try to influence Chinese behavior.[58] But Bowles's early suggestions did not produce major changes in policy.

A bureaucratic shake-up in November 1961, however, gave impetus to the food project. Bowles was asked to resign as Under Secretary. Personal and administrative difficulties, rather than East Asian policy, explain his removal. At the same time, Harriman became Assistant Secretary of State for the Far East. The consummate Washington insider, Harriman began to promote certain personnel shifts.

Edward Rice and Robert Barnett, who favored new approaches to the People's Republic, were given positions of increased importance. Rice and Barnett were veteran China specialists who had managed to escape the purge of the "China hands" in the early 1950s. They joined James Thomson, who had worked for Bowles, as advocates of the Bowles position on the food issue. Harriman created a separate mainland China desk in the Far Eastern bureau. This promised to give greater leeway to new suggestions for China policy. By early 1962, the new Assistant Secretary also had a "Harriman man" on the White House staff—Michael Forrestal.[59] Bowles, while pushed aside, also continued to make a good deal of noise about the food question in his new capacity as a roving ambassador.

Within the State Department, a lengthy analysis by Edward Rice served as the basis for discussion about new economic initiatives. Rice's report called for a lifting of the United States embargo on exports of food and medicine to China.[60] In the White House, Carl Kaysen, a prominent member of the National Security Council staff, led discussions on the question. The White House participants rejected the idea of a government food program for China as too politically risky. Such direct aid was seen as likely to touch off a major political battle in the United States. The discussants did support the idea of approving export licenses for private American groups which desired to sell or give food supplies to China.[61] Thomson, who took part in the White House talks, was hopeful that Kennedy would approve this shift in policy.[62]

The President seemed to be open to sending food to China. White House meetings that considered some change in food policy suggest at least that the President invited new thinking on the subject. Kennedy's interest in the issue was also demonstrated in February 1962. Bowles was scheduled the next month to tour Asia. He asked if he could contact U Nu, the Burmese Premier, about Burma's serving as a conduit through which American food might reach China. U Nu's amicable relationship with Beijing was offered as the reason for sounding out the Burmese leader. Kennedy gave Bowles the go-ahead, but the inquiry was never made. Before Bowles reached Rangoon, U Nu's government had been overthrown.[63]

In the State Department, the idea of changing food policy met considerable opposition. Secretary Rusk allowed a full discussion of the issue, but he indicated early he did not support the idea.[64] The Bureau of Intelligence and Research claimed that sending food to

China was not likely "to lead to any amelioration of Chinese Communist hostility to the West." In response to a request for a specific policy recommendation, the bureau recommended the United States do no more than adopt a policy of neither encouraging nor discouraging American allies from providing food products to the Chinese Communists.[65] The European Division also opposed a change in policy. A bureau memorandum again made the point that there was little reason to believe Chinese behavior would be changed by American assistance. The memorandum contended that relieving economic pressure in China might actually make the People's Republic more aggressive in international politics. The European section also argued that recent Sino-Soviet tension was in part a result of China's contention that the Soviet Union was insensitive to China's dire economic needs. If the United States shipped food to China, this would benefit Moscow by diminishing one of the factors which produced tension between the Soviet Union and China.[66]

The Harriman group in the State Department did not relent on the food question. In early April, Harriman suggested to Rusk that the Warsaw channel be used to inform the Chinese the United States was willing to reconsider its policy. Harriman was careful not to predict that millennial changes would follow such an overture. He argued, instead, that policy debates surely existed in the Beijing regime. The United States needed to send a sign to those officials in China who might be seeking to moderate Chinese policy. "Evidence that the United States would be willing to play a part in moving our relationship away from one of implacable hostility," Harriman contended, "might strengthen the hand of any elements which might favor doing so, now or later."[67]

The advocates of a change in food policy were destined to be disappointed. The Warsaw channel was not employed to sound out the Chinese. The proposal to approve export licenses never got beyond the discussion stage. It is possible Kennedy used an oblique press conference statement in May as a careful signal about a change in food policy. Asked if the United States would offer American surplus grains to China, Kennedy responded that "there's been no indication of any expression of interest or desire by the Chinese Communists to receive any food from us." This left open the possibility that, if the Chinese asked, the United States might respond positively. The Chinese did not ask. Chinese Foreign Minister Chen Yi responded shortly thereafter that China did not "need to be a beggar."[68] The combination of Beijing's attitude, the divided counsel, and the perceived political riskiness of the issue seems to have convinced Kennedy to back away from the question. By summer 1962, the matter had become a dead issue. At the end of June, Rusk informed British officials the United States was not going to alter its policy on food for China. According to Rusk, "an initiative on our part in this connection would play into Peiping's hands." The Secretary took the position that food for China would amount to rewarding Chinese belligerence.[69]

The willingness of some Kennedy officials to consider more flexible positions toward China did not mean they thought Chinese expansion no longer presented a problem. The Sino-India border clash in 1962 demonstrated that the drive to contain the People's Republic remained a firm American commitment. Chinese and Indian differences over the border between the two countries had existed long before the fall of 1962.[70] When violence flared along the contested territory, Washington considered aid to India in the face of what was seen as Chinese aggression. American officials sought to keep Chinese Communist power out of the Indian plain and hoped to prevent a humiliating defeat for India that would enhance Chinese prestige.[71] The Chinese offensive of mid-November brought these concerns very much to the fore (see Chapter 8).

The President responded to Prime Minister Jawaharlal Nehru's request for assistance by providing fire arms, light artillery, and transport planes. Kennedy also dispatched a special mission, headed by Harriman, to symbolize American concern, evaluate Indian requests for assistance, pacify the Pakistanis, who protested American aid to their rival India, and investigate whether the Chinese threat had improved chances for an India-Pakistan reconciliation.[72] Just as the Harriman mission was about to depart, the Chinese suddenly declared a cease-fire and set about consolidating their gains in the northeastern frontier and the Ladakh area of Kashmir.

President Kennedy's estimates of Chinese actions seem to have been guided by the State Department's Bureau of Intelligence and Research.[73] Roger Hilsman, the Bureau's director, was also a member of the Harriman delegation. The reports sent to Kennedy emphasized the necessity of deterring Chinese "aggression" by displaying United States firmness. They also predicted that China did not intend to move onto the Indian plain. The Chinese, instead, were only seeking to improve their position in the contested areas in Ladakh and in the North East Frontier Agency. It was important, the President was told, to send a strong American warning so the Chinese would be encouraged to moderate their military actions and not become tempted to enlarge their limited objectives. In the context of the Sino-Soviet dispute, the reports added, China was attempting to demonstrate the efficacy of its strategy of boldness and assertiveness. It was essential, therefore, not to reward this risk-taking strategy. How the United States reacted in India, Hilsman's reports argued, "may well affect future courses of Chinese Communist action, not only in India but in Burma, Laos, and elsewhere in Asia."[74]

While the Administration's firm backing for India did make clear Washington's resolve, the sudden Chinese cease-fire raised the question of whether the United States should accept the pre-cease-fire Chinese gains. Hilsman informed Kennedy that the Indians could not regain territory on their own. New Delhi had to accept the cease-fire on at least a de facto basis unless the United States decided to take strong new measures to help India roll back the Chinese positions.[75] By the beginning of December, it had also become evident that the United States did not have to contest a rampaging China on the Sino-India border. China had been careful not to press its military advantage in a reckless manner. The Chinese unilateral declaration of a cease-fire forced India to assume the onus of renewing the fighting or accept for the time being the Chinese advances. Beijing proved politically adept and cautious.[76] Kennedy, therefore, became content to see the cease-fire hold and Chinese Communist gains remain intact. In the weeks following the cease-fire, however, the President stated publicly several times that the United States and all of Asia remained quite concerned about Chinese designs.[77] In other words, China had better be satisfied with its limited achievements in the border war.

By 1963, American policy toward China began to turn on the emerging relationship between the United States and the Soviet Union. As Soviet-American relations moved toward some accommodation that year, the Kennedy Administration in essence started to take sides in the worsening Sino-Soviet dispute. Relations between the two Communist nations rapidly deteriorated during 1963. The Chinese asserted that the Soviet Union was cowering in the face of United States imperialism. China contended, for example, that the Soviet withdrawal of its missiles from Cuba was "capitulationism." According to President Liu Shaoqi of China, the differences between Beijing and Moscow centered on the question of "whether the people of the world should carry out revolutions or not and whether proletarian parties should lead the world's people in revolution or not." The Chinese Communist party wanted to assume revolutionary leadership, Liu contended, whereas the Soviet Communist party did not.[78]

American intelligence estimated in 1963 that the bitter squabble between Russia and China was consuming more and more of each's attention. Both Beijing and Moscow, moreover, were shaping their foreign policies in response to the widening schism. The Chinese and the Soviets were also evaluating the actions of other nations in terms of their impact upon the split. As had been the case at the time of the Indo-Chinese conflict, American intelligence reports noted that the Chinese Communists probably wanted to demonstrate that their more assertive international stance was more productive than the "peaceful coexistence" posture of the Soviet Union. This did not mean that major Chinese military aggression was imminent. Rather, the intelligence estimates pointed to a step-up in support for neighboring revolutionary movements as the most likely Chinese response.[79]

The Kennedy Administration's seeming movement toward détente with the Soviet Union carried with it implications for United States China policy. The Administration recognized that agreements with the Soviet Union such as the Limited Test Ban Treaty meant the United States was leaning to the Soviet side in the dispute between Moscow and Beijing. An unsigned White House memorandum made this point at the time of Kennedy's famous American University commencement address. "The President," the memorandum pointed out, "is not choosing sides, in any ostentatious way, between Moscow and Peiping, but his speech is designed to emphasize the positive opportunities for a more constructive and less hostile Soviet policy."[80] A "more constructive . . . Soviet policy" meant Washington would likely avoid acts of accommodation with China that might disturb Moscow and diminish the chances of agreement. It is not surprising, then, that in the last year of the Kennedy Administration little was done to make its China policy more flexible. Even the appearance of accommodation would have seriously troubled a Soviet Union grown increasingly sensitive to any gains achieved by its Communist rival.

The Administration's policies toward China and the Soviet Union were linked in another way. President Kennedy hoped improved American-Soviet relations and the test ban treaty in particular would be the basis for dealing with China's acquisition of a nuclear capability. Kennedy frequently justified the pursuit of a test ban treaty by claiming that it would arrest China's nuclear program. He hoped Soviet-American cooperation would produce the means to stop or delay the Chinese program. Kennedy instructed Harriman, the chief test ban negotiator, to "try to elicit Khrushchev's views of means of limiting or preventing Chinese nuclear development and his willingness either to take Soviet action or to accept U.S. action aimed in this direction."[81] It is not yet clear just exactly what actions Kennedy had in mind, although he might have been contemplating joint military action with the Soviet Union against nuclear sites in China. Khrushchev's unwillingness to make firm commitments deterred Kennedy from formulating a definite course of action.[82]

While the Kennedy Administration's Vietnam policy is discussed elsewhere in this volume, one aspect of China's role in Southeast Asia deserves some mention here. The Administration grew alarmed over Communist China's standing as an inspiration for and supporter of wars of national liberation. Kennedy came to the White House with the view that Communist-inspired wars of national liberation posed a major challenge to the United States. He insisted his Administration develop a counter-insurgency capability to deal with revolutionary warfare.[83] American leaders needed to study and comprehend this type of warfare in order to counter it. Kennedy himself read Mao on guerrilla warfare and went about urging others in the Administration to do the same.[84] Given this frame of reference, Southeast Asia became for Kennedy a test case measuring the ability of the United States to handle the mode of warfare which had been practiced so successfully in China before 1949 and which was being promoted by the Chinese Communists in the 1960s. The stakes, according to a national intelligence estimate in August 1961, were high:

> Thailand, Cambodia, Burma, Indonesia, the Philippines, and Nationalist China have all to some extent viewed developments in Laos as a gauge of U.S. willingness and ability to help an anti-Communist Asian government stand against a Communist "national liberation" campaign. They will almost certainly look at the struggle for Vietnam as a critical test of such U.S. willingness and ability. All of them, including the neutrals, would probably suffer demoralization and loss of confidence in the prospects for maintaining their independence if the Communists were to gain control of South Vietnam. This loss of confidence might even extend to India.[85]

Because we cannot know what Kennedy would have done in 1964 and beyond, any analysis of China policy can only review what did unfold in 1961–1963. The fundamental premise of the Kennedy Administration was that the People's Republic of China was a threat which had to be contained by the United States. What flowed from this assumption was a continuation of American ties with Jiang Jieshi and support for other regimes or political factions which seemed to be threatened by an expansionist Beijing. The Kennedy Administration followed a two-China policy in fact if not always in public acknowledgment. The Administration both recognized that the Communist regime in China was permanent and remained committed to the survival of the Nationalist government. Kennedy and some of his advisers also entertained ideas about making American policy more flexible. The "successor states" approach in the United Nations and the re-evaluation of food policy demonstrated this tendency. But none of the new initiatives reached fruition. The difficulties associated with new measures, particularly the perceived domestic political risks, were seen to outweigh the advantages which might flow from new initiatives.

This American policy turned on what President Kennedy believed about China and on what he was willing to do in light of his beliefs. Above all else, American policy grew from the President's belief that the People's Republic of China was an expansionist and threatening power. The restraint demonstrated by the Chinese Communists in circumstances such as the Taiwan Straits crisis and the Sino-India border conflict did not alter Kennedy's view that the United States confronted an aggressive Chinese expansionism. Kennedy's fear of domestic political reprisals also worked to prevent him from introducing new elements into China policy. While new measures did entail domestic political risk, Kennedy did not test in a sustained manner just how serious this risk was. There is reason to believe, for example, that some leeway existed for the President concerning the food-for-China issue. A Gallup poll in mid-1962 indicated the respondents approved by a margin of 48 to 43 percent the shipment of food to China.[86] In this case as in others, however, the fear of political reprisals outweighed the appeal of sending a major new signal to Chinese leaders. Instead, Kennedy chose to keep China policy in the rigid pattern he had inherited. The challenge of enacting new initiatives toward one-fifth of mankind was left to John Kennedy's successors.

8

Choosing Sides in South Asia

ROBERT J. McMAHON

On October 20, 1962, long-simmering border tensions between India and China erupted in full-scale hostilities. Chinese forces launched major attacks against Indian positions in the rugged terrain of both Ladakh and the Northeast Frontier Agency, quickly driving Indian defenders into retreat. Over the next several days India suffered stunning reverses. The once flourishing self-confidence of its leaders and the general public became profoundly shaken. "We were getting out of touch with reality in the modern world," Prime Minister Jawaharlal Nehru conceded in an address to the nation, "and we were living in an artificial atmosphere of our own creation. We have been shocked out of it, all of us, whether it is the government or the people."[1] Immediate external assistance, Nehru and his chief advisers realized, had become essential.

Top policymakers in the Kennedy Administration viewed the Sino-Indian War as a unique opportunity to accomplish a significant foreign policy objective: the alignment of India with the West. National Security Council aide Robert Komer ranked the border clash as "potentially one of the most crucial events of the decade."[2] Within days of the Chinese attack in the Himalayas, he predicted that "we may have a golden opportunity for a major gain in our relations with India."[3] Kennedy had worked toward this goal from the very inception of his presidency; suddenly the prospect for a fundamental reorientation in New Delhi's foreign policy appeared genuine. Certain that Indian complacency toward the Communist threat would be shat-

198

tered by the Chinese offensive, the President and his principal foreign policy advisers reasoned that prompt and generous military aid from the United States might convince India simultaneously of American reliability and the folly of non-alignment. Although preoccupied by the Cuban missile crisis, Kennedy moved quickly. In a personal letter of October 28 to Nehru, he came right to the point: "I want to give you support as well as sympathy."[4] Before long, substantial United States aid was flowing to India and American planners were discussing the possibility of a long-term military assistance agreement, some even conjuring up images of India's transformation into a staunch ally of the United States.

The Administration also recognized that significant risks inhered in its decision to provide India with emergency military aid. Pakistan, India's arch-rival on the subcontinent ever since the bitter partition of 1947, would almost surely balk at the prospect of a hostile neighbor being fortified by United States military equipment and diplomatic support. The Administration consequently believed Pakistan's response would be critical to the outcome of its policy initiative. The war "can give us a major breakthrough in Asia," noted the NSC Subcommittee on South Asia, "provided we can find ways to help India stand firm against the Chinese without disrupting our relationships with Pakistan."[5] American analysts considered Pakistan a valuable strategic asset they could not afford to lose. Not only was Pakistan formally allied to the West through two regional security agreements, the Southeast Asia Treaty Organization and the Baghdad Pact, but it ranked as one of the leading recipients of American military assistance and it provided the United States with intelligence installations that senior policymakers judged indispensable to American security. Only a comprehensive settlement of Indo-Pakistani differences, White House and State Department officials concurred, could render their initiative successful and lay the groundwork for a more stable, prosperous, and Western-oriented region. Their conclusion: the United States must play an active role in fostering an Indo-Pakistani rapprochement by pressing the two sides to reach a mutually acceptable resolution of the Kashmir dispute, the major bone of contention between the two countries since independence.[6]

The Kashmir dispute had defied all previous efforts by the United States and the United Nations to achieve a settlement. When the ruler of that predominantly Moslem state chose to accede to India under the British-negotiated partition agreement of 1947, Pakistan challenged the legality of his decision and fighting soon erupted between Indian and Pakistani forces. Following a United Nations-sponsored cease-fire in 1948, an uneasy peace had prevailed in the state, with each nation occupying part of it and rejecting the claims of the other. American officials often likened the Kashmir problem to the Arab-Israeli dispute in terms of both the emotional intensity that it generated and its intractability.

Kennedy's agenda for South Asia was thus a bold and ambitious one. Reflecting the "can do" spirit so many observers have found characteristic of the Kennedy years, Administration planners seemed undaunted by the failures of the past. Unfortunately, the New Frontiersmen also proved insensitive to the lessons of history and too blinded by Cold War geopolitical ambitions to grasp unpleasant regional realities. Their initiative did not succeed; American intervention did not transform South Asia. To the contrary, by the end of Kennedy's presidency, American-Pakistani relations had deteriorated drastically while Indo-American relations had barely improved. For all his hope of forging new relationships with the Third World, then, Kennedy's record in South Asia reveals a gaping chasm between promise and performance, between objectives and results.

Before he reached the Oval Office, Kennedy had already developed strong views regarding India's importance to the United States. As a junior senator from Massachusetts he discussed India more forcefully and more frequently than any other nation. In an essay he penned for *The Progressive* in January 1958, Kennedy said that, of all the nations of the Third World, India had most successfully pointed the way toward progressive economic development under a democratic system. Expressing a view that he would propound often, Kennedy declared: "If India collapses, so may all of Asia." If India succumbed to internal disintegration or joined the Communist camp with China, "the Free World would never be the same."[7] In March 1958, along with Republican colleague John Sherman Cooper, he offered a joint resolution to the Senate calling for increased economic aid to India.[8] Kennedy regularly called attention to the historical significance of the economic competition between India and China. "The outcome of this competition," he said in one speech, "will vitally affect the security and standing of this nation." If India does not "demonstrate an ability at least equal to that of China" to move from stagnation to economic growth, then "Communism would have won its greatest bloodless victory."[9] During his campaign for the presidency, the Massachusetts Democrat emphasized those themes repeatedly, promising that his Administration would pursue a more active and enlightened policy toward India and the Third World as a whole.[10]

The Eisenhower Administration, Kennedy and his foreign policy advisers argued, had committed a monumental strategic and geopolitical blunder when in 1954 it began to provide Pakistan with military aid. Within a year Pakistan was firmly aligned with the West; by the end of 1950s it ranked as one of the six leading recipients of United States military aid in the developing world. The Eisenhower Administration judged Pakistan a major strategic asset and an important anchor in its worldwide alliance system aimed at checking Soviet expansion. The diplomatic and strategic advantages of Pakistan's alignment with the West thus seemed clearly to outweigh the chill in Indo-American relations that followed.[11]

The incoming Administration disagreed vigorously with that analysis. It considered Eisenhower's approach to South Asia disastrously counterproductive. Instead of cultivating Indian friendship as the key to regional stability, Eisenhower and Secretary of State John Foster Dulles had foolishly undercut India by arming its chief rival. The results of that policy had proven as unfortunate as they were predictable: American military support for Pakistan stimulated an arms race on the subcontinent, rendered an amicable resolution of Kashmir and other Indo-Pakistani disputes increasingly unlikely, alienated Afghanistan, and opened the door for greater Russian involvement in both India and Afghanistan.[12] Kennedy, as his Senate and campaign speeches testified, was determined to forge a new policy, one that would reverse Eisenhower's priorities by tilting toward non-aligned India. The tricky aspect of such a policy reorientation, he recognized from the outset, was to accomplish it without alienating Pakistan in the process. Kennedy wanted to loosen the ties that bound the United States to Pakistan; he did not want to dissolve the alliance.[13]

Actually, Eisenhower had already taken some significant strides toward a new India policy during the closing years of his presidency. When it became apparent in 1957 that India faced a potentially catastrophic economic crisis due to serious shortfalls in its second Five-Year Plan, Dulles publicly announced the United States would look favorably on an Indian request for financial assistance. The United States soon offered a program of substantially increased economic aid to India. A variety of foreign policy considerations prompted Washington's generosity. Despite numerous differences between American and Indian perceptions of world affairs, and despite its displeasure with India's adherence to a policy of non-alignment or neutralism, the Eisenhower Administration plainly believed it was of critical importance for New Delhi to remain independent and free from Communist influence. To the extent that India remained stable, the security and prosperity of South Asia would be enhanced. In addition, the United States had an important stake in India's economic development, because Indian prosperity would demonstrate to the Third World the advantages of the capitalist model of economic development over the communist/socialist model. Consequently, in early 1958 the United States agreed to loan India $225 million and to provide large quantities of wheat and other food grains under the Public Law 480 program.[14]

Aware that the thaw in Indo-American relations would anger the Pakistanis, the Eisenhower Administration simultaneously developed a "package plan" for resolving tensions between India and Pakistan. The initiative sprang logically from the view that United States relations with the two nations were indivisible—that Washington could have friendly relations with *both* New Delhi and Karachi only if they were able first to compose their longstanding differences. To that end, the State Department drafted and Eisenhower approved an integrated approach to the subcontinent's problems. It called for the President personally to offer United States assistance to India and Pakistan in mediating the three principal problems dividing the two countries: Kashmir, the disposition of the waters of the Indus River, and the escalating arms race. In the absence of a comprehensive settlement, American analysts feared improved United States relations with one state would inevitably alienate the other. While Pakistani President Iskander Mirza leaped at the offer, Nehru politely rebuffed the American overture, leaving the carefully planned initiative stillborn.[15]

As predicted, the Administration's deepening financial commitment to India's development efforts drew Pakistan's ire. Pakistani leaders began to argue, with much justification, that alignment brought few advantages if a non-aligned nation could not only receive economic aid from Washington but receive substantially *more* economic aid. Indeed, in 1957 the United States supplied Pakistan with $170.7 million in economic assistance while providing India with $374.8 million, a disparity that continued to widen over the next three years. In fiscal year 1961 the United States committed $570 million in development and commodity aid for India compared with $168 million for Pakistan. American financial assistance to India, Pakistan complained, facilitated Indian military spending, a charge that Washington found difficult to refute.[16]

The Soviet downing of an American U-2 intelligence aircraft in May 1960 further strained the United States-Pakistani alliance. It soon became public knowledge that the plane had flown from an American-operated base near Peshawar in West Pakistan. Pakistan stood publicly with the United States in the face of vigorous Soviet denunciations and saber-rattling; but privately, Pakistani leaders began to wonder if the alliance with the United States was worth risking the hostility of its powerful neighbor to the north.[17]

In the wake of the U-2 incident, Pakistan began to move away from what it considered a dangerous over-reliance on the United States. President Mohammed Ayub Khan gave the signal for a fresh start in Soviet-Pakistani relations in June 1960 by announcing that he saw no reason why Karachi could not "do business" with Moscow. Subsequent technical assistance and oil exploration negotiations culminated in a $30 million Soviet loan to Pakistan in early 1961. At the same time, Pakistan announced its interest in negotiating a border demarcation agreement with China, demonstrating Karachi's interest in developing warmer ties with its other Communist neighbor. The latter offer reflected in part Pakistan's willingness to profit from the recent deterioration of Indo-Chinese relations by applying the ancient maxim "the enemy of my enemy is my friend." It also signified, along with the opening toward the Soviet Union, a tentative search for new friends to balance what Pakistani leaders viewed as an unhealthy dependence on an unreliable superpower. These moves carried profound implications for United States diplomacy.[18]

As the Eisenhower Administration came to a close, Indo-American relations also bore some ominous portents. To be sure, those relations had improved immeasurably from the 1954–1955 chill. Increasingly, Indian leaders viewed American aid dollars as critical to their economic development priorities. And, from a public relations standpoint, Eisenhower's goodwill trip to India in December 1959 (following an earlier visit to Pakistan) was a "brilliant success."[19] The impact of Ike's trip, Ambassador Ellsworth Bunker predicted, "is likely to be lasting, I believe due to the fact that the visit has for India broken down [the] last of [the] psychological barriers . . . that have stood in the way of giving trust and confidence to [the] U.S."[20] Yet, as the President himself acknowledged during his final year in office, the military relationship between the United States and Pakistan set definite limits on Indo-American friendship. India's deepening economic ties to the Soviet Union bluntly drove home that point. By the end of Eisenhower's tenure India ranked as the leading recipient of Soviet aid in the entire Third World. Bunker reported in May 1959 "a sharp increase in the tempo and scope of the Soviet economic offensive in India." There will be a large measure of Soviet success, he warned, "unless [the] U.S. takes rapid effective countermeasures in terms [of] specific decisions, revisions in programs and additional actions."[21] Such a response, however, barring a near-miraculous disappearance of the mutual suspicion that had for so long plagued Indo-Pakistani relations, would almost surely come at the expense of American ties to Pakistan. That dilemma, inherent in the decision to provide Pakistan with military assistance, lay unresolved as Eisenhower turned over the reins of power to John F. Kennedy in January 1961.

India, along with the developing world as a whole, occupied a position of central importance to the Kennedy Administration's overall diplomatic goals. Convinced the Soviet Union had gained the initiative in the Cold War, the new Administration believed it essential to pursue innovative strategies in the Third World lest the balance of forces shift decisively against the United States. One of those related to the so-called neutralist bloc. The new President and his top advisers agreed their predecessors had placed too much emphasis on the establishment of formal alliances and military assistance relationships with certain developing nations and paid too little attention to the cultivation of friends among the non-aligned countries. As a result, the Soviet Union had gained influence with such key non-aligned states as India, Indonesia, the United Arab Republic, and Ghana. Kennedy hoped to reverse that trend by demonstrating a more tolerant attitude toward neutralism and offering a more generous financial commitment to the economic development plans of neutralist nations. Toward that end, the President-elect appointed a special, pre-inaugural task force for India that recommended $500 million in annual American aid for the duration of India's third five-year plan (1961–1966). "Of all the neutral countries," White House adviser Arthur M. Schlesinger, Jr., later recalled, "Kennedy was most interested in India, which he had long regarded as 'the key area' in Asia."[22] With tact, patience, and dollars, Kennedy thought India and the other non-aligned states could eventually be won for the West; at a minimum, Communist influence could be arrested and increased support for United States policies gained. "We cannot permit all those who call themselves neutrals to join the Communist bloc," the President told his National Security Council. If we "lose" the neutrals, "the balance of power could swing against us."[23]

India's importance to Kennedy Administration strategists derived also from their fixation with China's presumed threat to the Asian equilibrium. "The central problem we face in Asia," Under Secretary of State Chester Bowles wrote the President, "is the existence of Communist China." Kennedy and his national security specialists viewed China as an increasingly hostile and militant adversary. As the Sino-Soviet split deepened, they feared Chinese policy might become even bolder and more aggressive, especially in Southeast Asia. Some senior officials believed New Delhi could play a critical role in containing Beijing's power and influence. Bowles insisted that India, along with Japan, "must be encouraged to recognize its own stake in the containment of China, the limitations of American power in dealing with this danger, and the consequent necessity" for those two Asian powers "to take the initiative in 'guaranteeing' the security of Asia against China's aggressions." All of those ideas, however inchoate and imprecise, helped elevate India to a diplomatic priority of the first order for the Kennedy Administration.[24]

India responded warmly to the new Administration. Nehru had been impressed by Senator Kennedy's persistent efforts to garner additional economic aid for India and by candidate Kennedy's repeated pleas for a more realistic approach to the Third World. The new President's reference to Nehru's "soaring idealism" during his State of the Union address helped reinforce those positive impressions, as did Kennedy's appointment of well-known friends of India to key diplomatic positions: including Chester Bowles as Under Secretary of State; Phillips Talbot as Assistant Secretary of State for Near Eastern and South Asian Affairs; and John K. Galbraith as Ambassador to India.[25] After a visit to New Delhi and a long private talk with Nehru following the election, Senator John Sherman Cooper, a former Ambassador to India, wrote Kennedy that the "relations of India and the United States [were] the best I have known."[26] In order to capitalize on that favorable trend and develop more intimate personal ties with the redoubtable Indian leader who had guided his nation since independence, Kennedy exchanged a series of increasingly friendly letters with Nehru during the early months of his presidency. "I want you to know how much I appreciate your continuing efforts to create a peaceful world community," Kennedy said in one. Referring to India's economic growth under its five-year plans, he exclaimed: "This progress augurs well not only for the future of India but is an example for the whole world of the achievements possible to a free society."[27] In his reply, Nehru waxed equally effusive: "Our task, great as it is, has been made light by the goodwill and generous assitance that has come to us from the United States. To the people of the United States and more especially to you, Mr. President, we feel deeply grateful."[28]

Vice President Lyndon B. Johnson's visit to New Delhi in May 1961, part of a larger Asian trip, reflected the new cordiality and mutuality of interest in Indo-American relations. Although a more unlikely pair is difficult to imagine, the earthy Texan and the austere, aristocratic Prime Minister held a series of friendly and constructive meetings. Johnson found that Nehru's "pleasant attitude and friendliness" well exceeded American expectations.[29] Ambassador Galbraith, the Harvard economics professor and Kennedy intimate, reported that the trip was a "first rate success."[30] He thought Johnson's mission had "markedly strengthened [the] Indian picture of [the] new administration as liberal and compassionate and much interested in Indian problems."[31] Upon his return to Washington, Johnson sent a report to the President that captured the Administration's optimism about its new India policy: "Nehru, during our visit, was clearly 'neutral' in favor of the West. This administration is highly regarded and well received in India. . . . Mainly, there is an intellectual affinity, or an affinity of spirit. This, in my judgment, should be exploited not with the hope of drawing India into our sphere—which might be as unnecessary as it is improbable—but, chiefly, with the hope of cementing under Nehru an India-U.S. friendship which would endure beyond any transition of power in India."[32]

Kennedy's accession to the presidency produced the opposite effect in Pakistan. President Ayub Khan feared the new leader's emphasis on promoting warmer ties with the non-aligned states would lead to a devaluation of Pakistan's alliance with the United States. The appointment of prominent critics of the Pakistan alliance, such as Bowles, Talbot, and Galbraith, to important policy posts fueled those fears. In order to allay Pakistan's concerns, in March 1961 Kennedy dispatched Ambassador-at-Large W. Averell Harriman to Karachi to clarify American intentions. Harriman assured Ayub that the United

States intended to continue its strong support for collective security pacts, and that it intended to maintain a close working relationship with valued allies like Pakistan. At the same time, he pointed out that the United States considered it essential for non-aligned nations to receive American support and help, for, although nominally neutral, they were determined to preserve their independence and to avoid Communist takeover. Ayub, for his part, explained that, although he hoped to normalize relations with China and the Soviet Union, the focal point of Pakistan's foreign policy remained its friendship with the United States. He struck a discordant note in the otherwise amicable conversation when he argued that the United States should press Nehru to settle the Kashmir dispute.[33]

Johnson's visit to Pakistan in May, immediately following his trip to India, revealed the growing importance Ayub attached to the Kashmir issue. When Ayub urged that the United States use its influence with India to break the current impasse, Johnson rejoined that Pakistan overestimated United States influence with Nehru. Ayub disagreed. India, he remarked, relied heavily upon American economic aid; the deterioration in its relations with China only increased that dependence, thus strengthening United States leverage. Johnson tried to reassure Ayub that Washington maintained a distinction between allies and neutrals, but the Kashmir imbroglio dominated the talks. The American response to that tangled question, Ayub made clear, would serve as a litmus test for Pakistan in its assessment of the new Administration's reliability.[34]

On the eve of Ayub's first state visit to the United States, scheduled for July 1961, criticisms of the United States reached unprecedented proportions in Pakistan. The *Civil and Military Gazette* pointed to the "developing crisis in relations" between the two countries caused by America's growing support for India. Decrying Washington's newfound sympathy for neutralists, the *Pakistan Times* railed: "No country can advocate two diametrically opposite philosophies without getting into a mess."[35] Ayub himself stoked the fires in a series of candid interviews prior to his arrival in Washington. He told an Associated Press reporter that Pakistan was "reexamining its membership" in SEATO and complained that American aid to India posed a direct threat to Pakistan's physical security. "Can it be," he asked rhetorically, "the U.S. is abandoning its good friends for the people who may not prove such good friends?" Washington, he added, did not "realize [the] gravity of the situation."[36] He also bluntly told a *London Times* correspondent that the United States was "too shy or too frightened" of India to use its influence to induce a Kashmir settlement.[37]

On July 1, Ambassador William M. Rountree cautioned the State Department that the current drift in relations would most likely accelerate if the United States "turned a deaf ear" to Pakistan's position on Kashmir. The Pakistanis believed strongly and passionately that their claim to Kashmir was just, that Nehru had repeatedly reneged on India's commitments to a plebiscite, and that the United States, as an ally, must use its leverage with the Indian leader to induce a fair resolution of that all-important problem. "Furthermore, their intense apprehension over [a] fundamental shift in American policy in favor of India, and to their disadvantage, can find expression and be tested against the U.S. reaction to [the] Kashmir problem." If Pakistan brought its case before the United Nations once again, the Ambassador warned, and the United States took no action to support it, there would be "foreseeably serious, probably lasting, repercussions on [the] whole gamut of our relations with Pak[istan] and Pak[istan]'s position in [the] East-West conflict."[38] Although sympathetic to the Pakistani position, Administration experts remained pessimistic about the chances for a breakthrough. "About the best we can hope for," observed Bowles, "is the gradual acceptance of the present *de facto* situation."[39]

During Ayub's Washington visit, the Pakistani leader repeatedly stressed the singular importance of the Kashmir dispute to his nation. He urged the President to use American economic assistance as a lever to force India to break the current deadlock. Kennedy countered that American aid was intended to keep India free, not to force India to follow Washington's direction. He agreed, however, to speak with Nehru about Kashmir during the Indian's scheduled visit to the United States in November. If his overture to Nehru proved unsuccessful, Kennedy promised, the United States would then support Pakistan's position on Kashmir at the United Nations. Ayub worried too that the United States might someday provide military assistance to India, especially in view of its escalating border tensions with China. Kennedy replied that the United States did not intend to provide arms to New Delhi. If a Sino-Indian conflict ever erupted, and India asked the United States for military aid, he would first consult with Ayub before making any commitment. Having secured Kennedy's assurances on both Kashmir and military aid to India, the Pakistani President departed Washington convinced his visit had been a major success. American officials also evaluated the Kennedy-Ayub talks as a success, believing that the face-to-face meetings had helped repair what was promising to become a dangerous crack in the United States-Pakistani alliance.[40]

In contrast, the Kennedy-Nehru talks of November 1961, in which the President and his top advisers had lodged so much more hope, produced only disappointment and disillusionment. The two leaders clashed over Southeast Asia, Berlin, and nuclear disarmament. Particularly frustrating to American officials was Nehru's refusal to accept the mantle of leadership in Southeast Asia. Kennedy later described the meetings as "a disaster." It was "the worst head-of-state visit I have had."[41] The President did most of the talking, since, in Galbraith's recollection, "Nehru simply did not respond."[42] According to Schlesinger, Kennedy remarked that talking to Nehru was "like trying to grab something in your hand, only to have it turn out to be just fog."[43] Many Administration officials judged Nehru an aging, tired leader who would not be capable of playing the active world role that the Administration wished to assign him.[44]

Kashmir was the most controversial topic Kennedy raised. Keeping his promise to Ayub, the President emphasized the importance that the United States attached to a peaceful and fair resolution of that question. He asked Nehru if he could see any possible line of settlement that would prove acceptable to both India and Pakistan. The Prime Minister discussed the history of the Kashmir dispute in great detail and with considerable emotion, concluding that no solution, aside from minor boundary adjustments, would be acceptable to India short of a formal recognition of the status quo. Kennedy pressed the Indian leader on several points, but found no flexibility. Recognizing his initiative was doomed, Kennedy instructed Galbraith to break the bad news to Ayub in a personal visit to Karachi. For his part, Nehru departed Washington with a deep sense of unease about the young President's brashness, aggressiveness, and inexperience.[45]

Even more distressing to American policymakers than Nehru's intractability on the Kashmir dispute was his decision to invade Portuguese Goa. The Indian ruler viewed the December 17 attack as justifiable on several grounds: the enclave was an imperial anachronism that culturally, economically, and ethnically belonged with India; Portugal's rule was both repressive to its subjects and provocative to India; the United Nations had repeatedly condemned Portuguese colonialism; all other means short of force had been tried. Although sympathetic to such arguments, the Kennedy Administration protested India's resort to force. Nehru's rejection of last-minute pleas for restraint from Kennedy and Galbraith especially annoyed Washington. "If the United Nations is not to die as ignoble a death as the League of Nations," declared Ambassador Adlai Stevenson at the United Nations, "we cannot condone the use of force in this instance and thus pave the way for forceful solutions of other disputes."[46] Stevenson's strong language infuriated Indians as much as Nehru's "brick exercise in Machtpolitik" appalled Americans.[47] In a long personal letter to Kennedy, Nehru sought to defend India's action while expressing his concern that the Goa invasion might harm Indo-American relations. Galbraith and the State Department agreed that, even though the invasion violated an important principle and thus warranted public condemnation, Indo-American relations were too important to allow such a relatively minor affair to cause permanent damage.[48]

In the wake of the Goa invasion, the Kennedy Administration reassessed its South Asia policy, but continued to lean toward India. In spite of the frustrations engendered by the Nehru visit, the failure of the Kashmir initiative, and the Goa affair, the State Department and the National Security Council staff appraised Indo-American ties as essentially sound. India's border dispute with China and its continued reliance on American economic aid inexorably pushed India closer to the West. Total development and commodity assistance for India had risen to $744 million in fiscal year 1962 (compared with $416 million for Pakistan).[49] At the same time, Administration analysts were relatively pleased with the recent trend in relations with Pakistan. They believed Kennedy had helped reassure Ayub about the Administration's intentions, thereby checking his flirtations with China and Russia.

Still, fundamental problems persisted. In order to advance regional stability and check Chinese and Soviet influence—the Administration's overarching goals—top policymakers agreed that an easing of tensions beween India and Pakistan would be essential. Yet current trends appeared highly unfavorable. Pakistan, unnerved by India's resort to force in Goa and frustrated by the failure of Kennedy's demarche to Nehru, threatened to bring the Kashmir dispute before the United Nations once again. Only American diplomatic intervention, Administration planners concurred, could block that unpromising avenue and stop the "painful confrontations looming in [the] subcontinent." Another United States initiative, however, also brought risks. "We will never be able to get the compromise solutions . . . which are in our own strategic interests," argued NSC aide Robert Komer, "without getting some people mad at us in the process. . . . The gut question is whether the risks of so doing outweigh the gains."50 He thought that they did and most senior officials agreed.

On January 11, 1962, Kennedy endorsed that view at a White House meeting. He authorized a formal offer to India and Pakistan for United States assistance in negotiating a settlement of the Kashmir dispute; a well-respected American citizen would be proposed as mediator. Expressing his personal concern with the state of Indo-Pakistani relations, Kennedy said he "wanted it emphasized to both India and Pakistan that their 'arms race' was ruining our economic aid program by diverting their assets from economic development."51

Kennedy extended the offer in personal letters to Nehru and Ayub, indicating that World Bank President Eugene Black had agreed to serve as mediator. Again, Nehru rejected American counsel. Direct negotiations between India and Pakistan were the only road to a solution, he said; third-party intervention might not help matters and might even complicate them. Administration officials were disappointed and angered by Nehru's intransigence. "This effort has clearly been a bust and leaves matters worse than before," admitted Galbraith. "However well-intentioned, it was based on a clear miscalculation of what we could get the Indians to do."52 Reflecting a view widely held by the government's South Asia specialists, Komer wrote Kennedy that Nehru's explanation for the turndown "was merely a cover for India's basic satisfaction with the present *status quo*. The Indians no doubt feel that any compromise solution would inevitably involve some change in the status quo to their disadvantage; therefore they prefer to spin out the matter, hoping that Pakistan will eventually relax." But, the adviser added solemnly, "we do not think Ayub will let the issue die down."53

Komer was right. Kashmir remained a virtual obsession with the Pakistani general, as did the Kennedy Adminstration's mounting commitment to India's economic development. In June 1962 the United States did support Pakistan's position on Kashmir in the Security Council—essentially a reaffirmation of previous United Nations resolutions calling for a plebiscite—but a Soviet veto, as expected, killed the measure. Ayub warmly thanked Kennedy for his backing, but he continued to suspect that the alliance in which Pakistan had invested so much was eroding. Its support for Beijing's representation on the Security Council and its continued efforts to normalize relations with China, measures that deeply disturbed American officials, stemmed logically from the calculation that an exclusive reliance on the United States could no longer be justified.[54]

On September 24, 1962, Kennedy and Ayub discussed those problems with great friendliness but little accomplishment during an informal three-and-a-half-hour meeting at Newport, Rhode Island. Ayub once again called upon the United States to use its economic aid to India as a lever to moderate Nehru's policy on Kashmir. Kennedy, in turn, insisted that American aid to India could not be used as a weapon. Similarly, the President warned the Pakistani leader against moving too close to the Chinese. Ayub parried that he was only normalizing relations with a potentially troublesome neighbor and that the United States had nothing to fear. On the eve of the Sino-Indian War, then, the Kennedy Administration had yet to deal effectively with the strains in Pakistani-American relations that flowed inexorably from its manifest tilt toward India.[55]

Nor had the Administration, on the eve of that conflict, effected the dramatic turnaround in Indo-American relations that it sought. A number of irritants prevented the development of closer ties between Washington and New Delhi. Nehru's refusal to accept outside mediation of the Kashmir dispute, of course, was one.

India's decision in May to purchase Soviet MIG aircraft as a counterweight to Pakistan's recent acquisition of sophisticated American F-104s presented Washington with another problem. Some policymakers urged that the United States try to block the transaction; others suggested that it subsidize the sale—or make an outright gift—of American aircraft to India if New Delhi agreed to repudiate its deal with Moscow. Komer advised caution: "It would raise hob with [the] Paks who will see in it final confirmation of their suspicions [that] we are shifting to a pro-Indian stance—true, we are but now is not the time to push [the] Paks to [the] wall."[56] Kennedy recognized that, after launching vigorous protests, the Administration could do little but acquiesce in the Indian purchase. Still, the incident heightened tensions between the two nations. Nehru took exception to American pressure, denouncing the United States before Parliament, while Kennedy fumed about India's unreliability.[57]

Periodic congressional displeasure with the Administration's massive economic commitment to India also strained relations between

Washington and New Delhi. Led by Stuart Symington (Democrat of Missouri), in May 1962 the Senate cut the President's proposed aid package for India by 25 percent. Symington explained his position to Kennedy: "Where is the logic in providing such multi-billion dollar assistance to a country whose Secretary of Defense constantly attacks us, whose military plans and programs build up the Soviet economy at the expense of our allies and ourselves, and whose chief leaders constantly threaten with military aggression some of the most steadfast and loyal friends the United States has in the free world?"[58] Strenuous Administration lobbying eventually restored the budget cuts, but not before the episode had generated additional ill will between the two countries.[59]

The outbreak of open hostilities between India and China in late October 1962 carried profound implications for American interests in the subcontinent—and beyond. Kennedy Administration strategists almost immediately interpreted the war as a watershed event, one that, if handled properly, would enable them to accomplish valuable policy objectives. They believed that India, awakened finally to the reality of the Chinese threat, would need—and request—American military aid, thereby tacitly abandoning its non-aligned stance and enabling Washington to draw New Delhi into its orbit. In addition, United States policymakers reasoned that the conflict would impale Moscow on the horns of a dilemma since it would be forced to choose "between (1) its obligations to Communist China as a military ally and fellow Communist state and (2) its assiduously cultivated ties with India." The Soviets would likely remain neutral and urge negotiations, but "as long as the conflict continues, Moscow cannot escape its dilemma and the longer it lasts the more persistent and intense is its divisive impact on the Sino-Soviet relationship." American officials thus saw the border fight as a means both to cement Indo-American friendship and to exacerbate the Sino-Soviet rift.[60]

The origins of the war are complex. Sino-Indian relations had deteriorated drastically following Beijing's brutal suppression in 1959 of a revolt in Tibet. Nehru's decision to grant political asylum to the Dalai Lama, Tibet's spiritual leader, and thousands of his followers angered the Chinese, who suspected the Indians of complicity in the revolt. By the summer of 1959, Indian and Chinese armed patrols clashed in the remote reaches of Ladakh and the North East Frontier Agency, where the two countries maintained overlapping border claims. In the view of United States intelligence experts, the Chinese offensive of

October 1962 reflected Beijing's desire "to consolidate its control over Tibet and to safeguard it against infiltration and subversion." China's longer-range goal sprang from "its expansionist ambitions south of the Himalayas" where it hoped "eventually to detach Nepal, Sikkim, and Bhutan from India's influence and make them satellites of China." American analysts dismissed the possibility that China's ambitions included the conquest of India.[61]

Reeling from the suddenness and surprising effectiveness of the Chinese attack, several Indian diplomats, as expected, sounded out their American counterparts about the possibility of emergency military aid. Kennedy responded promptly to the Indian feelers. On October 28 he offered American aid in a personal letter to Nehru, an offer the Prime Minister immediately accepted.[62]

For the offer of military aid to India to accomplish larger American objectives, however, Kennedy realized Pakistan's acceptance had to be gained. Accordingly, he also dispatched a letter to Ayub on October 28, explaining that United States aid to India was designed solely to counter Communist aggression. "These are interests which we all share," he wrote. "Certainly the United States as a leader of the free world must take alarm at any aggressive expansion of Communist power, and you as the leader of the other great nation in the subcontinent will share this alarm." Kennedy called upon Ayub to play the role of statesman by offering a unilateral no-war pledge to India, thus allowing India to shift all its forces to the border fight in the Himalayas. From Washington's perspective, the suggestion was eminently practical: Pakistan, by making a friendly gesture to India at its time of greatest trouble, would prove to India its intentions were honorable, thus laying a solid foundation for a new era of Indo-Pakistani harmony and regional stability.[63]

Pakistan's reaction to the United States announcement of its decision to aid India punctured those optimistic scenarios. It "has been the precise opposite to that for which we eventually hope," conceded Komer.[64] Throughout the nation rabid anti-American demonstrations and vitriolic newspaper editorials greeted the United States disclosure. An indignant Ayub felt personally betrayed by his ally. Kennedy had promised him in Washington and again at Newport that the United States would consult Pakistan before offering military aid to India; yet Ayub had been informed after the decision had already been reached, and not even consulted. In his response to the American President, Ayub downplayed the significance of the Sino-Indian border clash. Rather than signaling a new phase of Communist aggression, the Pakistani general called it a minor incident. Ayub predicted that any arms that India acquired for use against China would eventually be turned against Pakistan. "Is it in conformity with human nature," he implored Kennedy, "that we should cease to take such steps as are necessary for our self-preservation?"[65] In evaluating the significance of Pakistan's "violent reaction," Roger Hilsman, Director of the State Department's Bureau of Intelligence and Research, noted that "there have been strong intimations that Pakistan is considering a change in its policy of alignment with the West. The government is apparently giving serious consideration to a withdrawal from CENTO and SEATO and to the establishment of closer relations with Bloc countries."[66]

The Kennedy Administration soon directed American policy along three related tracks: first, it decided to provide India rapidly with appropriate military assistance; second, it chose to use its new leverage with New Delhi to break the Kashmir stalemate; and, third, it sought to mollify the Pakistanis with the prospect of a more moderate Indian position toward that dispute while, at the same time, warning them against the consequences of drawing closer to the Chinese. To accomplish these ends, Kennedy dispatched W. Averell Harriman, now Assistant Secretary of State for Far Eastern Affairs, on a mission to the subcontinent. Great Britain's Secretary of State for Commonwealth Relations Duncan Sandys, whose government's interests paralleled Washington's in this area, joined him. The President instructed Harriman to assess India's specific military needs, impress upon Nehru the importance of renewed negotiations with Pakistan, and convince Ayub that cooperation with the United States and India would best serve the interests of his nation.[67]

Kennedy expected the latter task would prove especially difficult. In a personal cable to Harriman, he acknowledged that "frank" discussions with the Pakistani leader would be necessary. "I do not want to push Ayub so hard as to get his back up," Kennedy said, "yet I think it imperative that he be under no illusion as to where we stand." As a result of the Chinese offensive, "the subcontinent has become a new area of major confrontation between the Free World and the Communists." India had been compelled to recognize that fact; Pakistan had to as well in order to meet its alliance commitments. "Were Pakistan to move closer to the Chinese at a time when we were assisting India to confront Communist China," the President pointed out, "it would cut across the deep commitments of the entire free world. . . . Pakistan must realize that there are certain limits which should not be overstepped if a fruitful Pak[istan]-US relationship can continue." Kennedy's message also exuded cautious optimism. Referring to the "one-time opportunity" for bringing about a reconciliation between India and Pakistan afforded by the border war, he ventured that, "with a lot of nursing along from us," issues such as Kashmir could be resolved. "I am proceeding on the assumption that in the last analysis he will go along with us," the President said. "I am convinced that with the right combination of patience and firmness we can bring Ayub to take a reasonable course in his own interest."[68]

The Harriman mission accomplished its immediate goals. Not only did Harriman and Sandys assess India's military requirements but, after some delicate negotiations, they also gained Nehru's assent to a reopening of the long-stalled Kashmir talks. Even the meetings with Ayub proved relatively successful. The Pakistani ruler acknowledged that limited aid to India was understandable and desirable. He also stressed, however, that Pakistani interests demanded tangible progress toward a Kashmir settlement, and he urged the United States to make additional military aid to India contingent upon such progress.[69]

In its final report, the Harriman mission emphasized the enormity of the stakes involved for the United States in the South Asian crisis. India's military defeat would enhance China's prestige, especially in Asia, and "a refusal to come to India's aid would bring in doubt our basic posture toward Communist aggression." The war provided "a unique opportunity" to advance a closer Indo-American relationship even with the unilateral Chinese cease-fire of November 21. It also brought, along with obvious risks, a "unique opportunity for the easing of tensions between India and Pakistan." The report declared that only a Kashmir settlement could ease those tensions and suggested that the United States continue to press both sides to accept a compromise.[70]

Following the advice of the Harriman mission and the NSC Subcommittee on South Asia, Kennedy on December 10 authorized increased military, financial, and diplomatic involvement in the subcontinent. He approved an emergency military aid program for India of up to $60 million, a figure contingent upon a comparable amount from a British-Commonwealth program. He also approved in principle an American commitment to provide air defense support for India as well as a renewed American commitment to help achieve a resolution of the Kashmir problem. Later that month he and British Prime Minister Harold Macmillan jointly endorsed this approach. After a meeting in Nassau, they publicly unveiled an Anglo-American emergency military aid package for India amounting to $120 million. The announcement, which was widely castigated within Pakistan, underscored once again the necessity of breaking the Kashmir deadlock.[71]

In an effort to reassure Ayub, Kennedy informed him that the United States and Great Britain had "agreed on a reasonable and frugal program of military assistance designed solely to enable India to defend itself better should the Chinese Communists renew their attacks at an early date." He stressed the importance of the upcoming Indo-Pakistani discussions, calling a Kashmir settlement the key to the subcontinent's security. On a matter critical to the Pakistani leader, however, Kennedy provided him no succor. The United States believed Chinese aggression posed "as grave an ultimate threat to Pakistan as to India." Therefore, the supply of arms to India to help thwart that threat "should not be made contingent on a Kashmir settlement."[72]

On December 26, just days before the Indo-Pakistani talks formally commenced, Pakistan and China announced the conclusion of a provisional border demarcation agreement. American officials feared that this convention—and the general strengthening of ties between Pakistan and China it symbolized—would poison the atmosphere for the Kashmir negotiations. Ayub tried to reassure American diplomats that his intentions were honorable, but to no avail. Plainly, it looked as if the Pakistanis were seeking common cause with the enemy of India—and America. Foreign Minister Zulfikar Ali Bhutto's much ballyhooed visit to Beijing in February 1963 to sign the border agreement further compounded the problem. "History can be idiotic," Galbraith wrote in his diary. "A staunch American ally against communism is negotiating with the Chinese Communists to the discontent of an erstwhile neutral."[73]

The Kennedy Administration tried persistently to keep the Kashmir talks on track, probing both sides at various junctures for possible points of compromise. In late February Kennedy reiterated his commitment to use all possible American influence to achieve a settlement. "Up to now we have been in up to our ankles, now we will have to get in up to our knees," remarked Secretary of State Dean Rusk.[74] Yet no amount of American prompting could bridge the fundamental differences separating the Indian and Pakistani positions. In April, following a short visit to the subcontinent, Robert Komer and Walt W. Rostow, head of the State Department's Policy Planning Council, reported that no one familiar with the talks believed any longer that they could be brought to a successful conclusion. By May, the Indo-Pakistani negotiations had reached a standstill, and Galbraith sadly observed that there was little the United States could do to revive them.[75] What had originally "looked like a vigorous initiative," the Ambassador admitted, "became a disastrous bungle. When it was all over, we were about back where we started."[76]

Despite the collapse of the Kashmir initiative, the State Department, the NSC staff, and Galbraith urged Kennedy to deepen United States support for the Indian military. "To make all military assistance contingent on Kashmir in coming months," argued Rusk, "is to risk losing out on the main chance." India remained Asia's richest prize; it was "the only non-communist country in Asia capable of becoming a counterpoise to Communist China."[77] From New Delhi, Galbraith concurred. Unless the Administration could soon make a concrete commitment to India regarding future military assistance, he warned Kennedy, "we are in danger of [a] grave loss here." The outlook for a Kashmir accord was "not promising," the Ambassador admitted, but "with continued foot-dragging we will have no progress on Kashmir and no Indians either." Acknowledging that such a decision would cause "problems" with Pakistan, Galbraith reiterated the thinking that undergirded so many of the Administration's policy decisions toward South Asia: "India is the biggest and most stable country in this part of Asia. With it our position is unassailable and without it we have none."[78] During his final months in office, the President acted on those assumptions. In May 1963 he approved a plan to strengthen Indian air defenses and to provide active American air support, if needed, in the event of another Chinese attack. Subsequently, Kennedy authorized continued military aid for India.[79]

But *how much* aid should India receive? Komer, Galbraith, and Bowles, whom Kennedy tapped in April to become Ambassador to India, urged that the United States substantially increase its assistance to New Delhi. Although none thought the Administration should meet India's request for a five-year military aid package of $1.3 billion, they considered a five-year commitment in the range of $500 million feasible and justifiable. Summarizing that perspective, Bowles said its proponents "saw the present situation in India as a major windfall for U.S. strategic interests which, if played skillfully, can lead to a close association with the second largest nation in the world, evolving into a de facto alliance and ultimately, under favorable circumstances, even into a formal alliance." A well-trained and equipped Indian army of some one million men could help balance Chinese military pressure in South Asia.[80] McNamara, Rusk, and Talbot, on the other hand, more concerned with budgetary pressures and more sensitive to the expected outcry from Pakistan, recommended a more circumscribed commitment. Their view prevailed. By November 1963, the White House, the State Department, and the Defense Department had agreed tentatively upon a military aid package to India in the range of only $50 million per annum. Nehru and his top aides, already stung by renewed congressional efforts to cut American economic aid to India, calculated that Washington would never meet New Delhi's mounting military needs. They thus came to depend ever more heavily on Soviet military supplies, deepening a relationship with Moscow that has continued to the present.[81]

According to Ambassador Bowles, a one-time chance to align India with the West had been squandered by short-sighted leadership. America's "strictly limited commitment to India," he told one State Department official, diminishes its leverage and "plays into the hands of the Soviets." Years later he recalled: "If we'd been able to get the agreement then, the history of the whole area would have been different because India would have worked with us at that stage. Russia would have pulled away."[82]

Although the available evidence is not conclusive on this point, it appears that Kennedy sided with his top cabinet officers in this important policy debate not because he had abandoned his long-held desire to align India with the West, but because he shared their apprehension about Pakistan's likely response to a generous, long-term military assistance agreement with India. Like them, he feared such a commitment would push Pakistan further into the arms of China, lead to the dissolution of Pakistan's alliance with the West, and jeopardize continued American use of the intelligence facilities at Peshawar. He recognized, in sum, that the breakdown of the Kashmir talks had placed definite limits on the emerging Indo-American military relationship. As Hilsman explained in his memoirs: "The more the United States gave India aid in the absence of a settlement, the more Pakistan would move toward an accommodation with Communist China, and there clearly was a limit to what the United States could give India and still maintain friendly relations with Pakistan."[83]

Plainly, the failure of the Kashmir negotiations strained American relations with Pakistan almost to the breaking point, revealing a deep cleavage between the national interests of the two countries. Pakistan had always considered India the chief threat to its security. Since the early 1950s Pakistani leaders accordingly had sought protection through a network of alliances with the West. Now, they saw that policy unraveling as their principal ally furnished military aid, however modest, to their principal adversary. Ayub recognized—correctly— that the Kennedy Administration would never favor Pakistan over India, despite the alliance ties. As a consequence, by mid-1963 he had embraced a policy of limited disengagement from the West, a policy based on the cultivation of closer relations with both China and the Soviet Union. Ayub, Ambassador Walter P. McConaughy reported from Karachi, believed he could no longer rely solely on the United States for his nation's security. "I feel that we have perhaps only a limited amount of time," the Ambassador warned Washington, "in the order of a year or two, to stem the trend away from Pakistan's current fundamental link with [the] West, before it picks up momentum which could make it irreversible."[84]

The Kennedy Administration considered Pakistan's limited disengagement from the West a dangerous development that undercut American global and regional interests while contradicting the original rationale for the alliance. Reacting to the recent announcement of a proposed air link between China and Pakistan, on July 4 Harriman told the Pakistani Ambassador that "in this period, no member of the Free World should do anything [to] aid and abet" the Chinese Communists. "Pakistan," he cautioned, "should be very careful in its dealing with the Chicoms and not jeopardize its relations with the Western world." Further "rapprochement" between Karachi and Beijing could cause "a very unfortunate reaction" in the United States.[85]

In early September 1963 Kennedy sent Under Secretary of State George Ball to Pakistan for a series of frank and wide-ranging discussions with Ayub. The terms of reference for the Ball mission were quite explicit: "To arrest the deterioration in U.S.-Pakistan relations so that our major interests in the security and stability of the subcontinent and in the Peshawar facilities can be protected without at the same time endangering the development of our new relationship with India."[86] During the discussions, held over three days at Pakistan's new interim capital of Rawalpindi, the two sides aired familiar positions in a candid but friendly manner. Ayub persistently emphasized his central concern: large-scale American military assistance to India had gravely jeopardized Pakistan's security. Although he had been compelled to normalize relations with China and other neighboring states in order to offset India's enhanced military strength, Ayub insisted such actions were not aimed at the United States. Ball tried to reassure the Pakistani general that Western military aid to India had become an essential part of Washington's global strategy for containing Communism. He reiterated earlier promises to Pakistan that it could depend upon American help in case of an attack from India or any other nation. But Ayub remained skeptical. The Under Secretary also expressed dissatisfaction with the current state of United States-Pakistani relations. He implied that further steps toward the normalization of relations with China might "nullify" the alliance between Washington and Karachi. While "gratifyingly direct," in Ball's view, the talks accomplished little of substance.[87]

The Ball mission revealed with disturbing clarity that the United States and Pakistan were embarked on a collision course. Kennedy's final months in office provided no respite from the "corrosive" trends in Pakistani-American relations.[88] Shortly after the Under Secretary returned to Washington, American intelligence sources learned that Ayub had invited Chinese Premier Zhou Enlai to Pakistan for a state visit. Combined with a succession of recent agreements between the two countries governing trade, aviation, borders, and cultural exchanges, the invitation convinced Administration officials that Pakistan's emerging entente with China had become an essential, and probably irreversible, element of Pakistani foreign policy.[89] Bhutto later argued correctly that American military support for India had "revealed the irreconcilable contradictions between the different assumptions on which Pakistan and the United States had built their special relations."[90]

Therein lay the ultimate failure of Kennedy's policy toward South Asia. United States military aid to India had radically undermined American relations with Pakistan—driving an ally to find common cause with one of Washington's chief adversaries. Yet that aid did not lead to a significant extension of American influence in India. The President had hoped simultaneously to promote regional stability and prosperity, foster an Indo-Pakistani rapprochement, and check Chinese and Soviet influence in the subcontinent. Instead, his initiatives promoted precisely the opposite effects. Kennedy bequeathed to Lyndon Johnson an increasingly explosive situation in South Asia. With the Indo-Pakistani War of 1965, Johnson would reap the bitter harvest of his predecessor's legacy.

The Kennedy Administration failed to achieve its policy objectives in South Asia not for want of trying but because its actions rested on a number of dubious assumptions: first, that the United States could have friendly relations with *both* India and Pakistan and not at the expense of one or the other; second, that the problems dividing the two countries could be solved with timely American encouragement and support; third, that the ominous shadow cast by China would induce India to abandon its cherished policy of non-alignment and Pakistan to join forces with India against a common enemy; fourth, that Pakistan's dependence on American aid would deter it from pursuing closer ties with China. Each of those premises proved deeply flawed. Kennedy and his advisers, driven by visions of Cold War victories, disregarded the impediments of history and underestimated the deep divergence between the national interests of the United States, India, and Pakistan. At the same time, they exaggerated the leverage Washington could bring to bear on those traditional rivals and nurtured the mistaken idea that an outside power could provide answers for regional questions. From their very inception, then, Kennedy's initiatives in South Asia were probably doomed.

The Administration's decisions were rooted not in regional realities, but in a series of global illusions: the illusion that China posed an immediate threat to the security of Southeast Asia; the illusion that India could—and would—contain Chinese expansion; the illusion that India, in spite of its poverty, military weakness, and vast internal problems, could offer meaningful support to American Cold War policies; the illusion that a Sino-Pakistani entente posed a major threat to United States interests. In retrospect, the largely symbolic value that Kennedy attached to bringing India into "our sphere" appears grossly disproportionate to India's true significance. The available documentation suggests that American policy toward India and Pakistan derived less from a careful analysis of the subcontinent's strategic, economic, and political value than from a Cold War *mentalité* that judged the world in terms of a "zero sum game": any victory for the United States, in other words, meant a loss for the Communist camp. That Cold War ethos so dominated Administration thinking about South Asia that it severely impeded any realistic appraisal of American interests and capabilities in the area.

9

The Failed Search for Victory: Vietnam and the Politics of War

LAWRENCE J. BASSETT AND
STEPHEN E. PELZ

Two weeks before the United States's defeat at the Bay of Pigs, John Kenneth Galbraith, John F. Kennedy's new Ambassador to India, warned the President against "the surviving adventurism in the Administration. . . ." The always frank Galbraith recalled that the "futile campaign to the Yalu ruined the Democrats in 1950. . . . We Democrats with our reputation for belligerence and our basically hostile press have far less margin for mistakes than had the Republicans." During the following months, Galbraith also told Kennedy that South Vietnam was "a can of snakes," and speculated that Premier Ngo Dinh Diem's desperate efforts to cling to power might falter and draw the United States deeper into Indochina. Galbraith recommended that Kennedy send an emissary to explain the problem of Diem's pigheadedness to the State Department—"with pictures. . . . We are increasingly replacing the French as the colonial military force and we will increasingly arouse the resentment associated therewith." "Incidentally," he continued, "who is the man in your administration who decides what countries are strategic? I would like to have his name and address and ask him what is so important about this [Vietnamese] real estate in the space age." Galbraith concluded that "it is the political poison that is really at issue. The Korean war killed us in the early 50's; this involvement could kill us now."[1]

John F. Kennedy himself decided that South Vietnam was strategically vital. He did so because he viewed the world and the methods for dealing with it differently from Galbraith, although he certainly

223

agreed with the Ambassador about the domestic political dangers of ordering American infantry units to fight in South Vietnam. While Galbraith called for continuing a "conservative, thoughtful, non-belligerent stance" toward the world, Kennedy wanted to lead his South Vietnamese allies to victory over the Vietnamese Communists without sending large numbers of American troops into battle.[2] To this end the President stated repeatedly and publicly that the United States would help suppress the insurgency in South Vietnam; he warned the Soviets both publicly and privately against assisting the guerrillas; he increased economic aid to South Vietnam; he enlarged the South Vietnamese Army and police forces; he increased the number of American military advisers, logistic units, and pilots from approximately 700 to approximately 16,700; he allowed a number of the advisers to participate in combat; he ordered assistance to the South Vietnamese for covert raids against North Vietnam; he helped launch the South Vietnamese strategic hamlet program; he encouraged the South Vietnamese military to assume political power; and he rejected suggestions that he try to neutralize South Vietnam—a solution which he had been willing to accept in Laos.

Early in his career Kennedy had formed an image of South Vietnam as a nation whose nationalist elite was caught between French colonialists and Communist insurgents. Since Kennedy believed Americans were not seen as colonialists, he expected that American advisers would be able to work with Vietnamese nationalists to establish and defend a pro-Western state in South Vietnam. Drawing the containment line at the South Vietnamese border was all the more important, because he had reluctantly accepted a neutralized Laos. In his determined search for victory in Vietnam, President Kennedy kept trying different tactics and personnel, but his efforts played into the hands of the National Liberation Front (NLF), a coalition of anti-Diem groups for which the Communists provided most of the leaders. By giving Diem money and men, Kennedy backed a system of landlord rule in the countryside, which was deeply unpopular with the peasants, and by aiding the South Vietnamese security forces in their attempts to impose Diem's will on the villages, he identified the Americans with a repressive *ancien regime*.

Peasants joined the NLF in increasing numbers, because the NLF cadres helped them achieve a rural revolution. Kennedy's program of industrialization, rural aid, resettlement, and helicopter assaults carried little appeal in the countryside. Kennedy nonetheless persisted in his quest for victory in Vietnam, even after repeated warnings that his methods were failing. He did so in part because he and his small senior staff did not spend much time searching for the realities behind the flow of daily cables from Saigon. Given the current state of documentation, Kennedy's motives for this persistant quest for victory must remain something of a mystery. It appears, however, that he persevered in Vietnam not only to preserve his credibility as a successful practitioner of containment but also to maintain his reputation as an anti-Communist in the face of Republican attacks at home.

Indochina had a special meaning for Kennedy, because it was the first issue on which he had gained some recognition as an expert on foreign policy.[3] He formed his views during a brief trip to the Middle East and Southeast Asia in October 1951, and he never changed them. Both he and his brother Robert concluded that unrest in the area stemmed from nationalist revolutions against exploitative, white colonialists and that, in some areas, such as Indochina, the Communists were winning over the nationalists by default. When Congressman Kennedy arrived in Saigon, Vietnam, he doubted the French predictions of victory and took an immediate dislike to Bao Dai, the French puppet ruler, whom he described as looking as if he were "fried in Crisco." When Kennedy returned home, he reported that "the majority of the people are on the side of the guerrillas," and he urged the French to permit Vietnam to establish "a non-communist native government so that it can move safely toward independence."[4]

Kennedy appears to have relied heavily in the 1950s on the views of Edmund A. Gullion, a young foreign service officer who shared Kennedy's doubts about French willingness to work with Vietnamese nationalists (in 1963 Kennedy considered sending Gullion to Saigon as Ambassador). Gullion argued that a grant of indepcndence would produce a "feeling of nationhood" for Vietnam and give the fledgling French-trained officer corps of the Vietnamese army an ideal around which to rally. Even with the Communist-led Vietminh in control of much of thc countryside, Gullion believed that the Communists lacked appeal as social revolutionaries, because Vietnam did not suffer the "grinding poverty" of other Southeast Asian nations. Gullion concluded that "the principal communist appeal is to nationalism." Kennedy thought the harsh methods of the Communist cadres alienated the nationalist elite, which was sitting on the fence between the two conquerors—the French and the Communists. The hope of the future, he believed, rested in this educated nationalist minority and in a trained corps of military officers, because the semiliterate peasantry's "main concern is their bowl of rice." The peasants would follow leaders who provided them with economic security and national independence.[5]

In 1953 Senator Kennedy asked the Eisenhower Administration to use foreign aid to force a French grant of independence to the Vietnamese, and a year later he told the Senate that it would be "self-destructive . . . to pour money, material, and men into the jungles of Indochina," unless the people there supported the cause of the West wholeheartedly. If the French granted them freedom and recruited "a reliable and crusading native army with a dependable officer corps," then victory might be possible in Vietnam—the key to all of Southeast Asia. And if American troops tried to prop up the French colonial regime, Kennedy predicted they would suffer the same fate as the French, making it necessary "to move back to a secondary line."[6]

After the French withdrawal from Vietnam in 1954–1955, events in South Vietnam seemed at first to confirm Kennedy's diagnosis. Kennedy claimed that Ngo Dinh Diem and "a determined band of patriotic Vietnamese around one man of faith, President Diem," had released and harnessed "the latent power of nationalism to create an independent, anti-Communist Vietnam."[7] In reality, far from being a full-fledged nationalist, Diem had served the Japanese during World War II. Yet in 1956 Kennedy praised the new South Vietnam with a barrage of mixed clichés such as "the cornerstone of the Free World in Southeast Asia, the keystone to the arch, the finger in the dike," "a proving ground of democracy in Asia," "a test of American responsibility and determination." And he concluded, "We must supply capital . . . , technicians . . . , [and] guidance to assist a nation taking those first feeble steps toward the complexities of a republican form of government."[8]

In spite of considerable American economic and military aid, Diem was in trouble by 1959. In 1957–1958 he had restored landlord-gentry rule to many of the rural areas and put his northern and central Vietnamese Catholic Can Lao party members in control of much of the government, army, and police.[9] In 1959 the southern Vietminh began reclaiming the countryside for the peasants, while decrying the harsh rule of "American Diem's" minions. In Long An province, not far from Saigon, for example, armed squads drove Diem's officials almost completely out of the villages with a campaign of terror which killed twenty-six people during the New Year's celebration of 1960. Vietminh cadres established peasant committees in the liberated areas and encouraged the newly empowered peasants to reduce land rents and redistribute the land of those Diemist officials who had fled.[10] By 1961 the campaign had swayed about 80 percent of South Vietnam's villages toward their side, and Diem's government had to rely almost totally on American economic and military assistance to replace the taxes and recruits lost in the villages.[11]

The Vietminh offensive in South Vietnam appeared to confirm Kennedy's picture of world politics in 1961. Although the United States was far superior to the Soviet Union in nuclear weaponry, Kennedy believed the United States faced a challenge to the global balance of power from both the Soviets and the Chinese Communists, who he claimed were merely vying with one another over the best way to bury the West. Because the Soviets possessed hydrogen bombs, Kennedy complained, Eisenhower's reliance on nuclear weapons represented a dangerous illusion; neither side could use such weapons for fighting conventional and brushfire wars. Kennedy therefore adopted a flexible response strategy to counter Communist-led insurgencies like the one in South Vietnam. The President and Secretary of State Dean Rusk also became particularly alarmed by the aggressive rhetoric of the People's Republic of China, which seemed to be gaining influence in Hanoi in 1962 (see Chapter 7).[12]

Kennedy had other reasons for taking the NLF challenge seriously. He had learned during the 1950s that he could win political rewards by advocating an anti-Communist counter-offensive. After all, he had grown up in the Massachusetts politics of anti-Communism, and Bay State voters had provided some of Joseph R. McCarthy's most loyal supporters. As a young congressman Kennedy had actually joined Republicans in criticizing the Democrats for losing East Germany, Poland, and China to the Soviets.[13] He had also made headlines by pursuing alleged Communists in labor unions, and during his senatorial campaign of 1952, he charged that Henry Cabot Lodge, Jr., was soft on Communism.[14] During his political campaigns he solicited support from a wide range of anti-Communist ethnic organizations— Italians, Poles, Germans, Hungarians, Czechs, Greeks, Lithuanians, and Russians.[15]

The political arithmetic was simple—ethnic voters had supported Truman by a two-to-one margin in 1948, but they shifted in large numbers to Eisenhower in 1952. Due in part to his public McCarthyism, Kennedy was one of the few Democrats to buck the Republican tide in 1952. Although ethnic voters did not support McCarthyism in larger proportions than the general population, McCarthyism became the bridge over which formerly loyal Democratic voters in critical electoral college states left the decaying New Deal coalition. In 1956, 35 percent of Catholic *Democrats* voted against Stevenson. Kennedy knew good politics when he saw it.[16] During his campaign, Kennedy portrayed himself as the man who could stand up to the Communists better than the Republicans, whom he accused of losing both Cuba and the Cold War. In the electoral college, Kennedy achieved a net gain of 22 votes due to the fortuitous concentration of ethnic blocs in key Northern and Midwestern states, and these votes were critical in the very close election of 1960.

The Republicans would hold Kennedy to his campaign promises of victories in the Cold War. In 1960, Richard M. Nixon had predicted that Kennedy was "the kind of man Mr. Khrushchev will make mince-meat of," and during his final briefing of the President-elect, Eisenhower told Kennedy he had to intervene militarily in Laos, with or without allies, if the Laotians appealed to the Southeast Asian Treaty Organization (SEATO).[17] Kennedy had sought a second meeting with Eisenhower during the transition because he himself was leaning toward escalation in Laos, where leftist guerrillas were defeating American-backed rightists. For Eisenhower, an independent Laos was vital for holding the rest of Southeast Asia.[18] According to one participant in this meeting, however, Eisenhower did leave an opening for a peaceful solution by saying that a coalition government which included the Communists might succeed in keeping Laos neutral indefinitely, but Kennedy concluded from this meeting that Eisenhower would prefer United States military intervention to any substantial Communist success in Laos.[19] During this second meeting neither Eisenhower nor Kennedy thought Vietnam required emergency measures, for they did not mention the country.

At the start of his Administration, Kennedy believed Indochina demanded decisions. In spite of the best efforts of Central Intelligence Agency advisers, America's allies in Laos were in disarray, and the neutralist factions there were tilting toward cooperation with the Communists; the NLF was making steady gains in South Vietnam; Diem's regime was almost completely dependent upon the United States for funds; and the 675 American advisers in South Vietnam could not stir Diem's security forces to fight effectively. With Eisenhower's support, Kennedy might have declared the region a vital security zone and stationed regular American armed forces in South Vietnam, Laos, and Thailand, exposing those units to attrition by the guerrillas. Or he might have decided to increase military, economic, and political aid and advice to the Laotians and Vietnamese and rely on them to hold the line, exposing only American advisers to danger. Or, finally, he might have tried to negotiate a neutralization agreement with the Communist powers, leaving American allies in Laos and Vietnam to fight on with American dollar aid only, while drawing the military containment line at the Thai border. Kennedy chose the middle course—escalation short of sending United States combat troops—though he had to retreat from Laos and apply his strategy to South Vietnam.

Why did Kennedy intervene in Southeast Asia? Domestic politics played its part, but international factors were also important. Kennedy perceived the Laotian civil war as yet another Sino-Soviet challenge, and he became even more alarmed when Premier Nikita Khrushchev placated the Chinese by declaring Soviet support for wars of national liberation.[20] Khrushchev added to Kennedy's uneasiness in 1961 by increasing Soviet airlifts to Congolese and Laotian insurgents and by augmenting aid to Castro's Cuba and to North Vietnam.[21] Even more disturbing was Khrushchev's threat to resume the Berlin blockade. In October, just before the Berlin crisis eased, Kennedy told Arthur Krock of the *New York Times* that "it was a hell of a note . . . that he had to try to handle the Berlin situation with the Communists encouraging foreign aggressors all over the place . . . in Viet-Nam, Laos, etc."[22]

In early 1961 Kennedy believed the United States lacked the strength to intervene with conventional forces in both Southeast Asia and Europe simultaneously, and, with the Berlin crisis looming, he certainly wanted enough troops available for service in Europe. Landlocked Laos presented difficult logistical problems, and the anticommunist Laotians showed little desire for combat. General Maxwell D. Taylor and Walt W. Rostow of the National Security Council (NSC) staff urged the President to commit the United States to direct military intervention if the Communists renewed their Laotian offensive. Kennedy demurred, replying that President Charles de Gaulle of France "had spoken with feeling of the difficulty of fighting in this part of the world." He also "emphasized the reluctance of the American people and of many distinguished military leaders to see any direct involvement of U.S. troops in that part of the world." Consequently, Kennedy chose to negotiate, and in April 1961 the Soviets and Chinese agreed to meet in Geneva to discuss Laos.[23]

By careful maneuvering, Kennedy was able to limit Republican criticism of his plan for a Laotian coalition government. He neutralized Eisenhower by having British Prime Minister Harold Macmillan appeal directly to the ex-President, and on July 20 he arranged for General Douglas MacArthur to lecture congressional leaders on the inadvisability of deploying American troops in Southeast Asia.[24] Kennedy hoped he could persuade the South Vietnamese and Thais to send their own forces into Southern Laos, if the need arose. Rostow concluded that Kennedy wanted "indigenous forces used to the maximum," and "should we have to fight, we should use air and seapower to the maximum and engage minimum U.S. forces on the Southeast Asian mainland."[25] The Geneva Conference on Laos began in May 1961 and lasted until June 1962, when the conferees agreed to set up a neutral government. Although they promised to respect Laotian neutrality and avoid establishing foreign military bases in Laos, by late 1962 both sides were covertly violating the agreement. Nevertheless, the shaky arrangement held together, decreasing the need for overt American intervention after June 1962.

Kennedy's concessions in Laos raised the stakes for him in South Vietnam. During the Laos negotiations, Dean Rusk told Andrei Gromyko that "there must be a cessation of the increasingly open attacks against South Viet Nam by the DRV [North Vietnam]. . . . Both the Soviets and the DRV should understand that we are deeply committed to South Vietnam and cannot and will not accept its destruction."[26] In spite of Rusk's claim, the Eisenhower Administration had not formally committed Kennedy to defend South Vietnam. The SEATO treaty required only that member nations consult with one another and meet common dangers according to their own "constitutional processes." Eisenhower had conditioned the large United States aid program on proper performance by Diem—a performance which Elbridge Durbrow, the United States Ambassador in Saigon, 1960–1961, found lacking.[27] Eisenhower's policy toward South Vietnam left Kennedy with options other than to support a Diemist regime, but Kennedy was determined to help the South Vietnamese defeat the Communists.

Even before deciding to negotiate a Laotian settlement, Kennedy had gradually increased American military and economic aid to South Vietnam. At the outset of his Administration Kennedy had expressed doubt that Eisenhower had been doing enough in South Vietnam, and he asked his NSC staff, "How do we change morale; how do we get [South Vietnamese] operations in the north [North Vietnam]; how do we get moving?" In order to shift "from the defense to the offense," Kennedy authorized a 50,000-man increase in ARVN, sent in more American training staff, deployed 400 Green Berets to lead 9,000 border tribesmen against North Vietnam's infiltration routes, ordered the Central Intelligence Agency to organize commando raids against North Vietnam, armed the South Vietnamese provincial Civil Guard forces with heavy weapons, and added $42 million to an aid program which was already spending $220 million per year. In May 1961 Diem assured Vice President Lyndon B. Johnson that this impressive military and economic buildup would enable the ARVN to go on the offensive.[28] Kennedy also prompted SEATO to declare publicly that it would refuse to "acquiesce in [a] takeover of [South Vietnam by] . . . an armed minority . . . supported from outside. . . ." In spite of these emergency actions, 58 percent of South Vietnam was under some degree of Communist control in May 1961, according to the Department of Defense.[29]

When Kennedy personally tried to warn off the Russians, however, he hit a roadblock. At the Vienna summit in June, Kennedy brought up Khrushchev's speech in support of national liberation wars, and he told the Soviet leader that the "problem was how to avoid direct contact between [the] two countries as we support respective groups; [he] referred to Vietnam guerrilla activity and said we do not believe they represent [the] popular will. . . ." Khrushchev said the Soviets found it necessary to support such wars, because they were the only way oppressed peoples could throw off their oppressors. He also warned that American meddling in such wars might bring the "terrible prospect of mutual destruction."[30] While Kennedy found Khrushchev to be threatening in this encounter, the young President may well have misperceived the degree of Soviet aggressiveness. During the Vienna summit, Kennedy gave as good as he got, and Khrushchev's moves in Germany, Laos, and the Congo might well have been defensive. In Berlin, the East Germans were losing growing numbers of refugees to the West; in Laos, the Communists were counterattacking against an American-backed rightist offensive; and in the Congo, Eisenhower had winked at the Belgian-sponsored Katanga secession and had driven Patrice Lumumba, a nationalist leader, to seek Soviet military aid. Even Khrushchev's much quoted speech called for disarmament negotiations and increased East-West trade, not just national liberation wars.[31] The Soviet Union was not a principal opponent in South Vietnam.

Who was the enemy in South Vietnam? The People's Republic of China was hardly a consistent or enthusiastic ally of the Vietnamese Communists, for Beijing had joined Moscow in forcing Ho Chi Minh to accept the division of Vietnam during the 1954 Geneva Conference, and the Chinese Communists continued to compete with the North Vietnamese for influence over the Pathet Lao in Laos. Until 1960 the Chinese had not been enthusiastic about reviving the insurgency in South Vietnam. Given this record, the majority of the North Vietnamese preferred to lean to the side of the more distant Russians rather than to the side of the nearby Chinese. And just before Kennedy decided to escalate American efforts drastically in South Vietnam, Zhou Enlai walked dramatically out of the Twenty-second Congress of the Communist Party of the Soviet Union on October 23, 1961. As the Sino-Soviet dispute widened in 1961–1963, the North Vietnamese were able to play off both Communist powers to secure somewhat increased aid, but even the Chinese stressed that the independent strength of internal revolutionaries, not outside aid, was the prerequisite for victory in national liberation wars.[32] Although the 1950s' line of peaceful coexistence did disappear from Communist rhetoric, neither the Chinese nor the Russians wanted to press national liberation wars to a direct superpower confrontation, and both recognized the centrality of indigenous sources to revolutionary success.

The North Vietnamese were not even the primary enemy in South Vietnam, for they hoped to avoid a full-scale conventional war with the American-advised Army of the Republic of Vietnam (ARVN). They planned to mobilize the peasantry by a socio-political campaign and convert urban dwellers and disgruntled ARVN officers to their cause by nationalistic appeals, and then set up a coalition government after a general uprising and coup. In order to appeal to nationalists, the North Vietnamese urged the Southern Vietminh to organize the NLF. After the coup, the North Vietnamese probably planned to ease the Americans out of the country and then move the noncommunist elements out of the coalition. This program would let Hanoi finish its new five-year economic plan for the north by 1966.[33] The North Vietnamese, then, did not constitute the *primary* enemy in South Vietnam during the Kennedy Administration, though they certainly provided leadership, some supplies, and encouragement to southern NLF fighters.

The two main enemies of the United States in South Vietnam were the peasants, who supported the NLF for reasons which Kennedy did not understand, and the southern Vietminh (later NLF) leaders who had suffered or gone into exile under Diem. Under Ho Chi Minh's direction from 1945 to 1954 the southern Vietminh had established the legitimacy of their movement by helping to defeat the Japanese, by driving the French colonialists from the country, and by extending the Vietminh revolution to at least 60 percent of the South, only to see Diem re-impose landlord control in the rural areas and arrest those suspected of Communist connections or opposition sympathies.[34] By 1961 the NLF-inspired peasants were steadily liberating themselves from Diemist rule, while supplying their village militias with arms purchased or captured from the ARVN or brought home by numerous ARVN deserters. Although they received trained leaders from among the southerners who had fled North and returned, and although they received some arms from China, the NLF-led peasants could sustain a guerrilla campaign and control the countryside without major infiltration or arms shipments from North Vietnam or China.[35]

The NLF had so many advantages that the insurgency spread rapidly. Its land program carried great appeal in the Delta region, where tenant farmers comprised the great majority, as well as in central Vietnam where landholdings were very small. Tenants customarily paid around 50 to 60 percent of their crop to the landlord, in addition to taxes and bribes, leaving them far poorer than Kennedy and Gullion supposed. The Diemists also represented an old, Westernizing, landlord regime, symbolized by Catholicism, which distinguished it from the majority of its Confucian, Buddhist, and Animist countrymen. By the fall of 1961, the peasant revolutionaries had won control of the villages in many regions of South Vietnam, although some experts have maintained that the Delta region was still hotly contested as late as 1963.[36] Walt Rostow and Roger Hilsman, Kennedy's principal counter-insurgency war theorists, did not understand the attraction of the people's war strategy for the peasantry. They believed the Communists were primarily terrorists and guerrilla fighters, whose challenge was as much military as socio-economic, though Rostow stressed the military side of the struggle more than Hilsman.[37] If Kennedy had felt politically free to do so, and if he had understood the strength of the people's war strategy, he might well have accepted coalition governments in both Laos and South Vietnam and drawn the counter-insurgency line instead in Thailand, a country which had not suffered the social divisions of colonialism and which did not suffer from a major insurgency.

By fall 1961 Diem's regime was in far deeper trouble than Kennedy had realized. In September, NLF armed forces tripled their attacks and consolidated their hold on much more of the countryside. Diem requested a bilateral security treaty with the United States and, with less enthusiasm, the dispatch of regular American combat forces. Kennedy then sent General Taylor, his personal military counselor, and Rostow of the NSC staff, two hawkish advisers, to South Vietnam to explore the seriousness of the setback and the need to meet Diem's requests. After their return the President began to consider his options. Through early November, the debate among Kennedy's principal advisers centered on a variety of escalatory alternatives. There were five main policies suggested, each of which reflected the organizational origins of its sponsor. Defense Secretary Robert S. McNamara and the Joint Chiefs of Staff recommended sending 40,000 regular United States troops to deal with the NLF, and 205,000 if the North Vietnamese and Chinese intervened with regular troops. The Joint Chiefs believed that regular American troops were quite capable of dealing with lightly armed guerrillas and that North Vietnamese and Chinese logistical difficulties and American air attacks could prevent the Communists from mounting a conventional campaign in South Vietnam on the scale of Korea. McNamara also wanted to warn North Vietnam that it would suffer "punitive retaliation" if it continued to support the southern guerrillas.[38]

McGeorge Bundy, Kennedy's National Security Adviser, joined Taylor and Rostow in arguing for a second alternative. They believed a smaller commitment of American troops—on the order of 5,000 to 25,000—would deter the North Vietnamese from aiding the NLF, and they expected this deployment to galvanize the South Vietnamese effort, provided that Kennedy also agreed to send a large number of American advisers, helicopters, tactical bombers, transport planes, logistical detachments, and intelligence units. Taylor believed helicopters and improved intelligence efforts would allow ARVN to move from static defensive positions to active pursuit of the guerrillas.[39] McGeorge Bundy claimed that the United States was already committed to the survival of South Vietnam and that a victory there would "produce great effects all over the world." He contrasted South Vietnam with Laos: "Laos was never really ours after 1954. South Vietnam is and wants to be. Laotians have fought very little. South Vietnam troops are not U.S Marines, but they are usable."[40]

Taylor, Rostow, and Edward Lansdale predicted that spreading American advisers throughout the South Vietnamese government would spur ARVN to action and shorten military reaction times, which had been slow because of Diem's personal control of all military movements. General Lansdale was a CIA agent who had helped direct the successful counter-insurgency effort of Ramon Magsaysay in the Philippines, and he had also helped advise Diem during the latter's consolidation of power in South Vietnam. "A U.S. operating presence at many working levels," Lansdale predicted, would force the South Vietnamese "to get their house in order."[41] This proposal reflected Kennedy's continuing desire to use local troops in Southeast Asia, though it bowed slightly toward the Pentagon by including small formations of American combat troops. This recommendation also reflected Taylor's belief that air mobility and tactical bombing provided a way for technologically superior forces to take the offensive in limited wars.[42]

The State Department was much more ambivalent about Diem's regime and offered a third alternative: a hard line on Diem to go with more advisers and aid. As McGeorge Bundy summarized Dean Rusk's views, the Secretary of State "knows we may lose, and he knows we want no Korea but he . . . thinks we *must* meet Khrushchev in Vietnam or take a terrible defeat."[43] Nevertheless, Rusk had grown frustrated with Diem's repeated rejection of Ambassador Frederick Nolting's requests to revise the military command arrangements which prevented ARVN generals from responding quickly to NLF attacks (and also from mounting a coup against Diem). Rusk feared Diem's continued refusal to "trust [his] military commanders" and "to consolidate non-communist elements into [a] serious national effort" would eventually make him "a losing horse."[44]

Sterling Cottrell, the head of State's Vietnam task force, which oversaw day-to-day implementation of Vietnam policy in 1961, was less polite, when he called Diem "an oriental despot." Ambassador Galbraith added that Diem's family dictatorship was marked by "intrigue, nepotism . . . , corruption . . . , administrative paralysis and steady deterioration."[45] George C. McGhee, the counselor at the Department of State who had run the American counter-insurgency program during the Greek civil war in the 1940s, had argued earlier that South Vietnamese insurgents derived support from inside the country and therefore American regulars would not be of much help, since "alien troops simply lack the bases for discriminating between friend and foe. . . ."[46] State Department officials urged the use of foreign aid as a lever to force Diem to revise his chain of command and broaden his government.

Kennedy's political advisers warned him against the dangers of sending American troops into combat and offered a fourth alternative. Senator Mike Mansfield, a former supporter of Diem, feared the Chinese might overwhelm American troops with regulars of their own, while Diem and the South Vietnamese would regard the deployment of United States regulars as a "revival of colonial force." Mansfield argued that the way to secure the South Vietnamese countryside was to introduce "democratic practices at the village and provincial levels" and couple them with economic and social reforms. "If the necessary reforms have not been forthcoming over the past seven years . . . then I do not see how American combat troops can do it today. . . . we must . . . avoid another Korean-type involvement on the Asian mainland." Mansfield recommended a different solution: give Diem all the money and weapons he needed, but let him do the job, while keeping the number of Americans in the field extremely limited.[47] Theodore Sorensen, the President's political alter-ego, later explained the rationale for this position. No effective way seemed to exist to use a division of American troops against "guerrilla-terrorist tactics," and the South Vietnamese government in any case had a 10 to 1 manpower advantage. Sorensen concluded:

> This battle must be won at [the] village level; and thus only the Vietnamese can defeat the Viet Cong. . . . Troops of a different country, color and culture are not as suitable or effective . . . as long as the local troops are in the preponderance. If such troops have the will, we can supply the weapons, training and financing—no more should be needed.[48]

W. Averell Harriman, the head negotiator at the talks on Laos, suggested a fifth, very different alternative. He advised that the Soviet Union was interested in stabilizing Southeast Asia, at least for a time, and that the United States should agree to reduce its military presence in South Vietnam as peace was restored in the area. For their part, the North Vietnamese and the NLF would agree to a cease-fire, accept a strong United Nations Control Commission, and achieve eventual reunification, possibly through elections.⁴⁹ Harriman's proposal was not likely to have appealed to the NLF leaders, for unlike the Communists in Laos, they would have gotten no role in a coalition government. Galbraith and Chester Bowles, the former Under Secretary of State whose influence was waning rapidly, also backed the idea of an independent, neutral South Vietnam; otherwise, Bowles warned, "we are headed full blast up a dead end street."⁵⁰

Kennedy briefly considered the neutralization proposal, but in the end he did not pursue it, or even order preliminary diplomatic contacts with the North Vietnamese or the NLF. He rejected neutralization, even though the international reasons for maintaining a hard line had moderated. By November 1961 the Berlin crisis had eased considerably, while the Sino-Soviet split had worsened. Even so, Rusk and McNamara warned that a retreat from South Vietnam would destroy SEATO and undermine the credibility of American commitments elsewhere. But they also added that "extreme elements" would seize on such a withdrawal "to divide the country and harass the Administration."⁵¹ After the failure of the Bay of Pigs invasion in April 1961, the Republicans began charging that Kennedy was yielding ground to the Communists around the world. They criticized him for canceling air strikes during the Bay of Pigs operation; for talking "big" and then backing "down when the chips were down" in Laos; for agreeing to negotiate on Berlin; and for failing to respond to the construction of the Berlin Wall in August. Senator Barry Goldwater made the cover of *Time* magazine in the summer of 1961 by criticizing Kennedy's softness. The President moved to head off criticism. In October, he told Sorensen to ask Walter Lippmann, Joseph Alsop, and other columnists how to counter increasing Republican charges of appeasement, and he publicly urged Americans to display "national maturity" in the face of temporary gains and setbacks in the Cold War.⁵²

Kennedy ruled out neutralization, but he also vetoed the Pentagon's plan to send regular combat troops to South Vietnam. Although the proposal for troops had gained wide support within the Administration, Taylor reported that Kennedy was "instinctively" against it. The CIA supported the President by predicting that the North Vietnamese would match American deployments with increased infiltration.⁵³ On November 11, Kennedy vetoed sending regular combat troops. Instead, he decided to increase economic aid as well as send more advisers to ARVN and to South Vietnamese intelligence and government agencies. The United States also promised air reconnaissance, air transport, and helicopter units to improve ARVN reactions to NLF movements. Kennedy ordered that American advisers be assigned to ARVN field battalions, rather than division headquarters (thereby allowing them to help plan and direct operations). The President also followed Lansdale's advice by seeking the insertion of American advisers into the South Vietnamese government to provide operational guidance at all levels.[54] The advisory effort, he said, "should be substantial otherwise we will give the wrong impression. . . . Are we prepared to send in hundreds and hundreds of men and dozens and dozens of ships? If we would just show up with 4 or 5 ships this will not do much good. . . . As I said on Saturday concerning Laos—we took actions which made no difference at all."[55] In return for all of this United States assistance Diem would have to mobilize his nation fully, broaden his government, and give his generals the power to move troops without prior clearance from Saigon.[56] Kennedy directed Ambassador Nolting to tell Diem that the "missions being undertaken by our own forces . . . are more suitable for white foreign troops than garrison duty or seeking out of Viet Cong personnel submerged in the Viet-Nam population."[57] Nevertheless, Kennedy had committed Americans to fly helicopters and planes and accompany ARVN troops when they engaged the NLF.

In mid-November, Kennedy tried to dissuade Bundy, Taylor, Rostow, McNamara, and the Joint Chiefs from their campaign to send regular troops by telling them foreign troops were only "a last resort." The President added that he did not want a war with China. He did agree to allow the Pentagon to plan for the introduction of SEATO troops, but that was as far as he would go. Vietnam, he explained, was unlike Korea, because it was not a clear-cut victim of aggression, and, consequently, neither the Democrats in Congress nor the British nor the French would support SEATO intervention there. And the United States did not have enough troops to go around. Nor was it clear why American soldiers should be sent into South Vietnam, but not into Cuba: "The President said that he could even make a rather strong case against intervening in an area 10,000 miles away against 16,000 guerrillas with a native army of 200,000, where millions have been spent for years with no success." The Joint Chiefs remained unconvinced, replying that they favored invading Cuba as well.[58] The Chiefs doubted that the Lansdale counter-insurgency approach would work, for Vietnam was not like the Philippines or Malaya. They told General Taylor in October that the Malay counter-insurgency campaign was not comparable to Vietnam, because the Thais and British were able to control Malaya's borders; because colonial police were able to isolate ethnic Chinese insurgents from the majority of the population; because food was scarce, enabling strategic hamlet programs to work; and because the British, not the Malays, were in command. In January 1962 the Joint Chiefs reiterated their request for the dispatch of regular American troops, but by then the alternative program was well under way.[59]

Diem expressed disappointment and anger. He had requested a bilateral alliance and massive aid, not an Americanization of his government. He told Nolting, "Viet Nam did not want to be a protectorate."[60] After tense negotiations, he agreed only to *consult* American advisers whom he helped select, and he avoided significant changes in his military command structure, because he remained fearful of a coup.[61] Kennedy was trapped by the contradictions in his own policy toward Diem. He could not force a supposedly independent nationalist leader to accept American tutelage without appearing to undermine him, and Diem was already publicizing Kennedy's demands.[62] Kennedy gave way. On December 15, the two governments announced their joint partnership—but on Diem's terms. A solid political foundation was essential to successful prosecution of the war, but the State Department had lost another round in its fight to make Diem more efficient, democratic, and popular. And on February 18, 1962, Robert F. Kennedy confirmed the State Department defeat by declaring unconditionally during a visit to Saigon, "We are going to win in Viet-Nam. We will remain here until we do win."[63]

Diem regained some favor with Washington by accepting another part of the Kennedy plan for South Vietnam—strategic hamlets. Roger Hilsman, director of the State Department's Bureau of Intelligence and Research, correctly concluded that the villages of South Vietnam willingly provided supplies and the great majority of recruits to the NLF. He argued that the South Vietnamese government had to provide villagers with civic action programs and physical security by creating fortified hamlets linked by radio. The strategic hamlets would receive developmental aid and close police scrutiny. In addition, the hamlets' own militias would defend them and call in roving Civil Guard units if the NLF attacked. Because they lacked food and replacements, the NLF bands would have to attack in strength, rather than starve, and the Civil Guard and newly mobile ARVN could then crush them by ambush or conventional engagement.[64]

While Hilsman had a somewhat more accurate perception of the insurgency than the Pentagon, his proposed solution proved unrealistic. His proposed village militias consisted of the fathers, uncles, and brothers of the NLF village guerrillas, and his expectation that one relative would starve or even shoot another in return for a medical clinic, a school, and a new well was strange at best. Diem, and his brother Ngo Dinh Nhu, who was in charge of the secret police and internal security, pushed the hamlet program rapidly as a means of reclaiming the villages. Land reform was notably absent and other benefits slow in coming, while the peasants often had to purchase the building materials and barbed wire which they used to fence themselves in.

At first, the military side of Kennedy's counter-insurgency campaign appeared to show progress. Aided by helicopters and growing numbers of American advisers, the ARVN bedeviled the NLF in the first half of 1962.[65] With ARVN's fortunes appearing to prosper, the Kennedy Administration flirted briefly with negotiations. In July 1962, Harriman, who was just wrapping up the Laos settlement, offered the North Vietnamese a neutrality agreement similar to the one he had just concluded for Laos. Ho Chi Minh replied that the NLF had already suggested such a plan: the United States would withdraw its advisers; a cease-fire would go into effect; the great powers would guarantee the neutralization and independence of Vietnam; the Vietnamese would establish a coalition government, which would include both Diem and the NLF; and the coalition government would end the strategic hamlet program, hold free elections, and begin talks to reunify the country. In late 1962 the NLF also offered a cease-fire which did not first require the withdrawal of the Americans.[66] Given the strength of the NLF in the countryside, free elections would almost certainly have resulted in a government dominated by the NLF. Although the NLF proposal opened the prospect of a decent interval between the time of American withdrawal and the time of a prospective defeat of Diem, Kennedy rejected the NLF offer. The President preferred to seek victory, rather than accept defeat, however much disguised or delayed.

By the end of 1962 Kennedy had sent 11,000 American military personnel to South Vietnam, along with 300 military aircraft, 120 helicopters, and additional heavy weapons. American pilots helped to fly combat missions, and the Americans supplied napalm bombs to the South Vietnamese air force.[67] At Binh Hoa in January 1962 an air strike killed five civilians, including a two-year-old boy, a five-year-old girl, and a seven-year-old boy.[68] If their parents had not been active supporters of the NLF before the raid, they most probably joined after this tragedy. Kennedy put General Paul D. Harkins, a former tank officer, in charge of the military assistance program in Saigon, and Harkins adopted a strategy based on the United States Army's tradition of achieving victory via attrition and destruction of the enemy's army. Harkins left the problem of village militias largely to the Vietnamese Civil Guards and Self Defense Corps, while he tried to break the enemy's will by using ARVN regulars to smash the enemy's main guerrilla forces. Taylor and Harkins wanted to put continuous pressure on the NLF regulars by exploiting American air mobility—a strategy which they believed had worked against guerrillas in both Greece and Korea. When ARVN succeeded in surrounding the NLF regulars with overwhelming numbers, they were supposed to use artillery and air strikes to flush them into combat with superior blocking forces.[69]

For a variety of reasons ARVN could not implement this strategy. Its divisions were trained and armed to deter a conventional invasion from the north, and they were unsuited to chase lightly armed guerrillas who disappeared into the countryside. Nor did many of the units in the field want to fight. A number of senior officers were mercenaries who had served in the colonial French Army, and Diem compounded the problem by putting his favorite officers in charge of the best units and keeping them in garrison, while sending poorly trained units into combat. American advisers could not energize ARVN because they did not speak Vietnamese, control promotions, make aid allocations (which came through Diem), or command troops (as they had done in Korea). Intelligence operations also faltered. American and South Vietnamese intelligence officers sought order-of-battle information on regular NLF units, rather than try to identify members of the local village militias and political committees, who were the mainstays of the insurgency. In 1962 air mobility allowed ARVN to achieve some early surprise victories, but the NLF soon adapted to the helicopters by making quicker hit-and-run attacks and placing heavy machine guns in village tree lines.[70] Even if ARVN had been able to destroy the main force units which they were vainly chasing, they would still have faced the much more numerous village militias.

The only solution to the village militias was to occupy the villages, reduce land rents, and recognize the NLF's land redistributions. But American military advisers believed in the Clausewitzian goal of destroying their enemy's army, not clearing and holding peasant villages, and Diem believed in control by his bureaucrats and the landlords, not reform for peasant hamlets.

Given the advanced state of the NLF revolt, Kennedy's counter-insurgency strategy was proving unworkable. As 1962 gave way to 1963, the strategic hamlet program also developed trouble. Diem, Nhu, and Harkins had pushed the program far out into enemy territory, resettling some hamlets in which as many as one-third of the men were missing—they had probably joined the NLF. The sullen strategic hamlet militias often did not defend their villages against the insurgents, and the Self-Defense Corps and Provincial Civil Guard units were unable or unwilling to take on company-sized NLF attacks. By the spring of 1963 only 1500 of 8500 strategic hamlets remained viable. By contrast, in June 1963 the NLF was levying taxes in 42 of South Vietnam's 44 provinces.[71]

Organizational problems also undermined Kennedy's strategy. General Lyman Lemnitzer, the Chairman of the Joint Chiefs of Staff, and General Earle G. Wheeler, Army Chief of Staff, proved unsympathetic to counter-insurgency ideas. Kennedy failed to appoint anyone of stature to ride herd in South Vietnam on Harkins, Diem, and Nhu, while in Washington the successive Vietnam task force directors also lacked the rank to force independent government departments to coordinate their activities. Consequently the military campaigns and strategic hamlet programs did not mesh well.[72] Kennedy kept most of the decisions in his own hands, and he lacked the time or energy to be an effective Vietnam desk officer. Nor could he play the role of an Under Secretary of State or Defense in seeking intelligence or reviewing policy, except in crises such as occurred during the fall of 1961. Most NSC staffers were primarily European-oriented generalists who lacked Asian expertise or the time to develop a sophisticated set of questions which would have revealed the nature of the NLF revolution. The NSC staff members maintained the illusion of being in touch by having mountains of cables routed through the White House, but they lacked the time and background to put them in their proper perspective.[73] Sorensen is correct in saying that Vietnam "never received the attention it should have . . . at the highest levels."[74] Kennedy remained convinced that the methods of counter-insurgency would gradually bring victory in the countryside. In his State of the Union message of 1963, he confidently declared, "The spearpoint of aggression has been blunted in Viet-Nam."[75]

In early 1963 Kennedy's optimism waned briefly after Senator Mansfield reported on his recent trip to Southeast Asia. Mansfield warned that the United States might ultimately be forced to accept a dominant combat role if Kennedy did not withdraw the American advisers. Mansfield's prediction reportedly angered the President, who was even less pleased when he heard of the very poor ARVN showing in combat at Ap Bac in the Delta.[76] With the American press present, a large ARVN force, aided by American-donated helicopters and armored personnel carriers, allowed a much smaller NLF force to escape. In the process, the NLF inflicted heavy casualties on ARVN and shot down five helicopters. Three American advisers died.[77] Kennedy was puzzled by "the Vietnam troops and their lack of courage,"[78] and he asked his aides to reassess the rice paddy war. Hilsman and Michael V. Forrestal, the NSC staffer assigned to expedite Vietnam policy, saw no need to "make any sudden and dramatic change," though they questioned Harkins's penchant for large-scale operations.[79] The generals themselves remained optimistic. Wheeler reported that "[we] are winning slowly on the present thrust," and Harkins trumpeted that "improvement is a daily fact . . . and we are confident of the outcome."[80]

Besides ARVN and strategic hamlet failures, Kennedy had to contend with charges that the United States was using "dirty-war" tactics in Vietnam. Kennedy had indeed ordered a limited, experimental program of trail clearing and crop destruction using defoliants and herbicides such as Agent Orange. In doing so, he not only set an unfortunate precedent for much larger applications of chemicals during the Johnson Administration but he also provided the NLF and North Vietnam with an opportunity to launch a propaganda campaign and appeal to the International Control Commission. It was a high political price to pay for a program which proved militarily worthless.[81]

Much worse problems arose when South Vietnamese troops fired into a crowd of Buddhists in Hué on May 8, 1963. The Buddhist marchers were flying religious banners during a celebration of Buddha's birthday, in spite of a ban on such symbols issued by Diem's brother, Ngo Dinh Thuc, the Archbishop of Hué. The ARVN killed nine marchers and wounded many others, triggering Buddhist demonstrations and self-immolations. In the major South Vietnamese cities students took to the streets to support Buddhist charges of religious discrimination and authoritarianism against the Ngos. Diem and Nhu countered with raids on pagodas, mass arrests, and martial law, each of which provoked more marches and self-immolations, creating a cycle which would persist through the Ngos' collapse in November. Madame Ngo Dinh Nhu, the security chief's wife and Diem's sister-in-law, callously dismissed the immolations as "barbecues" and offered to supply matches and gasoline in the future. The Kennedy Administration attempted repeatedly to induce Diem to compromise with the Buddhists. Diem said he would seek reconciliation, but he never kept his promise.[82]

During his first two years in office Kennedy had tried to minimize the seriousness of the Vietnam problem, and he had largely succeeded. In spite of Sorensen's advice, Kennedy chose not to make a major speech at the end of 1961 explaining his decision to escalate, and thus he delayed public debate. As American advisers went into combat, congressmen yielded to Kennedy's appeals for support and Congress routinely approved increases in American aid programs to South Vietnam.[83] In the summer of 1963, however, the Buddhist crisis brought increasingly critical newspaper reports from Homer Bigart and David Halberstam of the *New York Times* and Neil Sheehan of United Press International. At first Kennedy believed that having the American mission in Saigon bring reporters "into our confidence" would generate an "accurate story [of] our Viet-Nam program," but the journalists' well-founded distrust of the Diem regime and the American mission doomed the effort.[84] In late October Kennedy even tried to persuade *New York Times* publisher Arthur H. Sulzberger to remove Halberstam from South Vietnam, but to no avail. Vietnam became a big story in August and September 1963, and increasingly the criticism included both Kennedy and Diem. Kennedy finally had to conclude, "The way to confound the press is to win the war."[85]

As the election campaigns for 1964 began, bipartisan support for Kennedy's foreign policy broke down. During the summer and fall of 1963, conservatives attacked the foreign aid bill, the American wheat sale to the Soviet Union, and the nuclear test ban treaty. Nelson Rockefeller, Nixon, and Goldwater were waiting for Kennedy to make serious mistakes in South Vietnam and then exploit such errors in the presidential campaign. Senator Richard Russell of Georgia, a member of the President's own party, presaged the debate by chiding the Administration for "trying to fight this [Vietnam] problem as if it were a tournament of roses." He called for the "dirty-tricks department" to offer rewards for NLF guerrillas—dead or alive.[86] To Kennedy, experienced as he was in the politics of anti-Communism, these criticisms foreshadowed another debate about "who lost China?"

While Kennedy watched the Buddhist crisis in South Vietnam with growing dismay, he faced a similar crisis closer to home: the civil rights conflict in the American South. The civil rights issue worried Kennedy's pollsters and political advisers, who warned that he might lose critical Southern and Midwestern votes in the next election.[87] By August 1963, half of those polled said he was pushing integration too fast. Louis Harris's analysis of the 1960 results indicated the Republicans might make real inroads in the region in 1964, and a Lubell survey of former Kennedy voters in Birmingham, Alabama, turned up only one white who would again vote for Kennedy.[88]

The probable political loss of the South made the retention and expansion of the Democratic vote in the North vital, but Kennedy's advisers warned him he was in trouble there as well. States such as Ohio, Indiana, and Wisconsin, with their large ethnic blocs, were critical to victory, but Harris warned that urban Poles and Italians required "immediate and hard work" by the Democrats, because they were frustrated by their stagnant wages and by increased competition from blacks for jobs and housing. Harris concluded that the Republicans might win in 1964 by adding Southern segregationist and Northern working-class voters to their traditional strength in the Western states.[89] Ithiel de Sola Pool, a pollster and political analyst, reported that Kennedy had successfully appealed to these "urban Catholic Democratic" swing voters in 1960 with a hard line on Cold War containment.[90] At the same time, however, mass public opinion placed limits on the possibility of military escalation, since surveys showed that the average American feared the Democrats as the party of war.[91] This mass opinion actually remained inattentive to the Vietnam issue through 1963, but the potential for a strong reaction remained ever-present, especially if escalation occurred or defeat loomed. If any case, it was the swing votes, and not mass opinion, which counted in the Electoral College.[92] The Republican party turned demonstrably further to the right as Barry Goldwater moved ahead of Nelson Rockefeller in the polls, and Republican pundits predicted that Goldwater's states' rights stand would win the formerly solid South and Northern white ethnics over to the Republican banner in 1964.[93]

Thus, in addition to Kennedy's personal and ideological commitment to containment in South Vietnam, there also existed a political imperative to quiet the Buddhist crisis, stabilize the South Vietnamese regime, and convince the South Vietnamese to fight effectively. But Kennedy had little luck with Diem. In fact, Kennedy's efforts to persuade Diem to mollify the Buddhists aggravated the underlying conflict between Saigon and Washington. Diem resented the rapid American advisery buildup and the American advisers' penchant for meddling in Vietnamese decisions. The South Vietnamese dictator also feared—quite correctly—the Americans might encourage his enemies among the South Vietnamese generals to depose him. The CIA reported that Diem might request a reduction in the number of American advisers.[94] When asked about Diem's complaints at a news conference, Kennedy responded that withdrawal of the advisers would be premature, with "still a long, hard struggle to go" and no "brightening in the skies that would permit us to withdraw troops or begin to by the end of this year."[95] Actually, back in 1962 when the war seemed to be going well, the Pentagon had prepared plans for an orderly withdrawal. If Kennedy had wanted to, he might have used these plans to implement a withdrawal of aid and advisers in stages as a means of forcing the generals and Diem to reform.[96]

During June and July intelligence officials warned Kennedy that Diem had alienated the nationalist elites which Kennedy had identified in the 1950s as vital to building a stable Third World. Thomas Hughes of the State Department reported that discontent was widespread in the civil bureaucracy, in the military establishment, among students, and even within the Catholic hierarchy. Hughes, Hilsman, and the CIA warned that a coup against Diem was a distinct possibility, and Hughes and the CIA assured Kennedy that "a reasonably large pool of . . . experienced and trained manpower" existed which "could provide reasonably effective leadership for the government [of South Vietnam] and [for] the war effort."[97]

On June 27 the Administration announced the nomination of Henry Cabot Lodge, former senator from Massachusetts and Republican candidate for Vice President in 1960, as Ambassador to Saigon. According to the CIA, a "considerably disturbed" Diem correctly interpreted the appointment to mean "that the United States [now] planned to wield a 'big stick.' . . ."[98] Lodge's appointment also gave the Administration political sea room to act against Diem; one magazine predicted Lodge's appointment would "make the Republicans think twice before attacking Administration policy in troublesome South Viet Nam."[99] Lodge arrived in Saigon on August 22, the day after Nhu's American-trained Special Forces raided Buddhist pagodas in Saigon, Hué, and elsewhere and made mass arrests. Diem had presented Lodge with a fait accompli: he had curbed the Buddhists before Lodge could press him to accommodate them. Rumors even circulated that Diem and Nhu were considering serious negotiations with North Vietnam.[100] Kennedy had instructed Lodge to persuade Diem to treat his non-Communist opponents better, and if Diem resisted, work for Diem's removal. In fact, since July a group of ARVN generals led by Duong Van Minh, Tran Van Don, and Tran Thien Khiem had been exploring with American CIA agents the possibility of an American-supported coup.[101]

In Washington, many senior officials were on vacation at the time of the August raids on the pagodas, and the anti-Diem faction in the White House and State Department urged swift action. Forrestal urged the President to "move before the situation in Saigon freezes."[102] With the aid of George Ball, the Under Secretary of State, who was filling in for Rusk, Harriman, Hilsman, and Forrestal persuaded Kennedy over the telephone to instruct Lodge on August 24 to compel Diem to drop Nhu from his administration and accept American advice on how to run his government and army. If Diem did not comply, then the United States was to give "direct support" to the ARVN generals in the event of Diem's ouster. Kennedy assured Lodge, "We will back you to the hilt on actions you take to achieve our objectives."[103] Perhaps with the Bay of Pigs fiasco in mind, Kennedy did want time to review plans for the coup to assure that the American-backed generals would succeed. He warned Lodge on August 29, "I know from experience that failure is more destructive than the appearance of indecision. . . . When we go, we must go to win. . . ." Consequently, Kennedy reserved the right to "change course and reverse previous instructions." But he continued to allow the Ambassador wide discretion in the execution of his Vietnam policy, authorizing Lodge to suspend aid to Diem "at a time and under conditions of your choice."[104] Although Lodge was eager to act immediately, the ARVN generals were unable to line up enough military support in the Saigon area to risk a coup.

Kennedy continued to apply pressure to Diem. On television on September 2 he remarked that the war could not be won without popular support from the South Vietnamese, and, he added, "in my opinion, in the last 2 months, the government has gotten out of touch with the people." Kennedy predicted that Diem could only regain such support "with changes in policy and perhaps with [changes in] personnel." Otherwise, the chances for victory "would not be very good." But Kennedy disagreed "with those who say we should withdraw. That would be a great mistake. . . . Forty-seven Americans have been killed in combat with the enemy, but this is a very important struggle even though it is far away."[105] Between October 2 and October 5, Kennedy signaled his displeasure with Diem by applying a variety of "selective pressures": Kennedy canceled some future economic aid shipments; threatened to cut off American support for Nhu's Special Forces, unless they were placed under the command of the ARVN General Staff and moved from Saigon into the field; recalled the CIA station chief in Saigon, who was too closely identified with Nhu; and announced publicly that 1,000 American advisers would be withdrawn from South Vietnam by the end of 1963 and all American advisers would be out by the end of 1965, provided that the war in the countryside continued to go well.[106]

By cutting aid to Diem, Kennedy helped revive—apparently unwittingly—the ARVN generals' interest in a coup. On October 3, Duong Van Minh, Chief of the General Staff, asked for reassurance that the Americans would not oppose a coup, and he suggested the possibility that the plan might include the assassination of two Ngo brothers, Nhu and Can. Lucien Conein, Minh's CIA contact, assured him that Washington would provide economic and military assistance to a new regime which promised to cooperate with the United States, regain popular support, and try to win the war. CIA Director John McCone neither encouraged nor deplored the recommendation for the assassination of Diem's brothers, although he did warn Saigon that Diem himself should not be killed.[107] On October 25, Lodge alerted Kennedy that a coup would occur sometime before November.[108] In the days just before the coup, Kennedy and McGeorge Bundy worriedly questioned Lodge about prospects for success and the possibility of achieving plausible deniability of the American role in the coup. Once the attempted overthrow began, however, they told Lodge it was "in the interests of the U.S. Government that it should succeed."[109]

On the morning of November 1, Lodge met for the last time with Diem. A few hours later the coup finally began, with CIA agent Conein at coup headquarters to report to the embassy, advise the coup leaders, and distribute cash, if needed. At 4:30 p.m. that same day a frantic Diem telephoned the United States Ambassador. Lodge relayed an offer of safe conduct out of the country from the coup leaders, but he claimed disingenuously that the United States government had no policy toward the coup. While Diem and Nhu escaped to the Cholon section of Saigon, both to die the following day at the hands of General Minh's lieutenants, Lodge went to bed.[110] On November 8, Washington officially recognized the new military regime in Saigon. A week later, in response to a *New York Times* editorial which suggested a negotiated settlement of the war, Rusk instructed Lodge to tell the generals that the United States government "cannot envisage any points that would be negotiable." The Secretary of State reassured the South Vietnamese government that North Vietnam would have to end its "subversive aggression" and allow the new South Vietnamese regime to "extend its authority throughout South Vietnam before the United States would withdraw."[111]

The events of 1963 shattered one expectation—that Diem would listen to American advice, reform his government, and win the war—and created another—that the generals would do the same. Before the coup Kennedy and his Washington advisers simply assumed that the ARVN generals would be an improvement over Diem, but they were wrong. Many of the members of the South Vietnamese Military Revolutionary Council had been collaborators with the French colonialists, and Robert Thompson, the British counter-insurgency expert, thought they "lacked the experience or ability to command much more than a regiment, let alone a country."[112] Within three months, another military faction overthrew Minh and the Revolutionary Council, starting a topsy-turvy pattern of coup and counter-coup which continued for some time. Even the Buddhist protest marches and self-immolations continued to occur.[113]

Before Minh fell, however, Kennedy himself died. His remarks prepared for delivery on November 22 in Dallas, Texas, a destination he never reached, included the words: "We in this country in this generation are—by destiny rather than choice—the watchmen on the walls of world freedom. . . . Our assistance to . . . nations can be painful, risky and costly, as is true in Southeast Asia today. But we dare not weary of the task." And in another speech he intended to deliver that night can be seen the outline of his anticipated 1964 campaign. The New Frontier had gotten the country moving again—America's economy was growing, its space effort thriving, its military power expanding, and its containment policy working from Berlin to Latin America to Southeast Asia.[114] On the day he died he still hoped for victory in South Vietnam and vindication of the doctrine of counter-insurgency.

Why did Kennedy persist in Vietnam under such unpromising conditions? After all, many leaders, ranging from Charles de Gaulle and Douglas MacArthur to Mike Mansfield and John Kenneth Galbraith, had warned Kennedy against a deepening Vietnam adventure. He chose to ignore their warnings. His defenders claimed that the Eisenhower Administration left him no choice but to pursue the war in Vietnam.[115] But he might well have drawn the containment line in Thailand, while letting Diem fight his own battles with generous grants of money and arms. Instead, he sent in 16,000 advisers, 100 of whom had died by the end of 1963; he sponsored the strategic hamlet program; he unleashed a war of attrition against the NLF; and he allowed the military to use napalm, defoliation, and helicopter envelopment tactics, rather than a clear and hold strategy. Why did he do it? Both Khrushchev and Mao Zedong may have helped to draw him in, for they had exaggerated their support for national liberation wars, thereby lending substance to Kennedy's fears. In fact, however, the fragmentation of the Communist world was accelerating in these years, as Kennedy could read in his own intelligence reports.[116] If Kennedy had negotiated a deal on South Vietnam, he might have encouraged détente with the Soviet Union and hastened a Sino-Vietnamese split.

Kennedy's self-confident definition of the South Vietnamese problem was an important reason for his persistence. The President believed that Diem and the generals constituted a third force of nationalists who could lead peasants and workers in a fight against Communism. Because Americans were nation-builders, not colonialists, they could persuade the South Vietnamese to apply American technology, tactics, and organizational techniques to the problems of the Vietnamese countryside, wracked by continued underdevelopment, terrorism, and guerrilla warfare. The struggle would be long and hard, but success would come eventually—if only the right combination of Vietnamese nationalist leaders could be found. The misapplied analogs of Greece and Malaya reinforced his belief in nation-building and counter-insurgency.[117] Kennedy's image of Vietnam proved false. In the minds of the peasants, Diem and the generals represented the old regime. The people of the countryside craved land, power, and the promise of economic justice and national liberation, not wells, clinics, films, strategic hamlets, or infantry sweeps through their villages. The NLF program also contained more political and economic change and less coercion and violence than Kennedy comprehended. Kennedy's expectations for the future were unrealistic as well. American advisers could not transform the ARVN into an effective force, nor persuade Diem and Nhu to appeal to the peasantry.

Kennedy's decision-making system failed to correct the President's false image of Vietnam's prospects. His small staff lacked an understanding of the socio-economic appeal of the Chinese and Vietnamese revolutions to the peasantry. The NSC did not produce an accurate picture which would shatter the President's strongly held image of a nationalist elite waiting for outside inspiration to mobilize a neutral peasantry against Communist terrorists. Although Kennedy's collegial style of decision-making has received considerable praise,[118] it did not work very well in the case of Vietnam. Until the Buddhist crisis of 1963 Kennedy usually treated Vietnam as a fairly routine foreign policy problem, which he assumed he could handle with limited resources. His staff, with the exception of the hyperactive Walt Rostow, tended to coast along the lines of established policy, recommending more of the same. Not until November 1961 did a major review of the options emerge. Even then, however, the list of options which were staffed out and fully considered was incomplete, for none of the key debaters, with the brief exception of Harriman, was a serious advocate of neutralization and a retreat to Thailand. Kennedy never gave negotiations a chance. Nor were there many advocates for withholding advisers while giving Diem enough money and arms to sink or swim on his own. Instead of a sophisticated image of the problem of rural revolution in Southeast Asia, ingrained Cold War thinking about the credibility of containment shaped Administration deliberations. Consequently, the debate always centered on escalation, with Kennedy curbing the hawks in the Pentagon and choosing counter-insurgency.

The politics of anti-Communism also played a large role in shaping Kennedy's decisions. He had survived and prospered in the McCarthyite atmosphere of the fifties, and he feared the loss of swing anti-Communist votes to the Republicans and the Dixiecrats in the increasingly turbulent politics of the sixties. The lesson of the so-called loss of China remained with him, and the Republicans repeatedly peppered him with charges of appeasement on a host of issues. During the 1960 campaign he had promised to turn the tide of the Cold War, and he was preparing to claim considerable progress in 1964. With Laos neutralized, Cuba hostile, and East Berlin sealed off, Vietnam became a testing ground by his own definition. Though some of his defenders have claimed he would have withdrawn the United States from Vietnam after his re-election in 1964,[119] they underestimate the degree to which Kennedy had committed himself and the country to supporting a non-Communist Vietnam. Kennedy would have had to admit the failure of his major counter-insurgency effort, which was designed to discourage national liberation wars everywhere. More likely than withdrawal was a continued search for the right combination of means and men to win the war in South Vietnam. Kennedy would probably have ruled out sending in United States Army infantry divisions, but short of that limit, he would probably have continued to make a major effort to succeed.

In any case, by late 1963 Kennedy had radically expanded the American commitment to Vietnam. By putting American advisers in harm's way and allowing the press to chronicle their tribulations and casualties, he helped to engage American patriotism in a war against the Vietnamese people. By arguing that Vietnam was a test of the West's ability to defeat the people's war strategy and a test of American credibility in the Cold War, he raised the costs of withdrawal for his successor. By launching a strategic hamlet program, he further disrupted peasant society. By allowing Harkins and the ARVN to bomb, shell, search, and destroy, he made so many recruits for the NLF that he encouraged North Vietnam and the NLF to move the war into its final military phase. By participating in Diem's removal, he brought warlord politics to Saigon. By downplaying publicly the American role in Vietnam, he discouraged a constitutional debate about the commitment of American advisers to battle. By publicly and privately committing the United States to the survival of an anti-Communist state in South Vietnam, he made it much more difficult to blame the South Vietnamese government for its own failures and to withdraw. And by insisting that military victory was the only acceptable outcome, he ignored the possibility that negotiations might lead to an acceptable process of retreat. Kennedy bequeathed to Lyndon B. Johnson a failing counter-insurgency program and a deepened commitment to the war in South Vietnam.

10

New Frontiers and Old Priorities in Africa

THOMAS J. NOER

On July 12, 1961, John F. Kennedy scanned a Department of State briefing paper in preparation for an afternoon meeting with the Foreign Minister of Mali. Since gaining independence from France a ycar earlier, Mali had bccome a vocal critic of American foreign policy, had accepted Soviet aid, and had supported Moscow on most international issues. Kennedy worried that Mali "was going down the drain," and the briefing paper echoed his pessimism.[1] The President's frustration with Mali stemmed from his belief that his Administration had reversed America's traditional lack of interest in Africa and the close identification with the European colonial powers that had characterized foreign policy in the Eisenhower years. But Mali and other African nations had failed to acknowledge and respond to such changes. At the meeting, Kennedy asked why Mali's leaders "see us as an adversary, not as a friend?" Foreign Minister Jean-Marie Kone responded by quoting an African proverb: "The friend of my enemy is my adversary." He charged that the United States remained too closely aligned with the European nations who had "divided Africa among themselves." Kone also claimed that "Americans tend to see communists everywhere" and judged African nations solely on their commitment to anti-Communism. Although both leaders pledged to try to "liquidate the past," the meeting ended without reconciliation.[2]

The frosty encounter illustrated the dilemmas of the New Frontier's approach to Africa. Kennedy was elected president in 1960, the "Year of Africa," when seventeen black nations gained independence. By the end of his life, only British Rhodesia, the Republic of South Africa, and the Portuguese colonies of Angola and Mozambique still had white rule. Kennedy recognized that the "new Africa" required a new American foreign policy, less closely identified with the European powers and more tolerant of neutralism and nonalignment. The President found, however, that the need for continued close cooperation with Europe and the tenacious dominance of Cold War anti-Communism limited any major shift in Washington's African diplomacy.

Lacking the proximity of Latin America, the assumed economic potential of Asia, and the cultural influence of Europe, Africa sat at the periphery of American diplomacy until the late 1950s. Gaining their image of Africa from Tarzan movies, missionary slide shows in church basements, and Ernest Hemingway short stories, Americans saw the continent as a land of jungles and animals, not of nations in the international system. The rapid rise of the independence movement in Africa and the growth of the American civil rights struggle following the Second World War finally combined to make the "dark continent" an area of United States diplomatic activity.

The Second World War had served as the catalyst for African independence. The conflict weakened the imperial powers and fired the imaginations of African leaders. Encouraged by the anti-colonial statements of Franklin D. Roosevelt and Cordell Hull, African leaders became convinced that at the close of the war European control would end and that America would actively support the independence movement. The postwar conflict between the United States and the Soviet Union raised further African expectations. American Cold War rhetoric emphasized a global struggle between freedom and slavery—a battle for self-determination, democracy, and human rights. African nationalists pointed out that they also lacked majority rule and political freedom and interpreted such lofty statements as an implied United States commitment to decolonization.

Washington's position on decolonization, however, grew more timid as the Cold War intensified. Although officials in the Truman Administration called for self-determination in Eastern Europe, they became reluctant to extend such demands to the colonies of their NATO and Marshall Plan allies. American leaders feared rapid decolonization would cripple European economic recovery (and the ability to resist Communism) and produce weak and unstable African nations unable to prevent Soviet subversion. Increasingly the United States tried to restrain the very nationalism it had helped create.

The Administration of Dwight D. Eisenhower became actively hostile to African independence. Secretary of State John Foster Dulles grew convinced that Soviet intrigue lay behind the anti-colonial movement and judged Third World neutralism "a transitional stage to communism."[3] Eisenhower observed that African nationalism "resembled a torrent over-running everything in its path, including, frequently, the best interests of those concerned."[4] American officials warned repeatedly against the dangers of "premature independence" by peoples unprepared to resist "the new imperialism" of Moscow. Assistant Secretary of State George Allen bluntly noted that "all of the so-called colonial powers are our friends in the worldwide contest between the Free and the Communist worlds." Their continued friendship was more crucial than alignment with Africans.[5]

In 1957 Ghana became the first black African nation to secure its independence. Guinea followed a year later. With most other British and French colonies scheduled for independence, American policy gradually changed as Washington recognized that decolonization had become inevitable. Vice President Richard M. Nixon began to push for a more active African policy. He represented the United States at Ghana's independence ceremony and returned from Africa persuaded that America's neglect of the emerging nations was hurting its battle with Communism. He lobbied for a separate Bureau of African Affairs in the State Department, increased economic aid to Africa, and improvements in civil rights at home, because segregation had become a potent Communist propaganda issue in Africa.[6]

During its final two years the Eisenhower Administration worked to demonstrate a new commitment to Africa. The President offered American aid to Ghana, despite the neutralism of its mercurial leader, Kwame Nkrumah. Eisenhower also supported the United Nations effort to maintain unity in the Congo after the former Belgian colony degenerated into violence in the summer of 1960. Following the massacre of black demonstrators near Sharpville, South Africa, the United States for the first time supported United Nations condemnation of the white government of South Africa. Such gestures were probably designed as much to help Nixon in his 1960 presidential campaign as to implement a new approach to Africa. After the election, the Administration rapidly abandoned its "new"

Africa policy and returned to a "Europe-first" stance. When more than forty African and Asian nations sponsored a United Nations resolution denouncing colonialism, Eisenhower rejected pleas from the American delegate to support the symbolic gesture and ordered him to abstain.[7]

To John F. Kennedy, Republican diplomacy in Africa constituted a prime example of the failure of leadership that had led to the decline of American prestige. In his 1960 presidential campaign, Kennedy chastised Eisenhower for neglecting the new African nations and for his reluctance to support African independence. He noted repeatedly that he had chaired the Senate Foreign Relations Committee's sub-committee on Africa and courted black American voters by promising to send more black diplomats to Africa. Kennedy also made several dramatic gestures to illustrate his interest in Africa. When the State Department refused funds to transport African students to the United States, Kennedy arranged for the Joseph Kennedy Foundation to pay the $100,000 cost. When Guinea's President Sékou Touré expressed interest in meeting the Democratic candidate, Kennedy chartered a helicopter to fly the African leader to Disneyland for a much-publicized conference.

Clearly Kennedy was using Africa to try to appeal to liberals and blacks, two groups rather lukewarm about his candidacy, but the continent was more than just a campaign issue for him: he saw Africa as a major opportunity for gain in the Cold War. Dulles's moralizing and Eisenhower's indifference had created an area of potential Soviet expansion, but also a source of possible triumph for the new Administration. To Kennedy the battle against the Soviets in Africa was being lost because of American inaction and misunderstanding of African nationalism. "We cannot simply sit by and watch on the sidelines," he explained in a speech on Africa. "There are no sidelines. Under the law of physics, in order to maintain the same relative position to a moving body, one cannot stand still."[8] When the United States had acted, Kennedy argued, it had displayed an inability to comprehend the sources and effects of Third World nationalism. In 1957 Kennedy had criticized Eisesnhower for failing to accept and support the inevitable end of European colonization. "The sweep of nationalism is the most potent factor in foreign affairs today," he concluded.[9] Having refused to support African independence, the Republicans had further alienated African states by trying to force them to choose between East and West. To Kennedy, neutralism necessarily emerged from the colonial experience: Africans could never align with their former rulers because they feared compromising their newly-won independence.

Kennedy's interpretation of neutralism and non-alignment lay at the heart of his critique of Republican diplomacy and shaped his own response to Africa. Although Kennedy and his advisers claimed to "welcome a world of diversity," they did not advocate a passive acceptance of the policies of Third World nations. To the New Frontiersmen, there was an acceptable form of neutralism (called variously "true" neutralism, "real" neutralism, or "objective" neutralism) that consisted of balanced criticism of both the United States and the Soviet Union, a mixed economy, tolerance of political dissent, and the maintenance of stability and order. What America could not tolerate was a neutralism that disguised partiality toward the Soviet Union and Marxism. If the African states embraced "real" neutralism, it would be to the direct advantage of the United States. America "welcomed diversity," Kennedy argued, "but the Communists cannot." Because Communist ideology demanded eventual acceptance of the Soviet system, Moscow could not accept true non-alignment in the Cold War. By encouraging and preserving "true" neutralism, America would triumph. The containment doctrine, with different methods, could be applied to independent Africa.[10]

Kennedy neatly reversed Dulles's dictum that neutralism was a "transitional stage to communism." Neutralism actually worked to America's benefit and against Soviet interests. The United States could "win" in Africa merely by not "losing" the new nations to Communism. G. Mennen Williams, Kennedy's Assistant Secretary of State for African Affairs, explained that it was unnecessary for any African nation "to align itself with us and seek the exact world we seek." America had only to persuade African countries to deny "the subservience communism demands."[11] Kennedy's goal in Africa was victory through denial, a defensive diplomacy that defined success as not losing. His pre-inaugural transition team on Africa summed up the new strategy by concluding that "non-alignment of African states in the Cold War is in no sense detrimental to our interests." The goal should not be "winning the African states to capitalism or military alliance," but merely "to prevent the dominance of the continent by the Communist bloc."[12] This conservative goal still required an intense American effort. The new Administration's official "Guidelines of U.S. Policy and Operations Concerning Africa" warned that "the United States . . . probably cannot 'win' Africa" through "outright alignment," but "could, by failing to put forward a major effort, 'lose' Africa by default."[13]

Kennedy and his advisers viewed Africa more as an area of symbolic significance and as a battleground for international prestige than as a region of dominant economic and strategic interests. Although the continent had the potential for major economic development, it was of only minor importance to United States commerce. In 1960 Africa accounted for less than 4 percent of American imports and only 3.5 percent of the nation's exports. American investments in Africa were less than 3 percent of its global total. South Africa was the only African nation of direct strategic importance, as it was the major provider of gold, platinum, and other minerals. South Africa also controlled the key shipping lanes of the South Atlantic and was the site of American missile-tracking facilities.[14] More than direct economic or strategic interests, it was the fluidity and uncertainty generated by the rapid decolonization of the continent that concerned Kennedy. Africa held the potential for disorder, radicalism, and major-power conflict. American involvement thus became necessary.

Kennedy became even more convinced of the importance of Africa following Nikita Khrushchev's January 6, 1961, speech on the inevitable spread of Marxism through "wars of national liberation." To the new Administration, Khrushchev appeared to have announced a major new tack in the Cold War. If the battleground of an accelerated East-West conflict was the Third World, Africa took on increased importance.

Although Americans were alarmed by the possibility of a major Soviet effort in Africa, the Russians actually pursued conservative goals quite similar to those of the United States. Moscow sought, in the words of one analyst, "cheap prestige" in Africa through modest aid programs and vocal support of decolonization and the end of white rule. The Soviets managed to gain some influence in Ghana, Guinea, and Mali and tried to exploit the chaos in the Congo, but they did not make Africa a major priority in their foreign policy. Only in the mid-1960s, when China began to compete with the Soviet Union for the allegiance of African states, did the Soviets increase their efforts in Africa.[15]

Kennedy nonetheless saw Africa as an arena of significant Cold War rivalry that required active American involvement. But an activist African policy faced obstacles. Bureaucratic battles, the press of other issues, and domestic considerations all complicated Kennedy's efforts to realign American diplomacy toward Africa. First, American officials disagreed among themselves as to the significance of Africa for the United States. "Africanists" such as Mennen Williams, Under Secretary of State Chester Bowles, United Nations Ambassador Adlai Stevenson, and many of the new ambassadors to Africa contended that the continent should be a major priority for America. They argued that Washington had to break dramatically with its European allies on African issues. In contrast, a vocal group of "Europeanists" advocated a continued "Europe first" position. Many in the Defense and State departments contended that close ties with Europe were far more important than courting the new African states. The United States should defer to the Europeans in dealings with their former colonies and encourage continued European influence in Africa.

A second restraint lay in the Administration's fear of domestic reaction to a strong African policy. American liberals and blacks pressed for increased attention to Africa, but many Southerners and conservatives were opposed. Just as Kennedy temporized on civil rights issues to maintain the support of Southern congressional leaders, so did he tailor his African policy to avoid a conservative revolt at home.

The repeated intrusion of other issues constituted another limit on Kennedy's activism in Africa. As the Administration lurched from crisis to crisis, immediate interests often undercut long-range goals in Africa. Tension over Berlin reaffirmed the importance of NATO and cooperation with European allies. The deteriorating situation in Southeast Asia increasingly drew American resources and energies. A government confronted with nuclear weapons in Cuba had less time for distant Africa.

After his election, Kennedy worked early to revise the image and style of Washington's relations with Africa. His first announced appointment was former Michigan Governor G. Mennen Williams as Assistant Secretary of State for African Affairs. Kennedy's selection of the flamboyant "Soapy" Williams even before naming a Secretary of State emphasized the importance of Africa for the new Administration. Advocates of somber, quiet diplomacy disliked Williams's outspokenness, frequent overseas trips, and colorful tactics (such as holding a square dance at the State Department for African diplomats with himself as the caller), but the President remained impressed with the energy Williams injected into the African Bureau.[16] Kennedy's selection of Chester Bowles and Adlai Stevenson, two other strong advocates of making Africa a major policy priority, proved to be less successful. Bowles's perceived arrogance, imprecision, and unrelenting lobbying irritated White House officials. His seemed out of touch with the Administration's emphasis on pragmatism and toughness. In November 1961 Kennedy removed Bowles and gave him a meaningless assignment as a special adviser. Stevenson quickly earned a reputation in the White House as soft and lazy and lost influence throughout Kennedy's term. More in accord with Kennedy's style were a group of young American ambassadors to Africa, especially the journalists William Attwood (Guinea) and Edward Korry (Ethiopia) and diplomats Edmund Gullion (Congo) and Philip Kaiser (Senegal). Impatient, demanding, and assertive, they shared the President's disdain for the glacial pace of the State Department. Many enjoyed personal access to Kennedy and often used it to try to influence policy.

Aside from his appointments, Kennedy attempted to demonstrate a new concern for Africa through his personal diplomacy. Eisenhower had rarely invited Africans to the White House, but Kennedy opened the doors of the mansion to eleven African leaders in 1961, ten in 1962, and seven in 1963. The President was extremely effective at such meetings. Well-briefed on African issues, he impressed the visitors with his knowledge of their nations. Tom Mboya of Kenya was amazed that the President of the United States could discuss in detail factions of the labor movement in Nairobi.[17]

Kennedy's appointments and personal diplomacy were symbolic of a new emphasis on Africa, but the President soon needed to develop specific policies. He faced four areas of immediate concern. Most pressing was the ongoing chaos in the Congo, where succession, civil war, and foreign intervention had produced an instability Kennedy so feared. The second was the anti-colonial insurrection in Portuguese Angola which threatened to become a prototype of Khrushchev's wars of national liberation. Third, Kennedy had to handle the continued problem of American policy toward the white minority regime in South Africa and its repressive program of apartheid. Finally, the President confronted "non-neutral" nations such as Ghana and Guinea which had strayed from "true" neutralism.

According to Kennedy adviser Roger Hilsman, "history could hardly have devised a more baffling and frustrating test" for the new Administration than the Congo.[18] Leaders, factions, and issues changed daily, and just to keep track of the various regimes and incidents became a formidable task. Each crisis in the volatile nation also had an impact on United States relations with its European allies, the independent African states, the United Nations, and on domestic policies.

The rise of the Congo to an arena of international dispute began within hours of its independence on June 30, 1960. Belgium had made no attempt to prepare the Congo for self-rule. There were fewer than twenty college graduates in the new nation and Europeans still controlled its civil service, economy, and military. On independence day, Congolese troops mutinied against their white officers. Within days the Western press reported horror stories of the murder of whites, the rape of Belgian nuns, and violent clashes between rival army factions. The disarray in the Congo led to intervention and secession. Claiming the need to protect its citizens, Belgium soon airlifted troops to the Congo. Congolese President Joseph Kasavubu and Premier Patrice Lumumba demanded that the United Nations intervene to drive out the former colonials. The copper-rich province of Katanga declared itself a separate nation under the leadership of the pro-Belgian Moise Tshombe. Kasavubu fired Lumumba. Lumumba dismissed Kasavubu. If it were not for the sustained violence and random brutality, the Congo had the makings of a comic opera.

To many Americans, the Congo confirmed their worst fears of "premature independence." Eisenhower expected the Soviets to exploit the disorder when Lumumba threatened to ask for Russian military aid to regain Katanga. American leaders quickly became fixated on Lumumba. Although Lumumba claimed he was not a Marxist and sought only national unity and neutralism, CIA Director Allen Dulles told Eisenhower that Lumumba had been "bought by the communists."[19]

Lumumba came to the United States in July 1960 to lobby for support, but his behavior only confirmed the worst American assumptions and prejudices. Upon his arrival at Blair House in Washington, he asked his State Department host for "a white, blond woman" for the night and a pistol to protect himself from the criminals roaming the American capital. The next day, United States officials found evidence that Lumumba had smoked hemp in his bedroom, and they concluded that he was "a drug addict." Persuaded that the Congolese leader was an immoral, unstable radical, Eisenhower refused to meet with him.[20] Outraged by his rejection in Washington, Lumumba accepted Khrushchev's offer of military aid and advisers. American officials acknowledged that no other Congolese had the following of Lumumba, and concluded that the only solution was to eliminate him. At a National Security Council meeting on August 18, Eisenhower, Alan Dulles, and others discussed the assassination of Lumumba. The next day the CIA began the first of a series of elaborate plots to murder Lumumba that continued throughout the fall of 1960. Eventually, Colonel Joseph Mobutu seized power in the Congo, expelled Soviet diplomats and advisers, and placed Lumumba under house arrest.[21]

When Kennedy took office, direct Soviet influence in the Congo had diminished, but the country was still in chaos. The President feared that continued violence and disorder might produce "another Laos" with endless civil war or that the Congo would be united under a radical leader and become "another Cuba" exporting revolution throughout Africa.[22] Like Eisenhower, Kennedy sought a stable Congo united under a strong, non-Marxist leader. Unlike his predecessor, he was certain the United States would have to take the lead in obtaining these goals. Two weeks after he took office, Kennedy endorsed a major new American initiative that called for all factions in the Congo to be forced under United Nations authority, the release of all political prisoners, and the reconvening of the Congolese parliament to select a coalition government.[23]

Some members of the Administration disapproved of granting such power to the United Nations, while others feared the "Kennedy plan" would result in the release of the ever-dangerous Lumumba. In a secret briefing to the Senate Foreign Relations Committee, Williams admitted Lumumba was "the best rabble-rouser" in the Congo and, if released, "will end up having control of everything." Williams made it clear that even though the Kennedy proposal called for release of all political prisoners, "we do not feel that Lumumba should be released until such a time as neutralism of the military forces and the government are pretty well along."[24]

The Administration's initiative did not lead to stability, but, instead, indirectly to the death of Lumumba. The CIA had not informed the new President of its assassination plots against Lumumba. Agency officials thought Kennedy naïve and his plan for the Congo misguided. They were sure a release of prisoners would include Lumumba. Once free, Lumumba would quickly regain power and turn the Congo into a Communist state. When CIA sources in Washington learned of Kennedy's proposal, they persuaded Kasavubu (now sharing power with Mobutu) to transport the prisoner out of the capital of Léopoldville and away from United Nations troops. On January 17, 1961, Congolese troops loaded Lumumba and two of his followers on a Belgian plane. The troops beat the three throughout the eight-hour flight to Elizabethville. Shortly after the plane landed, they executed Lumumba and his two associates.[25]

The Congolese government did not announce Lumumba's death until February 13. The Soviet Union and many African states immediately blamed America for the executions. Kwame Nkrumah of Ghana publicly labeled Kennedy "a murderer," and Sékou Touré of Guinea accused the President of direct responsibility. Most African nations and the Soviet Union recognized Lumumba's protégé Antoine Gizenga as the legitimate ruler of the Congo.[26]

American officials grimly endured the attacks from African leaders while they searched for an acceptable alternative to Gizenga. Washington finally settled on Cyrille Adoula, a leader of the Congolese labor movement. Adoula had supported the expulsion of the Soviets from the Congo, but did not have the liability of too close an identification with the West. Secretary of State Dean Rusk judged Adoula "the strongest and most attractive of the moderate Congolese leaders."[27] For the next two years Adoula would be America's candidate to restore unity and order in the Congo.

Although Kasavubu and Mobutu still ruled in the capital of Léopoldville, Gizenga controlled the area near Stanleyville, and Tshombe governed in Katanga. In accordance with the Kennedy plan, the United Nations called a session of the Congo's parliament to meet at Louvanium University near Léopoldville in the summer of 1961. American officials were confident Adoula would emerge as the leader of the new government. Intelligence reports had concluded that Gizenga had little support, and Tshombe announced he would boycott the meeting. Despite such optimism, early votes at Louvanium showed strong support for Gizenga. Kennedy became outraged at the CIA and the State Department for assuring him Adoula would win control of the Congo. After a stormy meeting with the President, Rusk ordered American agents in the Congo to "use all means" to block Gizenga and to help Adoula.[28] CIA operatives distributed bribes to the delegates and the conference soon became an open auction as representatives shopped among American, Soviet, and assorted Congolese lobbyists. Besides offering cash and automobiles to Adoula supporters, American officials hinted openly that the United States would support a military coup if Gizenga were elected. In the end, American agents "simply outbid" the competition, and Adoula emerged victorious.[29] Rusk hailed the results as "a major Soviet defeat," while Assistant National Security Adviser Walt W. Rostow wrote to Kennedy that Adoula's victory was "the most encouraging development since you became President."[30]

Having used its dollars and the threat of a military coup to secure an acceptable leader for the Congo, the Kennedy Administration turned to its second goal, unification. Great Britain and Belgium had offered strong support for the secessionist regime in Katanga, and Eisenhower had refused to aid in efforts against the pro-Western province. Kennedy's advisers, however, argued that America must now take action to unite the Congo. Adoula could never hold power if he could not unify his nation, and the Congo would not survive economically without the wealth of Katanga.

Following demands from African and Asian nations, the United Nations began military operations against Katanga in August 1961. Although Belgium had withdrawn its troops from Katanga, Tshombe had hired a formidable force of white mercenaries. When the United Nations attack bogged down, Secretary General Dag Hammarskjold and "Africanists" in the Administration urged Kennedy to provide military aid to defeat Katanga. The President wavered. He acknowledged that Congolese unity was essential to preserve Adoula, but, mindful of the disaster at the Bay of Pigs, was reluctant to approve military action. The President was also sensitive to European support of Katanga and did not want to strain relations with allies at a time of crisis over Berlin. He refused to make any commitments. On September 17 a United Nations plane crashed after leaving Léopoldville. Dag Hammerskjold died in the accident and the United Nations military effort against Katanga seemed to die with him. Williams, Bowles, and Stevenson argued that the United Nations forces were desperate and the United States must act, but Kennedy again refused to approve military aid.[31]

A week later, the Under Secretary of State for Economic Affairs, George W. Ball, made a forceful case for United States activism. As one of the leaders of the "Europeanist" bloc in the Administration, Ball seemed an unexpected source for American engagement in the Congo. A strong admirer of former Secretary of State Dean Acheson, Ball had chided the Administration for being too solicitous toward nations "with names like typographical errors." But, to Ball, the Congo was different from most Third World nations because it carried the potential for a direct Soviet-American clash. He became convinced that Washington must restore unity and order or the Congo would return to the chaos of 1960 and invite renewed Russian meddling. On September 23, Ball sent Kennedy a plan to avoid the possibility of a Soviet state in Africa. To save the Congo, Ball insisted, America had to preserve Adoula; to preserve Adoula, the United States should provide direct military aid to the United Nations forces, offer massive economic assistance to Adoula, and pressure Belgium and Britain to end their support of Katanga.[32] Although Kennedy held Ball in high regard (Ball replaced Bowles in November), the President first expressed doubt that the United Nations could defeat Katanga even with American aid, and later explained that "he did not want to completely crush Tshombe until we know who will inherit this."[33] While Kennedy pondered, others echoed Ball's counsel. Edmund Gillion, the American Ambassador to the Congo and a personal favorite of Kennedy, rushed to Washington to plead with the President to act. Even Rusk, heretofore neutral in the battle over Congo policy, urged some support for the United Nations. But the President still hesitated.[34]

Part of Kennedy's reluctance to offer direct support to the United Nations stemmed from his fear of domestic reaction. Many American conservatives strongly supported Katangan independence. Senators Barry Goldwater of Arizona and Thomas Dodd of Connecticut (known in the State Department as "the Senator from Katanga"), charged that the Communist-dominated United Nations was trying to crush Katanga, the only stable, pro-capitalist regime in the Congo. Under attack for foreign policy setbacks in Cuba and Berlin, Kennedy did not want to provide critics with another issue by committing America to support a military campaign against Katanga.

Searching for a way to avoid domestic criticism, if he aided the United Nations, and criticism from African nations, if he took no action to support Congolese unity, Kennedy seized upon a personal letter from Katangan leader Tshombe, who asked the President to arrange negotiations with Adoula. Tshombe had repeatedly used negotiations in the past to delay and rearm, and nearly all of Kennedy's advisers concluded that this offer was yet another ploy. The President, however, saw an opportunity to achieve peace and unity in the Congo without using the American military or the United Nations, and he promptly accepted Tshombe's offer. When Adoula vowed to boycott the conference, Kennedy threatened to cut off American economic aid. Adoula reluctantly agreed to attend. Stevenson persuaded the United Nations Security Council to call for a cease fire, and the President ordered Ambassador Gullion to act as mediator. Kennedy even dispatched the presidential plane, *Columbine*, to transport the participants to an abandoned Belgian airbase at Kitona for the talks.[35]

After intense efforts by Gullion, Tshombe finally agreeed to turn his troops over to the central government and to rejoin parliament. Katanga's secession seemed at an end and the United States had produced an accord without firing a shot. Kennedy waxed jubilant. He told British Ambassador David Ormsby Gore, "Maybe they *aren't* paying me too much!"[36] But within a week Tshombe repudiated the Kitona agreement and the fighting resumed. Kennedy's Congo policy lay in shambles. Katanga was as strong as ever and Adoula, unable to unify his nation, was losing power. The United States had alienated its European allies by refusing to support Katangan independence and had angered the new African nations by negotiating with the despised Tshombe. Rather than the boldness he had promised, Kennedy's efforts in the Congo had been marked by hesitation and vacillation. As one scholar of American policy in the Congo has noted: "despite the brave talk . . . the record in 1961 showed that [Kennedy] had been little more than a practitioner of wait-and-see diplomacy."[37]

The President was determined to overcome the failures of 1961, but there was no consensus in Washington on what to do. In 1962 the simmering battle between "Africanists" and "Europeanists" erupted over every option. Certain that Kennedy would never follow his suggestions for military action to destroy Tshombe, Ball now called for complete United States "disengagement" from the Congo. Williams, Stevenson, and others renewed demands for American military aid to the United Nations. Hawks became doves and doves talked like hawks. Ball demanded that Williams's African Bureau cease its insistence on Administration support of military efforts against Katanga. Williams refused. Ball then told Bureau officers he would personally clear all of their speeches, press releases, and position papers. To counter Ball, Williams called on Stevenson, Bowles, Gullion, and others outside of the African Bureau to lobby with Kennedy. Ball called the bureau's analysis of the Congo "a bunch of mush," while

"Africanists" privately claimed the Administration was "as bad as Eisenhower" on the Congo.[38]

Rather than side with either faction or silence the bickering, Kennedy again chose a personal initiative. He sent to Katanga Under Secretary of State for Political Affairs George McGhee, a conservative Democrat not associated with either side, to explore once again the possibility of negotiations. As with the Kitona conference, the President's action led to near disaster. McGhee became infatuated with Katanga's anti-Communism, and hailed Tshombe as "the father of Congolese federalism." To show his good intentions, Tshombe promised to donate a portion of Katanga's tax revenue to the central government. When McGhee departed, Tshombe repudiated his promise. Adoula denounced unilateral American negotiations with his avowed enemy, and he called in the Soviet ambassador to discuss possible U.S.S.R. military assistance to use against Katanga. Kennedy's continued efforts to work with Tshombe seemed to have created the very Soviet threat he had so feared.[39]

As American officials sorted out the diplomatic debris of the failed McGhee mission, Kennedy became preoccupied with the Cuban missile crisis. When he returned to the problems of the Congo in November, he seemed to be moving toward the disengagement Ball had advocated. It was Belgian Foreign Minister Paul-Henri Spaak who finally succeeded where the President's advisers had failed. Belgium had been Katanga's leading supporter, but when Spaak met with Kennedy in late November the Belgian diplomat argued strongly for Western efforts to unify the Congo. He proposed a joint program of military aid to the United Nations and economic sanctions against Katanga. Kennedy was greatly impressed that Spaak would risk the collapse of Belgium's government to oppose Tshombe.[40]

Equally important in prodding Kennedy to new action were reports of increased Soviet influence among groups opposed to Adoula. Roger Hilsman, Director of the State Department's Bureau of Intelligence and Research and a self-described "cold-war technocrat," had largely avoided the vitriolic debate on the Congo. In December 1962, however, Hilsman prepared for Kennedy a long appraisal of potential Communist gains if Adoula's government collapsed. Hilsman repeated the familiar logic: the fall of Adoula meant civil war and possible victory for a radical regime; Adoula's survival required Tshombe's defeat. If America did not help crush Katanga it might have to intervene later to counter Soviet influence. In a gentle criticism of the President, Hilsman noted that past American "hesitancy" had helped create the current crisis. The fact that "we have not yet made up our mind on policy in the Congo" was "inexcusable." Hilsman suggested an immediate and massive American military package to United Nations forces. He argued that force probably would not have to be used as its very threat would compel Tshombe to surrender. American weapons would dictate a political solution. Now persuaded that Kennedy would never disengage from the Congo given the new threat of Soviet influence, Ball strongly supported Hilsman. "We have to fish or cut bait," he concluded, "and fishing involves a willingness to commit American forces."[41]

At a December 14 National Security Council meeting, Hilsman, Ball, and others argued strongly for a show of force in support of the United Nations. Kennedy remained dubious and made no decision. Three days later the group met again and the President announced he was sending an American military mission to study the Congolese situation and to consider the possibility of aiding United Nations forces.[42]

On Christmas eve, without a clear commitment of United States support, the United Nations launched "Operation Grandslam" against Katanga. To the surprise of American officials, United Nations troops rapidly overran Katangan defenses. From his vacation spot in Palm Springs, Kennedy expressed alarm at the United Nations success. Tshombe had vowed a scorched earth policy that included plans to destroy Katanga's mines, and Kennedy believed his threat. The President ordered Rusk and Stevenson to remind United Nations officials that the goal was "a political solution, not a military one."[43] Despite Kennedy's concerns, the United Nations forces continued their assault. In mid-January Tshombe surrendered with Katanga's mines undamaged.

Kennedy's advisers claimed it was the threat of American military aid that had finally ended Katanga's secession, and they showered the President with congratulations. Kennedy agreed that the Administration was entitled to "a little sense of pride" in securing stability and unity in the Congo.[44] In a sense he was correct, as America had gained both of its major objectives: the Congo was temporarily united under an anti-Communist leader. But Katanga's defeat owed little to American diplomacy. For nearly two years Kennedy had resisted any clear military commitment to the United Nations forces, despite repeated urgings of his advisers. Even at the end he had permitted only a fact-finding mission rather than direct support. With his Administration deeply divided over the role of the United States in the Congo, Kennedy sought a middle path between withdrawal and a direct use of American power. His fear of failure led to indecision rather than boldness; his policy was 'the product of pure caution.'"45

Kennedy showed a similar caution in his response to the rebellion in Portuguese Angola. Unlike the other colonial powers, Portugal refused even to consider independence for its African colonies of Angola and Mozambique. Portugal's dictator, Antonio de Oliveria Salazar, claimed that his nation had no "colonies," only "overseas provinces." Angola was, in short, as much a part of Portugal as Lisbon. Militantly anti-Communist and a member of NATO, Portugal also controlled a key military base in the Azores Islands that American defense experts considered vital. Portugal's own failure to prepare its colonies for freedom also worked to make Kennedy reluctant to push for immediate independence. Less than 1 percent of Angolans had ever attended a school. With the constant reminder of the turmoil in the Congo, American officials feared the rapid decolonization of Angola could lead to chaos and resulting Communist inroads. Salazar's personality and ideology compounded Washington's diplomatic dilemma. A self-proclaimed "nineteenth century man"—critics argued "sixteenth century"—Salazar saw the United States as the embodiment of decadent modern materialism with no right to dictate the abandonment of Portugal's "civilizing mission" in Africa.

Kennedy had repeatedly criticized Eisenhower for not supporting decolonization, and black Africa expected the Administration to put strong pressure on Portugal. But the President also feared a disruption in NATO, the loss of the Azores base, and the instability resultant from too rapid a rush to independence by the seemingly unprepared Portuguese colonies. Two weeks after he took office, Kennedy had to decide on a policy. On February 4, Angolans stormed the main prison in Luanda, the capital, to free nationalist leaders. Police fired into the crowd, killing thirty-three people. African and Asian states introduced into the United Nations Security Council a resolution that called on Portugal to end colonialism and demanded an investigation into the causes of the incident. Throughout the 1950s the United States had rejected similar resolutions directed at Portugal, but the Kennedy Administration saw an opportunity to break with past policies. After intense debate among American officials, Rusk informed

Lisbon that the United States would support the pending resolution. He explained that the African nations "hold us responsible for Portuguese actions . . . which clash with America's traditional position in regards to colonialism and self-determination." Washington could no longer "remain silent" or tolerate continued "inaction." If Portugal developed a "realistic time-table" for decolonization of its African possessions, America would offer economic aid to help Lisbon overcome the loss of its colonies.[46]

On March 15 the United States voted in favor of the resolution. France, Britain, and four others abstained, and the motion failed. That same day blacks in Angola attacked white farms, police stations, and army bases. Portugal sent troops, and what had begun as an isolated incident in February was by late March a large-scale rebellion. Portugal claimed American support for the defeated United Nations revolution had provoked a "communist revolution" in Angola.[47] Domestic critics also hammered at the Administration for its vote against a NATO ally. Led by Dean Acheson, they charged Kennedy with "misguided idealism" and "crumbling to the pressure of the new nations." More important, many military and State Department officials feared that the new "tough" line against Portugal risked loss of American use of the Azores base. They considered the facility crucial for the airlifting of troops to Europe or to the Middle East. The Azores lease expired at the end of 1962 and Portugal had refused even to discuss its renewal.[48]

Concern about the Azores would eventually dominate American diplomacy, but the most pressing issue in 1961 was the revolt in Angola. Administration officials publicly argued that Portuguese intransigence had made violence inevitable. Privately they struggled with the decision over which independence group to support. Two major organizations vied for control of the Angolan liberation movement: the União das Populaçõ de Angola (UPA), led by Holden Roberto, and the Movimento Popular de Libertação de Angola (MPLA), under Agoshinho Neto and Mario de Andrade. Although Roberto had close ties with Lumumba and Nkrumah, he rejected Marxism. On the other hand, MPLA leaders had repeatedly claimed that only through socialism and class struggle could Angola achieve freedom. To Washington, the choice became evident. State Department officials met secretly with Roberto in March and tried to persuade him to abandon violence. Roberto argued that Portugal had ignored all peaceful attempts to work for independence, and if he rejected violence, he would lose control of the liberation struggle. Roberto asked for American aid to compete with his radical MPLA rivals. Late in 1961 Washington began to supply UPA with non-military matériel and placed Roberto on the CIA payroll. (The United States ended direct aid to UPA in 1969, but continued to pay Roberto $10,000 a year "look-in" money.)[49] American officials accompanied their covert support for Roberto with demands that Portugal agree to eventual independence for Angola. Williams, Bowles, and Stevenson charged that Portugal was insuring the rise of radicalism in Angola by refusing to negotiate. Stevenson also cast affirmative votes for additional United Nations resolutions critical of Portugal. Lisbon responded by accusing Kennedy of "betraying a friend of freedom" and encouraging Communism in Africa.[50]

The Administration expected such criticism from Portugal, but they were dismayed their new stance at the United Nations had not gained the gratitude of the African nations. Nkrumah of Ghana dismissed American votes in the United Nations as "propaganda" and claimed that Portugal was using NATO weapons to kill Angolan freedom fighters. If Washington really wanted to demonstrate its commitment to African independence, it should expel Portugal from NATO.[51] Such remarks caused deep resentment in the Kennedy government. American officials believed they had made a significant break with past "Europe-first" policies, with little or no acknowledgment from African nations. Caught once again between old allies and the new African states, the Administration had to endure criticism from Portugal and other European states for "betraying" the Western community and charges from Africans that Washington was aiding Portugal's war in Angola. The Department of State Policy Planning Council conceded that America's "diplomatic offensive" to secure eventual independence for Angola had failed either to alter Portugal or to win support in Africa. It concluded that "it is doubtful any useful purpose would be served by the United States applying further pressure against Portugal."[52]

Kennedy was in the process of a complete re-evaluation of his Angolan policy when he went to Europe for his summit meeting with Khrushchev in the summer of 1961. Kennedy first discussed Angola with France's Charles de Gaulle. De Gaulle cautioned against pushing Salazar too far because such pressure might generate "revolution in Portugal" and a Communist regime in Angola. During his stormy talks with Khrushchev in Vienna two days later, Kennedy asked if the revolt in Angola was an example of "wars of national liberation." Khrushchev denied Soviet involvement, but declared all wars against colonialism to be "sacred" and warned against any American intervention.[53] Kennedy seemed to face a diplomatic dilemma: if he ended American pressure on Portugal, he risked the wrath of the African nations and the possibility of a protracted war leading to increased radicalism. If he continued to demand that Salazar accept Angolan independence, it could disrupt NATO and perhaps even topple Portugal's government.

As the revolt against Portugal intensified, "Africanists" in Washington argued that time was running out for a transition to a stable, non-Marxist, independent Angola. The longer the war continued, the greater the chance of a radical result. In June 1961 Williams organized a Task Force on the Portuguese Territorites that recommended increased pressure on Salazar to endorse a "timetable" for Angolan freedom. If Salazar failed to respond, the United States should terminate all economic aid to Portugal and develop contingency plans for the loss of the Azores and the withdrawal of Portugal from NATO. Only such a dramatic move could break the stalemate in Angola. Predictably, "Europeanists" were appalled at the idea of risking the Azores and the break-up of NATO in the vague hope of securing the liberation of Angola.[54]

On July 14, 1961, Kennedy met with his National Security Council to discuss Angola. As with most African issues, he sought a compromise. Worried about Berlin, he wanted to avoid weakening NATO or diminishing American military capabilities. He did agree to offer again economic aid to Portugal if Salazar agreed to negotiations leading to eventual independence.[55] "Africanists" noted the President's preoccupation with Europe and feared he would ease pressure on Portugal. In early 1962 they supported a new attempt to force Lisbon to grant independence. In late 1961 the CIA had assigned Paul Sakwa to prepare a study of insurgency and subversion in emerging nations. Sakwa had just completed two years as chief of the CIA's Vietnam covert action section. Claiming that "Vietnam was going to hell" and only decisive action by Washington could prevent a similar disaster in Angola, Sakwa prepared a nine-part plan to insure Angolan freedom by 1970. His January 1962 recommendations called for a massive American-funded educational program to prepare Angola for independence. The United States would give Roberto "a salaried consultative status" and he would be "groomed for the Premiership."

Angolans would form political parties in 1965 to prepare for elections in 1967 and complete independence three years later.[56]

Sakwa conceded that "an aged potentate like Salazar is not likely to accept the above plan without benefit of a frontal lobotomy"; still, America had "tacit responsibility" to prevent Portugal's "suicide" in Africa. To insure acceptance, Washington should offer aid that would double the per capita income of Portugal in five years. The economic incentive must be so large "as to capture the imagination of the average literate Portuguese to whom it will be leaked if turned down by Salazar." If Salazar rejected the offer, the United States should turn to "Phase two—an overthrow of the Salazar regime by pro-American officers." Sakwa estimated the plan would cost $500 million a year for eight years—"a cheap way to avoid disaster." He defended the coup by claiming that Salazar had used the Azores lease to blackmail the United States, and "counter-response to blackmail never has been regarded as a positive criminal act." An economic incentive to produce a Portuguese commitment to decolonization was not new, but Sakwa's suggestion of a possible overthrow of Salazar was. At a National Security Council meeting in March, the Administration approved a part of Sakwa's economic program, but rejected any plans for a coup. The President ordered the American Ambassador in Lisbon to offer up to $70 million in direct aid if Portugal agreed to negotiate the eventual independence of its African colonies.[57]

While he awaited Salazar's response, Kennedy ordered a new review of the importance of the Azores base. When William Attwood, American Ambassador to Guinea, met with the President to urge "a showdown" with Salazar, he found Kennedy preoccupied with the Azores. "What would they say if there was a tidal wave, and the Azores just disappeared?" Kennedy mused. "Are they all that vital?"[58] To American military experts the base was deemed vital. The lease for United States use of the Azores expired at the end of 1962 and Salazar still refused to negotiate for renewal. Washington began to temper its demands on Portugal as the expiration date neared. The State Department ordered an end to all direct contacts with Roberto. At the United Nations, America reversed itself and abstained on two Security Council resolutions condemning Portugal. The CIA concluded that Salazar would allow continued use of the Azores without any formal agreement as long as Washington did not renew its demands for Angolan independence. Kennedy thus instructed Stevenson "to sit back and let others take the lead" on issues involving

Portugal at the United Nations. When Stevenson nonetheless helped draft a resolution moderately critical of Lisbon, the President angrily ordered him to abstain from voting on the resolution he had helped to write.[59]

In August 1963 Salazar finally responded to the American offer of economic aid in exchange for a pledge to abandon Africa. He accused the United States of pushing for an independent Angola so American corporations could dominate the new nation. Salazar noted that Washington had offered "compensation for the loss of Africa," but declared, "Portugal overseas is not for sale!" He vowed to continue the "fight for freedom" in Angola.[60]

Salazar's rejection of the economic incentive for decolonization illustrated the Administration's inability to moderate Portugal. American diplomatic efforts in 1961 had led only to condemnation from Lisbon and other NATO allies, while the relaxation of pressure in 1962 and 1963 convinced African nations that Washington had abandoned Angola in favor of a military base in the Atlantic. Although Kennedy had demonstrated American opposition to continued Portuguese colonialism, he eventually judged the price of sustaining pressure on Lisbon to be too high. After more than a decade of guerrilla war, Angola finally gained independence in 1975. As many in the Kennedy Administration had predicted, the protracted struggle ended in a Marxist regime, unrecognized by the United States.

While he tried to moderate Portugal's intransigence, Kennedy also faced the problem of designing a policy toward the white minority regime of South Africa and its program of apartheid. When the National Party gained political control of South Africa in 1948 it instituted a complex system of racial classification, separatism, and absolute white control. Although whites were less than 20 percent of the population, they controlled over 80 percent of the land of South Africa, including all major urban areas, and were the only group allowed the vote. As the rest of Africa moved toward black rule, the white minority in South Africa united to prevent political action by the black majority. Unlike Europeans in other African nations, whites in South Africa had been on the continent for over three hundred years and had no "mother country" to return to. They were convinced that majority rule meant economic and political suicide. Since 1948 every American President had verbally condemned apartheid, but had also continued normal political and economic relations with South Africa.[61] Liberals and blacks in the United States and

African leaders pressed Kennedy to end this compromise policy and to use American power to moderate and eventually eliminate apartheid.

Economic and strategic considerations limited American actions against apartheid. United States trade with South Africa was modest compared with other regions, but was by far the largest of any African nation. In 1960 America exported $277 million to South Africa and imported $108 million. United States investment in South Africa totaled $286 million. More crucial than the amount of trade was South African dominance of a number of strategic minerals necessary for American manufacturing and defense.[62] A direct confrontation with Pretoria risked the cut-off of gold, diamonds, manganese, platinum, and chrome. Kennedy was also aware that South Africa allowed the United States to use its ports and to operate missile-tracking stations in its territory.

Despite American dependence on South African minerals, critics of apartheid contended that economic sanctions were the only way to force South Africa to share power with its black majority. To Kennedy and most of his advisers, however, economic sanctions were impractical and dangerous. They doubted if American economic pressure would force whites to yield power, and they expected that the black majority would bear the burden of any sanctions. American officials also assumed other nations would quickly replace United States trade and investment. While some in the Administration pushed hard for economic sanctions, the consensus in both the State Department and the While House stood steadfastly against economic pressure.

The United States thus had few options to demonstrate its opposition to apartheid. American leaders did verbally criticize the South African government with a sternness rare for a country that enjoyed normal relations with the United States. Throughout 1961, Williams, Bowles, and American representatives at the United Nations assailed apartheid as an unjust system paving the way for eventual violence. Bowles defended "opening up on apartheid" against critics who complained that Washington was engaged in "selective rage." Bowles told Kennedy that the New Frontier must make it clear that its dedication to equal rights "was absolute" both at home and abroad.[63]

Strength in policy did not match strength of language. Kennedy rejected suggestions that he end International Monetary Fund loans to South Africa or "discourage" new American investment. Most influential in resisting such efforts were Dean Rusk and Joseph Satterthwaite, the American Ambassador to South Africa. Rusk was as dedicated to racial equality as anyone in the Administration, but argued the need to separate domestic from foreign policy. He contended that dozens of nations did not share American notions of human rights and to single out South Africa meant selective enforcement and a misguided attempt to impose American values. Satterthwaite agreed. He dismissed Williams and Bowles as idealists who did not understand that external pressure on South Africa would only increase white obstinacy and encourage black violence.[64]

Rusk prepared a carefully worded statement of official policy that condemned apartheid as "repugnant" but called for the continuation of normal diplomatic and economic relations. He later explained that the United States would "distinguish between non-cooperation in matters directly or indirectly related to apartheid policy, and cooperation in all other fields." To Rusk, economic sanctions constituted "excessive pressure" that encouraged racial war and possible "communist infiltration."[65]

Having rejected a major break with past policies, the Administration was left largely with symbolic gestures to illustrate its opposition to apartheid. The State Department ordered Satterthwaite to integrate social events at United States facilities in South Africa, even though Satterthwaite protested that such a policy violated local law. At the United Nations, Stevenson supported general resolutions that condemned racial discrimination, but opposed specific demands for economic pressure against South Africa. When the United Nations vowed to refuse to seat South African delegates to the World Health Organization and to the International Labor Organization, American representatives devised a compromise whereby South Africa refused to send delegates and the United States was spared the need to vote on whether they should be seated.[66]

African leaders denounced America's compromise policy as hypocrisy. At home, black Americans charged that Kennedy was unwilling to make a clear commitment to equal rights in either the American South or in South Africa. Martin Luther King, Jr., told the American Negro Leadership Conference on Africa that in the segregated South and in segregated South Africa "there seems always the choice between political expediency and that which is morally compelling," and the New Frontier had opted for the former. Only strong pressure from the White House prevented King from attacking Washington's policy toward South Africa at the United Nations.[67]

Under attack from African and civil rights leaders for not confronting South Africa, the President seized upon a suggestion from Mennen Williams that the United States announce a unilateral arms embargo toward South Africa. "Africanists" had earlier suggested a weapons ban as a prelude to economic sanctions and Kennedy had rejected the recommendation. But in 1963 he saw benefits in such a move. An arms embargo would demonstrate American opposition to apartheid without involving other sanctions.[68] Kennedy ordered special assistant Ralph Dungan to survey opinion on a weapons ban. Dungan found strong opposition in the Defense and Commerce departments, but general support elsewhere. Ball endorsed the move, but warned the President that some in the Administration would see it as a first step toward complete sanctions.[69]

Convinced of the benefits both at home and abroad of a dramatic gesture against apartheid, Kennedy instructed Stevenson to announce the embargo at the United Nations, but to make it clear that it was a unilateral American action. He also ordered Stevenson to include "an escape clause" allowing the United States to repeal the embargo if a future need arose to "maintain world peace." Stevenson argued that such a clause made the weapons ban virtually meaningless. He also noted that the President had recently ordered him to abstain on a resolution calling for an arms embargo toward Portugal.[70] Despite Stevenson's reservations, on August 2, 1963, he announced America's intent to ban the sale of all weapons to South Africa by the end of the year. He included the "escape clause" by noting that the United States reserved the right to alter the policy in the future "in light of requirements for assuring the maintenance of international peace."[71] The arms embargo constituted the Administration's major effort to illustrate its opposition to apartheid and its sympathy with black Africa. The ban was neither total (Washington continued to supply spare parts to South Africa long after January 1, 1964) nor irreversible. Because South Africa produced nearly all the weapons it needed by 1963, the embargo also had little direct impact. Some in the Administration tried to lobby the President to expand the embargo to other products, but Kennedy refused. The Administration continued instead with symbolic protests. When South Africa denied a visa to a black State Department official, Rusk summoned its ambassador and vehemently denounced apartheid and the South African Government. Williams attended the meeting and noted he had never seen Rusk so furious. The Secretary of State paced the room and slammed his fist on his desk, demanding an immediate apology. When the South African left, Rusk turned to Williams and asked: "Did I really give it to him tough enough? If not, I'll follow him downstairs and finish the job!"[72] Rusk's anger was real, and so too was the Kennedy Administration's distaste for apartheid. But, as Stevenson summarized two weeks after Kennedy's death, "in dealing with so intractable an issue as apartheid there are no easy solutions."[73]

Kennedy's goals in the Congo, Angolo, and South Africa were to restore lost American prestige among black Africans and to prevent the rise of Soviet influence. His policy toward independent, neutralist African nations had the same objectives. Despite claims that the New Frontier welcomed a world of diversity, Kennedy and his advisers still viewed Africa as an arena of Cold War competition. Pro-Western or "truly" neutral nations constituted American victories while nations close to the Soviet Union counted as defeats. The Eisenhower Administration had judged the former French colony of Guinea and the former British colony of Ghana as pro-Soviet. Kennedy shared this interpretation, but he believed a combination of personal diplomacy and American power could bring each to "real" neutralism.

Most of the former French colonies in Africa had maintained close economic and political ties with the mother country. Kennedy continued Eisenhower's policy of undertaking only token programs of economic assistance to these nations, because he thought France "should logically bear most of the necessary aid burden." America had limited resources and there was no need to expend them in countries already aligned with the West.[74] The one exception to Washington's deference to Paris in French Africa was Guinea. Under the leadership of Sékou Touré, Guinea had been the only French colony to reject de Gaulle's plan for increased autonomy within a French Union of African states and to demand complete and immediate independence. France responded by withdrawing its aid and technicians after Guinea became free in 1958. Touré then turned to the Soviet Union for assistance. By the time Kennedy took office, most officials in Washington regarded Guinea as firmly in the Russian camp, but the new Ambassador, former *Look* magazine journalist William Attwood, persuaded the President that "the time is ripe for an American initiative" to win the nation from Soviet control.[75] Attwood courted Touré and hinted that Washington would provide significant economic aid if Guinea cut its ties with Moscow. Kennedy also sent Sargent Shriver, head of the new Peace Corps, to Guinea to woo Touré. After Guinea agreed to accept volunteers, Shriver told Kennedy that the Peace Corps could help "move a country from an apparently clear [Communist] Bloc orientation to a position of neutrality or even one of orientation to the West."[76]

More important than the efforts of Attwood and Shriver was a bungled Soviet attempt to topple Touré's government. In December 1962 Guinea expelled the Russian Ambassador and refused further Soviet aid. Kennedy soon invited Touré to the White House where Jacqueline Kennedy conversed with the Guinean leader in French at a formal luncheon and the President listened to a plea for aid. American officials made it clear to Touré that aid depended on Guinea displaying "objective" neutralism. Williams told Guinean representatives that Congress would never approve aid funds unless Guinea expelled all "bloc technicians as quickly as they can be replaced by technicians from the Free World." American diplomats also demanded that Touré refrain from his frequent criticism of United States foreign policy and racial problems.[77] Having alienated the French in 1958 and having expelled the Russians in 1962, Touré was desperate for economic assistance and complied with American demands. He rejected pressure from other African leaders that he join their condemnation of violence against blacks in Alabama and Mississippi. Touré also ended his persistent attacks on America's efforts in the Congo and even publicly praised Kennedy for promoting unity in the divided nation.

Kennedy had a more difficult time in his attempts to influence Ghana and its President Kwame Nkrumah to follow "true" neutralism in the Cold War. Nkrumah was the leading African critic of Western "neocolonialism." He had been censorious of American foreign policy and a strong supporter of the Soviet Union at the United Nations. Ghana had welcomed Russian economic aid and Nkrumah had moved toward a dictatorship by jailing critics, censoring the press, and ruling by decree. In late 1960 Secretary of State Christian Herter publicly announced that Nkrumah "was very definitely in the communist camp."[78]

The President had one major weapon to force Nkrumah to alter his policies. In 1958 the Eisenhower Administration had arranged for a consortium of private American investors to finance a massive hydro-electric dam and aluminum smelter on Ghana's Volta River. The United States hoped to regain prestige in the emerging world after a stormy withdrawal from the Aswan Dam project in Egypt two years earlier.[79] In response to Nkrumah's support of the Soviet Union and criticism of American foreign policy, Eisenhower had delayed formal approval of loan guarantees for the Volta project. When Kennedy took office, his advisers urged him to continue to delay final funding. The American Ambassador to Ghana concluded, "If the present virulent anti-American campaign . . . plus growing rapprochement with the Soviet bloc should continue, it would be self-defeating for the West to proceed with the financing of the Volta project." He urged the President to "wait and see" if Nkrumah continued "to follow the Soviet line" before making a decision.[80]

Nkrumah had staked his domestic and international reputation on the Volta project, and he recognized the proposal was in trouble. In late February 1961 he requested a pesonal meeting with Kennedy, who agreed. Presidential advisers urged Kennedy to use the meeting to pressure Nkrumah to alter his vocal criticism of the United States and to moderate his authoritarian rule in Ghana. The CIA concluded Nkrumah was not a true Marxist, but rather "a showboat and vain opportunist." Kennedy could use the issue of Volta funding to change the African leader's behavior.[81] Despite the President's plans to discuss Volta, the meeting at the White House became, in the words of one observer, "an Nkrumah monologue on the Congo." The two leaders never discussed directly funding for the project.[82]

Despite disappointment at his meeting with Nkrumah, Kennedy still believed he could use American aid to end Ghana's drift to the left. He dreaded the results of another Aswan, wherein the United States had first agreed to aid Egypt and then backed out, and the Soviets had moved in. In late June 1961, Kennedy rejected advice that he continue to wait and see and sent a warm personal letter to Nkrumah announcing he was "delighted" to approve funding for the Volta project.[83]

Kennedy assumed that American economic aid would moderate Nkrumah, but the President's letter had the opposite effect. Free from the need to court the United States, Nkrumah embarked on an eight-week tour of Eastern Europe, Russia, and China. He called for diplomatic recognition of the People's Republic of China, the acceptance of two Germanies, an end to all colonialism within one year, and total disarmament. He condemned Kennedy for increased military spending but refused to criticize the Soviet Union for resuming nuclear testing. Nkrumah further angered American officials when he agreed to send 400 of his troops to Russia for training. When the head of Ghana's armed forces protested, Nkrumah fired him.[84]

Kennedy grew outraged by Nkrumah's actions. Many in Congress and the press had criticized the President's decision to aid Ghana, and Nkrumah's actions seemed to confirm their charges that the African nation was pro-Moscow. Attorney General Robert Kennedy claimed that Nkrumah was "playing footsies with the Soviet Union." By granting aid to Ghana, Washington was teaching other African nations to "play the Soviet Union off against the United States." Even the President's father reportedly told Kennedy: "What the hell are you up to with that communist Nkrumah?"[85] Kennedy responded to such criticism by leaking a story to the *New York Times* that the Administration was "re-assessing" its commitment to the Volta project. The National Security Council prepared a summary of the possible consequences of abandoning the project, and legal experts in the State Department concluded that the United States was not "legally bound" to go ahead with Volta.[86]

Despite the reassessment, the June letter to Nkrumah had trapped the President. Nkrumah had already informed African leaders that Kennedy had agreed to fund Volta. He wrote the President threatening to make public Kennedy's letter if America reneged. Both the CIA and the State Department concluded that a refusal to proceed followed by release of the President's letter would "be interpreted as an open renunciation of the Administration's oft-stated policy of aid without political strings."[87]

At a National Security Council meeting on December 5, Kennedy asked, "How could we justify a decision to help Nkrumah in light of the leftward and authoritarian course of his domestic policies and his unhelpful positions on international issues?" The President read aloud his June note to Nkrumah and observed that "this seems a fairly warm letter and asked who had drafted it." The ever-blunt George Ball reminded Kennedy that "it had been made warmer by the President's own direction." After lengthy discussion, Kennedy observed that Treasury Secretary C. Douglas Dillon and the Attorney General opposed funding the project, but the others believed

America had to go ahead. A week later the President formally approved a $37 million loan to Ghana and $96 million in loan guarantees to the American consortium.[88]

Kennedy remained suspicious of Ghana's neutralism throughout his presidency. When Nkrumah criticized American policy during the Cuban missile crisis, the President again ordered the National Security Council to study ways to abandon the Volta project. Although NSC staffers agreed it "would be useful to make an example of one of the left-leaning neutrals," they concluded it was far too late to withdraw aid to Ghana.[89]

Kennedy's efforts to lure Guinea and Ghana away from the Soviet Union illustrated his view of diplomacy as a continuous competition with Moscow for influence and prestige. Despite pledges to keep the Cold War out of Africa, the President and his advisers viewed the continent in the traditional framework of East-West competition. His sustained interest in Africa and his effective personal diplomacy with African leaders altered dramatically the style of United States relations with the continent, but the substance was largely unchanged. Kennedy's 1960 campaign statements and early appointments raised expectations for a major realignment of American policy toward Africa, but his own goals were actually modest. He recognized that decolonization and the force of African nationalism made it unrealistic for Washington to expect the new nations to align with the West against the Soviet Union. He did, however, expect to avoid losing the continent to Communism. Merely by denying Khrushchev's apparent challenge of Third World revolution and wars of national liberation, Kennedy thought he could win the struggle in Africa.

Although he was persuaded of the importance of Africa in the Cold War, Kennedy was unwilling to adopt a clear "Africa first" position that would have jeopardized relations with the European powers. The split within the Administration between "Africanists" and "Europeanists" reflected a divison in the President's own thinking about Africa. He sided with neither faction because he shared some of the asumptions of both camps. With Williams, Bowles, and Stevenson, Kennedy agreed that Africa had major symbolic significance in the Cold War and required sustained American involvement. The President, however, also accepted the "Europeanist" view that Africa did not carry such immediate and crucial strategic interest to the United States as to warrant major risks in policy. He did not believe new friends should be gained at the expense of old allies.

As a result of the diplomatic dichotomy within the Administration and in Kennedy's own analysis, the New Frontier's policies toward Africa were generally the result of compromise. Kennedy accepted the need for American involvement in the Congo, but was reluctant to commit American power to the destruction of Katanga. He pressured Portugal to accept Angolan independence but was unwilling to jeopardize the Azores base or European solidarity to force the issue. The United States engaged in symbolic protest of South Africa's policy of apartheid, but rejected economic sanctions. The Administration claimed to understand and accept African neutralism, but only within carefully prescribed limits. Kennedy's efforts satisfied neither "Africanists" nor Africans, "Europeanists" nor Europeans, but they did help him meet his goal of not losing Africa to Communism. Kennedy knew that an independent Africa required a new American diplomacy, but he was unwilling to abandon prevailing priorities of anti-Communism and support of European allies.

11

Passing the Torch and Lighting Fires: The Peace Corps

GARY MAY

August 9, 1962, was oppressively warm and humid, like most summer days in Washington, D.C., but few among the proud six hundred men and women gathered on the White House lawn complained. They had volunteered to become members of the Peace Corps and had been summoned to meet the man who had called them to national service: President John F. Kennedy.

Shortly past 4 o'clock the President appeared, accompanied by Harris Wofford, former presidential assistant for civil rights and recently appointed Peace Corps Director for Ethiopia. The President told the trainees that they had "committed themselves to a great adventure" for America and the world. "I think that by the end of this year we'll have more than 5,000 Peace Corpsmen serving abroad," he said. Then Kennedy called the roll: "Georgetown University, 307 secondary school teachers for Ethiopia. Perhaps those of you going to Ethiopia could hold up their hands." He next acknowledged those bound for Nepal, Turkey, British Honduras, Ecuador, Venezuela, and Cyprus. "I hope that when you come back that we can persuade you to serve in the United States Government," the President told the group. "I hope that you will regard this as the first installment in a long life of service in the most exciting time. . . . The White House belongs to all the people, but I think it particularly belongs to you."[1]

The President then waded in to the crowd, shaking hands, posing for pictures, and chatting with the future volunteers. For most, seeing the President was a "real highlight" of the training period. Kennedy was "wonderful" recalled Linda Bergthold, twenty-one, of Pasadena, California, "but underneath those words you could feel this wry, sarcastic, sardonic, cynical thing. I felt he thought, 'What the hell, why not? Send those people out. What's the worse they can do?' "[2]

Bergthold had correctly sensed Kennedy's ambivalence about the Peace Corps. The President took great pleasure in its success—that, stirred by his words, thousands of Americans were asking to be sent to Africa, Asia, and Latin America, but he was reluctant to embrace the idea and eventually established the Peace Corps only after the public demanded it. Kennedy "thought the Peace Corps was good public relations and very American," Wofford later said. "But I don't think he saw any central role for it" in the conduct of American foreign policy.[3]

John F. Kennedy was not the first politician to call for the establishment of a Peace Corps. In 1958, Wisconsin Congressman Henry Reuss asked Congress to explore whether a "Youth Corps" could be created, and Senator Hubert Humphrey made the "Peace Corps" a part of his brief campaign for the presidency in 1960. After his withdrawal in June, he urged the Senate to create immediately such an agency. Later, Humphrey sent all of his research on the proposed corps to Senator John F. Kennedy.[4]

Kennedy did not take immediate advantage of Humphrey's gift. Although his staff was researching the idea, he remained publicly silent until a campaign appearance at the University of Michigan on the night of October 13, 1960. "How many of you who are going to be doctors are willing to spend your days in Ghana?" Kennedy asked the crowd of 10,000. "Technicians or engineers, how many of you are willing to work in the foreign service and spend your lives travelling around the world? On your willingness . . . to contribute part of your life to this country . . . will depend the answer to whether we as a free society can compete."[5] "The thrust of the Peace Corps idea was there," Wofford later noted, "but Kennedy's questions gave no clear sense of the program."[6] Indeed, despite a positive student response to the speech, two more weeks passed before Kennedy finally adopted the Peace Corps.

On November 2, 1960, Kennedy gave a major foreign policy address in San Francisco attacking the Eisenhower Administration for failing to prosecute vigorously the Cold War. "We must do better," Kennedy insisted. One way was to send Americans abroad: "I therefore propose," Kennedy said, "that our inadequate efforts . . . be supplemented by a Peace Corps . . . , well qualified through rigorous standards, well-trained in the language, skills, and customs they will need to know. . . . Our young men and women, dedicated to freedom, are fully capable of overcoming the efforts of Mr. Khrushchev's missionaries who are dedicated to undermining that freedom."[7] It is against this background of Cold War competition that Kennedy adopted the Peace Corps.

Although the Peace Corps was launched in dramatic fashion, Kennedy, in the weeks between his election and inauguration, said almost nothing about it. While "Peace Corps fever" spread throughout the nation's colleges and universities,[8] and mail poured into Kennedy headquarters in Boston and Washington, Kennedy simply issued a statement announcing that a small "International Youth Agency" would be proposed "on a limited pilot basis." On January 21, 1961, President Kennedy asked his brother-in-law, R. Sargent Shriver, to study "how the Peace Corps could be organized and then to organize it."[9]

The first man Shriver called for help in creating the Peace Corps was Harris Wofford. Wofford was thrilled: as a student World Federalist in the late 1940s, he had proposed a similar volunteer force, and later helped to create the International Development Placement Association, an organization which sent qualified Americans abroad. Shriver himself had been active in the Experiment for International Living in the 1930s, and in the 1950s he had recommended the creation of a Peace Corps-type agency to President Eisenhower. Now, in 1961, Wofford and Shriver had an opportunity to give new life to old ideas.[10]

They quickly assembled a task force of representatives of organizations with overseas experience. For the first week their discussion was guided by the various proposals already in existence: Congressman Reuss's "Youth Corps", Senator Humphrey's "Peace Corps", and reports from academics and other interested groups. Although different in conception, the first programs all envisioned a small organization, moving cautiously. Shriver and Wofford rejected this approach: they wanted to start big and move fast. They were therefore more attracted to the proposal of Warren W. Wiggins, a deputy director of the International Cooperation Agency, whose report proclaimed that it was both possible and desirable to send thousands of volunteers abroad within eighteen months; Wiggins's report, "The Towering Task," became the blueprint which guided the Peace Corps during its formative years.[11]

Unlike Kennedy, Shriver and Wofford believed that the Peace Corps should *not* be a weapon in the Cold War but "a genuine experiment in international partnership."[12] Its purpose would be threefold: "First, to make available to interested countries qualified men and women to help in meeting their needs for trained manpower. Second, to promote a better understanding of the American people on the part of the peoples served. [And] third, to promote a better understanding of other peoples on the part of the American people."[13] In late February, Shriver sent his report to the President urging the "immediate establishment" of the Peace Corps, and on March 1, Kennedy issued an executive order launching the Peace Corps "on a temporary basis" until Congress approved.[14]

Had Kennedy finally become a believer in the Peace Corps or was he simply responding to the widespread public interest in the agency? The latter seems more likely given Kennedy's behavior then and during the next crisis to face the Peace Corps—its struggle for independence. Shriver (appointed Peace Corps Director on March 4) strongly believed his organization should be "an identifiable . . . body of people, a corps . . . ," not an appendage of the existing foreign aid bureaucracy. Unfortunately, this view was not shared by the White House: a draft of Kennedy's Special Message to the Congress on Foreign Aid indicated that the President believed the Peace Corps should be part of the new Agency for International Development (AID).[15]

Shriver was in India when he received the news from Wiggins. "I was really stunned . . . and discouraged," he recalled. "It was final—the President had decided."[16] Nevertheless, Shriver cabled Wiggins instructing him to ask Vice President Lyndon Johnson (a Peace Corps supporter) to plead their case with the President. Kennedy and Johnson met privately on May 1, and the Vice President apparently "badgered him so much that Kennedy finally said all right."[17] On May 2, the White House announced that the Peace Corps would be "organized as a semi-autonomous unit within the Department of State . . . ,"[18] but, in fact, the Peace Corps was on its own—free to recruit and train volunteers and administer its own programs.

One final obstacle remained: congressional enactment—and here too the President displayed his customary coolness. "Jack feels that you and Lyndon Johnson demanded that the Peace Corps be separate and that therefore the two of you ought to get your damn bill through Congress by yourselves," Shriver's wife Eunice told him after speaking with her brother, the President. "Let them put the son of a bitch through," Kennedy was reported to have said. The President's words galvanized Shriver: "By God, I will never ask anything from the White House as long as I live," he said. "The one thing I was certain of—I was going to put the goddamned Peace Corps through the House and Senate."[19] For the next three months, Shriver prowled the halls of Congress—day and night—converting critics and wooing the undecided until Congress approved the Peace Corps by comfortable margins on September 22, 1961.

Within twenty-seven months, there were almost seven thousand volunteers working overseas in forty-four countries—in Asia, Africa, and Latin America. More than 50 percent were involved in education, 25 percent in community development, and the rest in public works, health care, and agricultural extension. Education was the Peace Corps' "biggest activity" during the Kennedy years because the agency's political, bureaucratic, and ideological interests coincided with the needs of many Third World countries. Nowhere was this more true than in Ethiopia.[20]

This ancient empire, located in northeastern Africa and ruled since 1930 by His Imperial Majesty, Haile Selassie, entered the 1960s with a serious "educational emergency," which threatened to retard permanently its economic development. Out of a secondary school-age population estimated at approximately one million, only six thousand were enrolled in 1960, and there were few college-trained Ethiopians qualified to teach them. This crisis had its origins during the Italian occupation (1935–1941), when the Italians killed nearly 20,000 Ethiopians, "reportedly concentrating on the professional, educational, and political leaders." When Selassie returned to Ethiopia in 1941 he found "almost no educated people left in the country." Over the next two decades he attempted to fill this gap by importing teachers from abroad, sending talented Ethiopian students to be educated in the United States, and asking his own countrymen to build new schools voluntarily and encourage their children to attend them. The emperor considered education so important to the modernization of Ethiopia that he personally assumed the position of Minister of Education. The Peace Corps seemed ideally suited to assist Ethiopia in overcoming these problems.[21]

Ethiopia's need for teachers provided the Peace Corps with an opportunity to become an agency that was large in number and bold in purpose. Most volunteers were college graduates who had majored in the liberal arts—Peace Corps officials thought they were the best suited to be teachers. Furthermore, Shriver and his aides believed education was not only "good in itself" but was the "key to progress and development" in Ethiopia and elsewhere. Ethiopia's crisis thus served the Peace Corps' desire to expand and extend its influence with "developing nations."[22] In October 1961, Selassie informed the Peace Corps that he would be interested in receiving as many as three hundred volunteers. In April 1962 Wofford negotiated the final agreement.[23] Wofford himself was appointed Country Director to lead what would become "the largest Peace Corps contingent ever to come to any country at one time."[24] The Ethiopian story reveals the complex nature of the Peace Corps at work and provides a prism through which to examine the Kennedy style in foreign affairs. "The New Frontiers are not in Washington," Harris Wofford told a group of volunteers in 1962, "they are out where you are going. . . ."[25]

On July 8, 1962, the 340 men and women who were selected as volunteer trainees for Ethiopia arrived at Georgetown University. Country Director Harris Wofford and Father George H. Dunne, head of the Georgetown training program, greeted them. Wofford spoke about the majesty of the ancient empire in which they would serve. "Each school yard will have a beautiful view—mountains in the background," he said. "But as for all the facilities you may be used to . . . well, the view is beautiful." Associate Director Bascom H. Story apologized for his exuberance, telling the volunteers that his words of enthusiasm "will be adequately modified by the hours of medical testimony you will hear about the country." After the nervous laughter subsided, Story explained the importance of their mission: in Ethiopia only 5 percent of the children attended school, and "it was a tremendous responsibility when you consider that one half of all secondary school education will be carried on by Americans within four or five years." Peace Corps officials expected that, with the volunteers, the number of students enrolled in Ethiopia's secondary schools would double.[26]

The next morning the trainees awakened at 5:45 a.m. and spent the first forty minutes in physical training. They did "push-ups, headstands, all manner of twisting, bending, turning, hopping, leaping, and jumping." Exhausted, they "drooped back to their dormitories, perspiration-soaked and muddy kneed, but no longer sleepy eyed."

·

After a shower and breakfast, they entered the classroom where they studied Ethiopian and American history, "world affairs," "teaching methods," and Amharic—Ethiopia's national language.[27]

"Chaos" was the word that almost everyone used to describe the training period.[28] Just six weeks earlier, Georgetown had received the contract to train the volunteers, so Father Dunne was given little time to assemble instructors, psychiatrists, and other personnel. His most difficult task was finding a competent Amharic instructor, and after searching throughout the United States and Canada, he finally turned to Ethiopia for his choice. To act as teaching assistants, Dunne also hired twenty Ethiopians who were studying in the United States; but of that group only a few were actually able to teach the language. Finding no "sound textbook," he was forced to rely on one he thought "pedagogically unsound." The result was language instruction that was almost legendary for its poor quality. Peace Corps officials described the program as "weak" and "inadequate"; the volunteers reported later that "language was the major shortcoming of the Ethiopian project and the one [they] are most embarrassed about." It was a rare volunteer who had a basic command of Amharic. Some would later joke that the most they could say was *Tenaystelin* ("Hello") and *Babor Tabyaw Yetinew?* ("Where is the railroad station?").[29]

More serious was Dunne's fear that the Peace Corps was guilty of "pressurized and hasty recruitment" of volunteers. Those concerned about the rapid growth of the Peace Corps called this the "Numbers Game": selecting volunteers either to meet the country's demands or to satisfy the "empire building tendencies of the Peace Corps' leaders." In the case of Ethiopia, both seemed likely. The Ministry of Education was asking for hundreds of volunteers, and Wofford, who believed that the Peace Corps should "move into Africa on a big scale," was eager to comply. Dunne thought the Peace Corps was determined "to supply three hundred people to Ethiopia" rather than three hundred qualified teachers. "Some of those sent to this project clearly had no particular competence at all," he later noted.[30]

The volunteers were too busy to sense the conflicts between Wofford and Dunne. Their day was filled with hikes and classes, lectures from visiting dignitaries such as diplomat Chester Bowles and anthropologist Margaret Mead, and examinations by psychiatrists who, they thought, searched for weaknesses that would lead to "de-selection"—removal from the program. Trainee Carol Miller believed that "the people doing the screening needed as much help as the volunteers."

Most thought the "best way" to avoid de-selection "was to keep your mouth shut."[31] The unit on health and medical training was "terrible, absolutely awful," recalled trainee Linda Bergthold. "They showed us microscopic slides of every Ethiopian or African disease known to the Public Health Service. They had us convinced that schistosomiasis, elephantitis, and leprosy were just around the corner." Almost all of the volunteers found the briefing equally "frightening" and tried to follow the doctors' orders: "If you can't boil it or peel it— don't eat it."[32]

Like Father Dunne, Dr. J. L. Manuell, Director of Student Health, criticized the way the Peace Corps processed the volunteers. He discovered that the agency had failed to conduct or complete physical examinations on hundreds of trainees. "This phase of the entire program presented the most miserable experience that the entire staff of Georgetown's Student Health has ever faced," he later wrote to Dunne. Medical histories had to be re-checked, examinations performed, tests run—"up to and including the very last day of the program." Manuell blamed Peace Corps incompetence and ignorance for this "nightmare."[33] And because the Peace Corps had also left uncompleted the required civil service investigation of eighty volunteers, they were consigned to "limbo." "They herded us into a room and just told us we weren't going," one victim later complained, "and they didn't know how long it would be before they'd let us know. It was brutal."[34] Dunne waxed furious that the Peace Corps, in its haste to attract volunteers, treated them in such a "cavalier fashion."[35]

Most volunteers actually enjoyed their eight weeks at Georgetown. True, they learned little Amharic and little about Ethiopian history and culture, but beyond all of this was the fact that they were training to become Peace Corps volunteers and were, in a sense, celebrities. Their hometown newspapers and radio stations celebrated their courage and selflessness. They were welcomed at the White House and proclaimed Kennedy's "Ambassadors"—pioneers on their own new frontier. At dinners, in personal meetings, on hikes, Wofford spoke of Ethiopia's beauties and Africa's challenges: "It's all so wide open," he liked to tell trainees, "and limited by your imagination. . . . Africans are a young people, making history. . . . Peace Corps want[s] to encourage the African countries to think even bigger."[36] Wofford cast a spell that only the most cynical could reject. Tall, lean, handsome, and eloquent, he seemed the very personification of the New Frontier. Friends and critics alike called him the "Philosopher King" of the

Peace Corps. He preached that the Peace Corps could help to achieve world integration and also cure America's domestic ills. "We are a pioneering people, with the frontier still in our blood . . . ," he once said. "We do not want to stay at home in our safe suburbs while the city is burning and being rebuilt. . . . It is truly our need and our desire . . . to participate in the great adventure of world development. . . ."[37] Wofford "had an almost Pollyannaish view—he never talked about all the disasters that could befall us," Linda Bergthold recalled. "He always talked about this common vision which kept swirling around us and moving us forward . . . the New Frontier . . . in the Third World. Previously, we had sent technicians . . . now we are sending people to bring the message of democracy and individual initiative. . . . It was all very romantic and we believed it."[38]

The training program for Ethiopia ended on August 30, 1962, when 224 trainees were inducted into the Peace Corps and honored at a special dinner. They were then sent home for a brief visit and reassembled in New York for their flight to Ethiopia.[39]

The volunteers arrived in Ethiopia's capital, Addis Ababa, on September 7. As they disembarked, carrying musical instruments, cameras, and piles of luggage, the sun appeared—"most unusual in this period of heavy Ethiopian rains," one official remarked. Nature had "conspired to make [their] arrival [a] festive occasion."[40] The volunteers passed through customs quickly and hurried into the airport lobby. They "spoke to every Ethiopian that moved." "We were all trying our Amharic," volunteer John Coyne later wrote. "We wanted to prove immediately that we weren't 'Ugly Americans.' . . ." A few volunteers approached one Ethiopian, "shook his hand and said 'Babor Tabyaw?' " The Ethiopian pointed out the location of the railroad station and went on his way. The volunteers then climbed on buses for their ride to the University College, where they would live during a two-week orientation period.[41]

For some, "culture shock" set in as they passed "all the huts, the mud, the masses of people, donkeys, sheep, cattle and cars crowding the airport road. We had traveled back hundreds of years when we dropped out of the sky," Coyne observed, "and the sudden reality of life in Africa—our life for the next two years—filled us with fright."[42] Coyne and the others soon became too busy to worry. First, there was additional instruction at the college, then trips to the Merkado, the largest open marketplace in Africa, and the Koko Dam and the Wongi Sugar Plantations near Nazareth. September 11 was New

Year's Day, and the Americans were invited to celebrate the holiday with sixty Ethiopian families. For almost everyone it was their first taste of Ethiopia's traditional dishes of *Injera* and *Wat*. "We had not been accustomed to that kind of very hot, spicy food," volunteer Paul Tsongas recalled. "So we sat down in this man's house and he gave us . . . the real *Wat* . . . because he wanted to treat us with respect. And wanting to respond with respect, I began to eat the *Injera* and *Wat* and it began to eat me. My mouth was just burning. I looked on the table and there was a glass of a clear liquid. Whether or not we learned the language, or anything about teaching, one thing we learned in Georgetown was: Don't drink the water. . . . I gazed at that glass, and took another bite, and gazed at that glass. Finally, Washington seemed a long way away. My hand involuntarily took the glass and I drank. . . . It was not water. It was *Arake*—the Ethiopian's most potent drink. . . . I made a damn fool of myself."[43]

The highlight of their stay in Addis Ababa came on September 20 when the volunteers were invited to Jubilee Palace for a reception with His Imperial Majesty, Haile Selassie. Wofford had instructed them to follow royal protocol: when approaching the Emperor they should dip their heads and bow low with both hands extended. When Anne Martin shook his hand, Selassie looked into her eyes and said in French: "I am glad you are going to be in my country." Martin replied in Amharic that she was very happy to be there. Selassie smiled and said, "Your verb tenses need some work." Martin later wrote her parents that the criticism had not bothered her: "I'd never been insulted by an Emperor before."[44] The volunteers then listened to Selassie read a message thanking them for coming to Ethiopia to work towards the elimination of ignorance "which in itself helps bring peace and understanding." Wofford spoke next. The American volunteers "come here to teach and to serve your people," he told the Emperor. "But they expect to learn as much as they teach." The Peace Corps, he said, was "part of a pioneering process spreading inside many nations. . . . These men and women before you, ranging in age from 19 to 66, come from 47 American states; they are graduates from over 200 colleges and universities. On behalf of President Kennedy, who proposed the Peace Corps both as a contribution to the world community and as a way to restore the American spirit of pioneering," he concluded, "I present to Your Majesty these volunteers, who constitute the largest single contingent yet to go to any nation. *Ethiopia Lezelalem Timur* [Long Live Ethiopia]!"[45]

The reception at Jubilee Palace marked the end of their "in-country" training. Teaching assignments followed. Thirty-four per-cent of the group was assigned to Addis Ababa and Asmara, where the majority of the students were located; the rest were placed in twenty-eight towns throughout the empire. Wofford estimated that the Peace Corps' presence permitted the enrollment of approximately five thousand new students.[46]

On Friday morning, September 21, 1962, the 183 volunteers who were posted outside the capital began their departure by plane, train, Land Rover, and bus. Among them were nine Americans who had been selected to work in Debre Berhan, a small town about eighty miles north of Addis. They were John Rex, age 21, from Mt. Kisco, New York; Carol Miller, age 22, Longview, Washington; Anne Mar-tin, 23, Denton, Maryland; Robert Savage, 21, Rochester, New York; Marian Haley, 23, Greensburg, Pennsylvania; Camilla Chicker-ing, 21, Belmont, Massachusetts; Bruce Engle, 23, Seattle, Washing-ton; and two Philadelphians: Gerald Bieler and Russell Mischeloff, both 22. Three Californians—recently freed from "Limbo"—would join them shortly: Ronald Kazarian, 22, from Selma, and the group's only married couple: 24-year-old Lynn Linman and his wife, Mary Lou, 21, of Kingsburg.[47]

Their motives for joining the Peace Corps were mixed. John Rex, a recent graduate of Bowdoin College in Maine, was attracted "by the enthusiastic . . . young man who had just become the leader of our country. He was not the balding or grey-haired oracle who spoke in platitudes of complacency," Rex later wrote. "Not only did he seem to be telling the truth, but he seemed to be talking to me, and I wanted to answer." Idealism and self-interest drove him: he wanted to be "a missionary of democracy" and to "see the world—especially those places which other people do not see."[48]

Idealism also led Anne Martin to the Peace Corps. "My family is very service oriented—very humanitarian," she recalled. A graduate of Hood College in Maryland and for two years a school teacher, Martin thought it was an opportune moment to go abroad. "I'm single, unattached, had some professional training. . . . I might never be in a position again where I have two years when I can go out and do something for somebody else."[49]

As for Miller, Kazarian, and the Linmans, travel lured them. While a student at Washington State, Miller met Bascom Story, who was on campus recruiting for Ethiopia. She "was immediately excited," applied, and was invited to train. "For middle class Americans [the Peace Corps] opened up an opportunity for foreign travel that was previously available only to the affluent or those [on] scholarship," Miller noted.[50] Mary Lou Linman, a graduate of the University of California at Berkeley and the daughter of college professors who had taught abroad, yearned "to get back to India," where she had attended high school and still had close friends. Her husband Lynn thought joining the Peace Corps was "the public spirited thing to do." They applied and asked to be assigned to India. Ethiopia came as a shock—they were not even sure where the country was located. Ron Kazarian was also surprised: he had requested an assignment in Latin America. But, after four years at California State College at Fresno and uncertain about his future plans, Ethiopia seemed fine. He too loved to travel and considered the Peace Corps a way both to do service and "to see the world."[51]

The old school bus carrying the group to Debre Berhan started along the Asmara Road, crowded now with Ethiopians taking cattle, goats, and goods to market. The mountainous terrain of the country-side, with "its spectacular gorges," reminded the volunteers of the Rockies. In the distance, they could see groves of eucalyptus trees and *tukels,* round stone houses, "looking like clusters of mushrooms on the hillside."[52]

Five hours after beginning their journey, they came to Debre Berhan. Bouncing along a dirt road, which was the only main street in town, the volunteers saw a post office, a "great circular edifice" they learned was the Selassie Coptic Christian Church, and a government house owned by the Emperor. On the other side of the street was the cinema hall, and the town hospital, staffed, they were later told, "by an inefficient Egyptian doctor who usually cannot be found or awakened even for emergency cases. . . ." Up the road were the most important complexes: the Teacher Training School and the Haile Mariam Mammo Secondary School, where most of the volunteers would teach.[53] The volunteers spent their first night in a "luxurious guest house" on the Teacher Training School Compound, formerly occupied by an AID official who had reluctantly loaned the house to the Peace Corps.[54] They especially welcomed its fireplace—at 9,200 feet above sea level, Debre Berhan was both the highest and the coldest spot in the country.[55]

The Americans had a week to explore their new surroundings be-fore the school term began. Haile Mariam Mammo Secondary School appeared impressive by Ethiopian standards. Each classroom had new desks; the book room was filled with books; and the science lab was stocked with modern chemicals, beakers, and test tubes. Later, the imperfections would show: the blackboards were black-painted boards whose rough surfaces shattered chalk and were difficult to erase. The books looked new because the headmaster had prohibited them from being distributed to the students because they frequently lost or sold them. The equipment in the lab was pristine because it had never been used; none of the teachers could afford to replace chemicals or broken beakers, so no experiments had ever been conducted. Such drawbacks "amused us more than they annoyed us," Mary Lou Linman noted. After all, the Peace Corps was created to supply books and equipment, build latrines, and lay water lines (the school had no drinking fountains or lavatories) as well as teach.[56]

Their faculty colleagues consisted of seven Ethiopians and nine Indians, one of whom was headmaster. The volunteers found them cordial but sensed an underlying tension. The Ethiopian school system was run principally by Indians, and they feared that the Americans would disrupt traditional pedagogy and thereby undermine their authority and jeopardize their careers. For Indians, teaching was not a form of voluntary service but a permanent profession. "We heard that some of their contracts had not been renewed . . . and that we should expect some friction," John Rex observed.[57]

As the first day of school approached, the students began to arrive. Most were as much strangers to Debre Berhan as the Americans, because their homes were located miles away in the countryside. By the seventh grade, Ethiopian boys (and the few girls permitted to seek an education) were cut off from their villages and their families, and were responsible for taking care of themselves. Most wore no shoes and "dressed in tattered khaki trousers or shorts, with *netullahs* [shawls] draped around their shoulders." Some received a modest government stipend to defray expenses, but most found it difficult to feed, clothe, and lodge themselves. Their goal was to pass two examinations given at the end of the eighth and twelfth grades; without them, they could not enter the university or obtain a position with the government. A failing student could not go forward to a professional career nor return to his village since he was now considered too well educated to farm like his ancestors. Education for an Ethiopian student was not a luxury but a matter of life and death.[58]

The volunteers' first week in the classroom was exciting but troubling. Bob Savage found his students' "oral facility abominable. Even though it is the 11th grade it is very much like teaching in the 4th grade in the states," he observed.[59] Despite their difficulty with written and spoken English, John Rex's students were remarkably well-informed about the struggle to desegregate the University of Mississippi and the ensuing riot which, just the day before, left two dead and 300 injured. "It is extremely embarrassing to have [it] thrown in our faces," Rex told his family. "If the ignorant, stupid, prejudiced bastards in the South only realized how important and how well known all their actions are in the rest of the world, they might try to think for the first time in their lives. How," he wondered, "do you explain to Ethiopians that this form of prejudice can exist in a great democracy?"[60] Female volunteers learned that they were not especially welcomed in the classroom. Ethiopians "had not been accustomed to 10th grade women teachers who knew anything," Anne Martin recalled. "In Ethiopia women are good for bearing children and carrying clay jugs on their heads and so we fought that battle when we first got there and eventually proved to them that 'yes,' we did know English and we could teach it."[61] Everyone fought against the traditional system by which "Indian teachers give or dictate notes which the students memorize and vomit back on exams. They call this learning," Rex complained. "We PCVs are struggling like mad. . . . Every day we repeat over and over again that students must take their own notes. The result is chaos."[62]

As foreign teachers in a student town, without many Ethiopian counterparts with whom to socialize, the volunteers quite naturally felt lonely and drew together for support. On his way to the marketplace one Saturday, Rex's thoughts turned to "football games, [and] colored leaves . . . which I do miss very much."[63] He wrote home asking for photographs of his parents and sister, news of old friends, "and an occasional good theatre review from the *New York Times*. . . ." When one volunteer received "two colored maple leaves" enclosed in a letter, they were shared with the group: "We all gazed longingly at them," Rex noted, "the only trees around here are eucalyptus and they don't turn color."[64]

With the arrival of Ron Kazarian and Lynn and Mary Lou Linman in early October, the group was now complete. As the only married couple, the Linmans received separate quarters near the school; Kazarian joined the others in the guest house. After examining his new home and meeting three recently hired servants, he told his family: "This isn't how I pictured the Peace Corps." The guest house had not only a cook but modern kitchen facilities, so the volunteers dined together almost every evening. Most meals consisted of solid American fare like macaroni and cheese and meatballs.[65] "We are eating very well indeed," Rex noted.[66]

After dinner the volunteers would play charades or bridge, eat popcorn or fudge, listen to the tunes of the Kingston Trio and the Limelighters, then lounge around the fireplace correcting papers or writing letters. They had much in common, and this made for generally harmonious relationships. In general, the group typified the Peace Corps as a whole: their average age was 22, and most volunteers during the Kennedy era were usually between 22 and 28 years old; seven grew up in the East or in Mid-Atlantic states and five came from Washington and California, also typical of most volunteers, who grew up on the West Coast or in the industrial states of the East and Midwest; and they were all recent college graduates, most of whom had majored in the liberal arts.[67] The group had its occasional differences, but John Rex spoke for all when he told his family: "We all get along very well and make up one big happy family. Life overseas could be considerably unbearable under less favorable conditions."[68]

Every few weeks, the volunteers spent a weekend in Addis Ababa. In the capital, the volunteers shopped for food, books, school supplies, and personal items. "Generally speaking the Peace Corps houses are *very nice*," Rex observed after visiting the city in October. "As a matter of fact we have a saying that you can find if the Peace Corps is in any town by looking in the nicest house." The volunteers "go to parties every weekend with all the degenerate expatriates in Ethiopia and spend their money like any group of rich foreign plutocrats," Bob Savage noted. "Not exactly my idea of the Peace Corps spirit!" Savage later told his family how happy he was not to be stationed in the capital: "Teaching in Addis is much like teaching in an American city: very impersonal! In the country it is quite different and I am glad."[69]

Savage's view of the intimate country life seemed to be affirmed one Sunday night, when the governor of Debre Berhan honored the volunteers at a special dinner. They were served an endless array of Ethiopian dishes, including chicken and beef *Wat,* and potent drinks which left their heads spinning. After the feast, the governor thanked the Americans for coming to educate Ethiopia's children. Rex left the banquet feeling that "our town-PCV relationship is quite good," while Kazarian later boasted, "they treated us like kings."[70]

The governor's affair was another in a series of events which made the volunteers feel special, even royal. After all, these Americans were sent abroad personally by the President of the United States. Their celebrated arrival intensified their desire to fulfill their mission—to bring Ethiopia into the twentieth century. That effort would begin by transforming Haile Mariam Mammo into a modern secondary school. This meant changing the traditional ways that students were taught by their Indian and Ethiopian instructors. Promotion should not depend solely on passing a final examination at the end of the year in June; students would be tested each term and performance would count towards advancement. Rote memorization of facts would no longer be acceptable—students would be required to listen carefully, take their own notes, and complete assignments on time. "We were hell-bent on teaching them to think," recalled Carol Miller. "We were going to hold them accountable. . . . We knew that the Indian teachers would lay it out [and] and if the kids got it—fine, if they didn't, they'd pass them anyway. We thought that they were doing a disservice to the Ethiopians by promoting them without even giving them the basics."[71] Volunteers were especially shocked by student cheating, unaware that it was culturally acceptable. Anne Martin remembered how Ethiopians would write notes "on their cuffs, on their palms, on their erasers. And we'd take erasers, and tear up papers . . . and tell them 'you got an F on that test.'" She and the others would compose different tests for each class as one way to prevent widespread cheating.[72]

During these first months, students reacted to the new standards in a variety of ways. "Sometimes I would be teaching merrily along," Carol Miller recalled, "and I would be . . . ecstatic—my kids were looking at me and . . . nodding their heads; I thought: My God! They're getting it! And then I'd realize that they wanted so badly to convey their good will and I wanted so badly to teach them, but in fact they weren't getting anything." Some students burst into tears; others acted "arrogant and insolent" and argued until they quieted down or left the classroom. The volunteers felt no joy in seeing their students experience the pain of having their papers destroyed, but believed it was in the students' best interest.[73]

One special target of the volunteers' wrath was the Indian headmaster, Mr. Ratneswami. He seemed to symbolize the corruption of the Ethiopian school system. The Americans continually demanded that he call a meeting to discuss promotion policy, but he balked—until two volunteers refused to participate in a volleyball match important to the headmaster. The group expressed dismay that the final examination was "the only factor" which decided the fate of their students. "This encourages the students not to work for the first two terms," the Linmans argued, "and means that the teacher has little influence in the class because students know that they do not have to do any homework or take any tests, since none of that will be counted." The volunteers hoped the assembled staff would choose a different promotion policy, but during the October meeting, the stubborn headmaster announced that promotion policy would not be decided until the day before school closed.[74] The volunteers were disappointed but not surprised that tradition had—for the moment—triumphed over innovation. In the future they ignored the headmaster and continued to teach their classes in a way that reflected the spirit of the Peace Corps.

If volunteer morale needed a boost, it received one in late October when Sargent Shriver visited Ethiopia. He was determined to meet all 275 voluteers, so he raced "around in a jeep from sun-up to sunset," recalled Donovan McClure, who accompanied him, "shattering the poise of countless volunteers by suddenly appearing in their classrooms or at the doors of their houses, hand extended: 'Hi! I'm Sarge Shriver. Greatameecha. . . . President Kennedy is behind you all the way."[75]

A chartered bus was sent to bring the Debra Berhan volunteers to Peace Corps Headquarters to meet their boss. They drank beer and Cokes while Shriver spoke. "He was completely honest," Martha Stonequist later wrote home, "and admitted that we had 'very poor training' at Georgetown, also that things here in Ethiopia were not planned nearly as well as they might have been—said it was to our credit that we had thus far done so well."[76] While some volunteers thought Shriver "hopelessly positive" and "disgustingly upbeat,"[77] Stonequist found him impressive: "He's completly dedicated, and his whole life is the Peace Corps. . . . His enthusiasm, his humor, his dedication, his hopes—all are contagious. . . . He was most forthright and helped morale considerably."[78] Later that evening, Rex and the others dined in the "plushest Addis restaurant" and went to the movies before returning to Debre Berhan.[79]

One result of Shriver's visit was Country Director Wofford's order that the volunteers must find new homes, less ornate and more spartan as befitted the Peace Corps. This meant that the men of Debre Berhan (like their female colleagues who had departed earlier) had to leave the guest house. "I may be living in a grass hut yet!" Rex noted the night before he and the others went house-hunting.[80]

The homes they eventually selected were—in their view—"African" and "Peace Corps." Located in the middle of town, Rex's home, which he would share with three fellow volunteers, had wood floors and walls made of dung and straw.[81] The Kazarian-Savage "stables" were even more primitive: the house had a roof, Kazarian noted, "and absolutely nothing else."[82] When his parents expressed their concern about his new home, he told them that it was "for the better because the [guest] house isn't very Peace Corps. . . . If [some] U.S. Senators were visiting Ethiopia and they saw us in this beautiful house, they would be wondering about these dedicated Americans who have given up the conveniences of modern living to live with the people of underdeveloped countries at their level. We'll also be closer to our students."[83]

Now living in town, the volunteers sought to broaden their relationships with Ethiopian students. Those contacts were of two types: extracurricular and familial. Nearly every volunteer initiated some scholastic project: Lynn Linman sponsored a science club; Anne Martin taught French; Carol Miller planned a new library; Bob Savage coached basketball; Ron Kazarian coached soccer and baseball and created a service organization for civic improvement; and John Rex taught drawing and established a drama club.[84]

The volunteers' relationships with students often extended beyond the classroom; sometimes they "adopted" them. Such was the case of John Rex and his ninth grader, Damene. Rex had met Damene one Saturday at the marketplace and the boy had helped the American "bargain" for his goods. A few days later, he told Rex that he would have to quit school and seek work in the capital; with no parents to support him and lacking a stipend, he simply could not afford to continue his education.[85] So Rex decided to become, at age twenty-two, a surrogate father: he paid Damene $15 Ethiopian a month, gave him clothes to wear, and arranged for the boy and a fellow orphan named Wondafresh to live in a "little dirt house" behind Rex's new home. "I got the landlord to put in an electric light and allow them to get water," Rex wrote his family. "You'd be amazed at what a luxury these things are to kids who have been existing on next to nothing. . . . I have been very concerned about all the boys and I'm glad to help at least a couple of them. They don't have much of a chance if they leave school—and they know it!"[86] Ron Kazarian also supported a student. In return for help around the house and other chores, Kazarian paid the seventeen-year-old boy $15 Ethiopian a month, bought him his first pair of shoes, and planned "to fix him a place on the back of the house." One day, the boy told him: "I think of you as my Father because you take good care of me."[87]

Rex and his students became settled in their new home shortly before the beginning of first-term final examinations. "I'm really putting the pressure on the kids to think," Rex noted, "and a few of them are coming through admirably."[88] Examinations started on December 19 and continued for the next ten days. Students took their tests during the morning hours, so volunteers had afternoons free to correct their examinations (which usually numbered around one hundred). Some days they acted as "invigilators," or proctors. They also made preparation for their two-week Christmas vacation, part of which was to be spent at a Peace Corps conference in Asmara.[89]

The Americans' Christmas Eve was spent at the "girls' house." Gifts were put under a cedar Christmas tree decorated with strings of popcorn and Italian lights. They ate home-made ice cream and Christmas cookies and drank egg nog with brandy. The volunteers then marched down the main street, singing "White Christmas" and "Jingle Bells." "The Ethiopians laughed their heads off," Kazarian later wrote. "They must have thought we were all drunk."[90] Perhaps they did—the Ethiopian Christmas was celebrated in January.

On Christmas morning, the volunteers returned to the "girls' house" to exchange gifts. Then they all hopped into their Peace Corps jeep and toured the countryside, taking pictures, and singing "God Bless America" and other patriotic favorites. "We really went all out to keep the American tradition," Ron Kazarain noted following the group's Thanksgiving celebration, and Christmas dinner was no different—chicken, stuffing, and "jello salad like you make at home." "It was a magnificent holiday," Rex observed.[91]

In January they and two hundred of their Peace Corps colleagues journeyed to Asmara, second largest city in the empire and former capital of the Italian-dominated colony of Eritrea. They attended a Peace Corps conference and teachers' workshop, during which they renewed old friendships, discussed mutual problems, and studied, in Harris Wofford's words, how to become "better servants of the Twentieth Century."⁹² The volunteers found Asmara "magnificent," with its wide, immaculate palm-lined streets, Italian shops, and restaurants. It was also the site of Kagnew Station, an enormous American communications center whose PX was officially "off-limits" to the Peace Corps volunteers.⁹³ However, the group from Debre Berhan managed to sneak in for a taste of home. They ate cheeseburgers and hot fudge sundaes and watched "Twilight Zone," "Popeye," and "some other swinging programs."⁹⁴

The conference, held at Haile Selassie I Secondary School, brought all the volunteers together for the first time since September. "That first morning . . . was rather shattering," one volunteer noted. "In the months since we had last been together we've had pretty rough going—we've taken a beating and looked it. Most of us have lost weight, a few gained, but we're all different. We've toughened . . . for better or worse." During the working sessions, volunteers discussed the subjects they taught and prepared reports for the Ministry of Education. "We put our battered heads together and . . . talked about the problems that plague us."⁹⁵

Those problems, Martha Stonequist noted, were "lack of enough or suitable equipment, classes too large, lack of standard curriculum uniform throughout [the] Empire, or just lack of a curriculum period. Too heavy student load, . . . lack of English comprehension, [and] too much basis on [the] final exam. . . ."⁹⁶ Volunteers who taught history and geography complained that the curriculum did not meet the needs of their students; they proposed alternative courses emphasizing the African experience. English instructors desired "literature . . . appropriate for Ethiopia in the 20th Century and not for England in the 19th Century. . . ." Those teaching other subjects (science, mathematics, music, home economics, industrial arts) had experienced similar difficulties and recommended radical changes.⁹⁷

The Americans also discussed their conflicts with students and headmasters. Science teachers noted "that some students tend to act as though they control school practices. They contradict and disobey teachers." Mathematics teachers believed that the students "need discipline and from time to time punishment. . . ." English teachers complained that "discipline is poor because the teachers cannot enforce disciplinary measures and are often not backed up by their headmasters." But most criticized the common practice of corporal punishment as ineffective.⁹⁸

The volunteers returned to Debre Berhan "tired [but] happy to be home."[99] The second term, which began in February and ended in mid-April 1963, was a static period for the volunteers. After six months in Ethiopia, life was less exotic and more routine. Frequently now the volunteers sought "diversion": they bought horses and spent many afternoons on cross-country rides where they "galloped and raced, climbed hills and crossed streams, and had a wonderful time." At night they played poker or partied, and, if all this was not diverting enough, there was always "a good Victorian novel for escape. . . ."[100]

Suddenly, in the middle of the third term, the calm of the volunteers' lives was shattered. Ron Kazarian was the first to sense a certain restlessness in his class on that Monday morning, May 6. A test was underway and the students were cheating and acting unruly. "I started to lose my temper," he later wrote, "but managed to keep my self-control. I went into my next class and started to give another test. A few students . . . began to cheat. I told them to shut up three or four times and took a few papers from [those] who were cheating. They continued—so I walked out of class. . . ."[101]

Next door, Anne Martin was also having trouble teaching math to her tenth graders; finally, they all stood up and left the room. Marian Haley, also teaching tenth-grade math, experienced similar resistance. Kazarian's third-period class refused to speak to him, so he left the room. His fourth-period class was also uncooperative, and they too left the room. By day's end, it was clear that Haile Mariam Mammo was experiencing its first student strike since the arrival of the Peace Corps.[102]

Student strikes were something of a scholastic tradition in Debre Berhan and throughout the country. The previous May, the tenth grade had left their classes, yet the Indian teachers had promoted the entire group. But the Americans were not knowledgeable about such practices. To Martin, "the strike was . . . a real kick in the face because I had thought things were going fairly well and that we had established a good rapport. . . . We were almost in shock that this could happen. . . ."[103]

Within days, surprise turned to hurt, and anger. The students drafted a petition, written in Amharic, and gave copies to the headmaster, the Provincial Education Officer, the Ministry of Education, and, last, to the volunteers. The Americans asked for a written translation but did not receive one, so they turned to a sympathetic Ethiopian who read the document to them. The volunteers were accused of insulting their students, calling them "lazy," "goofy," "dogs," "animals," and "wild black beasts." "Utterly fantastic and generally untrue" was John Rex's first response to the "complaints." The Americans were certain that they had never used such derogatory language, but, as the group thought it over, they realized painfully that the Ethiopians might have misunderstood certain facetious remarks made in the classroom. Marian Haley sometimes told her students they were acting "wild" or "goofy" and frequently used the expression "okey-doke." Barely understanding English, the Ethiopians could not appreciate American colloquialisms and had mistaken joshing remarks for serious insults—doke—for dog or donkey.[104] Georgetown had not offered a course in such cross-cultural misunderstandings.

The leaders of the rebellion were the boys in "10B," whom most volunteers characterized as "poor students" who "didn't want to be taught and who had influence—in some cases that of physical threat—over their classmates." Kazarian learned about the source of the trouble one night when a group of students "sneaked" up to his house. They had been forced to sign the petition, the students said. And if they returned to class they would be beaten, perhaps killed. "One kid was so scared," Kazarian noted, "he had to stay the night with us."[105]

Despite threats of violence, one group of tenth graders apologized to the volunteers and returned to class on May 8. But a sizable number, including many of the best students, remained on strike against Kazarian; Haley, Martin, and Lynn Linman. "The situation is very bad and extremely tense," Rex wrote on May 9. "The Indian teachers blame it on our more familiar methods in the classroom. The ninth grades have been very good, but there is still a very uncomfortable atmosphere in the classroom, a tenseness which puts everybody on his guard. . . ."[106] The striking students received no support from the Ministry of Education, which threatened to punish them if they did not return to class. So, fearing a monetary fine and bored after a week of inactivity, they decided to return to school. The headmaster declared the strike over and ordered the four volunteers to resume teaching. They refused.

Stung by the students' petition and disgusted with the headmaster's lack of support, the group decided it was time to take "a definite stand." They informed Ratneswami they would "not return to classes until the students produced a written apology and retraction of their false statements." "We refused," Ron Kazarian explained, "because we felt that we were insulted and some [form] of punishment should be given to the students. . . . [They] run the school and we have to make a firm stand to regain respect for the teachers and restore some type of discipline. . . ." Now, for the first time in its brief history, the Peace Corps was on strike.[107]

On May 16, 1963, Harris Wofford came to Debre Berhan to resolve the dispute. After conferring with the headmaster, he met with the volunteers and told them that Kazarain, Martin, Haley, and Linman could, if they wished, transfer to another post. It was up to them; he would not tell the volunteers what to do: "Let your conscience be your guide," he remarked.[108] This is not what the four Americans expected or wanted to hear, and their colleagues came quickly to their defense. If the four had to leave, they said, the entire group would follow. Impressed, finally, by the group's passion, Wofford told the headmaster that once the volunteers received a "written apology and retraction," they would return to classes. After Ratneswami "promised" to comply, the volunteers resumed teaching and Wofford returned to Addis Ababa. But "nothing was done," Ron Kazarian wrote home. "So today, Monday [May 21], the four teachers, including myself, refused to go back to class. Everybody thought the thing was over and peace was restored. They couldn't believe it when we walked out on them."[109]

The volunteer strike continued for three weeks, and as the days passed, the group became polarized between Anne Martin and Ron Kazarian. "Once the strike started I was willing to compromise," Martin recalled. "It was becoming very bitter. Kazarian was the hardnose. He said: 'I am not going to compromise on this, it's a matter of control and we need to have the control here as teachers.' " Marian Haley and Lynn Linman found themselves "in the middle"— sometimes supporting Martin, sometimes "pulling very hard for Kazarian."[110]

For Kazarian, the strike was a matter of honor: "You know how I get when it comes to principle," he wrote his family on May 15. "I am stubborn and obstinate." Looking back on the strike years later, Kazarain admitted that perhaps he had been "too tough": "I didn't want to be a tough person. . . . But when I got over there . . . I became hard as a rock mentally. . . . I had to be or I wouldn't have survived—it would have gotten to me emotionally—poverty, sickness. . . . You don't know until you go over there what it's like."[111] Kazarian was also expressing frustrations shared by most of the volunteers, including those not on strike. "The strike is only one example of how bad our school really was," John Rex wrote in 1964. "Marking, keeping records, promotion policy, book distribution, and discipline were handled so foolishly . . . that we continually felt that we were walking through the looking glass when we went to school."[112]

Another feeling also explains Kazarian's posture: a sense of personal injury. Of all the volunteers, it was Kazarian who spent the most hours in extracurricular activities with his students—camping, horseback riding, demonstrating that manual labor (not highly prized in Ethiopian culture) had value. As Kazarian built his house—laying the floor, constructing a toilet and hot-water heater—the students would gather around in fascination. "I would show them how to do it," he said, "and pretty soon I'd teach them how to make something. They always thought it was too hard: they didn't have the tools, they didn't know how to start." Kazarian began by teaching them how to build lamps, which they sold to the townspeople, generating enough money to pay some of their expenses. And how was he rewarded? he asked. With insults and false accusations. Indeed, the ringleader of the strike was a member of Kazarian's service club: "He was in my house. I helped him. I showed him a lot of things. . . . I really felt bad because he was the leader of the strike."[113]

During the last week of May, Wofford sent his deputy, Chester Carter, to Debre Berhan to resolve the strike. Carter told the volunteers, in a heated meeting, that the four must return to school. Had they forgotten they were guests in Ethiopia and employees of the Ministry of Education? They must "work within the system." "There was no system," the volunteers replied, "except corruption and dishonesty in our school—should we simply become a part of it?" What of the apology that Wofford had demanded on their behalf? Carter explained that there would be no formal apology, but the strikers would be punished with 7 days' hard labor.[114]

The volunteers fumed at Carter and faulted the settlement. "Carter probably thought we were all a bunch of spoiled American shits, racist to boot [and] in over our heads . . . ," Carol Miller remembered. "We all believed that we would be going against our beliefs, our integrity, if we capitulated."[115] John Rex identified the fundamental cultural conflict: "When we work within a system which is foreign to our own ideas, should we be forced to compromise our basic ideals concerning honesty, truth, and honor?" "The decision . . . is a complete evasion of the truth . . . ," he wrote his parents. "[It] has made us all quite sick at heart and cut the ground from under any enthusiasm which we may have left. I do not believe that there can be compromise when there is no truth, and I shall continue to support those who have been hurt . . . even against the Peace Corps. . . . We have no power and the Peace Corps wants us to work within the system. It's enough to give one ulcers. Nobody here seems to care except us, and they don't like us for caring. Gads!"[116]

Despite their disappointment, Anne Martin, Marian Haley, and Lynn Linman decided to return to their tenth-grade classes, but Ron Kazarian rejected the settlement. He refused because he felt that the students owed their teachers an apology and that there was "no effective way" to carry out the punishment. The punishment—digging holes—proved to be as "idiotic" as Kazarian had predicted. There were only five shovels for the ninety boys and most sat around doing nothing. "They were laughing in our faces, telling us: 'We won—we got away with it,' " he said later.[117] In part, they did: Kazarian's three sections were taught by Indian teachers, and although he offered to make up a comprehensive final examination, the students received a test that covered just two weeks and the grade counted for the entire year. To the volunteers, it seemed like the students were actually "rewarded for striking."[118]

The volunteers had little time to worry about the outcome of the strike—suddenly, their own future was in jeopardy. They learned in mid-July that the headmaster had asked that all Peace Corps volunteers be transferred. None wished to go, so they rushed to see Wofford, who reported that nothing could be done until their request to stay was discussed with the headmaster and District Education Officer.[119]

It seemed like "limbo" again: they were to complete their academic work and proceed with their summer plans knowing that, for the moment, they were to return to Debre Berhan. But they should be prepared to move if the authorities ordered it. And so, in late July, they set off for various destinations. Part of the summer the volunteers worked on special projects: Rex prepared a textbook for the eighth grade while living in Addis Ababa; Kazarian and Savage helped construct a new school in the desert near Dire Dawa; and the Linmans studied Amharic at University College in the capital. They spent one month of free time traveling in India and Egypt.[120]

They returned anxiously to Debre Berhan in late September, their future still in doubt. They soon learned about their status and what the Linmans called the "Indians' big plot." It began when the Ministry informed the Peace Corps that Ron Kazarian and Bob Savage should be transferred for "personal reasons." While investigating the Ministry's request, Wofford's staff discovered that the headmaster had falsified documents to indicate he had two more teachers than the school needed and could, therefore, easily dispense with Savage and Kazarian. When Wofford's aides came to Debre Berhan they found a different situation: the school was actually short three teachers. The Linmans were astonished: "It is really unbelievable to us that this kind of dishonesty and conniving can really exist."[121] In the end, all volunteers who wished to remain in Debre Berhan were allowed to— "somewhat of a moral victory," Rex noted.[122]

November brought even more welcome news: "Our Headmaster has been transferred!" the Linmans exulted. "The impossible has happened! Supposedly it is for matters of health . . . since he is a chain smoker and looks like he is consumed with something. . . ." Ato Berhanu, assistant headmaster and an Ethiopian admired by the volunteers, was appointed as the new headmaster. Later that month, at a dinner held in Ratneswami's honor, Mary Lou Linman noticed the changes time had wrought: when the volunteers first arrived at Haile Mariam Mammo there were nine Indian teachers and an Indian headmaster. Now there were just four Indians and an Ethiopian headmaster. And those volunteers "that they most wanted to transfer (including me) are still there."[123]

Ato Berhanu brought new leadership and needed changes to the school. He immediately called a staff meeting to resolve examination and promotion policies. This year, "class marks" would count toward final grades, and no one was required to submit final examinations in advance. Students found cheating were sent directly to Berhanu. And report cards—"the most noteworthy innovation of all"—finally came to Haile Mariam Mammo.[124]

That month's pleasant developments were overshadowed by the terrible news of November 22. Shortly before 11 p.m. the women volunteers arrived unexpectedly at John Rex's home, and he could tell that something was terribly wrong. "The President was shot," Anne Martin told him. "He's dead." They quickly turned on the radio and heard the news confirmed. "My reaction of initial disbelief was soon followed by a sense of horror," Rex later wrote home. "The faith of my generation, especially of us overseas, had been placed in the hands of this one man. We have felt a closeness and trust in him. . . . He and his America have been the symbols of all that we have been working for. But for him, we would not be here."[125]

Throughout Ethiopia, volunteers reacted with similar shock and sadness. "We just could not visualize the strong, vigorous President lying bloody and dead somewhere," Linda Bergthold told her family. "The shock of last night's news has left me numb with . . . horror and grief," wrote Carolyn Wood from Asmara. "It feels like we have lost the living symbol of everything the United States stands for."[126] In the capital, volunteers found the Ethiopians "stricken with grief." Monday, November 25, was decreed a national day of mourning, and a high Coptic Mass was held, attended by the royal family and members of the Ethiopian government. The Emperor flew to Washington and joined the mourners who accompanied President Kennedy's casket to Arlington National Cemetary.[127]

As 1963 ended, the volunteers' thoughts turned toward the completion of their Peace Corps service in July and their return home. Their original decision to join the Peace Corps was, in part, the result of uncertainty about choosing a permanent career, and now they were forced again to confront the future. "I don't really want to go back to the usual routine and grind of 'living correctly before dying,' " Rex wrote his parents early in 1964. "Can't I write a book or travel, or do something different? I don't expect you to answer that question—I can't answer it myself."[128] The others were also uncertain; most planned to spend the first few months following termination traveling through Europe. Some looked back and felt discouragement about what they had achieved in Ethiopia: "It's rather terrifying to think of how little we have accomplished in the year and a half that we have been here," Rex observed. "I certainly have benefited from the experience, but I ask myself if anyone else really has."[129]

Rex learned that other volunteers shared such feelings when the Debre Berhan group and seventy-five of their colleagues met in Addis for a "Completion of Service Conference" in April. The conference, conducted by Dr. Joseph English, chief Peace Corps Psychiatrist, and Jane Campbell of the Division of Volunteer Support, was designed to elicit the volunteers' opinions on their Peace Corps experience. "I had thought that I had become very cynical," Mary Lou Linman noted, "but now I see that I am no more cynical than the other volunteers. Generally we are cynical and disillusioned about Ethiopians and their values, but we remain idealistic and enthusiastic about the Peace Corps and the importance of our work here."[130]

At the conference, many volunteers expressed the view that Ethiopians were "passive, apathetic, hostile, and suspicious of all foreigners, . . . and new ideas. They are not interested in working to help themselves," Linman wrote, "or in any work at all, but only in how much other countries will give them. This is not an underdeveloped country, it is an underdeveloping country! One anonymous comment summed it up very well: 'a lazy, seemingly useless people.' " To be sure, there were exceptions—like Ato Berhanu—but, she insisted, "the generalizations remain true." During training they had been told that Ethiopian students were "eager to learn," but the reality proved quite different.[131] Ethiopian attitudes—"mutual suspicion, non-cooperation with one another, the lack of prestige accorded manual labor"—all had to change, the volunteers believed, before Ethiopia could solve its profound educational or economic problems. In the classroom, volunteers had tried to change traditional attitudes, but they argued that the Peace Corps could do much more. The Ministry of Education should be forced to assign more Ethiopian teachers to their schools, especially in the provinces. "We are here to help the people help themselves," one volunteer said. "But so long as it's easier and cheaper for the Ethiopian government to rely on Peace Corps teachers than on their own, they're not going to do much . . . themselves. We must make them begin to assume full responsibility for their own educational system. . . ."[132]

The volunteers were as critical of themselves as they were of the Ethiopians. "They will admit that, on the whole, they did a poor job of learning the language," Jane Campbell wrote in her final report. "That they did not make the 'supreme effort' to overcome the cultural barrier between themselves and the Ethiopians, that they could have become better teachers. . . ." Many spoke openly about volunteers who they thought should have been sent home: the males who lived with prostitutes; the woman who was "obviously mentally disturbed"; the "opportunist" who was unable to teach so was given a sinecure in the Ministry of Education. "The Peace Corps," one volunteer stated, "is not a goddam rehabilitation center." Almost everyone detested the "image" of the volunteer promoted by the Peace Corps to win public support. "I'm sick and tired of the mud-hut hero image," said one volunteer. "It doesn't apply to us." "How can I live like my counterpart?" asked another. "I don't even have a counterpart."[133]

Despite their distaste for Ethiopian culture and Peace Corps public relations, 96 percent of Peace Corps Ethiopia as a whole believed their work had "made a contribution to [Ethiopia's] economic, cultural or social development." More children had been able to attend school, and the quality of teaching had improved. They helped "some students to reason rather than to memorize," and "perhaps" a few Ethiopians had learned that "there may be dignity in manual labor."[134]

Many volunteers were also greatly concerned about the struggle for black equality in America, having observed how the sometimes violent events at home produced negative foreign attitudes toward the United States. Although the volunteers were aware of their nation's flaws and the problems of readjustment ahead, "the overwhelming sentiment was pleasure at the prospect of going home."[135]

Rex's last major project was disposing of the special library which the volunteers had worked so hard to fill with new books, but which no one at Haile Mariam Mammo was willing to supervise once the American departed. "It's the kids who suffer," Rex complained, "and who, slowly but surely, became a part of the same ridiculous system. They can't escape. There really aren't any alternatives. . . . It is so totally rotten and yet so firmly entrenched."[136] He finally decided to create his own library system, dividing the stock (which included over 500 books and magazines) into groups which would be given to "responsible students" to start permanent reading centers in thirteen isolated areas. These would be "the first grass roofed libraries in Ethiopia."[137]

The semester ended in July 1964, after each teacher conferred with the headmaster to decide which students would be promoted ("quite a change from the total idiocy which we went through last year," Rex noted). His final days in Debre Berhan were spent closing up his house, "selling and giving away goods," and being fêted by his students. At a special school banquet, the volunteers were given handsome Shamas with colorful borders—"a very nice gesture," Rex thought.[138]

Not all the farewells were pleasant, however. "Damene left . . . two days ago," he told his family on July 4. "He has been declining swiftly in my opinion since the beginning of the year, and I finally ended all help at the beginning of the third term. True to form, I now find that he has cheated some people in town. . . . It's a sad story. . . ."[139] On Tuesday, July 7, in the midst of a "downpour and foot deep mud everywhere," Rex left Debre Berhan. In Addis

Ababa, he left the Peace Corps—exactly two years after arriving at Georgetown. The Ministry of Education honored the volunteers at a cocktail party, presenting each with a certificate and a gold pin.[140]

Only one final chore remained before departure—delivering books to Fitche and observing the opening of its first library. Accompanied by two students, Rex set out by jeep for the nearby town. "Just after I had come over the crest of Entoto Mountain . . . , I accelerated to go into third gear and all hell broke loose," Rex wrote. The jeep's axle had snapped and "we were going down hill with a drop off to our right with no breaks and picking up speed." To stop the jeep, he rammed it into an embankment, nearly overturning. No one was hurt. Rex hopped a truck back to Addis, picked up a car, and returned to get his friends. All decided that they had had enough excitement for one day and returned to the capital. Later that night, he took the Ethiopians to dinner. "I'm very sorry to say that I never did get to Fitche," he confessed. The next day he boarded an Ethiopian airplane bound for Athens, his first stop on a European tour which would eventually take him home.[141]

"The besetting sin of the New Frontier . . . was the addiction of activism," Kennedy aide Arthur M. Schlesinger, Jr., later observed.[142] Nowhere in Kennedy's Washington was this addiction greater than in the Peace Corps. "The Peace Corps' purposes are as large as the world," Harris Wofford wrote in 1963. "It is an invitation to the imagination, an invitation to large action, to moving fast, to thinking big, an invitation to its volunteers and to all Americans . . . to extend themselves. This extension . . . of ourselves into citizens of the world may be needed not just for our survival but for our salvation."[143] In the case of Peace Corps Ethiopia, reality rarely conformed to such passionate rhetoric. After just eight weeks of inadequate training, almost three hundred Americans were sent abroad—not just to teach but to be "agents of change." The result was tension between the Ministry of Education, which wanted classrooms filled with teachers, and the volunteers who dedicated themselves to bring Ethiopia into the twentieth century. The strike in Debre Berhan was one consequence of this conflict. The Emperor (and his American advisers) were mistaken: helping to "eliminate ignorance" did not necessarily "bring peace and understanding."

Handicapped by their inability to speak Amharic and lacking a sophisticated knowledge of Ethiopian history and culture, the volunteers in Debre Berhan, through no fault of their own, remained ethnocentric. They tended to "Americanize" their experience: they lived together, they ate American food, they celebrated American holidays, sang American songs, played American games, and generally believed that their values were superior and exportable to Ethiopia. Looking back on the strike after twenty-four years, the former volunteers had a better understanding of the cultural dynamics which had produced it. Carol Miller Reynolds said in 1987:

> The basic issues were deep seated and antagonistic to easy resolution. It had to do with us imposing what we considered to be reasonable academic standards. From the students' point of view our requirements were unreasonable. None of this had ever been done before. We thought our standards were just dandy and ought to be met. But we could not fully appreciate what devastation our demands could bring about in their lives. They could. We couldn't. . . . We thought: "We certainly can't pass these kids because they don't deserve to pass." We weren't thinking: "Gee, if they don't pass this means they're going to have to go back to their villages in failure and disgrace, every avenue of opportunity shut off to them." We weren't thinking along these lines. We mishandled it. Wofford mishandled it. The Peace Corps mishandled it.[144]

Despite their sincere efforts to establish close relationships with their students, the volunteers probably failed to fulfill the Peace Corps' goal of "promoting mutual understanding" between America and Ethiopia. After two years in Ethiopia, many of the volunteers began to question the importance of education to the country's social and economic development. "The sadness of the Peace Corps is that we are educating these people for nothing," wrote Paul Koprowski from Asmara. "Our students have nowhere to go, no jobs, no hopes of any. Many of us wonder if we aren't creating an educational and dissatisfied minority which may turn against democracy and seek answers in another form of government and philosophy. It could easily happen."[145] Although such concerns were expressed as early as 1964, the Peace Corps continued to send more and more volunteers to Ethiopia, almost always as teachers. In 1967, when there were 434 volunteers, Peace Corps Evaluators Meridan H. Bennett and Maureen J. Carroll accused the Peace Corps of misunderstanding Ethiopia's fundamental need for agricultural assistance. The agency, Bennett and Carroll argued, had chosen the incorrect "institutional answer—the secondary schools—to the problems of Ethiopia." Education, contrary to Wofford's belief, was not "fundamental" to Ethiopia's progress.[146] When a student-led revolution finally toppled Selassie's government in 1974 and a Marxist regime sympathetic to the Soviet Union took power, many volunteers wondered if the Peace Corps by commission or omission had contributed to the outcome. "We did such a good job that a few years after we left the whole place went Communist," Bob Savage joked in 1987. "It's amazing what a group of determined amateurs can do when they really try."[147]

The volunteers' Peace Corps experience also suggests that the Kennedy-Wofford view of the world was too romantic and chauvinistic. On Kennedy's New Frontier, the "protocol-minded, striped-pants officials" would supposedly be replaced by "reform-minded missionaries of democracy who mixed with the people, spoke the native dialects, ate the food, and involved themselves in local struggles against ignorance and want. . . ." Such "action diplomacy," Schlesinger has noted, "led American diplomats to try to do things in foreign countries that the people of the country ought to do for themselves. It nourished the faith that American 'know-how' . . . could master anything."[148] The Peace Corps was guilty of a similar cultural imperialism. Wofford believed that the volunteers—whom he called optimistic, energetic, and arrogant—could inspire the Ethiopians to shed their traditions as a snake sheds its skin. Ethiopians "are learning that all things are possible in time," he wrote in 1963, ". . . that it is time to change, and that peaceful, intelligent, responsible change is possible."[149] But Wofford's dreams foundered on the rocks of Ethiopian culture. Cultural values, the product of particular historical experiences, are not easily transferable, and foreign affairs is not a form of therapy designed to cure personal or national ills. The volunteers' efforts had unintended consequences: the "torch" that Kennedy passed to a new generation lit fires no one expected or desired.

Despite their difficulties, the volunteers considered their Peace Corps service personally invaluable. The chance to live abroad and travel and the exposure to different cultures—all had a profound effect on their lives. "I still think the Peace Corps is one of the most valuable forms of foreign aid, despite its inadequacies," Carol Miller Reynolds has said. "I still think it's a good basic way to approach problems—at the grass roots level—unlike the policymakers who never understand things at the grass roots." "I learned a lot over there," Ron Kazarian remarked in 1987. "I learned a lot about people, life, myself. Where I live [in central California] I'm an authority on one part of Africa. Everyday, somebody asks me about [Ethiopia]. . . . It's still being transmitted out of me. I'm like a piece of uranium. . . ." Many volunteers have remained teachers: John Rex, Anne Martin, Lynn and Mary Lou Linman, Bob Savage. Others have become foreign service officers, AID administrators, psychologists, social workers, novelists. One—Paul Tsongas—became a United States Senator from Massachusetts. The volunteers have gathered frequently to reminisce about their lives in Addis Ababa or Asmara or Dire Dawa, and they have also held three formal reunions since their Georgetown training.[150]

At a 1987 meeting, they were joined by their former Country Director, Harris Wofford, then the Secretary of Labor and Commerce for Pennsylvania. It seemed as if it was 1962 again, as the volunteers listened to Wofford describe his current plans to revitalize his department along the model of the Peace Corps. He also reminisced about the lost promise of John F. Kennedy in the era of Ronald Reagan. He feared that Americans had learned "almost nothing" about how to conduct foreign policy. "I wish we were plotting something big again," Wofford told them, "even if we fail."[151]

Abbreviations Used in the Notes

CIA	Central Intelligence Agency
CR	*Congressional Record*
DDEL	Dwight D. Eisenhower Library, Abilene, Kansas
DDEP	Dwight D. Eisenhower Papers
DDRS	Declassified Documents Reference Service, Carrollton Press
DS	Department of State
DSB	*Department of State Bulletin*
DSR	Department of State Records
FBI	Federal Bureau of Investigation
FOIA	Freedom of Information Act (documents declassified under)
JFKL	John F. Kennedy Library, Boston, Massachusetts
JFKP	John F. Kennedy Papers
LBJL	Lyndon B. Johnson Library, Austin, Texas
LBJP	Lyndon B. Johnson Papers
LC	Library of Congress, Washington, D.C.
NA	National Archives, Washington, D.C.
NSC	National Security Council
NSF	National Security File
OH	Oral History
OSANSA	Office of the Special Assistant for National Security Affairs
POF	President's Office Files
PrePP	Pre-Presidential Papers
PPP, JFK, year	*Public Papers of the Presidents, John F. Kennedy, year*
USIA	United States Information Agency
VPSF	Vice President's Security File
WHCF	White House Central File
WHOF	White House Office File

Notes

Introduction

Parts of this chapter found expression earlier in Thomas G. Paterson, "Bearing the Burden," *Virginia Quarterly Review,* LIV (Spring 1978), 193–212, Thomas G. Paterson, *Meeting the Communist Threat: Truman to Reagan* (New York, 1988), 191–210, 292–295, and Thomas G. Paterson, "John F. Kennedy and the World," in J. Richard Snyder, ed., *John F. Kennedy: Person, Policy, Presidency* (Wilmington, DE, 1988), 123–138.

1. Richard H. Rovere, "Letter from Washington," *The New Yorker* XXXIX (November 30, 1963), 51–53.
2. Arthur M. Schlesinger, Jr., *The Cycles of American History* (Boston, 1986), 405.
3. *The New Yorker* XXXIX (November 30, 1963), 51.
4. Quoted in Allen J. Matusow, *The Unraveling of America: A History of Liberalism in the 1960s* (New York, 1984), 31.
5. *PPP, JFK, 1961,* p. 429.
6. Theodore C. Sorensen, *Kennedy* (New York, 1965), 310.
7. See Montague Kern, Patricia W. Levering, and Ralph B. Levering, *The Kennedy Crises: The Press, the Presidency, and Foreign Policy* (Chapel Hill, NC, 1983); John Tebbel and Sarah M. Watts, *The Press and the Presidency* (New York, 1985); "Care and Feeding of the Kennedy Image," *U.S. News & World Report* LV (September 9, 1963), 92–93.
8. See works on specific topics cited in the Selected Bibliography and chapter endnotes, as well as these general assessments: Stephen E. Ambrose, *Rise to Globalism,* 4th rev. ed. (New York, 1985); David Burner, *The Torch Is Passed* (New York, 1984); William H. Chafe, *The Unfinished Journey: America Since World War II* (New York, 1986); Peter Collier and David Horowitz, *The Kennedys* (New York, 1984); John H. Davis, *The Kennedys* (New York, 1984); Henry Fairlie, *The Kennedy Promise* (New York, 1973); Doris Kearns Goodwin, *The Fitzgeralds and the Kennedys* (New York, 1987); Jim F. Heath, *Decade of Disillusionment: The Kennedy-Johnson Years*

(Bloomington, IN, 1975); Ralph G. Martin, *A Hero for Our Time* (New York, 1983); Matusow, *Unraveling;* Bruce Miroff, *Pragmatic Illusions: The Presidential Politics of John F. Kennedy* (New York, 1976); Herbert S. Parmet, *JFK* (New York, 1983); J. Richard Snyder, ed., *John F. Kennedy: Person, Policy, Presidency* (Wilmington, DE, 1988); Ronald Steel, *Imperialists and Other Heroes* (New York, 1975); Richard J. Walton, *Cold War and Counterrevolution* (New York, 1972); Garry Wills, *The Kennedy Imprisonment* (New York, 1981).

9. Dean Acheson to Max Lerner, August 5, 1971, Box 19, Series I, Dean Acheson Papers, Yale University Library, New Haven, CT.

10. *PPP, JFK, 1961,* p. 2.

11. Barry Blechman and Stephen S. Kaplan, *Force Without War: U.S. Armed Forces as a Political Instrument* (Washington, DC, 1978), 547–553.

12. Quoted in Heath, *Decade,* 80.

13. See A. Paul Kubricht, "Politics and Foreign Policy: A Brief Look at the Kennedy Administration's Eastern European Diplomacy," *Diplomatic History* XI (Winter 1987), 55–65; George F. Kennan, *Memoirs, 1950–1963* (Boston, 1972), 292–305.

14. C. Vann Woodward, "Kennedy and After," *New York Review of Books,* December 26, 1963, p. 8.

15. Schlesinger, *Cycles,* 417.

16. Robert A. Divine, "The Education of John F. Kennedy," in Frank Merli and Theodore A. Wilson, eds., *Makers of American Diplomacy* (New York, 1974), 317–343; Chafe, *Unfinished Journey,* 216–220; William E. Leuchtenburg, "Kennedy and the New Generation," in Snyder, *John F. Kennedy,* 11–24.

17. Quoted in William E. Leuchtenburg, *In the Shadow of FDR: From Harry Truman to Ronald Reagan* (Ithaca, NY, 1983), 119.

18. John F. Kennedy, "If the Soviets Control Space—They Can Control Earth," *Missiles and Rockets* VII (October 10, 1960), 12–13.

19. Walt W. Rostow, *The Diffusion of Power* (New York, 1972), 296.

20. J. B. Atn Hegemony and Modern American Foreign Policy," in Lloyd C. Gardner, ed., *Redefining the Past* (Corvallis, OR, 1986), 195–220; Terry Boswell and Albert Bergesen, eds., *America's Changing Role in the World System* (New York, 1987); Paul Kennedy, *The Rise and Fall of the Great Powers* (New York, 1988).

22. George W. Ball, *The Past Has Another Pattern* (New York, 1982), 175.

23. *Ibid.,* 176.

24. *PPP, JFK, 1961,* p. 2.

25. *PPP, JFK, 1961,* pp. 22, 23.

26. *PPP, JFK, 1963,* p. 659.

27. Charles Bartlett, "Portrait of a Friend," in Kenneth W. Thompson, ed., *The Kennedy Presidency* (Lanham, MD, 1985), 16.

28. Quoted in Leuchtenburg, *In the Shadow,* 83.

29. *PPP, JFK, 1963,* p. 669; John L. Gaddis, *Strategies of Containment* (New York, 1982), 211.

30. Bernard J. Firestone, *The Quest for Nuclear Stability: John F. Kennedy and the Soviet Union* (Westport, CT, 1982), 52.

31. Quoted in Stephen E. Ambrose, *Rise to Globalism,* 4th rev. ed. (New York, 1985), 201.

32. John F. Kennedy, *The Strategy for Peace,* Allan Nevins, ed. (New York, 1960), 7.

33. Quoted in Sorensen, *Kennedy,* 199.

34. Quoted in Heath, *Decade,* 120.

35. Quoted in Divine, "Education," 623.

36. *New York Times,* August 25, 1960.

37. Quoted in Walton, *Cold War,* 9.

38. Quoted in Patrick Anderson, "Clark Clifford 'Sounds the Alarm,' " *New York Times Magazine,* August 8, 1971, pp. 56, 58.

39. "Guerrilla Warfare in Underdeveloped Areas," in Marcus Raskin and Bernard B. Fall, eds., *The Viet-Nam Reader,* rev. ed. (New York, 1967), 113. For a discussion of Rostow's thinking and the Kennedy Administration's views on development, see Robert A. Packenham, *Liberal America and the Third World* (Princeton, NJ, 1973).

40. Memorandum by Arthur M. Schlesinger, Jr., n.d. (but probably 1961), Box 121, JFKP, JFKL.

41. Quoted in Seyom Brown, *The Faces of Power,* 2nd ed. (New York, 1983), 153.

42. Memorandum by Walt W. Rostow, March 29, 1961, Box 193, NSF, JFKL.

43. Quoted in Miroff, *Pragmatic Illusions,* 146.

44. Arthur M. Schlesinger, Jr., "JFK Plus 20: What the Thousand Days Wrought," *The New Republic* CLXXXIX (November 21, 1983), 25.

45. Walt W. Rostow to C.D. Jackson, February 17, 1961, Box 75, C.D. Jackson Papers, DDEL.

46. Quoted in Peter Joseph, ed., *Good Times* (New York, 1974), 54.

47. Arthur M. Schlesinger, Jr., *A Thousand Days* (Boston, 1965), 259.

48. See James Barber, *The Presidential Character* (Englewood Cliffs, NJ, 1972), 298.

49. Chafe, *Unfinished Journey,* 180.

50. William V. Shannon, "The Kennedy Administration," *American Scholar* XXX (Autumn 1961), 487.

51. Quoted in Kenneth P. O'Donnell and David F. Powers, *"Johnny, We Hardly Knew Ye"* (Boston, 1972), 287. For the view that Kennedy at the start may have wanted to test the Soviets, rather than vice versa, see George W. Breslauer, "Do Soviet Leaders Test New Presidents?" *International Security* VIII (Winter 1983–1984), 83–107.

52. Quoted in Hugh Sidey, *John F. Kennedy, President* (New York, 1964), 127.

53. Memorandum for the Secretary of State, n.d. (but probably 1961), Box 68, Departments and Agencies File, POF, JFKL.

54. Quoted in Gerald T. Rice, *The Bold Experiment: JFK's Peace Corps* (Notre Dame, IN, 1985), 59.

55. Quoted in Chester Bowles, *Promises to Keep: My Years in Public Life, 1941–1969* (New York, 1971), 449.

56. Quoted in Fairlie, *Kennedy Promise,* 180–181.

57. Quoted in Charles Roberts, "Image and Reality," in Thompson, *Kennedy Presidency,* 181.

58. Theodore H. White, "The Action Intellectuals," *Life* LXII (June 1967), 43.

59. Quoted in Midge Decter, "Kennedyism," *Commentary* XLIX (January 1970), 20.

60. Memorandum by Arthur M. Schlesinger, Jr., n.d. (but probably 1961), Box 121, POF, JFKL.

61. *PPP, JFK, 1961,* p. 1.

62. Schlesinger, *Cycles,* 412.

63. I.M. Destler, Leslie H. Gelb, and Anthony Lake, *Our Own Worst Enemy: The Unmaking of American Foreign Policy* (New York, 1984), 182.

64. John F. Campbell, *The Foreign Affairs Fudge Factory* (New York, 1971), 6. See also Charles E. Neu, "The Rise of the National Security Bureaucracy," in Louis Galambos, ed., *The New American State: Bureaucracies and Policies Since World War II* (Baltimore, MD, 1987), 91–98.

65. U. Alexis Johnson OH Interview, LBJL.

66. Warren I. Cohen, *Dean Rusk* (Totowa, NJ, 1980); John B. Henry and William Espinosa, "The Tragedy of Dean Rusk," *Foreign Policy,* No. 8 (Fall 1972), 166–189; Thomas J. Schoenbaum, *Waging Peace and War* (New York, 1988).

67. Sorensen, *Kennedy,* 270.

68. Quoted in Barry Rubin, *Secrets of State* (New York, 1985), 98.

69. Dean Rusk, "Reflections on Foreign Policy," in Thompson, *Kennedy Presidency,* 193.

70. Atkinson, "Kennedy Staff," 16.

71. McGeorge Bundy, "The History-Maker," *Massachusetts Historical Society: Proceedings* XC (1978), 79.

72. Dean Rusk OH Interview # 1, LBJL.

73. O'Donnell and Powers, *"Johnny,"* 241.

74. See Arthur M. Schlesinger, Jr., *Robert Kennedy and His Times* (Boston, 1978).

75. Quoted in Carl M. Brauer, *Presidential Transitions: Eisenhower Through Reagan* (New York, 1986), 73.

76. Quoted in Heath, *Decade,* 119.

77. Quoted in Jeffrey G. Barlow, "President John F. Kennedy and His Joint Chiefs of Staff" (Ph.D. dissertation, University of South Carolina, 1981), 15.

78. Bromley Smith quoted in Atkinson, "Kennedy Staff," 4.

79. Rostow, *Diffusion,* 126.

80. "Kennedy Notes 6/27/62," Box 12, Richard Rovere Papers, State Historical Society of Wisconsin, Madison, WI.

81. Ball, *The Past,* 167.
82. *Ibid.,* 164.
83. Quoted in William S. White, *The Making of a Journalist* (Lexington, KY, 1986), 153.
84. Quoted in Theodore H. White, *In Search of History* (New York, 1978), 461.
85. Quoted in John Bartlow Martin, *Adlai Stevenson and the World* (Garden City, NY, 1977), 634.
86. Chester Bowles OH Interview, JFKL. See also Bowles, *Promises to Keep,* Part III.
87. Arthur M. Schlesinger, Jr., "A Biographer's Perspective," in Thompson, *Kennedy Presidency,* 21. See also Hubert H. Humphrey, *Education of a Public Man* (Garden City, NY, 1976), 248; Anthony Hartley, "John F. Kennedy's Foreign Policy," *Foreign Policy,* No. 4 (Fall 1971), 86; *Wall Street Journal,* January 21, 1971.
88. *PPP, JFK, 1963,* pp. 459–464.
89. *Ibid.,* 464.
90. Quoted in Louise FitzSimons, *The Kennedy Doctrine* (New York, 1972), 15.
91. *PPP, JFK, 1963,* pp. 890–898.
92. Quoted in William J. Rust, *Kennedy in Vietnam* (New York, 1985), x.
93. William Bundy, "Kennedy and Vietnam," in Thompson, ed., *Kennedy Presidency,* 255.
94. Fred Kaplan, *Wizards of Armageddon* (New York, 1983), 307–314.
95. Quoted in Heath, *Decade,* 137.
96. Quoted in Schlesinger, *Thousand Days,* 615.

Chapter 1. Atlantic Community

1. For the American reaction, see Bradley S. Greenberg and Edwin B. Parker, eds., *The Kennedy Assassination and the American Public* (Stanford, CA, 1965). Part of the following was first published in Costigliola, "The Failed Design: Kennedy, de Gaulle, and the Struggle for Europe," *Diplomatic History* VIII (Summer 1984), 227–51, and Costigliola, " 'Like Children in the Darkness': The Impact on Europe of John F. Kennedy's Assassination," *Journal of Popular Culture* XX (Winter 1987), 115–24.
2. Leo M. Goodman (Bremen) to Department of State, December 2, 1963, A-43, EX FE 3-1/Kennedy, John F., WHCF, LBJL.
3. R.A. Lloyd, Jr., to DS, December 2, 1963, *ibid.* See also Robert S. Folsom (Thessaloniki) to DS, November 29, 1963, *ibid.;* P.F. DuVivier (Nice) to DS, November 29, 1963, *ibid.*
4. *Der Tagesspiegel,* November 23, 1963.
5. Quoted in David Nunnerly, *President Kennedy and Britain* (London, 1972), 221.
6. Bohlen to Secretary of State, November 23, 1963, WHCF, EX FE 3-1/Kennedy, John F., LBJL.

7. Bruce to Secretary of State, December 1, 1963, *ibid.*

8. Rusk in U.S. Senate, Committee on Foreign Relations, *Executive Sessions, 1963: Historical Series,* vol. XV (Washington, DC, 1986), 71.

9. U.S. Senate, Committee on Foreign Relations, *United States Policy Toward Europe (and Related Matters),* 89th Congress, 2nd Session (Washington, DC, 1966), 512.

10. U.S. Department of Commerce, *Statistical Abstract of the United States 1965* (Washington, DC, 1965), 856, 859.

11. John F. Kennedy, *The Strategy of Peace,* Allan Nevins, ed. (New York, 1960), 66–81, 99–102, 212–15.

12. Sidney Kraus, *The Great Debates* (Bloomington, IN, 1977), 414–16, 424–25.

13. Kennedy, *Strategy of Peace,* 99–102.

14. Myer Rashish OH Interview, JFKL; Joseph Kraft, *The Grand Design* (New York, 1962).

15. Dean Acheson to Robert J. Schaetzel, April 1, 1963, Box 28, Dean Acheson Papers, Yale University Library, New Haven, CT; Mike Mansfield OH, JFKL.

16. Kenneth W. Thompson, ed., *The Kennedy Presidency* (Lanham, MD, 1985), 228.

17. U.S. Senate, Committee on Foreign Relations, *Executive Sessions, 1962: Historical Seires,* vol. XIV (Washington, DC, 1986), 587.

18. Rostow to Secretary of State, September 17, 1963, Box 65, POF, JFKL.

19. Memorandum by David Bruce, February 9, 1963, Box 49-56, Theodore Sorensen Papers, JFKL.

20. Senate, *Executive Sessions, 1962,* XIV, 697–98. See also *ibid., 1961,* XIII, Part 2 (Washington, DC, 1984), 192; James Reston OH Interview, JFKL.

21. Senate, *Executive Sessions, 1962,* XIV, 570.

22. William R. Tyler letter to the author, August 25, 1983.

23. Schlesinger, *A Thousand Days,* 654; author's interview with C. Douglas Dillon, November 15, 1983.

24. "Remarks of President Kennedy to the National Security Council Meeting of January 22, 1963," No. 1986(2274), DDRS.

25. Theodore Sorensen OH, JFKL.

26. "Memorandum of Conversation Between French Foreign Minister Couve de Murville and Under Secretary Ball," May 25, 1963, Box 72, NSF, JFKL; "Memorandum of Conversation with the President, William R. Tyler, Couve de Murville, Hervé Alphand, and Charles Lucet," October 7, 1963, Box 73, *ibid.;* Bohlen to Secretary of State, September 22, 1965, Box 172, NSF, LBJL.

27. "Summary of the President's Remarks to the National Security Council—January 18, 1962," Box 313, NSF, JFKL.

28. Konrad Adenauer, *Erinnerungen 1959–1963* (Stuttgart, 1978), 147.

29. "US–German Military Cooperation: Status, Including Offset Arrangements, Sale of PERSHINGS/SERGEANTS, German MAP," June 11, 1963,

President's Briefing Book, June 1963 European Trip, No. 1979(305B), DDRS; "Italy: Scope Paper," June 17, 1963, *ibid.;* "U.S.–Italian Military Cooperation," June 7, 1963, *ibid.;* Gavin to Secretary of State, February 16, 1962, Box 71, NSF, JFKL; Rusk to French Defense Minister, February 20, 1962, *ibid,;* Gavin to President, March 8, 1962, *ibid.;* Memorandum of Conversation in Nitze's Office, March 13, 1962, *ibid.*

30. "The U.S. and de Gaulle—The Past and the Future," January 30, 1963, Box 116A, POF, JFKL.

31. Kennedy to James Gavin, (n.d. but early 1962), Box 116, POF, JFKL; Henry Owen, "A New Approach to France," April 21, 1961, Box 70, NSF, JFKL; Rusk to Gavin, May 5, 1961, Box 71, NSF, JFKL.

32. Robert Estabrook Interview with Elbridge Durbrow, November 2, 1962, Box 1, Robert Estabrook Papers, JFKL.

33. Owen, "A New Approach." See also "Memorandum of Conversation Between French Foreign Minister Couve de Murville and Under Secretary Ball"; "Memorandum of Conversation with the President, William R. Tyler, Couve de Murville, Hervé Alphand and Charles Lucet", May 25, 1963, Box 70, NSF, JFKL; Rostow to the President, February 19, 1963, Box 65, POF, JFKL; "The U.S. and de Gaulle—The Past and the Future."

34. Senate, *Executive Sessions, 1963,* XV, 332, 524.

35. Sorensen OH.

36. Fred Kaplan, *The Wizards of Armageddon* (New York, 1983), 291–327; Morton H. Halperin, *Nuclear Fallacy: Dispelling the Myth of Nuclear Strategy* (Cambridge, MA, 1987), 15–21; David Rosenberg, "Reality and Responsibility: Power and Process in the Making of United States Nuclear Strategy, 1945–68," *Journal of Strategic Studies* IX (March 1986), 43–50; John Lewis Gaddis, *Strategies of Containment* (New York, 1982), 198–236; William W. Kaufman, *The McNamara Strategy* (New York, 1964), 102–34; Desmond Ball, *Politics and Force Levels* (Berkeley, CA, 1980), 16–18, 31–34; Robert S. McNamara, *The Essence of Security* (New York, 1968), 32–67; Scott D. Sagan, "SIOP-62: The Nuclear War Plan Briefing to President Kennedy," *International Security* XII (Summer 1987), 22–51; David N. Schwartz, *NATO's Nuclear Dilemmas* (Washington, DC, 1983), 174–75.

37. Cyrus Sulzberger, *The Last of the Giants* (New York, 1970), 838; Gavin to DS, May 18, 1962, Box 71, NSF, JFKL.

38. Charles de Gaulle, *Memoirs of Hope: Renewal and Endeavor* (New York, 1971), 213–16.

39. Herbert S. Parmet, *Jack: The Struggles of John F. Kennedy* (New York, 1980), 401–08.

40 "Thoughts on Reading the Morning Papers," May 9, 1962, Box 71, NSF, JFKL.

41. Bohlen quoted in Note C, p. 41, File 4, Box W-13, Arthur M. Schlesinger, Jr. Papers, JFKL.

42. Acheson to Robert J. Schaetzel, April 1, 1963, Box 28, Acheson Papers.

43. Jean Lacouture, *De Gaulle* (Paris, 1986; 3 vols.), III, 343–66; Stanley

Hoffmann, *Decline or Renewal?* (New York, 1974), 283–362; Michael M. Harrison, *Reluctant Ally* (Baltimore, MD, 1981), 49–138.

44. Sulzberger, *Last of the Giants,* 647.

45. *Ibid.,* 45.

46. Adenauer, *Erinnerungen.* See also Pierre Melandri, "Le général de Gaulle, la construction européenne et l'alliance atlantique," in Elie Barnavi and Saul Friedlander, eds., *La politique étrangère du général de Gaulle* (Paris, 1965), 87–111.

47. For the quotation, Thompson, *Kennedy Presidency,* 198. See also Sulzberger, *Last of the Giants,* 54–57, 663–64, 671, 705–08, 715, 975; de Gaulle, *Memoirs of Hope,* 202–4, 208–9; Lawrence S. Kaplan, *NATO and the United States* (Boston, 1988), 69–92; "Tripartite Consultation Between France, the United States and the United Kingdom," March 10, 1961, Box 70, NSF, JFKL; Lacouture, *De Gaulle,* III, 363.

48. Acheson to McNamara, September 16, 1963, Box 22, Acheson Papers.

49. "President's European Trip June 1963, Miscellaneous Economic Matters—Germany," June 13, 1963, No. 1979(305B), DDRS; Harriman to President, September 1, 1961, Box 82-98, NSF, JFKL; Adrian Schertz, *John F. Kennedys deutschlandpolitisches Konzept im Rahmen der amerikanischen Strategie* (Prüfungsarbeit, Universität Trier, 1986), 27–30.

50. "Points which the President May Wish to Emphasize on Discussion with Foreign Minister von Brentano," February 16, 1961; Ball to Kennedy (n.d. but March 1961), Box 116A, POF, JFKL; Kennedy to Adenauer, October 16, 1961, Box 117, JFKL.

51. McGeorge Bundy to President Johnson, "Basic Talking Points for the President with Erhard," December 27, 1963, No. 1979(471A), DDRS; "US-German Military Cooperation: Status, Including Offset Arrangements, Sale of PERSHINGS/SERGEANTS, German MAP," June 11, 1963, President's Briefing Book, June 1963 European Trip, No. 1979(305B), *ibid.*

52. Carl Kaysen to President, March 12, 1963, Box 64, POF, JFKL.

53. George W. Ball, *The Past Has Another Pattern* (New York, 1982), 184–85.

54. Rostow to the President, April 11, 1961, Box 64A, POF, JFKL.

55. John Newhouse, *De Gaulle and the Anglo-Saxons* (New York, 1970), 59; Helga Haftendorn, *Abrüstungs-und-Entspannungspolitik der BRD 1955–1973* (Düsseldorf, 1974), 109–37; author's interview with George W. Ball, June 24, 1986.

56. Acheson to McNamara, September 16, 1963, Box 22, Acheson Papers. See also note 31.

57. *Frankfurter Allgemeine Zeitung,* December 21, 1961; January 12, 1962; *Die Zeit,* January 26, 1962; *Der Tagesspiegel,* January 4, 1962.

58. Senate, *Executive Sessions, 1961,* XIII, Part 2, 189.

59. "Memorandum of Conversation," October 8, 1963, Box 73, NSF, JFKL.

60. Kissinger to the President, April 6, 1961, Box 117, POF, JFKL.

61. Charles E. Bohlen OH Interview, JFKL.

62. Robert M. Slusser, *The Berlin Crisis of 1961* (Baltimore, MD, 1973); Jack M. Schick, *The Berlin Crisis 1958–1962* (Philadelphia, PA, 1971);

Honoré Catudal, *Kennedy and the Berlin Wall Crisis* (Berlin, 1980); Fritz Lenze, "U.S.–West German Relations During the Berlin Crisis, 1958–1962" (Ph.D. dissertation, Tufts University, 1982); "Talking Points Reviewing Conversations between President Kennedy and Chairman Khrushchev, June 3–4, 1961," Box 300, Chester Bowles Papers, Yale University Library.

63. Catudal, *Kennedy and the Berlin Wall Crisis,* 23, 48.

64. Rostow to Kennedy, "Miscellaneous Papers for Hyannisport, September 15–18, 1961," Box 318, NSF, JFKL.

65. Memorandum by David Bruce, February 9, 1963, Box 49-56, Sorensen Papers (emphasis added).

66. Sulzberger, *Last of the Giants,* 960–61.

67. Robert Estabrook, "Talk with President Kennedy," August 28, 1961, Box 1, Estabrook Papers.

68. Louis Harris to the President through Evelyn Lincoln (n.d. but summer 1961), Box 63a, POF, JFKL.

69. Kaplan, *Wizards,* 294–301; Halperin, *Nuclear Fallacy,* 35–36; Ball, *Politics and Force Levels,* 46, 55; Sagan, "SIOP-62," 24–29.

70. Senate, *Executive Sessions, 1961,* XIII, Part 2, 185.

71. Schlesinger, *A Thousand Days,* 379.

72. Catudal, *Kennedy and the Berlin Wall Crisis,* 30, 187.

73. *Ibid.,* 199.

74. Thompson to Secretary of State, February 4, 1961, No. 1977(74B), DDRS.

75. Senate, *Executive Sessions, 1961,* XIII, Part 2, 615.

76. *Ibid.,* 188.

77. Catudal, *Kennedy and the Berlin Wall Crisis,* 188.

78. Morrow to the President through McGeorge Bundy, July 20, 1961, Box 75, NSF, JFKL.

79. Catudal, *Kennedy and the Berlin Wall Crisis,* 188.

80. *New York Times,* August 3, 1961. See also George W. Johnson, ed., *The Kennedy Presidential Press Conferences* (New York, 1978), 132; Thilo Koch, *Tagebuch aus Washington* (Frankfurt, 1965), 60–61.

81. Catudal, *Kennedy and the Berlin Wall Crisis,* 201.

82. Lucius D. Clay Speech to Council on Foreign Relations, June 13, 1962, vol. 39, Council on Foreign Relations Archives, New York City; *New York Times,* August 14, 1986; *Berliner Morgenpost,* August 13, 1987.

83. Martin J. Hillenbrand OH Interview, JFKL; quotation in Catudal, *Kennedy and the Berlin Wall Crisis,* 38.

84. *Ibid.*

85. Vice President to the President, August 21, 1961, No. 1978(301B), DDRS.

86. Rostow to Bundy, "Initial Comments on Acheson Paper of August 1, 1961," August 7, 1961, Box 82-98, NSF, JFKL; Carl Kaysen to Bundy, August 22, 1961, *ibid.*

87. Kennedy to Mayor Brandt, August 18, 1961, *ibid.;* Allen Dulles to the President, August 22, 1961, *ibid.;* Costigliola, "Failed Design," 240.

88. Memorandum of Conversation in Mayor's Office, August 20, 1961, No. 1976(258B), DDRS.

89. Robert W. Komer to McGeorge Bundy, August 22, 1961, Box 82-98, NSF, JFKL.

90. William E. Griffith to Rostow, August 25, 1961, *ibid.*

91. Vice President to the President, August 21, 1961, No. 1978(301B), DDRS.

92. Nikita Khrushchev, trans. by Strobe Talbott, *Khrushchev Remembers* (Boston, MA, 1970), 455.

93. Slusser, *Berlin Crisis,* 157–66.

94. Acheson, "Berlin: A Political Program," August 1, 1961, Box 82-98, NSF, JFKL; Bundy, "Berlin Plans," August 10, 1961, *ibid.;* Kissinger to Bundy, August 11, 1961, *ibid.;* "Minutes of Inter-Departmental Coordinating Group on Berlin, July 26, 1961, 5:15 p.m.," July 31, 1961, *ibid.;* Thompson, *Kennedy Presidency,* 207–8; Schlesinger, *A Thousand Days,* 379–97; Warren I. Cohen, *Dean Rusk* (Totowa, NJ, 1980), 138–44.

95. *PPP, JFK, 1961,* pp. 533–40.

96. Herbert S. Parmet, *JFK: The Presidency of John F. Kennedy* (New York, 1984), 196–97; Sorensen, *Kennedy,* 627.

97. Schlesinger, *A Thousand Days,* 392.

98. Khrushchev, *Khrushchev Remembers,* 459–60; Curtis Cate, *The Ides of August* (New York, 1978), 476–87; Ball, *Politics and Force Levels,* 96–98.

99. Catudal, *Kennedy and the Berlin Wall Crisis,* 131; Schlesinger, *A Thousand Days,* 403; Slusser, *Berlin Crisis,* 440–41.

100. Kennedy to Secretary of State, August 21, 1961, Box 82-98, NSF, JFKL; Cate, *The Ides of August,* 470–72.

101. Bundy to the President, August 28, 1961, Box 82-98, NSF, JFKL.

102. Kennedy to the Secretary of State, August 21, 1961, *ibid.*

103. Schlesinger, *A Thousand Days,* 385.

104. Richard K. Betts, *Nuclear Blackmail and Nuclear Balance* (Washington, DC, 1987), 100.

105. "Summary of Remarks of McGeorge Bundy," November 1, 1961, Records of Meetings, vol. 39, Council on Foreign Relations Archives; Baron Axel von dem Bussche, "The German Public and the Crisis in Europe," November 20, 1961, *ibid.;* Schick, *Berlin Crisis,* 200–203; Adenauer, *Erinnerungen,* 173; Bruno Bandulet, *Adenauer zwischen Ost und West* (München, 1970), 165–70; Sulzberger, *Last of the Giants,* 886, 889; Robert Kleiman, *Atlantic Crisis* (New York, 1964), 42–43.

106. Adenauer, *Erinnerungen,* 136. See also pp. 137–49.

107. Gavin to Secretary of State, May 16, 1962, Box 71A, NSF, JFKL.

108. Kennedy to Gavin, May 18, 1962, Box 71, *ibid.*

109. Macmillan Diary, June 3, 1962, quoted in Harold Macmillan, *At the End of the Day* (London, 1973), 120.

110. Nunnerly, *Kennedy and Britain,* 76; Costigliola, "Failed Design," 243–44.

111. *Washington Post,* December 20, 1962.

112. Dean Acheson OH Interview, JFKL.

113. Senate, *Executive Sessions, 1963,* XV, 6–7 (emphasis added); author interview with McGeorge Bundy, January 21, 1988.

114. Estabrook, "Private Talk with Lord Privy Seal Edward Heath," June 12, 1962, Box 1, Estabrook Papers; author interview with Ball.

115. Senate, *Executive Sessions, 1963,* XV, 40–41.

116. Ball to Kennedy, December 8, 1962, Box 170A, NSF, JFKL; Costigliola, "Failed Design," 229–30, 238, 245.

117. Nunnerly, *Kennedy and Britain,* 131, for background, see 127–37; Henry Brandon, "Skybolt," *The Times* (London), December 8, 1963; Richard E. Neustadt, *Alliance Politics* (New York, 1970), 30–55; Richard E. Neustadt report to Kennedy, "Skybolt and Nassau," November 15, 1963, Box 319-324, NSF, JFKL.

118. Stuart Symington in Senate, *Executive Sessions, 1963,* XV, 622. See also Kennedy to Gavin, June 14, 1962, Box 71, NSF, JFKL; Sulzberger, *Last of the Giants,* 963, 992; "De Gaulle and Great Britain," *espoir* XLIII (June 1983), 83–84, 91.

119. Nunnerly, *Kennedy and Britain,* 157.

120. Neustadt, "Skybolt and Nassau," 97–98; Henry Brandon OH, JFKL.

121. *New York Times,* January 15, 1963; Newhouse, *De Gaulle and the Anglo-Saxons,* 237–40.

122. John J. McCloy to Adenauer, February 4, 1963, Box 31, POF, JFKL; Bandulet, *Adenauer,* 199–208; Ball, *The Past,* 272–73.

123. Quotations in Sorensen OH; see also Sulzberger, *Last of the Giants,* 51, 962; Ball to Bundy, January 23, 1963, Box 73a, NSF, JFKL; author's interview with Ball.

124. [Kennedy], "Questions to Be Settled by the United States in the Coming Months," January 31, 1963, Box 62, POF, JFKL.

125. Evelyn Lincoln to Bundy, February 1, 1963, *ibid.*

126. Acheson to Christopher Emmet (not sent, about March 21, 1963), Box 110, Acheson Papers.

127. Memorandum to David Bruce, February 9, 1963, Box 49-56, Sorensen Papers.

128. Author interview with Ball.

129. McCloy to Adenauer, February 4, 1963, Box 31, POF, JFKL; Acheson to Kurt Birrenbach, February 19, 1963, Box 3, Acheson Papers; Acheson, "Memorandum of Conversation (with W.A. Menne)," May 3, 1963, Box 68, *ibid.*

130. For background, see John D. Steinbruner, *The Cybernetic Theory of Decision* (Princeton, 1974); Schwartz, *NATO's Nuclear Dilemmas,* 82–135.

131. "Remarks of President Kennedy to the National Security Council Meeting of January 22, 1963," No. 1986(2274), DDRS.

132. Joseph Alsop, "Farce or Force" (n.d. but 1963), copy in Box 216, NSF, JFKL; Finletter to Rusk, March 16, 1963, *ibid.;* Bohlen to Secretary of State, February 28, 1963, *ibid.;* Kennedy to William R. Tyler, March 29, 1963, Box 23, NSF, LBJL.

133. Merchant to Secretary of State, March 10, 1963, Box 216, NSF, JFKL.

134. Merchant, "Overall Thoughts on the MLF Enroute from Ankara to Naples," April 29, 1963, Box 10, Livingston Merchant Papers, Princeton University Library, Princeton, NJ; "Initial West European Assessment of US

Multilateral Force Proposals," March 7, 1963, Box 216, NSF, JFKL; Morris to Secretary of State, March 18, 1963, *ibid;* Raymond F. Courtney, to Secretary of State, June 18, 1963, *ibid.*

135. Bundy to President, June 15, 1963, Box 23, NSF, LBJL.

136. Author interview with Bundy.

137. Thompson, *Kennedy Presidency,* 236.

138. National Security Action Memorandum No. 270, October 29, 1963, Box 342, NSF, JFKL.

139. Sulzberger, *Last of the Giants,* 985; Sorensen, OH; Senate, *Executive Session, 1963,* XV, 356.

140. *Ibid.,* 435.

141. *Ibid.,* 436 (see also p. 470); Kennedy to de Gaulle, July 24, 1963, Box 73a, NSF, JFKL; David Klein to Bundy, July 30, 1963, *ibid.;* Gordon H. Chang, "JFK, China, and the Bomb," *Journal of American History* LXXIV (March 1988), 1287–1310.

142. Maurice Couve de Murville OH Interview, JFKL.

143. Ibid., 14; Memorandum of Conversation Between President Johnson and President de Gaulle, November 25, 1963, No. 1975(94A), DDRS.

144. Averell Harriman quoted in Sorensen, *Kennedy,* 579.

145. *Ibid.,* 579.

146. *PPP, JFK, 1963,* pp. 516–21, 524–25; Schlesinger, *A Thousand Days,* 884–85; *Der Tagesspiegel,* June 27–30, 1963; *Frankfurter Rundschau,* June 27–28, 1963; *Berliner Zeitung,* June 27–30, 1963.

147. Arthur M. Schlesinger, Jr., Note on Conversation with Richard E. Neustadt, July 10, 1964, Box W-12, Schlesinger Papers.

148. "Wie populär ist Kennedy in der Bundesrepublik?" *Die Stimmung im Bundesgebiet,* No. 586 (Allensbach, West Germany, 1963).

149. Central Intelligence Agency Report, June 22, 1963, Box 72A, NSF, JFKL.

150. Sorensen, *Kennedy,* 601. For the President's success in Germany, see note 146; "Mit welchen Ländern soll die Bundesrepublik möglichst eng zusammenarbeiten?," *Die Stimmung im Bundesgebiet,* No. 588 (Allensbach, 1963). For French reaction to the assassination, see *Sondages* XXVI, No. 4 (1964), 58–62.

151. Antonio Gambino to Robert Neumann, January 3, 1964, Box W-12, Schlesinger Papers.

152. Patrick Devlin to Acheson, November 2, 1962, Box 8, Acheson Papers.

153. Hillenbrand to the Secretary, November 28, 1964, Box 24, NSF, LBJL; Memorandum by Bundy to Bruce, December 9, 1964, *ibid.;* David Klein to Bundy, January 8, 1965, *ibid.;* Bundy to the President with enclosures, January 12, 1965, Box 25, *ibid.;* Steinbruner, *Cybernetic Theory,* 299–310.

154. For German sentiment, see "Der Krieg in Vietnam—Die Kritik an den Amerikanern nimmt zu," *Die Stimmung im Bundesgebiet,* No. 777 (Allensbach, 1967).

155. Honoré M. Catudal, *The Diplomacy of the Quadripartite Agreement on Berlin* (Berlin, 1978); Erich Vogt, "The Role of Berlin and the Four-Power

Negotiations in the Foreign Policy Process of the Nixon Administration" (Ph.D. dissertation, Freie Universität Berlin, 1980), 33–58.

156. See David Calleo, *Beyond American Hegemony* (New York, 1987), 44–126.

Chapter 2. Foreign Economic Policy

1. Theodore Sorensen, *Kennedy* (New York, 1965), 456.

2. Walter Heller, Memorandum for the President, June 26, 1962, Box 16, Walter Heller Papers, JFKL.

3. David Calleo, *The Imperious Economy* (Cambridge, MA, 1982). David Calleo and Benjamin Rowland, *America and the World Political Economy* (Bloomington, IN, 1973), is one of the most thoughtful overviews of U.S. policy in the 1960s.

4. For discussions of world systems analyses of American foreign economic policy, see Thomas J. McCormick, " 'Every System Needs a Center Sometime,' " in Lloyd C. Gardner, ed., *Redefining the Past* (Corvallis, OR, 1986); Immanuel Wallerstein, *The Politics of the World Economy* (New York, 1984); Albert Bergesen, ed., *Studies of the Modern World System* (New York, 1980).

5. See William S. Borden, *The Pacific Alliance* (Madison, WI, 1984), 1–55.

6. Jack Behrman to Luther Hodges, May 4, 1962; George Ball to Kennedy, May 6, 1962, both in Box 5, Jack Behrman Papers, JFKL.

7. "Special Report to the President-Elect," January 18, 1961, Alan Sproul, Roy Blough and Paul McCracken, reprinted in Robert Roosa, *The Dollar and World Liquidity* (New York, 1968), 278.

8. DS, "Summary Record of Meeting with Economic Consultants," October 31, 1961, Box 32, Kermit Gordon Papers, JFKL.

9. Kennedy's personal summary of the economic situation is found in Kennedy to David Rockefeller, June 26, 1962, Box 29, Theodore Sorensen Papers, JFKL; Sorensen, *Kennedy*, 454; Bruce Miroff, *Pragmatic Illusions* (New York, 1976), 182–207; Luther Hodges OH Interview, JFKL; Seymour Harris, *Economics of the Kennedy Years* (New York, 1964), 1–22.

10. Walter Heller to Kennedy, November 28, 1961, Box 29, Sorensen Papers.

11. Rostow OH Interview, JFKL.

12. George W. Ball, *The Past Has Another Pattern* (New York, 1982), 205.

13. Rostow OH Interview.

14. Harry G. Johnson, *The World Economy at the Crossroads* (New York, 1965), 4.

15. David Calleo, *Europe's Future* (New York, 1965), 139.

16. Ball, *The Past*, 166.

17. Roosa, *The Dollar*, 265–270.

18. Heller to Kennedy, October 16, 1961; see also Heller, "Accentuating

the Positive in Our Balance of Payments," August 6, 1963; Heller to Kennedy September 15, 1961, all Box 16, Walter Heller Papers, JFKL.

19. Roosa, *The Dollar,* 265–270.

20. Heller To Kennedy, September 15, 1961, Box 16, Heller Papers.

21. Kennedy speech, February 6, 1961. *PPP, JFK, 1961,* 58.

22. See Roosa, *The Dollar,* 3–33.

23. Jacques Rueff, "The Gold Standard," in Benjamin Cohen, ed., *American Foreign Economic Policy* (New York, 1968), 155–159; Jacques Rueff, *The Balance of Payments* (New York, 1968).

24. See Roosa, *The Dollar,* 17, 112–113, 219–220; Calleo, *Imperious Economy,* 48–52; Robert Solomon, *The International Monetary System* (New York, 1977), 66–81. See also numerous references in Cohen, *American Foreign Economic Policy.*

25. See Triffin, *The World Money Maze* (New Haven, 1966).

26. Solomon, *International Monetary System,* 54.

27. Acheson OH Interview, JFKL. See also Roosa, *The Dollar,* 33; Fred Block, *The Origins of International Economic Disorder* (Berkeley, CA, 1977), 180–181; Ball, *The Past,* 206–207; Solomon, *International Monetary System,* 38–39.

28. Roosa, *The Dollar,* 221–222; Calleo, *Imperious Economy,* 53–54; Block, *The Origins,* 189–193.

29. The best summary of the TEA is found in the *Congressional Quarterly Almanac 1963* (Washington, DC, 1964), 264–265.

30. Ball, *The Past,* 197–198.

31. Department of Commerce, "Some Implications of Linear Tariff Cutting for the United States," Box 8, Behrman Papers.

32. Christian Herter, U.S. Congress, Joint Economic Committee, Sub-Committee for Foreign Economic Policy, *Foreign Economic Policy* (Washington, DC, 1961), 12; Kennedy Message to Congress, House Ways and Means Committee, *Trade Expansion Act of 1962* (Washington, DC, 1962), 3; Joint Economic Committee Report, *ibid.,* 114, 117–129.

33. Ball to Kennedy, October 23, 1961, Box 2, Howard Petersen Papers, JFKL.

34. Myer Rashish, "The Content and Timing of US Foreign Trade Legislation," attached to Howard C. Petersen to Kennedy, October 26, 1961, Box 2, Petersen Papers; Hale Boggs OH Interview, JFKL; Ernest Preeg, *Traders and Diplomats* (Washington, DC, 1970), 44–45.

35. Ball, *The Past,* 188–189; Thomas Zeiler, "Free Trade Politics and Diplomacy," *Diplomatic History* XI (Spring 1987), 127–142.

36. Ball, *The Past,* 190–191, 188.

37. DS Memorandum, November 16, 1961, and "Bulletin of the EEC," December 1961, both in Box 25, Myer Feldman Papers, JFKL. See also Luther Hodges in House, *Trade Expansion Act,* 99.

38. DS, "Summary Record of Meeting with Economic Consultants," October 3, 1961, Box 32, Gordon Papers.

39. Ernest Preeg, *Traders and Diplomats* (Washington, DC, 1970) 50, 51, 55.

40. *PPP, JFK, 1962,* pp. 14–15.
41. House, *Trade Expansion Act,* 5.
42. *Ibid.,* 79.
43. *Ibid.,* 159.
44. *Ibid.,* 2844, 2916. For the excessive optimism of TEA advocates, see *ibid.,* 1395, 1396, 2205, 2206, 2688.
45. Walter Salant and Beatrice Vaccara, *Import Liberalization and Employment* (Washington, DC, 1961).
46. Myer Feldman to Kennedy, January 5, 1962, Box 2, Peterson Papers.
47. Heller to Kennedy, November 21, 1962; Heller to Kennedy, April 6, 1963, both Box 16, Heller Papers.
48. House, *Trade Expansion Act,* 1164.
49. "Commerce Department/Industry Consultations in Preparation for the 'Kennedy Round,' " Box 8, Behrman Papers.
50. House, *Trade Expansion Act,* 137–154.
51. Gudeman to Ruder and Foley, April 23, 1962, Box 8, Behrman Papers.
52. "Company Positions on HR 11970," memo for Petersen, April 11, 1962, Box 6, Petersen Papers.
53. House, *Trade Expansion Act,* 2258, 2720, 3028.
54. *Ibid.,* 2258–2259.
55. *Ibid.,* 146.
56. *Ibid.,* 2213, 151.
57. *Ibid.,* 2213.
58. *Ibid.,* 1207.
59. *Ibid.,* 2870.
60. *Ibid.,* 1278.
61. Hodges OH Interview.
62. House, *Trade Expansion Act,* 1365.
63. DS, "Summary of Record of Meeting with Economic Consultants," October 3, 1961.
64. *Ibid.*
65. *Ibid.* For a list of trade groups and their positions on the TEA, see Memorandum to Petersen, April 11, 1962, Box 6, Petersen Papers.
66. *Congressional Quarterly Almanac, 1962,* pp. 254–297.
67. For the European attack on the American Selling Price, see Karin Kock, *International Trade Policy and the GATT* (Stockholm, 1969), 91.
68. Orville Freeman OH Interview, JFKL; Memorandum of Conversation, "Brussels Negotiations—Kennedy Round," December 28, 1963, Box 8, Christian A. Herter Papers, JFKL.
69. For the Kennedy Round, see Preeg, *Traders and Diplomats;* John W. Evans, *The Kennedy Round in American Trade Policy* (New York, 1971).
70. Freeman OH Interview.
71. Calleo, *Imperious Economy,* 16.
72. Freeman to Kennedy, December 4, 1962, Box 9, Orville Freeman Papers, JFLK.
73. Hodges OH Interview; Preeg, *Traders and Diplomats,* 139–140, 144; Freeman memorandum, "Summary for Use by the President in Meeting with

Spaak," November 1962, Box 9, Freeman Papers; Freeman to Feldman, August 30, 1963, Box 26, Feldman Papers.

74. Clay Shaw, International House of New Orleans, Joint Economic Committee, *Foreign Economic Policy* (Washington, DC, 1961), 269.

75. Freeman OH Interview.

76. For US threats to retaliate against EEC agricultural policies, see Chester Bowles to Kennedy, May 13, 1961, Box 170, NSF, JFKL; Murphy to Petersen, October 27, 1961, Box 2, Petersen Papers; Richard P. Stebbins, *The United States in World Affairs, 1961* (New York, 1962), 148; Memorandum of Conversation, March 26, 1963, Box 10, Herter Papers.

77. Murphy to Kennedy, November 13, 1962, Box 9, Freeman Papers; Preeg, *Traders and Diplomats,* 74–76.

78. Freeman to Kennedy, November 15 and November 26, 1962, Box 9, Freeman Papers.

79. Herter to Kennedy, April 8, 1963, Box 10, Herter Papers; Rusk to U.S. Embassies (DS Circular), May 7, 1963, Box 7, Herter Papers.

80. Herter to Kennedy, August 2, 1963, Box 10, Herter Papers.

81. Richard P. Stebbins, *The United States in World Affairs, 1963,* (New York, 1964), 133; Herter to Kennedy, October 12, 1963, Box 10, Herter Papers.

82. Freeman to Feldman, with attached "Major Agricultural Objectives in Trade Negotiations," Box 26, Feldman Papers.

83. "August 15 Meeting with Under Secretary Murphy," August 16, 1963, "A Statement on the Concept, Rationale, and Role of Market Sharing in World Agricultural Trade," December 19, 1963, both Box 5, Herter Papers; "Draft Memorandum for the President's Meeting with Erhard," December 10, 1963, Box 8, *ibid.*

84. "National Security Action Memorandum 11," February 6, 1961; NSAM 22, February 20, 1961, both Box 328, National Security Action Memoranda Files, JFKL.

85. Roosa, *The Dollar,* 99.

86. Paul Nitze, "Memorandum on the U.S. Balance of Payments," November 24, 1959, Box 1073, Pre-PP, JFKL.

87. House, *Trade Expansion Act,* 759–760.

88. Henry Kissinger, *The Troubled Partnership* (New York, 1965), 6–7.

89. Gregory F. Treverton, *The Dollar Drain and American Forces in Germany* (Athens, OH, 1978), 32; Solomon, *International Monetary System,* 36.

90. See, for example, Sproul Report, reprinted in Roosa, *The Dollar,* 283–284.

91. Acheson to Kennedy and Rusk, March 1961, Box 70, NSF, JFKL. For Acheson's role, see also Roswell Gilpatrick OH Interview, JFKL.

92. Gilpatrick OH Interview; Traverton, *Dollar Drain,* 10.

93. Heller to Kennedy, November 21, 1962, Box 16, Heller Papers.

94. Treverton, *Dollar Drain,* 32–33.

95. Memorandum of Conversation between Nitze and General Lavaud, March 13, 1962, Box 71, NSF, JFKL.

96. House, *Trade Expansion Act,* 2847; Hodges OH Interview.

97. Meeting of Inter-Departmental Committee of Under-Secretaries for

Foreign Economic Policy, December 22, 1961, Box 8, Behrman Papers; Emilio Collado before Economic Joint Committee, *American Foreign Economic Policy*, 203.

98. Emmerson to Rusk, December 7, 1962; Ball to Tokyo, December 14, 1962; Rusk to Embassies, March 23, 1963; Ambassador Thompson Memo, March 25, 1963; Bruce to Rusk, March 25, 1963; McGee to Ball, May 29, 1963; Bruce to Rusk, March 28, 1963; Reischauer to Rusk, May 8, 1963; Morris to Rusk, May 10, 1963; Farely to Rusk, May 21, 1963; Kohler to Rusk, May 31, 1963; Bruce to Rusk, May 17, 1963; Kohler to Rusk, July 22, 1963, all Box 223, NSF, JFKL.

99. Stebbins, *United States in World Affairs, 1963,* 107.

100. Allen Matusow, "Kennedy, the World Economy and the Decline of America," in J. Richard Snyder, ed., *John F. Kennedy* (Wilmington, DE, 1988), 111–122.

101. Robert Barnett Memorandum, June 5, 1962, Box 33, Gordon Papers. For American complaints about European and Japanese neo-mercantilism, see Douglass F. Lamont, *Forcing Our Hand* (Lexington, MA, 1986); Bruce Nussbaum, et al., *The Decline of American Power* (New York, 1980); Gordon K. Douglass, ed., *The New Interdependence* (Lexington, MA, 1979).

102. House, *Trade Expansion Act,* 4.

Chapter 3. Canada

1. Teno Roncalio OH Interview, JFKL.

2. On NORAD and the Arrow cancellation, see J.L. Granatstein, *Canada 1957–1967: The Years of Uncertainty and Innovation* (Toronto, 1986), 101–38; James Dow, *The Arrow* (Toronto, 1979).

3. See James M. Minifie, *Peacemaker or Powder-Monkey?* (Toronto, 1960.)

4. For one statement of economic nationalism, by the chair of the Royal Commission on Canada's Economic Prospects, see Walter Gordon, *Troubled Canada* (Toronto, 1961). The statistics are from F.H. Leacy, ed., *Historical Statistics of Canada* (Ottawa, 1983), G291–302, G401–14.

5. See especially the *Report of the Royal Commission on National Development in the Arts, Letters and Sciences* (Ottawa, 1951). For the formation of the Canada Council, see J.L. Granatstein, "Culture and Scholarship: The First Ten Years of the Canada Council," *Canadian Historical Review* LXV (December 1984), 441–74.

6. The best analysis remains John Meisel, *The Canadian General Election of 1957* (Toronto, 1962).

7. On 1958, see Granatstein, *Canada 1957–67,* pp. 35–38. On Diefenbaker after the victory, Peter Newman, *Renegade in Power* (Toronto, 1963), remains valuable.

8. On Diefenbaker's troubles, see Granatstein, *Canada 1957–1967,* pp. 62–100, and Robert Bothwell, et al., *Canada Since 1945: Power, Politics, and Provincialism* (Toronto, 1981), 197–99.

9. Still useful on defense procurement decisions is Jon B. McLin, *Canada's Changing Defense Policy, 1957–1963* (Baltimore, 1967).

10. See on Robertson and Green, J.L. Granatstein, *A Man of Influence: Norman A. Robertson and Canadian Statecraft, 1929–1968* (Ottawa, 1981), 322–63.

11. See Lt.-Gen. E.L.M. Burns, *A Seat at the Table: The Struggle for Disarmament* (Toronto, 1972). Burns led Canadian disarmament delegations from 1960 to 1968.

12. Howard Green OH Interview, York University Archives, Toronto.

13. Canada, House of Commons, Special Committee on Defence, *Minutes,* May 13, 1963, p. 510.

14. Canada, House of Commons *Debates,* February 20, 1959, p. 1223.

15. This was especially so because one of the main factors in the Eisenhower Administration's decision to continue Bomarc development had been Canada's choice of the SAM system. "Memo of Conversation with the President," June 10, 1959, Staff Notes, Whitman Files, DDEP, DDEL.

16. John G. Diefenbaker, *One Canada: The Memoirs of the Rt. Hon. John G. Diefenbaker* (Toronto, 1975–77; 3 vols.), III, 71.

17. Norman Robertson to Howard Green, February 14, 1961, vol. 3, Howard Green Papers, Public Archives of Canada, Ottawa (hereafter PAC).

18. Diary, August 30, 1960, vol. 2, Arnold Heeney Papers, PAC.

19. Heeney to Diefenbaker, February 20, 1961, vol. 15, U.S. Ambassador file, *ibid.*

20. Livingston Merchant OH Interview, JFKL.

21. Memorandum for the President, February 17, 1961, and attachments, Box 113, Canada Security 1961 file, POF, JFKP, JFKL. Howard Green in these notes was characterized much more harshly: "naive and almost parochial approach . . . self-righteousness and stubbornness . . . less flexible . . . almost pacifist attitude. . . ."

22. R.B. Bryce to Harkness, March 2, 1961, envelope 1, vol. 84, Douglas Harkness Papers, PAC; Memorandum, H.B. Robinson to Under Secretary, February 21, 1961, H.B. Robinson Papers, Historical Division, Department of External Affairs, Ottawa; Merchant OH Interview; Fred Dutton Memorandum for President, February 20, 1961, Canada 1961 file, Box 113, POF, JFKP.

23. Memorandum for Meeting with Prime Minister Diefenbaker, att. to Memorandum for the President, February 17, 1961, Canada Security 1961 file, *ibid.* On the February 1961 visit I have benefited from H. Basil Robinson's as yet unpublished "From Eisenhower to Kennedy." Robinson was External Affairs aide in the Prime Minister's Office.

24. "Trends in Canadian Foreign Policy," May 2, 1961, Canada Security 1961, box 113, Trip to Ottawa (D) file, POF, JFKP.

25. Telegram, External to Geneva, May 18, 1961, NATO and Nuclear Weapons file, vol. 8, Green Papers.

26. Donald M. Fleming, *So Very Near: The Political Memoirs of Donald M. Fleming,* Vol. II: *The Summit Years* (Toronto, 1985; 2 vols.), 586 reprints the memorandum.

27. Diary, March 18, 1962, vol. 2, Heeney Papers.

28. Fleming, *So Very Near,* II, 371–73. Fleming was Finance Minister in Diefenbaker's government.

29. House of Commons *Debates,* March 8, 1962, p. 1602. See also Ramesh

Thakur, *Peacekeeping in Vietnam* (Edmonton, 1984); James Eayrs, *In Defence of Canada,* Vol. V: *Indochina: Roots of Complicity* (Toronto, 1983), and especially Douglas Ross, *In the Interests of Peace* (Toronto, 1984).

30. See Victor Levant, *Quiet Complicity: Canadian Involvement in the Vietnam War* (Toronto, 1986), chaps. X–XII.

31. "The Cuban Situation," July 13, 1960, John Starnes Papers, Historical Division, Department of External Affairs, Ottawa; "Record of meeting on July 12–13, 1960," *ibid.*

32. March 12, 1961, *ibid.*

33. *Ibid.*

34. See H.H. Fowler to McG. Bundy, February 28, 1963, Treasury 2/63 file, Box 90, POF, JFKP.

35. Telegram, American Embassy, Ottawa, October 22, 1962, Box 20, NSF, JFKP.

36. "The Nuclear Arms Question and the Political Crisis Which Arose from It in January and February, 1963," August 19–27, 1963, file 2, vol. 14, Harkness Papers. A version of this document was printed in a number of Canadian newspapers. See *Ottawa Citizen,* October 22, 1977. See also Jocelyn Ghent, "Canada, the United States, and the Cuban Missile Crisis," *Pacific Historical Review* XVIII (May 1979), 159–84.

37. Air Marshal Slemon to Foulkes, March 3, 1965, NORAD Consultation file, Gen. Charles Foulkes Papers, Directorate of History, Department of National Defence, Ottawa.

38. "The Nuclear Arms Question," Harkness Papers. See also Jeffry V. Brock, *The Thunder and the Sunshine,* Vol. II: *With Many Voices* (Toronto, 1983; 2 vols.), 110, which attests to the Royal Canadian Navy's actions without authority from Ottawa.

39. Cabinet Conclusions, October 24, 1962, Cabinet Records, Privy Council Office, Ottawa; "Nuclear Arms Question," Harkness Papers.

40. See Robertson to Green, November 7, 1962, file 50309-40, Historical Division, Department of External Affairs.

41. Granatstein, *Man of Influence,* 352; Diefenbaker, *One Canada,* III, 83; Washington to External, October 23, 1962, file 2444-40, Historical Division, Department of External Affairs; House of Commons *Debates,* October 22, 1962.

42. See Peyton Lyon, *Canada in World Affairs 1961–1963* (Toronto, 1968), 52–54; Pierre Sevigny, *This Game of Politics* (Toronto, 1965), 253, 257.

43. See Granatstein, *Canada 1957–1967,* pp. 122–23.

44. Cabinet Conclusions, October 30, 1962, Cabinet Records; "Nuclear Arms Question," Harkness Papers; Jocelyn Ghent, "Did He Fall or Was He Pushed? The Kennedy Administration and the Fall of the Diefenbaker Government," *International History Review* I (April 1979), 246–70.

45. Canadian Joint Staff Washington to Chairman, Chiefs of Staff, February 14, 1963 (re talk with Paul Nitze), Defence Policy—Canada-US Relations file, Office of the Chief of the Defence Staff Records, Directorate of History, Department of National Defence.

46. Lyon, *World Affairs,* 130–36.

47. See J.T. Saywell, ed., *The Canadian Annual Review, 1963* (Toronto, 1964), 287. The most famous critique of Pearson's switch is Pierre-E. Trudeau, "Pearson où l'abdication de l'esprit," *Cité Libre* (avril 1963), 7.

49. House of Commons *Debates,* January 25, 1963, pp. 3125–28.

49. Lyon, *World Affairs,* 157–58.

50. Documents attached to Memorandum for Minister, February 1, 1963, and Robertson to Prime Minister, January 30, 1963, vol. 9, Green Papers.

51. Sorenson OH Interview.

52. Confidential interview.

53. Col. Burris to Vice-President Lyndon B. Johnson, February 6, 1963, No. (78)301E, DDRS.

54. Ghent, "Did He Fall?," 262.

55. Memorandum for Minister, February 7, 1963, file 50309-40, Historical Division, Department of External Affairs.

56. See Granatstein,, *Canada 1957–1967,* pp. 130–33.

57. Memorandum for Rusk, March 29, 1963, Canada Security 1963 file, Box 113, POF, JFKP; Lyon, *World Affairs,* 203–4.

58. Election 1963-Butterworth file, vol. 105, Gordon Churchill Papers, PAC; Churchill's mss "Recollections," chap. XII, which remained, before his death, in Churchill's possession; House of Commons *Debates,* May 27, 1963, pp. 319–22.

59. Butterworth to Lippmann, May 20, 1963, File 351, Box 59, Sec. III, Walter Lippmann Papers, Yale University Library, New Haven, CT.

60. See memorandum for Under Secretary, May 12, 1963, file 60, vol. 232, Paul Martin Papers, PAC.

61. Telegram, President to Prime Minister, April 22, 1963, Canada Security 1963 file, Box 113, POF, JFKP.

62. Nos. (78) 261C; (76) 54G; (76) 265D; (76) 54E; and (76) 54F, DDRS, originally from LBJL, constitute the U.S. briefing papers.

63. "Meeting Between the Prime Minister of Canada and the President of the United States, Hyannisport, Mass., May 10–11, 1963," vol. 232, Martin Papers.

64. Granatstein, *Canada 1957–1967,* pp. 276–79.

65. "Some Comments on the Budget," May 31, 1963, file LR76-549, Louis Rasminsky Papers, Bank of Canada Archives, Ottawa.

66. See memorandum for Mr. Pearson, May 7, 1963, file U-10, Walter Gordon Papers, Toronto (private collection).

67. "Discriminatory Measures in Canadian Budget," June 28, 1963, Box 19, NSF, JFKP; Butterworth Memo to McG. Bundy, July 16, 1963, *ibid.*

68. "Canadian Reaction to Proposed U.S. Balance of Payments Measures," July 19, 1963, Canada General file, Box 17, NSF, *ibid.* See also Paul Martin to Prime Minister, July 19, 1963, file 852.2 Conf., vol. 284, L.B. Pearson Papers, PAC.

69. Press Release, July 21, 1963, Office of the Minister of Finance, Ottawa.

70. "Meeting of Canadian and United States Officials . . . Washington, D.C., August 18, 1963," file LR76-5360-1, Rasminsky Papers.

71. Bundy to Secretary of State et al., November 11, 1963, Canada General file, Box 19, NSF, JFKP.

Chapter 4. Latin America

1. For Kennedy's speech, *DSB* XLIV (April 3, 1961), 471–74.
2. *DSB* XLIV (April 3, 1961), 474–78; *DSB* XLVI (January 29, 1962), 178–79.
3. Kennedy to President Víctor Paz Estenssoro of Bolivia, *DSB* XLIV (June 12, 1961), 920–21.
4. Text of Dillon's speech in *DSB* XLV (August 28, 1961), 356–60; Jerome Levinson and Juan de Onís, *The Alliance That Lost Its Way: A Critical Report on the Alliance for Progress* (Chicago, 1970), 59–73.
5. *DSB* XLIV (May 1, 1961), 617–21.
6. For economic aid, see U.S. Congress, Senate, Committee on Foreign Relations, *Foreign Assistance Act of 1962,* 87th Cong., 2nd sess. (Washington, DC, 1962), 19, 99; *DSB,* XLVIII (June 10, 1963), 920; Levinson and de Onís, *The Alliance,* 132–40.
7. For the international coffee agreement, see *DSB* XLVII (October 29, 1962), 667–68.
8. For United States-Cuban relations, see Chapter 5 in this volume.
9. Adolf Berle to Richard Goodwin, January 9, 1961, "Summary of Recommendations of Latin American Task Force," Latin America Task Force File, and Berle to Kennedy, July 7, 1961, Second Task Force Report File, both Box 94, Adolf A. Berle, Jr., Papers, Franklin D. Roosevelt Library, Hyde Park, NY.
10. Ball quoted in *DSB* XLIV (June 5, 1961), 864–68; Dillon quoted in Richard P. Stebbins, *The United States in World Affairs, 1961* (New York, 1962), 326.
11. Berle to Richard Goodwin, January 9, 1961, Latin America Task Force File, and Berle to Kennedy, July 7, 1961, Second Task Force Report File, both Box 94, Berle Papers.
12. Berle to Richard Goodwin, January 9, 1961, Latin American Task Force File, Box 94, Berle Papers; memorandum, Arthur Schlesinger to Kennedy, March 10, 1961, Latin American Report Folder, Box 14, Arthur M. Schlesinger, Jr., Papers, JFKL.
13. For direct investment, see U.S. Congress, Senate, Committee on Foreign Relations, Subcommittee on Multinational Corporations, *Multinational Corporations in Brazil and Mexico: Structural Sources of Economic and Noneconomic Power,* 94th Cong., 1st sess. (Washington, DC, 1975), 34–37; for trade, see U.S. Department of Commerce, Office of Business Economics, *Business Statistics, 1961* (Washington, DC, 1961), 106–13.
14. "General Considerations," in Statement of United States Policy toward Latin America (draft), November 15, 1960, United States Policy toward Latin America (1) Folder, Box 12, Briefing Notes Subseries, NSC Series, OSANSA, DDEL.
15. Dwight D. Eisenhower, *The White House Years,* II, *Waging Peace,*

1956–1961 (Garden City, NY, 1965), 539; Milton Eisenhower, *The Wine Is Bitter* (Garden City, NY, 1963), 161–63, 248–51. For an analysis of this issue, see Stephen G. Rabe, *Eisenhower and Latin America: The Foreign Policy of Anticommunism* (Chapel Hill, NC, 1988), 134–52.

16. Memorandum, Richard Goodwin to Kennedy, March 14, 1962, in Arthur M. Schlesinger, Jr., "The Alliance for Progress: A Retrospective," in Ronald G. Hellman and H. Jon Rosenbaum, eds., *Latin America; The Search for a New International Role* (New York, 1975), 91–92; R. Harrison Wagner, *United States Policy Toward Latin America* (Stanford, CA, 1970), 41.

17. "General Considerations," in Statement of United States Policy toward Latin America (draft), November 15, 1960, United States Policy toward Latin America (1) Folder, Box 12, Briefing Notes Subseries, NSC Series, OSANSA, DDEL.

18. Robert M. Smetherman and Bobbie B. Smetherman, "The Alliance for Progress: Promises Unfulfilled," *American Journal of Economics and Sociology* XXXI (January 1972), 79–86; Heliodoro Gonzalez (pen name), "The Failure of the Alliance for Progress in Colombia," *Inter-American Economic Affairs* XXIII (Summer 1969), 87–96; Simon G. Hanson, *Dollar Diplomacy Modern Style: Chapters in the Failure of the Alliance for Progresss* (Washington, 1970), 1–16; Víctor Alba, *Alliance Without Allies: The Mythology of Progress in Latin America* (New York, 1965), 1–74; Levinson and de Onís, *The Alliance*, 5–13, 23.

19. Edwin Lieuwen, *Generals vs. Presidents: Neo-Militarism in Latin America* (New York, 1964), 10–68.

20. Quoted in Senate, *Foreign Assistance Act of 1962*, p. 388; *DSB* XLIV (April 3, 1961), 475.

21. For Kennedy Administration on population control, see U.S. Congress, Senate, Committee on Foreign Relations, *Executive Sessions of the Senate Foreign Relations Committee (Historical Series), 1961*, Vol. XIII, 87th Cong., 1st sess. (Washington, DC, 1984), 432–40.

22. Levinson and de Onís, *The Alliance*, 10.

23. Memorandum, Schlesinger to Kennedy, March 10, 1961, Latin America Report Folder, Box 14, Schlesinger Papers, JFKL; Lincoln Gordon OH (1981), JFKL; Report of Task Force on Immediate Latin American Problems, January 1961, Latin America Folder, Box 1074, PrePP, JFKL; Rostow to Kennedy on "Economic Development Decade," March 2, 1961, Latin American Folder (3/1/61–3/7/61), Box 215, NSF, JFKL; W.W. Rostow, *The Stages of Economic Growth: A Non-Communist Manifesto* (New York, 1960); W.W. Rostow, "Guerrilla Warfare in Underdeveloped Areas," in Marcus G. Raskin and Bernard B. Fall, eds., *The Viet-Nam Reader* (New York, 1965), 108–16. A key scholarly exposition of the "middle-class revolution" thesis is John Johnson, *Political Change in Latin America: The Growth of the Middle Sectors* (Stanford, CA, 1958).

24. Lars Schoultz, *Human Rights and United States Policy Toward Latin America* (Princeton, 1981), 5–16; Guillermo A. O'Donnell, *Modernization and Bureaucratic Authoritarianism: Studies in South American Politics* (Berkeley, CA, 1973), 89–95.

25. Thomas Mann OH, DDEL. For Kennedy's view of history, see Thomas G. Paterson, "Bearing the Burden: A Critical Look at JFK's Foreign Policy," *The Virginia Quarterly Review* LIV (Spring 1978), 196–201.

26. Robert Packenham, *Liberal America and the Third World: Political Development Ideas in Foreign Aid and Social Science* (Princeton, 1973), 34–35, 59–75, 111–60.

27. *DSB* XLIX (December 9, 1963), 900–904.

28. Schlesinger, "The Alliance for Progress," 57–92.

29. Quoted in "A Biographer's Perspective," in Kenneth W. Thompson, ed., *The Kennedy Presidency* (New York, 1985), 35; David Rockefeller, "What Private Enterprise Means to Latin America," *Foreign Affairs* XLIV (April 1966), 403–16.

30. Eduardo Frei Montalva, "The Alliance That Lost Its Way," *Foreign Affairs* XLV (April 1967), 437–38. See also Ambassador to Chile Ralph Dungan OH, LBJL; Ambassador to El Salvador Murat Williams OH, JFKL.

31. Official quoted is Lincoln Gordon. Gordon OH. For other arguments that the Johnson Administration did not alter the Alliance, see AID Administrator William Gaud OH, and Assistant Secretary of State Covey Oliver OH, both LBJL.

32. Berle to Kennedy, July 7, 1961, Second Task Force Report File, Box 94, Berle Papers.

33. John Bartlow Martin, *Overtaken by Events: The Dominican Crisis from the Fall of Trujillo to the Civil War* (Garden City, NY, 1966), 64–301; Arthur M. Schlesinger, Jr., *A Thousand Days: John F. Kennedy in the White House* (Boston, 1965), 769–73. For a critical account, see Piero Gleijeses, *The Dominican Crisis: The 1965 Constitutionalist Revolt and American Intervention* (Baltimore, MD, 1978), 30–106. For the possible roles of President Kennedy and the CIA in the assassination of Trujillo, see U.S. Congress, Senate, Select Committee to Study Governmental Operations with Respect to Intelligence Activities, *Alleged Assassination Plots Involving Foreign Leaders*, Senate Report No. 465, 94th Cong., 1st sess. (Washington, DC, 1975), 209–15, 262–63.

34. Ambassador to Costa Rica Raymond Telles OH, JFKL; Stephen G. Rabe, *The Road to OPEC: United States Relations with Venezuela, 1919–1976* (Austin, TX, 1982), 144–50.

35. *DSB* XLVII (August 6, 1962), 213–14; *DSB* XLVII (September 3, 1962), 348–49; Schlesinger, *A Thousand Days*, 787–88.

36. Assistant Secretary of State Edwin M. Martin OH, JFKL; Schlesinger, *A Thousand Days*, 787–88; Lieuwen, *Generals vs. Presidents*, 116–18.

37. Schlesinger, *A Thousand Days*, 773; Martin OH; Juan Bosch OH, JFKL.

38. Theodore C. Sorensen, *Kennedy* (New York, 1965), 536.

39. Martin OH; Jonathan V. Van Cleve, "The Latin American Policy of President Kennedy: A Reexamination Case: Peru," *Inter-American Economic Affairs* XXX (Spring 1977), 29–44.

40. Testimony of Secretary Dean Rusk in U.S. Congress, Senate, Committee on Foreign Relations, *Executive Sessions of the Foreign Relations Committee (Historical Series), 1962*, Vol. XIV, 87th Cong., 2nd sess. (Washington,

DC, 1986), 691, 760; Ambassador to Argentina Robert McClintock to Rusk, March 28, 1962, Argentina Security, 1961–1963 Folder, Box 111, POF, JFKL; *DSB* XLVII (August 13, 1962), 253–54.

41. Lieuwen, *Generals vs. Presidents,* 117–18; Levinson and de Onís, *The Alliance,* 83–85.

42. Charles Burrows OH, JFKL.

43. *DSB* XLIX (November 4, 1963), 698–700.

44. Martin OH; Sorensen, *Kennedy,* 535–36. See also Kennedy's news conference of November 14, 1963, *PPP, JFK, 1963* (Washington, DC, 1964), 851.

45. Rusk quoted in Senate, *Executive Sessions, 1961,* XIII, p. 210; Ambassador to Haiti Raymond Thurston OH, JFKL; De Lesseps Morrison, *Latin American Mission: An Adventure in Hemisphere Democracy* (New York, 1965), 191–92. By 1963, however, the Kennedy Administration was restricting economic aid to Haiti to protest Duvalier's violations of human rights. See National Security Action Memorandum No. 246, "Future Policy Toward Haiti," May 23, 1963, NSF: Memoranda and Meetings Series, NSAM #246 Folder, Box 341, JFKL.

46. Memorandum of conversation between Kennedy, Martin, and Ambassador to Chile Charles Cole, August 3, 1962; Taylor Belcher (DS) to Martin on Recommendations of Ambassador Cole, January 8, 1963; and "Review of U.S. Policy in Regard to 1964 Election and American Copper Companies," January 10, 1963, all in NSF: Brubeck Series, Chile Folder, Box 384, JFKL; Charles Cole OH, JFKL; U.S. Congress, Senate, Select Committee to Study Governmental Operations with Respect to Intelligence Activities, *Covert Action in Chile, 1963–1973: Staff Report,* 94th Cong., 1st sess. (Washington, DC, 1975), 4–19, 57. For CIA covert activities in Ecuador, see Philip Agee, *Inside the Company: CIA Diary* (New York, 1975), 147–316.

47. Testimony of General William Enemark, Director of Western Hemisphere Region, and other Defense Department officers in Senate, *Foreign Assistance Act of 1962,* pp. 406–20; Rusk to American Embassy in Santiago on Kennedy's talks with Khrushchev, June 26, 1961, NSF: CO: Chile, Box 20, JFKL.

48. Senate, *Executive Sessions, 1961,* XIII, 185; Sherman Kent to CIA Director John McCone, April 22, 1963, "Cuba—A Year Hence," NSF: Meetings and Memoranda Series, Standing Group Meeting Folder, Box 315, JFKL.

49. Rabe, *Road to OPEC,* 152–54.

50. L.L. Lemnitzer, Chairman, Joint Chiefs of Staff, to President Kennedy, "Training of Police and Armed Forces of Latin America," May 19, 1961, POF: Countries, Latin America Security, Box 121A, JFKL; NSAM #114, "Review of Internal Security Programs," November 2, 1961, NSF: Memoranda and Meetings Series, NSAM #114 Folder, Box 332, JFKL; NSC memorandum to Kennedy on counter-insurgency efforts, March 22, 1962, NSF: Memoranda and Meetings Series, Special Group Folder (1/61–6/62), Box 319, JFKL; Robert Kennedy to President, September 11, 1961, NSF: Memoranda and Meetings Series, NSAM #88 Folder, Box 331, JFKL; NSAM #177, "Establishment of Police Assistance Programs," August 7,

1962, NSF: Memoranda and Meetings Series, NSAM #177 Folder, Box 338, JFKL.

51. "Summary of Training for Latin Americans in U.S. Military Schools and Institutions," October 16, 1961, and Chester Bowles to Kennedy, "Report on Police Training in Latin America," September 30, 1961, both in NSF: Memoranda and Meetings Series, NSAM #88 Folder, Box 331, JFKL; Schoultz, *Human Rights,* 179–83, 211–47.

52. MacNamara testimony in Senate, *Foreign Assistance Act of 1962,* pp. 60, 76; testimony of General Enemark, Senate, *Executive Sessions, 1962,* XIV, 433.

53. Bowles to Kennedy, September 30, 1961; NSF: Memoranda and Meetings Series, NSAM #88 Folder, Box 331, JFKL.

54. Office of Assistant Secretary of Defense, International Security Affairs, "U.S. Policies Toward Latin American Military Forces," February 25, 1965, Vol. III (1–6/65), and memorandum, Robert Sayre to Bundy, October 8, 1964, Vol. II (9–12/64), both in Box 2, NSC (Latin America-Country) Files, LBJL.

55. Lieuwen, *Generals vs. Presidents,* 127; U.S. Congress, Senate, Committee on Foreign Relations, *Foreign Assistance Act of 1963,* 88th Cong., 1st sess. (Washington, DC, 1963), 206–8. The Kennedy Administration actually discouraged Bosch from purging his security forces of Trujillist elements. See Briefing Memorandum for the President, "Principal Problems Confronting Dr. Bosch," January 2, 1963, Box 115A, POF, JFKL.

56. Burrows OH; Williams OH.

57. Memorandum of conversation, Kennedy and Brazilian Foreign Minister Clemente Mariani, May 16, 1961; CIA, Office of Current Intelligence, memorandum, "Communist Inroads in Brazil," September 27, 1961; memorandum of conversation, Gordon and President Goulart, January 13, 1962, all in NSF: CO: Brazil, Box 12, JFKL.

58. Standing Group on Brazil, "Proposed Short-Term Policy for Meeting of Standing Group on Brazil," September 30, 1963; NSF: CO: Brazil, Folder (10/1–1/15/63), Box 14A, JFKL; Jan Knippers Black, *United States Penetration of Brazil* (Philadelphia, PA, 1977), 138–78.

59. For the United States role in the overthrow of Goulart, see Black, *United States Penetration of Brazil,* 37–56; Phyllis R. Parker, *Brazil and the Quiet Intervention, 1964* (Austin, TX, 1979).

68. Martin OH; memorandum of conversation, Kennedy and Celso Furtado, Director of Brazilian Development Agency, SUDENE, July 14, 1961, NSF: CO: Brazil, Box 12, JFKL.

61. *DSB* XLVII (July 23, 1962), 137–38.

62. Burrows OH; Levinson and de Onís, *The Alliance,* 224–54. See also "An Evaluation of the Alliance for Progress in Costa Rica—A Country Team Report," in Ambassador Raymond Telles to SD, August 21, 1963, NSF: CO: Costa Rica, Box 35, JFKL.

63. Memorandum of conversation, Kennedy and Furtado, July 14, 1961, and memorandum of conversation, Goulart and Gordon, October 22, 1961, both in NSF: CO: Brazil, Box 12, JFKL; Riordan Roett, *The Politics of Foreign Aid in the Brazilian Northeast* (Nashville, 1972), 70, 92–93.

64. Roett, *Politics of Foreign Aid*, 112–38, 170. See also Ruth Leacock, "JFK, Business, and Brazil," *Hispanic American Historical Review* LIX (November 1979), 636–73.

65. Draft memorandum by Martin on "Problems of Alliance," 1963, Alliance for Progress Folder, Box 1, Schlesinger Papers.

66. *PPP, JFK, 1963*, p. 458.

67. Chester Bowles OH, JFKL.

68. Schlesinger, "The Alliance for Progress," 59; Jerome Slater, "Democracy Versus Stability: The Recent Latin American Policy of the United States," *Yale Review* LV (December 1965), 175. See also Abraham F. Lowenthal, "United States Policy Toward Latin America: 'Liberal,' 'Radical,' and 'Bureaucratic' Perspectives," *Latin American Research Review* VIII (Spring 1974), 3–25.

Chapter 5. Cuba

1. Quoted in Thomas Powers, *The Man Who Kept the Secrets* (New York, 1981), 174.

2. Richard Bissell in Peter Collier and David Horowitz, *The Kennedys* (New York, 1984), 278.

3. Claude Pepper to Kennedy, April 27, 1962, Box 23-G-4-2F, Senatorial Files, Hubert H. Humphrey Papers, Minnesota Historical Society, St. Paul, MN.

4. Paul Miller, "Confidential Memorandum—Conversation with President Kennedy," March 13, 1963, Box 48, Gridiron Club Records, LC.

5. Quoted in U.S. Senate, Select Committee to Study Governmental Operations with Respect to Intelligence Activities, *Alleged Assassination Plots Involving Foreign Leaders: An Interim Report* (Washington, DC, 1975), 142n.

6. See, for example, Ernest R. May, "Writing Contemporary International History," *Diplomatic History* VIII (Spring 1984), 105.

7. A 1968 comment in Harris Wofford, *Of Kennedys and Kings* (New York, 1980), 426.

8. William Attwood, *The Twilight Struggle: Tales of the Cold War* (New York, 1987), 257.

9. Theodore C. Sorensen, *Kennedy* (New York, 1965), 306; Frank Mankiewicz and Kirby Jones, *With Fidel* (New York, 1975), 145.

10. Kennedy to Elizabeth Swank, January 29, 1959, Box 717, Senate Files, PrePP, JFKL; Kennedy to C.A. Nolan, April 25, 1959, *ibid.;* John F. Kennedy, *The Strategy of Peace*, Allan Nevins, ed. (New York, 1960), 132.

11. U.S. Department of State, *Cuba* (Washington, DC, 1961); *PPP, JFK, 1961*, p. 369; Memorandum for the President, "Latin American Program," 1961, Box 121, POF, JFKL. Theodore Draper popularized the "betrayal" theme in his *Castro's Revolution* (New York, 1962) and *Castroism* (New York, 1965).

12. Richard N. Goodwin, *The American Condition* (Garden City, NY, 1974), 256.

13. Adolf A. Berle, *Latin America—Diplomacy and Reality* (New York, 1962), 77.

14. *CR* CIX (May 20, 1963), 8986.

15. Quoted in Kent M. Beck, "Necessary Lies, Hidden Truths: Cuba in the 1960 Campaign," *Diplomatic History* VIII (Winter 1984), 45.

16. Quoted in Arthur M. Schlesinger, Jr., *A Thousand Days* (Boston, 1965), 224.

17. Robert Anderson in Memorandum, January 19, 1961, Box 11, Postpresidential, Augusta, Georgia . . . Papers, DDEP, DDEL.

18. For American interest groups and Cuba, see Richard E. Welch, Jr., *Response to Revolution: The United States and the Cuban Revolution, 1959–1961* (Chapel Hill, NC, 1985).

19. "Notes on National Security Council Meeting, 15 November 1961," Box 4, VPSF, LBJL.

20. Arthur M. Schlesinger, Jr., Memorandum for the President, March 3, 1961, Box 65, Schlesinger Staff Memoranda, POF, JFKL.

21. Carlos Franqui, *Family Portrait with Fidel* (New York, 1984), 73.

22. Quoted in Cole Blasier, *The Hovering Giant: U.S. Responses to Revolutionary Change in Latin America* (Pittsburgh, PA, 1975), 185.

23. Quoted in Drew Pearson to Lyndon B. Johnson, May 24, 1964, Box G265, Drew Pearson Papers, LBJL.

24. Jorge I. Domínguez, *Cuba: Order and Revolution* (Cambridge, MA, 1978), 68, 149.

25. William D. Pawley, "Memoirs" (unpublished manuscript, Coral Gables, FL, n.d.), ch. 19; U.S. Senate, Committee on the Judiciary, *Communist Threat to the United States through the Caribbean,* Part 10: *Testimony of William D. Pawley* (Washington, DC, 1960), 739; Justo Carrillo, "Vision and Revision: U.S.-Cuban Relations, 1902 to 1959," in Jaime Suchlicki et al., eds., *Cuba: Continuity and Change* (Miami, FL, 1985), 166.

26. "Why the Cuban Revolution of 1958 Led to Cuba's Alignment with the USSR," February 21, 1961, CIA Records (FOIA).

27. For 1959–1961, see Stephen G. Rabe, *Eisenhower and Latin America* (Chapel Hill, NC, 1988); Stephen E. Ambrose with Richard H. Immerman, *Ike's Spies* (Garden City, NY, 1981), 303–316; Welch, *Response;* Blasier, *Hovering Giant;* Louis A. Pérez, Jr., *Cuba* (New York, 1988).

28. Bonsal to Secretary of State, November 6, 1959, 611.37/11-659, Box 2473, DSR, NA; Eisenhower quoted in Trumbull Higgins, *The Perfect Failure: Kennedy, Eisenhower, and the CIA at the Bay of Pigs* (New York, 1987), 48.

29. Memorandum for the President, "Current Basic United States Policy Toward Cuba," November 5, 1959, 611.37/11-559, Box 2474, DSR.

30. Quoted in Wayne S. Smith, *The Closest of Enemies* (New York, 1987), 64.

31. Philip W. Bonsal, *Cuba, Castro, and the United States* (Pittsburgh, PA, 1971), 192.

32. *Washington Post,* April 23, 1963.

33. Memorandum of meeting with the President, January 3, 1961, Box 22, OSANSA, WHOF, DDEL; Memorandum of conversation with Dean Rusk,

January 3, 1961, Box 10, Christian Herter Papers, DDEL; Memorandum by A. J. Goodpaster, January 5, 1961, Box 4, International Series, Office of the Staff Secretary, WHOF, DDEL.

34. For the Bay of Pigs, see Peter Wyden, *Bay of Pigs* (New York, 1979); Higgins, *Perfect Failure;* Gabriel Molina, *Diario de Girón* (La Habana, 1983); Haynes Johnson, *The Bay of Pigs* (New York, 1964); Karl Meyer and Tad Szulc, *The Cuban Invasion* (New York, 1962); Lucien S. Vandenbroucke, "Anatomy of a Failure: The Decision to Land at the Bay of Pigs," *Political Science Quarterly* XCIX (Fall 1984), 471–491.

35. Quoted in Herbert Parmet, *JFK* (New York, 1983), 159.

36. Discussion on Cuba, March 11, 1961, National Security Action Memorandum No. 31, Box 329, NSF, JFKL; Dulles in Schlesinger, *A Thousand Days*, 242.

37. Department of State, *Cuba*.

38. Quoted in Sorensen, *Kennedy*, 309.

39. *Ibid.*, 297.

40. Louis Halle to Walter Lippmann, May 3, 1961, Box 75, Walter Lippmann Papers, Yale University Library.

41. U.S. Senate, Committee on Foreign Relations, *Executive Sessions, 1961: Historical Series*, XIII, Part 1 (Washington, DC, 1984), 445; Roger Hilsman, *To Move a Nation* (New York, 1967), 32; Welch, *Response*, 72: Sorensen, *Kennedy*, 306.

42. Allen Dulles in *Meet the Press No. 61*, V (December 31, 1961); Sherman Kent, "Is Time on Our Side," memorandum for the Director, March 10, 1961, CIA Records (FOIA); Senate, *Executive Sessions, 1961*, XIII, Part 1, p. 401; Allen Dulles, *The Craft of Intelligence* (New York, 1963), 169.

43. Richard M. Bissell, Jr., OH Interview, OH Project, Columbia University, New York; Bissell, "Response to Lucien S. Vandenbroucke, 'Confessions of Allen Dulles,'" *Diplomatic History* VIII (Fall 1984), 379–380; Senate, *Executive Sessions, 1961*, XIII, Part 1, p. 392.

44. For these and other operational failures, see Senate, *Executive Sessions, 1961*, XIII, Part 1, pp. 342, 412; Bissell OH Interview; Lyman B. Kirkpatrick, "Paramilitary Case Study: The Bay of Pigs," *Naval War College Review* II (December 1972), 39; Tad Szulc, *Fidel* (New York, 1986), 550–551; Barton J. Bernstein, "Kennedy and the Bay of Pigs Revisited—Twenty Four Years Later," *Foreign Service Journal* LXII (March 1985), 32; Hilsman, *To Move*, 78; "Comments by Fidel Castro, 14 and 15 June, on the Invasion of 17 April 1961," Maxwell Taylor Papers, National Defense University, Washington, DC; Welch, *Response*, 80–81; CIA, Report No. 00-K-3/187,928, "Experiences Just Before, During, and After the 17 Apr 1961 Invasion Attempt," June 5, 1961, No. 1977 (12D), DDRS.

45. Interview with Richard Bissell by Lucien Vandenbroucke, May 18, 1984. See also Senate, *Alleged Assassination Plots;* Thomas Powers, "Inside the Department of Dirty Tricks," *Atlantic Monthly* CCXLIV (August 1979), 40.

46. Charles J. V. Murphy, "Cuba: The Record Set Straight," *Fortune* LXIV (September 1961), 92ff; Hanson Baldwin OH Interview, U.S. Naval Institute, Annapolis, MD; Allen W. Dulles to L. Paul Bremer III, April 28,

1965, Box 138, Allen Dulles Papers, Princeton University Library, Princeton, NJ; "Interview Between Paul D. Bethel . . . and Orlando Cuervo of Cuban Brigade 2506," January 30, 1963, Kenneth Keating Papers, University of Rochester Library, Rochester, NY; Bissell OH Interview; *Time* CXXIX (June 1, 1987), 29.

47. "Comments by Fidel Castro;" Bissell OH Interview.

48. Vandenbroucke, "Anatomy," 475; Joseph B. Smith, *Portrait of a Cold Warrior* (New York, 1976), 324.

49. Robert Jervis, *Perception and Misperception in International Relations* (Princeton, NJ, 1976), 356–406; Vandenbroucke, "Anatomy," 488–489.

50. Kirkpatrick, "Paramilitary," 41.

51. Admiral Arleigh Burke OH Interview #4, U.S. Naval Institute. See also Maxwell Taylor, *Swords and Plowshares* (New York, 1972), 188–189; Robert Dennison OH Interview#8, U.S. Naval Institute; Vandenbroucke, "Anatomy," 477; Jeffrey G. Barlow, "President John F. Kennedy and His Joint Chiefs of Staff" (Ph.D. dissertation, University of South Carolina, 1981), 177–200.

52. Dean Rusk, "Reflections on Foreign Policy," in Kenneth W. Thompson, ed., *The Kennedy Presidency* (Lanham, MD, 1985), 195. See also Warren I. Cohen, *Dean Rusk* (Totowa, NJ, 1980), 96–115.

53. Bonsal, *Cuba, Castro,* 179; Smith, *Closest,* 69.

54. Arthur M. Schlesinger, Jr., Memorandum for the President, "Joseph Newman on Cuba," March 31, 1961, Countries, POF, JFKL; Schlesinnger, "Howard Handleman on Cuba," *ibid.;* Schlesinger, *A Thousand Days,* 252–256.

55. J. William Fulbright, "Cuba Policy," March 29, 1961, Box 38, File 1, Series 48:14, J. William Fulbright Papers, University of Arkansas Library, Fayetteville; Schlesinger, *A Thousand Days,* 252.

56. Clayton Fritchey in Wyden, *Bay of Pigs,* 183n.

57. Ellis O. Briggs, *Farewell to Foggy Bottom* (New York, 1964), 192.

58. Schlesinger, *A Thousand Days,* 254; Bonsal, *Cuba, Castro,* 184–186.

59. Chester Bowles, "Notes on Cuban Crisis," May 1961, Box 392, Diary, Bowles Papers. Also, Bowles to the President, April 20, 1961, Box 297, *ibid.*

60. Memorandum, June 5, 1961, Box 10, Post-presidential Papers, DDEP, DDEL; "Off-the-Record Breakfast with Nixon . . . April 21, [1961]," Box 65, Schlesinger Staff Memoranda, POF, JFKL.

61. Wofford, *Of Kennedys,* 341.

62. *PPP, JFK, 1961,* pp. 304–306.

63. Taylor, *Swords,* 200.

64. On Laos, see "Background Dinner with Arthur Schlesinger, Jr.," May 10, 1961, Box 1, Robert H. Estabrook Papers, JFKL; Herbert L. Matthews, "Talk with Kennedy," July 2, 1962, Box 27, Herbert L. Matthews Papers, Columbia University Library. Quotation in Draft Record of Action, 478th NSC Meeting, April 22, 1961, Box 4, VPSF, LBJL.

65. Walt W. Rostow, *The Diffusion of Power* (New York, 1972), 210–211.

66. *Operation ZAPATA: The "Ultrasensitive" Report and Testimony of the Board of Inquiry on the Bay of Pigs* (Frederick, MD, 1981), 51–52.

67. Quoted in Taylor Branch and George Crile III, "The Kennedy Ven-

detta: How the CIA Waged a Silent War Against Cuba," *Harper's Magazine* CCLI (August 1975), 50.

68. CIA, Report No. CS-3/474,882, "Reaction Within Cuba to Attempt to Overthrow Castro Regime," May 19, 1961, No. 1977 (12C), DDRS; CIA, "Experiences"; CIA, Staff Memoranda No. 23-61, April 28, 1961, CIA Records, (FOIA); Justo Carrillo to Jose Miro Cardona, September 30, 1961, Box 23, Theodore Draper Papers, Hoover Institution Archives, Stanford, CA; NSC Action Memorandum No. 2413-C, May 4, 1961, Box 4, VPSF, LBJL; *New York Times*, July 17, 1961.

69. CIA, "The Situation and Prospects in Cuba," NIE 85-62, March 21, 1962, Box 9, National Intelligence Estimates, NSF, LBJL.

70. *Operation ZAPATA*, 52. For propaganda, see Edward R. Murrow (USIA) to the President, "Our Latin American Program," May 15, 1961, Box 121, POF, JFKL.

71. Quoted in Schlesinger, *Robert Kennedy*, 476.

72. Quoted in Senate, *Alleged Assassination Plots*, 139.

73. Branch and Crile, "Kennedy Vendetta," 52.

74. Schlesinger, *Robert Kennedy*, 481–498.

75. Quoted in Senate, *Alleged Assassination Plots*, 148–150.

76. Morris Morley, *Imperial State and Revolution: The United States and Cuba, 1952–1987* (New York, 1987), 191–203, 367–374; Domínguez, *Cuba*, 148; Margaret P. Doxey, *Economic Sanctions and International Enforcement* (New York, 1980), 39; *PPP, JFK, 1962*, p. 106; Gary C. Hufbauer and Jeffrey J. Schott, *Economic Sanctions Reconsidered* (Washington, DC, 1985), 315–323; Donald Losman, "The Embargo of Cuba: An Economic Appraisal," *Caribbean Studies* XIV (October 1974), 95–120; U.S. Department of State, "Success of the Economic Boycott," Draft Update to White Paper on Cuba, n.d. (but probably 1964), DSR (FOIA); CIA, "Situation and Prospects in Cuba"; Anna P. Schreiber, "Economic Coercion as an Instrument of Foreign Policy," *World Politics* XXV (April 1973), 387–405; Robin Renwick, *Economic Sanctions* (Cambridge, MA, 1981), 64–66; Interview with John Crimmins by Thomas G. Paterson, Washington, DC, February 4, 1985.

77. Bryce N. Harlow, Memorandum for the Record, March 4, 1960, Box 47, Staff Notes, DDE Diary Series, Whitman File, DDEP.

78. Christian A. Herter, Memorandum for the President, "Status of Possible OAS Action on Cuba," March 17, 1960, Box 10, Dulles-Herter Series, *ibid.*

79. Delesseps S. Morrison, *Latin American Mission* (New York, 1965), 152–197; Morley, *Imperial State*, 155–162.

80. Szulc, *Fidel*, 574.

81. *PPP, JFK, 1962*, p. 911; Milton S. Eisenhower, *The Wine Is Bitter* (Garden City, NY, 1963), 274–295; Diary, James B. Donovan Papers, Hoover Institution Archives; Rudolf A. Clemens, "Prisoners Exchange" (unpublished manuscript by Red Cross officer, Washington, DC, n.d.).

82. Richard N. Goodwin, "Annals of Politics: A Footnote," *The New Yorker* XLIV (May 25, 1968), 94.

83. Goodwin quoted in memorandum for the President, August 22, 1961,

Box 115, POF, JFKL; Schlesinger, *Robert Kennedy,* 542n; Goodwin, "Annals," p. 110.

84. Quoted in Mankiewicz and Jones, *With Fidel,* 150.

85. See, for example, Arnold Horelick, "The Cuban Missile Crisis: An Analysis of Soviet Calculations and Behavior," *World Politics* XVI (April 1964), 363–389; John L. Gaddis, *Russia, the Soviet Union, and the United States* (New York, 1978), 236–237; David Detzer, *The Brink* (New York, 1979), 41, 49; Graham Allison, *Essence of Decision* (Boston, 1971), 52–56.

86. Herbert S. Dinerstein, *The Making of a Missile Crisis: October 1962* (Baltimore, MD, 1976), 155–156, 186–187.

87. Lee Lockwood, *Castro's Cuba, Cuba's Fidel* (New York, 1969), 224; Mankiewicz and Jones, *With Fidel,* 152.

88. Quoted in J. Anthony Lukacs, "Class Reunion: Kennedy's Men Relive the Cuban Missile Crisis," *New York Times Magazine,* August 30, 1987, p. 27.

89. U Thant, "Summary of My Meeting . . . ," October 30, 1962, DAG-1/5.2.2.6.2-1, United Nations Archives, New York. See also Foreign Broadcast Information Service, "Radio Propaganda Report: Castro on Normalization of U.S.-Cuban Relations," March 2, 1964, Box 21, Country File-Cuba, NSF, LBJL; Anatolii A. Gromyko, "The Caribbean Crisis," *Soviet Law and Government* XL (No. 1, 1972), 3–53; Nikita Khrushchev, *Khrushchev Remembers* (Boston, 1970), 492–496; Herbert L. Matthews, "Return to Cuba," *Hispanic American Report,* special issue (1964), pp. 15–16; Szulc, *Fidel,* 578–580.

90. CIA, "The Military Build-up in Cuba," No. 85-3-62, CIA Records (FOIA). See also Thomas Mann to Secretary of State, Telegram 761, September 761, September 6, 1962, NSF, JFKL.

91. Department of State Airgram CA-3675, October 5, 1962, Box 43, Series B, Wayne Morse Papers, University of Oregon Library, Eugene, OR. See also Colonel Burris to the Vice President, October 2, 1962, Box 6, VPSF, LBJL.

92. "Evidence of a Soviet Commitment to Defend Cuba," OCI No. 2428/62, October 19, 1962, Box 51, NSF, JFKL.

93. Thomas L. Hughes to Acting Secretary of State, "Daniel's Conversation with Castro," December 13, 1963, Box 23-F-1-2F, Humphrey Papers.

94. Servando Gonzalez, "The Great Deception: Nikita Khrushchev and the Cuban Missile Crisis," undated paper by former Cuban army officer, Servando Gonzalez Papers, Hoover Institution Archives.

95. Mohamed H. Heikal, *The Cairo Documents* (Garden City, NY, 1973), 142, 148.

96. Quoted in Allison, *Essence,* 193.

97. *PPP, JFK, 1962,* p. 674.

98. "Off-the-Record Meeting on Cuba," 11:50 A.M.–12:57 P.M., October 16, 1962, transcript, Presidential Recordings, JFKL.

99. "Off-the-Record Meeting on Cuba," 6:30–7:55 P.M., *ibid.*

100. James M. Grimwood and Frances Strowd, "History of the Jupiter Missile System," July 27, 1962, U.S. Army Ordnance Missile Command, copy in National Security Archive, Washington, DC; Raymond L. Garthoff,

Reflections on the Cuban Missile Crisis (Washington, DC, 1987), 37, 43n; Barton J. Bernstein, "The Cuban Missile Crisis; Trading the Jupiters in Turkey?" *Political Science Quarterly* XCV (Spring 1980), 97–125.

101. Quoted in Lukacs, "Class Reunion," 58.

102. Much of what follows draws upon the "minutes" of Ex Comm meetings, Box 316, Meetings and Memoranda, NSF, JFKL, and Box 8, VPSF, LBJL.

103. Robert S.. McNamara, "Notes on October 21, 1962 Meeting with the President," National Security Archive. See also Robert F. Kennedy, *Thirteen Days* (New York, 1969), 31.

104. "Off-the-Record Meeting on Cuba," 6:30–7:55 P.M., October 16, 1962; George W. Ball to Thomas G. Paterson, December 17, 1984; Allison, *Essence,* 201–202.

105. Charles E. Bohlen, *Witness to History, 1929–1969* (New York, 1973), 489–492.

106. Quoted in John B. Martin, *Adlai Stevenson and the World* (Garden City, NY, 1977), 721–722.

107. *PPP, JFK, 1962,* pp. 806–809.

108. U.S. Department of Defense, *Annual Report for Fiscal 1963* (Washington, DC, 1964); Department of Defense, "Actions of Military Services in Cuba Crisis Outlined," November 29, 1962, Department of the Army Records (FOIA); Adam Yarmolinsky, "Department of Defense Operations During the Cuban Crisis," February 12, 1963, in *Naval War College Review* XXXII (July–August 1979), 83–99.

109. Marc Trachtenberg, "The Influence of Nuclear Weapons in the Cuban Missile Crisis," *International Security* X (Summer 1985), 158.

110. Bromley Smith, "Summary Record of NSC Executive Committee Meeting No. 6, October 26, 1962, 10:00 A.M.," Box 216, Meetings and Memoranda, NSF, JFKL; Lyndon B. Johnson notes, October 26, 1962, Box 8, VPSF, LJBJ.

111. Secretary to Ambassador, October 26, 1962, Box 8, VPSF, LBJL; U. Alexis Johnson to McGeorge Bundy, October 26, 1962, Box 316, Meetings and Memoranda, NSF, JFKL; Smith, "Summary Record . . . No. 6."

112. Hilsman, *To Move,* 216–219.

113. *DSB* LXIX (November 19, 1973), 640–645.

114. Bromley Smith, "Summary Meeting of NSC Executive Committee Meeting No. 7, October 27, 1962, 10:00 A.M.," Box 316, Meetings and Memoranda, NSF, JFKL.

115. Garthoff, *Reflections,* 43n. Bernstein, "Cuban Missile Crisis," 102–104.

116. Raymond Hare to Secretary of State, Telegram 587, October 26, 1962, National Security Archive. Also, Thomas Finletter to Secretary of State, Telegram 506, October 25, 1962, *ibid.;* Roger Hilsman to Secretary of State, "Trading US Missiles in Turkey for Soviet Bases in Cuba," October 27, 1962, *ibid.*

117. "Cuban Missile Crisis Meetings, October 27, 1962," transcript, Presidential Recordings, JFKL. See also Richard K. Betts, *Nuclear Blackmail and Nuclear Balance* (Washington, DC, 1987), 111–114.

118. Harriman, "Memorandum on Kremlin Reactions," October 22, 1962, National Security Archive.

119. Garthoff, *Reflections,* 12, 19.

120. Seymour M. Hersh, "Were Cuban Fingers on the Trigger in the Cuban Missile Crisis?" *Washington Post National Weekly Edition,* October 19, 1987.

121. Bromley Smith, "Summary Record of NSC Executive Committee Meeting No. 8, October 27, 1962, 4:00," Box 316, Meetings and Memoranda, NSF, JFKL.

122. Kennedy, *Thirteen Days,* 108.

123. "Cuban Missile Crisis Meetings, October 27, 1962."

124. Schlesinger, *Robert Kennedy,* 521–523.

125. "Cuban Missile Crisis Meetings, October 27, 1962."

126. Bromley Smith, "Summary Record of NSC executive Committee Meeting No. 10, October 28, 1962, 11:10 A.M.," Box 316, Meetings and Memoranda, NSF, JFKL.

127. "Chronology of the Cuban Crisis, October 15–28, 1962," n.d., Army Records (FOIA).

128. Barton J. Bernstein, "Bombers, Inspections, and the No Invasion Pledge," *Foreign Service Journal* LVI (July 1979), 8–12.

129. U Thant, "Summary . . . , October 30, 1962."

130. John Kenneth Galbraith, "The Plain Lessons of a Bad Decade," *Foreign Policy,* No. 1 (Winter 1970–1971), 32.

131. "Call from the Attorney General," W. C. Sullivan to A. H. Belmont, October 29, 1962, FBI Records (FOIA).

132. Quoted in Schlesinger, *Robert Kennedy,* 532.

133. Raymond L. Garthoff, "The Cuban 'Contras' Caper," *Washington Post,* October 25, 1987.

134. "Chronology of the Cuban Crisis"; Smith, "Summary Record . . . No. 6."

135. Lukacs, "Class Reunion," 51.

136. Scott D. Sagan, "Nuclear Alerts and Crisis Management," *International Security* IX (Spring 1985), 112–118.

137. Richard Ned LeBow, *Between Peace and War* (Baltimore, 1981), 302.

138. Ball, *The Past,* 295, 309. See also Kennedy, *Thirteen Days,* 22.

139. Alexander L. George, "The Impact of Crisis-Induced Stress on Decision Making," in Frederic Solomon and Robert Q. Marston, eds., *The Medical Implications of Nuclear War* (Washington, DC, 1986), 541.

140. Charles Wellborn OH Interview #10, U.S. Naval Institute.

141. Quoted in Schlesinger, *Robert Kennedy,* 507.

142. CIA, "Readiness Status of Soviet Missiles in Cuba," October 23, 1962, Box 316, Meetings and Memoranda, NSF, JFKL; CIA, "Major Consequences of Certain U.S. Courses of Action in Cuba," October 20, 1962, CIA Records (FOIA); McGeorge Bundy, "Kennedy and the Nuclear Question," in Thompson, *Kennedy Presidency,* 212; "The Cuban Missile Crisis," transcript of discussion conducted by Alfred P. Sloan Foundation, New York, NY, 1983, Reel #4, p. 13.

143. Thomas G. Paterson and William J. Brophy, "October Missiles and November Elections: The Cuban Missile Crisis and American Politics, 1962," *Journal of American History* LXXIII (June 1986), 87–119; Thomas G. Paterson, "The Historian as Detective: Senator Kenneth Keating, the Missiles in Cuba, and His Mysterious Sources," *Diplomatic History* XI (Winter 1987), 67–70.

144. "Off-the-Record Meeting on Cuba," 6:60–7:55 P.M., October 16, 1962. See also *Washington Post*, December 18, 1962.

145. "The Cuban Missile Crisis," Sloan Reel #5, p. 33.

146. "Cuban Missile Crisis Meetings, October 27, 1962."

147. Harriman to Under Secretary, October 26, 1962, No. 1977 (54B), DDRS; United Nations, *Official Records of the General Assembly*, 17th Session, *Annexes*, vol. III (New York, 1963), 12–13; Roger Hilsman to the Secretary, "Possible Soviet Attitude Toward Regional Denuclearization Proposals," October 26, 1962, National Security Archive; Smith, "Summary Record . . . No. 5," October 25, 1962; Smith, "Summary Record . . . No. 6."

148. Garthoff, *Reflections*, 114–116.

149. Szulc, *Fidel*, 588.

150. Rusk quoted in Peter Joseph, *Good Times* (New York, 1974), 58.

151. Glenn T. Seaborg and Benjamin S. Loeb, *Kennedy, Khrushchev, and the Test Ban* (Berkeley, CA, 1981); Michael Mandelbaum, *The Nuclear Question* (New York, 1979), 159–189; Ronald E. Powaski, *March to Armageddon* (New York, 1987), 101–112.

152. Herbert L. Matthews to John Oakes, November 5, 1963, Box 85, Hanson Baldwin Papers, Yale Univeristy Library. See also Charles O. Porter, "An Interview with Fidel Castro [October 3, 1963]," *Northwest Review* VI (Fall 1963), 109.

153. Presidential Memorandum for Director McCone, December 13, 1962, Box 68, Departments and Agencies, POF, JFKL; Frederick C. Dutton to Senator Humphrey, April 4, 1963, Box 23-J-6-7B, Humphrey Papers; Memorandum, February 13, 1963, DAG-1/5.2.2.6.1-2, United Nations Archives; *PPP, JFK, 1963*, p. 176.

154. "Review of the Cuban Situation and Policy," February 28, 1963, Box 115, POF, JFKL.

155. See FBI Director to Attorney General, April 1, 1963, FBI Records (FOIA).

156. *PPP, JFK, 1963*, p. 278.

157. Department of State, Memorandum of Conversation, "Cuban Exile Plotting," July 19, 1963, Box 14, Attorney General's Correspondence, Robert F. Kennedy Papers, JFKL; Schlesinger, *Robert Kennedy*, 540; Dean Rusk to the President, March 28, 1963, Box 4, VPSF, LBJL.

158. *PPP, JFK, 1963*, p. 305.

159. Robert Hurwitch OH Interview, JFKL; Press Release, Committee for the Monroe Doctrine, April 7, 1963, Box 66, Liebman Associates Papers, Hoover Institution Archives.

160. W.R. Wannall to W.C. Sullivan, April 2, 1963, FBI Records (FOIA).

161. "Lisa Howard Interview of Fidel Castro," 1963, Box 23-I-9-10F, Humphrey Papers; Lisa Howard, "Castro's Overture," *War/Peace Report,* September 1963, pp. 3–5. Also, Schlesinger, *Robert Kennedy,* 541.

162. Ernest Halperin, *The Rise and Decline of Fidel Castro* (Berkeley, CA, 1972), 210–246.

163. Department of State to American Embassy, Paris, May 11, 1963, DSR (FOIA); Foy Kohler (Moscow) to Secretary of State, July 31, 1963, *ibid.*

164. John A. McCone, Memorandum for NSC Standing Group Members, May 1, 1963, CIA Records (FOIA).

165. Reports by George Volsky (USIA-Miami), August 16, 23, September 16, and October 4, 25, 1963, Box 26, Draper Papers; D.J. Brennan to W.C. Sullivan, "Anti-Fidel Castro Activities," November 4, 1963, FBI Records (FOIA).

166. William Attwood, *The Reds and the Blacks* (New York, 1967), 142–146; Attwood, *Twilight Struggle,* 257–264; Schlesinger, *Robert Kennedy,* 551–552, 556.

167. Jean Daniel, "Unofficial Envoy: An Historic Report from Two Capitals," *New Republic* CXLIX (December 14, 1963), 20; Tad Sculz, "Friendship Is Possible, But . . . ," *Parade Magazine,* April 1, 1984, p. 6.

168. *PPP, JFK, 1963,* p. 876.

169. "Meeting with the President," December 19, 1963, Box 19, Aides Files-Bundy, NSF, LBJL.

170. Jean Daniel, "When Castro Heard the News," *New Republic* CLXIX (December 7, 1963), 7.

171. "Meeting with the President," December 19, 1963; Attwood, *Reds and Blacks,* 146.

172. Donald E. Schulz, "Kennedy and the Cuban Connection," *Foreign Policy,* No. 26 (Spring 1977), 57–139; U.S. House, Select Committee on Assassinations, *Final Report* (Washington, DC, 1979), 3; Carl F. Tagg, "Fidel Castro and the Kennedy Assassination" (M.A. thesis, Florida Atlantic University, 1982); Michael L. Kurtz, *Crime of the Century* (Knoxville, TN, 1982), 233–238; Anthony Summers, *Conspiracy* (New York, 1980); James W. Clarke, *American Assassins* (Princeton, NJ, 1982), 105–128.

173. Quoted in Herbert L. Matthews diary of trip to Cuba, October 24–November 3, 1963, Box 27, Matthews Papers.

174. Senate, *Alleged Assassination Plots,* 88–89.

Chapter 6. Middle East

1. Speech to Zionists of America, August 26, 1960, in U.S. Senate, Committee on Commerce, *The Speeches, Remarks, Press Conferences, and Statements of Senator John F. Kennedy, August 1 through November 7, 1960* (Washington, DC, 1961), 46–50. (Hereafter cited as *Speeches of JFK 1960.*)

2. John F. Kennedy, *The Strategy of Peace,* Allan Nevins, ed. (New York, 1960), 118.

3. Speech, May 14, 1947, quoted in Mordechai Gazit, *President Ken-*

nedy's Policy Toward the Arab States and Israel (Tel Aviv, 1983), 33–34; Ian J. Bickerton, "John F. Kennedy, the Jewish Community and Israel: Some Preliminary Observations," *Australasian Journal of American Studies* II (December 1983), 33–35.

4. Speech to B'nai Zion, February 9, 1959, in Kennedy, *Strategy of Peace*, 118–19; Gazit, *Kennedy's Policy*, 43.

5. Speech to Histadrut Zionist Organization, November 27, 1956, in Kennedy, *Strategy of Peace*, 112.

6. William Burns, *Economic Aid and American Policy Toward Egypt, 1955–1981* (Albany, NY, 1985), 8–35; Donald Neff, *Warriors at Suez* (New York, 1981), 253–72, 371–406; Wilbur C. Eveland, *Ropes of Sand: America's Failure in the Middle East* (New York, 1980), 240–55.

7. Kennedy, *Strategy of Peace*, 110–11.

8. *CR*, CIII (July 2, 1957), 10780–10793. For reaction to the speech, see Richard Mahoney, *JFK: Ordeal in Africa* (New York, 1983), 19–24.

9. Burns, *Economic Aid*, 128, 250 (n. 29); C. L. Sulzberger, *The Last of the Giants* (New York, 1970), 504–5; William Macomber OH Interview, JFKL.

10. Speech to B'nai Zion, February 9, 1959, in Kennedy, *Strategy of Peace*, 119–23.

11. Speech of November 9, 1959, *ibid.*, pp. 107–9.

12. Speech of August 26, 1960, *Speeches of JFK 1960*, 49.

13. Lawrence Fuchs, "JFK and the Jews," *Moment* IX (June 1983), 26–27; Steven Spiegel, *The Other Arab-Israeli Conflict* (Chicago, 1985), 96–97. On Goldberg's role, see Goldberg to JFK, (n.d. but mid-1962), Box 119a, POF, JFKL.

14. Herbert Parmet, *JFK: The Presidency of John F. Kennedy* (New York, 1983), 226; Spiegel, *Other Arab-Israeli Conflict*, 100; Philip Klutznick OH Interview, JFKL.

15. Edward Tivnan, *The Lobby: Jewish Political Power and American Foreign Policy* (New York, 1987), 59–61; William Quandt, *Decade of Decisions: American Policy toward the Arab-Israeli Conflict, 1967–1976* (Berkeley, CA, 1977), 37; Donald Neff, *Warriors for Jerusalem* (New York, 1984), 78–80; Isaiah L. Kenen, *Israel's Defense Line: Her Friends and Foes in Washington* (Buffalo, NY, 1981), 134–37, 172–74; Carl Solberg, *Hubert Humphrey* (New York, 1984), 183–84.

16. Rusk to Kennedy, May 5, 1961, Box 127, POF, JFKL; Warren I. Cohen, *Dean Rusk* (Totowa, NJ, 1980), 16–31; Talbot to the author, August 26, 1985.

17. John S. Badeau, *The Middle East Remembered* (Washington, DC, 1983), 169–85.

18. On Komer, see William Colby, *Honorable Men* (New York, 1978), 236, and I. M. Destler, Leslie Gelb, and Anthony Lake, *Our Own Worst Enemy* (New York, 1984), 184.

19. Memcon, "Algeria," March 10, 1961; Ambassador James Gavin (Paris) to Rusk, tel. September 21, 1961; and Walt Rostow to JFK, January 1962, all in Box 4, NSF, JFKL; Rusk to author, July 1, 1985; Arthur M. Schlesinger, Jr., *A Thousand Days* (Boston, 1965), 564–65.

20. Mohamed Heikal, *Sphinx and Commissar: The Rise and Fall of Soviet Influence in the Arab World* (London, 1978), 103–14; Oles Smolansky, *The Soviet Union and the Arab East under Khrushchev* (Lewisburg, PA, 1974), 125–49.

21. Nasser to JFK, February 20 and April 18, 1961; Chester Bowles to JFK, February 27 and April 27, 1961; and JFK to Nasser, May 3, 1961, all in Box 169, NSF, JFKL; Robert Komer OH Interview, JFKL.

22. Rusk to JFK, May 5, 1961 and undated enclosure from NEA, Box 127, POF, JFKL; Burns, *Economic Aid,* 133, John S. Badeau OH Interview, JFKL.

23. CIA, Office of Current Intelligence, "The Nonaligned Nations Conference," August 7, 1961, Box 721, POF, JFKL; Frederick Dutton to JFK, "Status of UAR Nuclear Development," July 7, 1961, and Nasser to JFK, August 22, 1961, both in Box 127, POF, JFKL.

24. Parker T. Hart OH Interview, JFKL; Badeau, *Middle East Remembered,* 190–91; Mohamed Heikal, *The Cairo Documents* (New York, 1973), 204–06. Kennedy quoted in Komer OH Interview.

25. DS Research Memorandum RNA-8, "The Outlook for Nasser," October 30, 1961, Box 127, POF, JFKL.

26. Walt W. Rostow, *The Diffusion of Power* (New York, 1972), 197–98; Burns, *Economic Aid,* 118–20, 126–27; Gazit, *Kennedy's Policy,* 19–22.

27. William Gaud OH Interview, JFKL.

28. "Action Program for the UAR," January 10, 1962, enclosed in Rusk to JFK, January 10, 1962, and Rusk to JFK, 20 January 1962, all in Box 127, POF, JFKL; Gaud OH Interview.

29. Bowles to JFK, Rusk, and Fowler Hamilton, tel. February 21, 1962, Box 127, POF, JFKL; Bowles to Edward S. Mason, February 20, 1962, Box 308, Chester Bowles Papers, Yale University Library, New Haven, CT. See also Chester Bowles, *Promises to Keep: My Years in Public Life 1941–1969* (New York, 1971), 371–72.

30. Lucius Battle to McGeorge Bundy, February 27, 1962, and "Report on Mission to the U.A.R.," by Mason (n.d. but Spring 1962), Box 127, POF, JFKL; Gaud OH Interview.

31. Kamel quoted in Burns, *Economic Aid,* 147–48.

32. Komer OH Interview.

33. Draft tel. to American Embassy (Tel Aviv) (n.d. but probably May 8, 1962), Box 303, Bowles Papers.

34. DS circular tels., May 10 and June 2, 1961, both in Box 118, NSF, JFKL; Lucius Battle to McGeorge Bundy, May 29, 1961, Box 119, NSF, JFKL; Gazit, *Kennedy's Policy,* 38–41; Parmet, *JFK,* 228.

35. Lucius Battle to Myer Feldman, September 15, 1961, Box 118, NSF, JFKL.

36. William Bundy to Talbot, May 23, 1962, Box 118, NSF, JFKL.

37. JFK to Ben Gurion, June 13, 1962, *ibid.*

38. Spiegel, *Other Arab-Israeli Conflict,* 110–12; Parmet, *JFK,* 228–31; Ambassador Walworth Barbour (Tel Aviv) to Rusk, tel. April 12, 1962, and SD circular tel. June 5, 1962, both in Box 118, NSF, JFKL.

39. Rusk to Barbour, tel. June 5, 1962, and State Department memoran-

dum, "Problems of U.S.-Israel Relations," July 6, 1962, both in Box 118, NSF, JFKL.

40. Ambassador Adlai Stevenson to Rusk, tel. June 1, 1962, and State Department memorandum, "Problems of US-Israeli Relations," July 6, 1962, both in *ibid.*

41. Talbot to Feldman,, August 9, 1962, *ibid.*

42. Feldman to JFK, August 10, 1962, *ibid.*

43. Komer to McGeorge Bundy and Feldman, August 13, 1962, *ibid.*

44. "Issues," August 14, 1962, and Komer to McGeorge Bundy, August 17, 1962, both in Box 118, NSF, JFKL; Feldman OH Interview, JFKL; Spiegel, *Other Arab-Israeli Conflict,* 108–9, 117; Parmet, *JFK,* 225–26, 232.

45. JFK to Ben Gurion, August 15, 1962, Box 118, NSF, JFKL; Feldman OH Interview.

46. Feldman to JFK and Rusk, tel. August 19, 1962, and Rusk to Feldman, tel. August 20, 1962, both in Box 118, NSF, JFKL; Feldman to author, August 30, 1985.

47. Rusk to Strong and Badeau, tel. August 22, 1962, Box 118, NSF, JFKL.

48. Strong and Badeau to Rusk, tel. August 24, 1962, Box 127, POF, JFKL; Burns, *Economic Aid,* p. 141; Badeau OH Interview; Badeau, *Middle East Remembered,* 175–77.

49. Feldman OH Interview.

50. Rusk, circular tel. September 14, 1962, Box 119, NSF, JFKL; Bickerton, "JFK & Israel," 41.

51. Parmet, *JFK,* 233–34; Spiegel, *Other Arab-Israeli Conflict,* 114–15; Kenen, *Israel's Defense Line,* 159–62; Feldman to author, August 30, 1985. Johnson is quoted in Parmet, *JFK,* 230. See also Joseph E. Johnson, "Arab vs. Israeli: A Persistent Challenge to Americans," *Middle East Journal* XVIII (Winter 1964), 1–13.

52. Tazewell Shepard, Jr., to JFK, September 21, 1962, Box 119a, POF, JFKL.

53. Stevenson to Rusk, tel. September 28, 1962, Box 119, NSF, JFKL.

54. Jones (Tripoli) to Rusk, tel. September 20, 1962, *ibid.*

55. Lewis (Amman) to Rusk, tel. September 27, 1962, and Ball to Macomber (Amman), tel. October 8, 1962, both in *ibid.*

56. Parker T. Hart to Rusk, tel. October 6, 1962, *ibid.*

57. Armin Meyer (Beirut) to Rusk, tels. September 28 and 29, 1962, *ibid.*

58. Lewis (Amman) to Rusk, tel. September 27, 1962, and Hart (Riyadh) to Rusk, tel. October 6, 1962, both in *ibid.;* DS to JFK, "Developments in Yemen" and "Talking Outline—Developments in Yemen" (n.d. but early October 1962), both in Box 158, NSF, JFKL.

59. Dana Schmidt, *Yemen: The Unknown War* (New York, 1968), 36–39; John S. Badeau, *The American Approach to the Arab World* (New York, 1968), 124–26; Edgar O'Ballance, *The War in the Yemen* (Hamden, CT, 1971), 46–50, 66–71.

60. Memo by Chester V. Clifton, May 4, 1961, and 3904/JCT to White House, tel. May 5, 1961, both in Box 115, NSF, JFKL; Komer OH Interview; Amin Seikal, *The Rise and Fall of the Shah* (Princeton, NJ, 1980), 75–77.

61. Meyer quoted in Seikal, *Rise and Fall,* 75.

62. "A Review of Problems in Iran and Recommendations for the National Security Council," May 15, 1961, Box 115, NSF, JFKL; Komer OH Interview.

63. Bowles to JFK, tel. February 17, 1962; Bowles to JFK, "The Shah's Visit," April 10, 1962; and Komer to Bowles, September 24, 1962, all in Box 297, Bowles Papers; Komer OH Interview; Seikal, *Rise and Fall,* 77–78.

64. DS to JFK, "Libya, June 1962: United States Objectives"; Komer to JFK, October 16, 1962; and JFK to Libyan Crown Prince Hasan, tel. October 22, 1962, all in Box 121a, POF, JFKL. See also Stephen Duncan-Peters, "Libya: An African Success Story," *Foreign Commerce Weekly,* February 5, 1962, pp. 208–9.

65. Macomber OH Interview, JFKL; Harold Chase, "United States Arms Aid to Jordan," in Anne Sinai and Allen Pollack, eds., *The Hashemite Kingdom of Jordan* (New York, 1977), 170–71; Komer to JFK, September 28, 1963, Box 121a, POF, JFKL.

66. Hart OH Interview and Komer OH Interview; SD to JFK, "U.S. Economic Assistance to Saudi Arabia," n.d. (early October 1962), Box 158, NSF, JFKL; Spiegel, *Other Arab-Israeli Conflict,* 98.

67. "President's Luncheon for Crown Prince Faysal," enclosed in William Brubeck to McGeorge Bundy, October 4, 1962, and Komer to JFK, October 4, 1962, all in Box 123b, POF, JFKL; DS scope paper, "Informal Visit of Crown Prince Faysal," October 4, 1962, Box 158, NSF, JFKL.

68. Hart OH Interview; Hart to author, August 27, 1985; Nadav Safran, *Saudi Arabia: The Ceaseless Quest for Security* (Cambridge, MA, 1985), 97–98.

69. Rusk to JFK, "Recognition of the Yemen Arab Republic," October 17, 1962, Box 207, NSF, JFKL.

70. Edward Weintal and Charles Bartlett, *Facing the Brink: An Intimate Study of Crisis Diplomacy* (New York, 1967), 38–39; Macomber OH Interview and Hart OH Interview; Harold Macmillan, *At the End of the Day* (New York, 1973), 270–74.

71. JFK to Nasser, November 17, 1962, and Nasser to JFK (n.d. but late November 1962), quoted in Heikal, *Cairo Documents,* 216–18; JFK to Hussein, n.d., appended to Rusk to Macomber, tel. December 7, 1962, Box 120, POF, JFKL; Hart OH Interview; Macmillan, *At the End of the Day,* 272–74.

72. "Elements of US Policy Toward the UAR," enclosed in Brubeck to McGeorge Bundy, December 11, 1962, Box 127, POF, JFKL; Komer to JFK, January 19, 1963; McGeorge Bundy to JFK, January 21, 1963; and "Remarks of President Kennedy to the National Security Council," January 22, 1963, all in Box 314, NSF, JFKL.

73. O'Ballance, *War in Yemen,* 92–99; Hart OH Interview; Komer OH Interview; George McGhee OH Interview, JFKL; Komer to author, April 25, 1985.

74. National Security Action Memorandum 227, "Decisions Taken at President's Meeting on Yemen Crisis, 25 February 1963," by McGeorge Bundy, February 27, 1963, Box 123b, POF, JFKL; Komer OH Interview; Komer to author, July 25, 1985.

75. JFK to Faisal, draft letter (n.d. probably February 23, 1963), Box 128a, POF, JFKL; Christopher J. McMullen, *Resolution of the Yemen Crisis, 1963* (Washington, DC, 1980), 13–25; Weintal and Bartlett, *Facing the Brink,* 45–48.

76. Komer OH Interview; Hart OH Interview; Badeau OH Interview; Badeau to Rusk, tel. March 3, 1963, Box 127, POF, JFKL; Komer to author, July 25, 1985; Hart to author, August 27, 1985; McMullen, *Yemen Crisis,* 31–37, 45–46.

77. "Conversation with Israeli Foreign Minister Meir," December 27, 1962, Box 119, NSF, JFKL.

78. Anthony Nutting, *Nasser* (New York, 1972), 323–37; Macomber OH Interview; "Weekend Reading January 12–13, 1963," McGeorge Bundy to JFK, Box 317, NSF, JFKL; Komer to McGeorge Bundy, March 6, 1963, Box 322, NSF, JFKL; "Syrian Coup," undated unsigned note to JFK, Box 124a, POF, JFKL.

79. "Near East Tour d'Horizon," April 2, 1963, Box 119, NSF, JFKL.

80. Shimon Peres, *David's Sling* (London, 1970), 93–94, 99.

81. Rusk, "Near East Tour d'Horizon," April 25, 1963, Box 119, NSF, JFKL.

82. Rusk to Barbour, tel. April 26, 1963, *ibid.* Rusk's cable contains a paraphrase of Ben Gurion's April 26 message to JFK. The verbatim text remains classified as of this writing.

83. Benjamin Read to McGeorge Bundy, May 13, 1963, Box 119, NSF, JFKL. Read's memo contained a summary of the decisions made on April 27 and their implementation over the next two weeks.

84. Feldman OH Interview; Macomber to author, June 25, 1985.

85. Barbour to Rusk, tel. May 5, 1963, and DS circular tel., May 9, 1963, both in Box 119, NSF, JFKL.

86. *PPP, JFK,* 1963 (Washington, DC, 1964), 373.

87. Harriman, "US Security Guarantees to Israel," May 8, 1963, Box 119, NSF, JFKL.

88. Komer to McGeorge Bundy, May 3 and 6, 1963; and Komer, "Memorandum for the Record," May 8, 1863, all in Box 322, NSF, JFKL. On Israeli nuclear developments, see Sherman Kent, "Consequences of Israeli Acquisition of Nuclear Capability," March 6, 1963, in Gazit, *Kennedy's Policy,* 116–20.

89. JFK to Nasser, n.d., appended to Rusk to Badeau, tel. April 18, 1963, Box 127, POF, JFKL.

90. Rusk to JFK, "Israel Security Assurance: Near East Arms Limitation," May 16, 1963, Box 119a, POF, JFKL.

91. "Weekend Reading July 4–7, 1963," McGeorge Bundy to JFK, Box 317, NSF, JFKL; Gazit, *Kennedy's Policy,* 52–53; Burns, *Economic Aid,* 142–43.

92. Komer to McGeorge Bundy, May 14, 1963, Box 322, NSF, JFKL; Glenn Seaborg (Atomic Energy Commission) to McGeorge Bundy, July 1, 1963; Barbour to Rusk, tel. August 16, 1963; and Read to McGeorge Bundy, September 24, 1963, all in Box 119, NSF, JFKL.

93. "United States Security Assistance for Israel," September 11, 1963, Box 119, NSF, JFKL; Gazit, *Kennedy's Policy*, 53–54; Sulzberger, *Last of the Giants*, 1029, 1031–32; Spiegel, *Other Arab-Israeli Conflict*, 110; Komer to author, June 23, 1987; Talbot to author, July 15, 1987.

94. Komer to JFK, October 7, 1963, Box 123b, POF, JFKL; *New York Times*, October 18, 1963, p. 7, and October 27, 1963, p. 6. As of this writing, key documents contained in "NSAM 262—Yemen Disengagement, 10 October 1963," Box 342, NSF, JFKL, have been withheld by the NSC despite repeated attempts to have them declassified.

95. JFK to Nasser, October 19, 1963, quoted in Heikal, *Cairo Documents*, 222–23.

96. Rusk, circular tel. November 8, 1963, and McGeorge Bundy to J. William Fulbright, November 11, 1963, both in Box 127, POF, JFKL; Schimdt, *Yemen*, 201–3; Burns, *Economic Aid*, 144–45, 155; Ernest Gruening, *Many Battles* (New York, 1973), 445–47.

Chapter 7. China

1. Arthur M. Schlesinger, Jr., *A Thousand Days* (Boston, 1965), 479.

2. For Truman and Eisenhower policies, see William W. Stueck, Jr., *The Road to Confrontation* (Chapel Hill, NC, 1981); Robert G. Sutter, *China Watch* (Baltimore, MD, 1978), 31–62; Foster Rhea Dulles, *American Policy Toward Communist China, 1949–1969* (New York, 1972), 1–187; and J. H. Kalicki, *The Pattern of Sino-American Crises* (London, 1975).

3. *CR*, XCV (January 25, 1949), 532–533.

4. John F. Kennedy, *The Strategy of Peace*, Allan Nevins, ed. (New York, 1960), 142; *CR*, CIV (June 6, 1958), 10399–10400, 10407; *CR*, CV (February 19, 1959), 2737.

5. John F. Kennedy, "A Democrat Looks at Foreign Policy," *Foreign Affairs* XXXVI (October 1957), 50.

6. W. W. Rostow OH Interview, JFKL; Roger Hilsman, *To Move a Nation* (New York, 1967), 302–303; Dulles, *American Policy*, 190–191.

7. *CR*, CVII (January 30, 1961), 1429.

8. Harold W. Chase and Allen W. Lerman, eds., *Kennedy and the Press* (New York, 1965), 119.

9. *PPP, JFK, 1962*, pp. 850–851. *PPP, JFK, 1963*, p. 616; Schlesinger, *A Thousand Days*, 903–909; Theodore C. Sorensen, *Kennedy* (New York, 1965), 665; Chase and Lerman, *Kennedy and the Press*, 85, 356, 358, 429.

10. Memorandum of Conversation, May 24, 1961, Box 22, NSF, JFKL.

11. Chester Bowles, Memorandum to President Kennedy, July 1, 1961, Box 297, Chester Bowles Papers, Yale University Library, New Haven, CT. See also George W. Ball, *The Past Has Another Pattern* (New York, 1983), 179.

12. See Dulles, *American Policy*, 191–192; James C. Thomson, Jr., "On the Making of U.S. China Policy, 1961–1969: A Study in Bureaucratic Politics," *China Quarterly* L (April/June 1972), 221–222.

13. Warren I. Cohen, *Dean Rusk* (Totowa, NJ, 1980), 45–76, 84–88, 163–173.

14. *Ibid.*, 96–99; Ball, *The Past,* 168–169.

15. W. W. Rostow OH Interview; Schlesinger, *A Thousand Days,* 207–210.

16. *PPP, JFK, 1963,* pp. 349, 658–660; W. W. Rostow, *The Diffusion of Power* (New York, 1972), 269–270.

17. Bureau of Intelligence and Research Memorandum, December 3, 1962, *The Pentagon Papers* (The Senator Gravel Edition) (Boston, 1971), 693–694..

18. W. W. Rostow OH Interview.

19. *PPP, JFK, 1963,* pp. 349, 887; Summary of the President's Views—NSC Meeting, January 22, 1963, Boxes 4–6, Roger Hilsman Papers, JFKL.

20. Report of the Sino-Soviet Task Force, April 1, 1961, Box 22, NSF, JFKL. On the development of the Sino-Soviet dispute see Herbert Ellison, ed., *The Sino-Soviet Conflict: A Global Perspective* (Seattle, WA, 1981); Alfred D. Low, *The Sino-Soviet Dispute* (Madison, NJ, 1976); Donald Zagoria, *The Sino-Soviet Conflict* (New York, 1980); O. E. Clubb, *China and Russia: The "Great Game"* (New York, 1971); John Gittings, *Survey of the Sino-Soviet Dispute* (London, 1968).

21. Analysis of Sino-Soviet dispute, December 19, 1961, Box 14, James C. Thomson, Jr. Papers, JFKL; CIA Draft Report—"Prospects for the Sino-Soviet Relationship," February 20, 1962, Box 15, Thomson Papers; Memorandum on Sino-Soviet Relations, Roger Hilsman to Secretary Rusk, May 14, 1962, Box 1, Hilsman Papers.

22. U.S. Senate, Committee on Foreign Relations, *Executive Sessions 1961: Historical Series,* XIII, pt. 1 (Washington, DC, 1981), 361.

23. *Ibid.,* 362, 453–455; Joint Chiefs of Staff to Secretary of Defense, January 13, 1962, *The Pentagon Papers,* 663–664.

24. Thomson, "On the Making," 226–227; Schlesinger, *A Thousand Days,* 614; Hilsman, *To Move,* 344.

25. Report of the Sino-Soviet Task Force, April 1, 1961, Box 22, NSF, JFKL; Analysis of Sino-Soviet dispute, December 19, 1961, Box 14, Thomson Papers; CIA Memorandum, January 14, 1963, Box 180, NSF, JFKL; CIA Memorandum, July 31, 1963, Box 314, NSF, JFKL; Hilsman, *To Move,* pp. 340–341.

26. Communist China Problem Research Series, *Communist China, 1961,* Vol. II (Hong Kong, 1962), 35–38.

27. Claudius M. Colombo, "Chinese Communist Perceptions of the Foreign Policy of John F. Kennedy, 1961–1963" (Ph.D. dissertation, New York University, 1982), 2–38; Kenneth Young, *Negotiating with the Chinese Communists* (New York, 1968), 236–238.

28. Report of the Sino-Soviet Task Force, April 1, 1961, Box 22, NSF, JFKL; CIA Memorandum, July 31, 1963, Box 314, NSF, JFKL; Hilsman to Rusk, July 31, 1963, Box 314, NSF, JFKL; Hilsman, *To Move,* 285, 291.

29. CIA Memorandum, May 11, 1961, Box 114, POF, JFKL; Huntington Sheldon to Walt Rostow, n.d., Box 22, NSF, JFKL; Sherman Kent to McGeorge Bundy, July 28, 1961, Box 22, NSF, JFKL.

30. "Talking Points on the Vienna Conversations," McGeorge Bundy to Rostow, June 11, 1961, Box 300, Bowles Papers.

31. Stanley Bachrack, *The Committee of One Million* (New York, 1976), 179–200; *CR*, CVII (July 28, August 31, 1961), 13943–13962, 17768–17778.

32. Frederick Dutton to Kennedy, February 1, 1961, Box 21, NSF, JFKL.

33. Bowles to Kennedy, January 11, 1961, Box 114, POF, JFKL; Chester Bowles, *Promises to Keep* (New York, 1971), 397–398.

34. *New York Times,* March 4, 7, 9, 10, April 13, May 15, 16, and June 3, 1961.

35. *Executive Sessions, 1961,* XIII, pt. 1, 205–220.

36. Robert Komer to McGeorge Bundy, March 1, 1961, Box 21, NSF, JFKL; Chiang Kai-Shek to Kennedy, April 1, 1961, Box 113A, POF, JFKL.

37. L. D. Battle to McGeorge Bundy, June 30, 1961, Box 22, NSF, JFKL; Memorandum of Conversation, May 24, 1961, Box 22, NSF, JFKL.

38. Memorandum of Conversation, May 24, 1961, Box 22, NSF, JFKL; "Talking Paper for Discussion with Mr. Luce," Box 22, NSF, JFKL; L. D. Battle to McGeorge Bundy, June 30, 1961, Box 22, NSF, JFKL; John Bartlow Martin, *Adlai Stevenson and the World* (New York, 1977), 638–639.

39. Robert Komer to McGeorge Bundy, June 15, 1961, Box 22, NSF, JFKL.

40. McGeorge Bundy to Kennedy, June 26, 1961, Box 22, NSF, JFKL; Robert Komer to McGeorge Bundy, June 15, 1961, Box 22, NSF, JFKL; Thomson "On the Making," 224–225.

41. Memorandum of Conversation, July 28, 1961, Box 22, NSF, JFKL; McGeorge Bundy to Kennedy, August 22, 1961, Box 22, NSF, JFKL.

42. Rusk to Adlai Stevenson, September 13, 1961, Box 22, NSF, JFKL; Martin, *Adlai Stevenson,* 654–655.

43. Memorandum of Conversation, July 28, 1961, Box 22, NSF, JFKL; Hilsman, *To Move,* 306–307.

44. Memorandum of Conversation, President Kennedy and General Ch'en Ch'eng (Vice President GRC), August 2, 1961, Box 22, NSF, JFKL; McGeorge Bundy to Kennedy, August 22, 1961, Box 22, NSF, JFKL.

45. McGeorge Bundy to Ray Cline, October 11, 1961; Cline to Bundy, October 14, 1961; Bundy to Cline, October 15, 1961; Rusk to Ambassador Drumright, October 16, 1961; Bundy to Kennedy, October 16, 1961, all in Box 22, NSF, JFKL.

46. Martin, *Adlai Stevenson,* 682–684.

47. Jacob D. Beam, *Multiple Exposure* (New York, 1978), 139–140.

48. *Ibid.,* 140–141.

49. Hilsman to Walter McConaughy, July 7, 1961, Box 22, NSF, JFKL.

50. Beam, *Multiple Exposure,* 142–143.

51. Ray S. Cline, *Secrets, Spies, and Scholars* (Washington, DC, 1976), 177–179.

52. Rusk to the American Embassy-Taipei, January 8, 1962, Box 23, NSF, JFKL.

53. Leonard H. D. Gordon, "United States Opposition to the Use of Force in the Taiwan Strait, 1954–1962," *Journal of American History,* LXXII (December 1985), 658; Thomson, "On the Making," 227–228.

54. President's Intelligence Checklist, June 19, 1962, Box 113a, POF, JFKL; Hilsman, *To Move*, 318.

55. *PPP, JFK, 1962*, pp. 509–510; Sorensen, *Kennedy*, 662.

56. Memorandum of Conversation, June 22, 1962, Box 1, Hilsman Papers.

57. Gary C. Hufbauer and Jeffrey J. Schott, *Economic Sanctions Reconsidered: History and Current Policy* (Washington, DC, 1985), 221–229. See also Jerome Alan Cohen, "China's Attitude Toward Trade with the United States," in Jerome Alan Cohen, ed., *The Dynamics of China's Foreign Relations* (Cambridge, MA, 1970), 57–68.

58. Bowles to Rusk, February 8, 1961, Box 15, Thomson Papers.

59. Thomson, "On the Making," 225–226; Michael Forrestal OH Interview, JFKL.

60. Robert Barnett to the Under Secretary of State, January 4, 1962, Box 15, Thomson Papers.

61. Memoranda of Conversations, December 21, 1961, January 10, 1961, *ibid.*

62. Thomson to Bowles, January 11, 1962, *ibid.*

63. Bowles to Kennedy, February 6, 1962, Bowles to Kennedy, May 23, 1962, Box 297, Bowles Papers; Bowles OH Interview.

64. Thomson to W. Averell Harriman, January 12, 1962, Box 15, Thomson Papers.

65. Bureau of Intelligence and Research Report, January 5, 1962, *ibid.*

66. Memorandum, February 28, 1962, Foy Kohler to Rostow, March 8, 1962, *ibid.*

67. Harriman to Rusk, April 13, 1962, *ibid.*

68. Chase and Lerman, *Kennedy and the Press*, 253; Hilsman, *To Move*, 317; Thomson, "On the Making," 227; Bowles to Kennedy, May 23, 1962, Box 297, Bowles Papers.

69. Memorandum of Conversation, June 24, 1962, Box 15, Thomson Papers.

70. On the origins of the border conflict see Neville Maxwell, *India's China War* (London, 1970).

71. Memorandum, "United States Policy in the Sino-Indian Conflict," November 3, 1962, Box 1, Hilsman Papers; John K. Galbraith, *Ambassador's Journal* (Boston, 1969), 428–477.

72. Hilsman, *To Move*, 328–329.

73. Robert Komer to Hilsman, November 21, 1962, Box 1, Hilsman Papers.

74. Hilsman to Rusk, November 17, 1962; Hilsman to Rusk, November 20, 1962, *ibid.*

75. Hilsman to Kennedy, November 21, 1962, *ibid.*

76. Hilsman, *To Move*, 338–339.

77. *PPP, JFK, 1962*, pp. 850–851, 887, 900.

78. *New York Times*, May 17, 1963; Clubb, *China and Russia*, 451–479; Gittings, *Survey*, 174–193.

79. CIA Memorandum, January 14, 1963, Box 180, NSF, JFKL; CIA Memorandum, July 31, 1963; Hillsman to Rusk, July 31, 1963, both in Box 314, NSF, JFKL.

80. Quoted in Glenn T. Seaborg, *Kennedy, Khrushchev, and the Test Ban* (Berkeley, CA, 1981), 217.

81. Quoted in Gordon H. Chang, "JFK, China, and the Bomb," *Journal of American History* LXXIV (March 1988), 1300. See also Summary of the President's Views—NSC Meeting, January 22, 1963, Boxes 4–6, Hilsman Papers; Sorensen, *Kennedy,* 736; Schlesinger, *A Thousand Days,* 903–909, 915; Franz Schurmann, *The Logic of World Peace* (New York, 1974), 384–387.

82. Chang, "JFK, China, and the Bomb," 1287, 1304–1305.

83. Roger Hilsman OH Interview; W. W. Rostow OH Interview; Maxwell Taylor OH Interview, JFKL; Rostow, *Diffusion of Power,* 265, 284–286.

84. Sorensen, *Kennedy,* 631–632. On the development and practice of revolutionary war doctrine, see Chalmers Johnson, *Autopsy on People's War* (Berkeley, CA, 1973), 10–45; Peter Van Ness, *Revolution and Chinese Foreign Policy* (Berkeley, CA, 1971), 1–77, 185–206.

85. *Pentagon Papers,* II, 72.

86. George H. Gallup, *The Gallup Poll: Public Opinion, 1935–1971* (New York, 1972), III, 1773.

Chapter 8. South Asia

1. Quoted in Sarvepalli Gopal, *Jawaharlal Nehru: A Biography,* III, *1956–1964* (Cambridge, MA, 1984; 3 vols.), 223. On the origins of the border conflict, see Neville Maxwell, *India's China War* (London, 1970).

2. Komer to Carl Kaysen, November 16, 1962, NSC History of South Asia, Vol. I, Box 24, NSF, LBJL.

3. Komer to Phillips Talbot October 24, 1962, *ibid.*

4. Kennedy to Nehru, October 28, 1962, Box 118a, POF, JFKL; Kaysen to Kennedy, October 26, 1962, NSC History of South Asia, Vol. I, Box 24, NSF, LBJL.

5. Memorandum for the NSC, undated (probably early December 1962), Box 5, VPSF, LBJP, LBJL.

6. See, for example, Talbot to the NSC, December 6, 1962, Boxes 338–342, NSF, JFKL.

7. John F. Kennedy, "If India Falls," *Progressive* XXII (January 1958), 8–11.

8. Kennedy to the Senate Foreign Relations Committee, March 1958, Holburn Files, India, PrePP, JFKP, JFKL; *CR,* CIV (March 25, 1958), 5246–5255. For Kennedy's advocacy of aid for India in the 1950s, see W. W. Rostow, *Eisenhower, Kennedy, and Foreign Aid* (Austin, TX, 1985).

9. Kennedy speech, May 4, 1959, Holburn Files, India, PrePP, JFKP, JFKL.

10. See speeches in John F. Kennedy, *The Strategy of Peace,* Allan Nevins, ed. (New York, 1960), esp. 141–158.

11. For the evolution of that policy, see Robert J. McMahon, "United States Cold War Strategy in South Asia: Making a Military Commitment to Pakistan, 1947–1954," *Journal of American History* (forthcoming); M. S. Venkataramani, *The American Role in Pakistan, 1947–1958* (New Delhi, 1982).

12. Chester Bowles, *Promises to Keep* (New York, 1971), 478–481.

13. Background Paper, "U.S.–Pakistan Relations," May 1961, Box 1, VPSF, LBJP, LBJL; Scope Paper for Ayub Khan visit, July 1961, Box 123, POF, JFKL.

14. U.S. Department of State, *Foreign Relations of the United States, 1955–1957,* vol. VIII: *South Asia* (Washington, DC, 1987), 363 ff; James H. Hitchman, "Parry and Thrust: Eisenhower, the Soviet Union, and India, 1953–1961," *World Review* XXIV (April 1985), 11–24; Dennis Merrill, "Bread and the Ballot: The United States and India's Economic Development, 1947–1961" (Ph.D. dissertation, University of Connecticut, 1986), chs. 5–6.

15. Dulles to Eisenhower, April 17, 1958, Dulles-Herter Series, Whitman File, DDEP, DDEL; Eisenhower to Dulles, April 21, 1958, *ibid.;* NSC Planning Board, Discussion Paper, May 22, 1959, NSC 5701 folder, OSANSA Records, DDEL.

16. For comparative aid figures, see William J. Barnds, *India, Pakistan, and the Great Powers* (New York, 1972), 226–227.

17. G. W. Choudhury, *India, Pakistan, Bangladesh, and the Major Powers* (New York, 1975), 34–35.

18. S. M. Burke, *Pakistan's Foreign Policy: An Historical Analysis* (New York, 1973), 266–267; CIA Special Report, "Pakistan and the Free World Alliance," July 10, 1964, Box 150, NSF, LBJL.

19. Bunker to the State Department, December 23, 1959, International Series, Office of the White House Staff Secretary, DDEL.

20. Bunker to the State Department, December 18, 1959, International Series, Whitman File, DDEL.

21. Bunker to the State Department, May 13, 1959, South Asia, Briefing Notes Subseries, NSC Series, OSANSA Records, DDEL; memorandum of conversation between Eisenhower and Bunker, April 25, 1960, International Series, Office of the White House Staff Secretary, DDEL.

22. Arthur M. Schlesinger, Jr., *A Thousand Days* (Boston, MA, 1965), 522.

23. Remarks of Kennedy to NSC, January 22, 1963, Box 314, NSF, JFKL; Chester Bowles to Kennedy, March 29, 1961, Kennedy folder, Box 297, Chester Bowles Papers, Yale University, New Haven, CT; Barnds, *India, Pakistan, and the Great Powers,* 165–167; George Ball, *The Past Has Another Pattern* (New York, 1983), 174–181; W. W. Rostow, *The Diffusion of Power,* (New York, 1972), 185–188; Merrill, "Bread and the Ballot," 306.

24. Bowles to Kennedy, July 1, 1961, Kennedy folder, Box 297, Bowles Papers.

25. Gopal, *Nehru,* III, 187.

26. Cooper memorandum, "Notes on My Talks in India," undated (probably January 1961), Box 118a, POF, JFKL.

27. Kennedy to Nehru, May 8, 1961, Boxes 111–112, NSF, JFKL.

28. Nehru to Kennedy, May 24, 1961, quoted in Gopal, *Nehru,* III, 187–188.

29. Johnson to Bowles, May 22, 1961, Box 1, VPSF, LBJP, LBJL.

30. Galbraith to the State Department, May 19, 1961, Box 242, NSF, JFKL.

31. Galbraith to the State Department, May 20, 1961, *ibid.*
32. Johnson to Kennedy, May 23, 1961, *ibid.*
33. *New York Times,* March 20 and 21, 1961; W. Averell Harriman OH Interview, JFKL.
34. William M. Rountree (Ambassador to Pakistan) to the State Department, May 21, 1961, Box 1, VPSF, LJBP, LBJL; Rountree to the State Department, May 22, 1961, Box 242, NSF, JFKL.
35. Quoted in Hall (Chargé in Pakistan) to the State Department, June 29, 1961, Box 123, POF, JFKL.
36. Quoted in Hall to the State Department, July 7, 1961, *ibid.*
37. Quoted in Hall to the State Department, July 6, 1961, *ibid.* For similar Ayub comments, see Mohammed Ayub Khan, *Speeches and Statements* (Karachi, n.d.; 6 vols.), IV, 7–11.
38. Rountree to the State Department, July 1, 1961, Box 123, POF, JFKL.
39. Bowles to Thomas Hughes (Acting Director, Bureau of Intelligence and Research), April 4, 1961, Hughes folder, Box 299, Bowles Papers.
40. President's Talking Paper, Scope Paper, and other briefing materials for the Ayub visit, July 1961, all in Box 123, POF, JFKL; Mohammed Ayub Khan, *Friends Not Masters: A Political Autobiography* (New York, 1967), 136–139; Choudhury, *India, Pakistan, Bangladesh,* 103–105; Position Paper, "Indo-Pakistan Relations," November 1961, Box 11, VPSF, LBJP, LBJL; Selig S. Harrison, "South Asia and U.S. Policy," *New Republic* CXLV (December 11, 1961), 12–13.
41. Quoted in Schlesinger, *A Thousand Days,* 525–526.
42. John Kenneth Galbraith, *Ambassador's Journal* (Boston, MA, 1969), 216.
43. Quoted in Schlesinger, *A Thousand Days,* 525.
44. *Ibid.,* 526. See also Theodore C. Sorensen, *Kennedy* (New York, 1965), 651–652.
45. Komer to McGeorge Bundy, October 23, 1961, Komer Staff Memoranda, NSF, JFKL; President's Talking Paper, Scope Paper, and other briefing materials for the Nehru visit, November 1961, all in Box 118a, POF, JFKL; Gopal, *Nehru,* III, 188–189; Galbraith, *Ambassador's Journal,* 242.
46. Quoted in Schlesinger, *A Thousand Days,* 527–528.
47. *Ibid.,* 527.
48. Galbraith to the State Department, December 5, 1961, Goa, Portugal Country File, NSF, JFKL; Galbraith to the State Department, December 20, 1961, *ibid.;* Nehru to Kennedy, December 29, 1961, Box 118a, POF, JFKL; Galbraith, *Ambassador's Journal,* 244–254; Gopal, *Nehru,* III, 190–203.
49. Barnds, *India, Pakistan, and the Great Powers,* 226–227.
50. Komer to Bundy and Kaysen, January 9, 1962, Komer Staff Memoranda, NSF, JFKL.
51. Komer to Bundy, January 12, 1962, NSC History of South Asia, Vol. I, Box 24, NSF, LBJL.
52. Galbraith to the State Department, January 27, 1962, Box 118a, NSF, JFKL; Kennedy to Nehru, January 15, 1962, *ibid.;* Kaysen to Bundy, January 28, 1962, Kaysen Staff Memoranda, NSF, JFKL.
53. Komer to Kennedy, January 30, 1962, Box 118a, POF, JFKL.

54. Ayub to Kennedy, July 26, 1962, Box 123, *ibid.;* Roger Hilsman to the Acting Secretary of State, "The Sino-Indian Border Dispute and Its Ramifications," May 7, 1962, Box 11, VPSF, LBJP, LBJL.

55. *New York Times,* September 25 and 30, 1962; Kaysen to Bundy, October 5, 1962, Kaysen Staff Memoranda, NSF, JFKL; Bundy to Kennedy, October 15, 1962, Box 123, POF, JFKL.

56. Komer to Bundy, May 9, 1962, NSC History of South Asia, Vol. I, Box 24, NSF, LBJL.

57. Komer to Bundy, May 22, 1962, NSC History of South Asia, Vol. I, Box 24, NSF, LBJL; Record of President's meeting, June 14, 1962, *ibid.;* Komer to Bundy, July 26, 1962, *ibid.;* Galbraith to the State Department, June 20, 1962, Boxes 111–112, NSF, JFKL; Ian C. C. Graham, "The Indo-Soviet MIG Deal and Its International Repercussions," *Asian Survey* IV (May 1964), 823–832; Gopal, *Nehru,* III, 327–329, 337–338; Galbraith, *Ambassador's Journal,* 333, 337.

58. Symington to Kennedy, May 11, 1962, Box 118a, POF, JFKL; *Executive Sessions of the Senate Foreign Relations Committee, 1962, Historical Series,* vol. XIV (Washington, DC, 1986), 411–412; *New York Times,* May 12 and 25 and July 29, 1962.

59. Galbraith, *Ambassador's Journal,* 328; Kennedy to Nehru, September 7, 1962, Boxes 111–112, NSF, JFKL; President's Talking Paper for meeting with Morarji Desai (Indian Finance Minister), September 1962, Box 118a, POF, JFKL.

60. Roger Hilsman to Rusk, "The Five-Fold Dilemma: The Implications of the Sino-Indian Conflict," November 17, 1962, Sino-Indian Border Clash folder, Box 1, Roger Hilsman Papers, JFKL. See also Komer to Talbot, October 24, 1962, NSC History of South Asia, Vol. I, Box 24 NSF, LBJL.

61. Hilsman to Rusk, "The Five-Fold Dilemma," November 17, 1962.

62. Kennedy to Nehru, October 28, 1962, Box 118a, POF, JFKL; Galbraith to the State Department, October 29, 1962, Boxes 111–112, NSF, JFKL; Galbraith, *Ambassador's Journal,* 386–387.

63. Kennedy to Ayub, October 28, 1962, NSC History of South Asia, vol. 1, Box 24, NSF, LBJL.

64. Komer to Kaysen, November 16, 1962, NSC History of South Asia, *ibid.*

65. Ayub to Kennedy, November 5, 1962, reprinted in Ayub, *Friends Not Masters,* 141–143.

66. Hilsman to Rusk, "The Five-Fold Dilemma," November 17, 1962.

67. Komer to Kaysen, November 16, 1962, NSC History of South Asia, Vol. I, Box 24, NSF, LBJL; memorandum for the record of presidential meeting, November 19, 1962, *ibid.;* Hilsman to Rusk, November 20, 1962, Sino-Indian Border Clash folder, Box 1, Hilsman Papers.

68. Kennedy to Harriman, November 25, 1962, Box 118a, POF, JFKL.

69. Memorandum of conversation between Nehru and Harriman, November 22, 1962, Sino-Indian Border Clash folder, Box 1, Hilsman Papers; Roger Hilsman, *To Move a Nation* (New York, 1967), 327–337; report of the Harriman Mission, undated (probably early December 1962), Box 6, VPSF, LBJP, LBJL; Kennedy to Ayub, December 5, 1962, Box 123, POF, JFKL.

70. Report of the Harriman Mission; NSC Executive Committee Record of Action, December 3, 1962, Box 313, NSF, JFKL.

71. Talbot to the NSC, December 6, 1962, Boxes 338–342, NSF, JFKL; Talbot to the NSC, December 7, 1962, *ibid.;* National Security Action Memorandum No. 209, December 10, 1962, *ibid.;* Ayub Khan, *Friends Not Masters,* 148–152; Ayub Khan, "The Pakistan-American Alliance: Stresses and Strains," *Foreign Affairs* XLII (January 1964), 200–203.

72. Kennedy to Ayub, December 22, 1962, NSC History of South Asia, Vol. I, Box 242, NSF, LBJL.

73. Galbraith, *Ambassador's Journal,* 457; Zulfikar Ali Bhutto, *The Myth of Independence* (London, 1969), 62–64; Gopal, *Nehru,* III, 256–257; Choudhury, *India, Pakistan, Bangladesh,* 178–181.

74. Memorandum of a presidential meeting, February 21, 1963, Komer Staff Memoranda, NSF, JFKL.

75. Kennedy to Nehru, March 9, 1963, Box 118a, POF, JFKL; Rostow to Kennedy, April 8, 1963, in Rostow, *Diffusion of Power,* 651–653; Burris to Johnson, April 9, 1963, Box 6, VPSF, LBJP, LBJL; Bundy to Kennedy, May 4, 1963, Index of Weekend Papers, NSF, JFKL.

76. Galbraith, *Ambassador's Journal,* 509. See also Galbraith to Bowles, April 24, 1963, Galbraith folder, Box 299, Bowles Papers.

77. Rusk to Kennedy, May 8, 1963, Box 13, VPSF, LBJP, LBJL.

78. Galbraith to Kennedy and Rusk, May 16, 1963, Box 118a, POF, JFKL. See also Komer to Kennedy, May 17, 1963, *ibid.*

79. NSC Record of Action, May 9, 1963, NSC History of South Asia, Vol. I, Box 24, NSF, LBJL; Komer to Kennedy, May 9, 1963, *ibid.;* National Security Action Memorandum, No. 243, May 10, 1963, Box 314, NSF, JFKL.

80. Bowles to Kennedy, May 18, 1963, Box 118a, POF, JFKL; Bowles to Kennedy, May 4, 1963, Kennedy folder, Box 297, Bowles Papers.

81. Chester Bowles OH Interview (July 1, 1970), JFKL; James P. Grant (Deputy Assistant Secretary of State) to Bowles, October 21, 1963, Grant folder, Box 330, Bowles Papers; memorandum by Bowles, "Toward a Balance of Political and Military Forces in South Asia," November 12, 1963, Box 118a, POF, JFKL; Komer to Kennedy, November 12, 1963, *ibid.;* Bowles, *Promises,* 439–440; Mahendra Singh, *Indo-U.S. Relations, 1961–64* (Delhi, 1982), 178–189. For Soviet-Indian relations, see also Michael Brecher, "Non-Alignment Under Stress: The West and the India-China Border War," *Pacific Affairs* LII (Winter 1979–80), 612–630.

82. Bowles OH Interview; Bowles to James C. Thomson, October 15, 1963, Box 8, James C. Thomson Papers, JFKL; Bowles, *Promises to Keep,* 481–484.

83. Hilsman, *To Move,* 337. On the vital importance of the Peshawar base, see Bowles, *Promises to Keep, 481.*

84. McConaughy to the State Department, June 22, 1963, Box 123, POF, JFKL.

85. Rusk to the Embassy in Pakistan, July 7, 1963, Box 123, POF, JFKL.

86. Scope Paper for the Ball Mission, August 1963, *ibid.* See also "Instructions for Mr. Ball's Mission," *ibid.*

87. Ball, *The Past,* 275–276, 282–285; *New York Times,* September 4 and 6, 1963.

88. Ball, *The Past,* 282.

89. Memorandum of conversation between Talbot and Mohammed Shoaib (Pakistani Minister of Finance), September 30, 1963, Box 123, POF, JFKL; Benjamin H. Read (Executive Secretary, State Department) to Kennedy, October 3, 1963, *ibid.;* Spielman (Chargé, Pakistan) to the State Department, October 21, 1963, *ibid.;* CIA Special Report, "Pakistan's Foreign Policy Under Ayub and Bhutto," April 16, 1965, Box 151, NSF, LBJL.

90. Bhutto, *Myth,* 105.

Chapter 9. Vietnam

1. J. K. Galbraith to J. F. Kennedy, April 3, October 9, November 28, 1961, and March 2, 1962, Boxes 29a, 30, POF, JFKL.

2. J. K. Galbraith to J. F. Kennedy, April 3, 1961, Box 29a, POF, JFKL.

3. Herbert S. Parmet, *Jack: The Struggles of John F. Kennedy* (New York, 1980), 284–287.

4. Arthur M. Schlesinger, Jr., *Robert Kennedy and His Times* (Boston, 1978), 96; Address, November 14, 1951, Box 95, Legislative Files, House Files, PrePP, JFKL; Ronald Joseph Nurse, "America Must Not Sleep: The Development of John F. Kennedy's Foreign Policy Attitudes, 1947–1960" (Ph.D. dissertation, Michigan State University, 1971), 56, 80, 81, 89, 126, 132.

5. Edmund A. Gullion, "Political Evolution in Southeast Asia," Discussion Meeting Report, Council on Foreign Relations, November 30, 1953; speech draft, "Indo-China," undated with January 21, 1954 attachment, Box 481, Legislative Files, Senate Files, PrePP, JFKL.

6. John F. Kennedy to John Foster Dulles, May 7, 1953, Box 481, Legislative Files, Senate Files, PrePP, JFKL; Nurse, "America Must Not Sleep," 114–119.

7. John F. Kennedy, *The Strategy of Peace,* Allan Nevins, ed. (New York, 1960), 61–65; Nurse, "America Must Not Sleep," 130–131, 180.

8. Quoted in William Conrad Gibbons, *The United States Government and the Vietnam War,* Part I: *1945–1960* (Princeton, NJ, 1986), 300–305.

9. George McT. Kahin, *Intervention: How America Became Involved in Vietnam* (New York, 1986), 78–88, 96.

10. Jeffrey Race, *War Comes to Long An* (Berkeley, CA, 1973), 106–134.

11. Joseph Buttinger, *Vietnam: A Political History* (New York, 1968), 460; Mark Selden, "People's War and the Transformation of Peasant Society: China and Vietnam," in *America's Asia,* Edward Friedman and Mark Selden, eds. (New York, 1969), 357–392.

12. Warren I. Cohen, *Dean Rusk* (Totowa, NJ, 1980), 164–187.

13. Donald F. Crosby, *God, Church, and Flag: Senator Joseph R. McCarthy and the Catholic Church 1950–1957* (Chapel Hill, NC, 1978), 6–19, 206.

14. Parmet, *Jack,* 132, 158, 172, 175–182, 245–246, 250–256.

15. Crosby, *God, Church, and Flag,* 104–114.

16. Michael Rogin, *The Intellectuals and McCarthy* (Cambridge, MA, 1967), 233–239, 247–248, 262; Ithiel de Sola Pool, Robert P. Abelson, and

Samuel L. Popkin, *Candidates, Issues, and Strategies* (Cambridge, MA, 1964), 88–92, 117–118; Allen J. Matusow, *The Unraveling of America* (New York, 1984), 21–29.

17. Robert A. Divine, *Foreign Policy and U.S. Presidential Elections: 1952–1960* (New York, 1974), 209, 234–235, 240–274, 275; Stephen E. Ambrose, *Eisenhower,* Vol. II: *The President* (New York, 1984), 614–616.

18. Wilton B. Persons, Assistant to the President, Memorandum, January 19, 1961, Box 11, Post-Presidential Files, DDEP, DDEL; Clark Clifford to the President, "Memorandum of Conference on January 19, 1961 between President Eisenhower and President-Elect Kennedy on the Subject of Laos," misdated September 29, 1967, probably 1961; Beacon Press, *The Pentagon Papers (The Senator Gravel Edition)* (Boston, 1971), II, 635–637; hereafter cited as *Pentagon Papers (Gravel)*; Clark M. Clifford to J. F. Kennedy, "Memorandum on Conference between President Eisenhower and President-elect Kennedy and their Chief Advisers on January 19, 1961," January 24, 1961, Box 29a, POF, JFKL.

19. Robert S. McNamara to J. F. Kennedy, Memorandum, January 24, 1961, Box 29a, POF, JFKL; J. F. Kennedy, Memorandum dictated to Evelyn Lincoln, January 19, 1961, *ibid.*

20. *PPP, JFK, 1961,* pp. 19–28; R. B. Smith, *An International History of the Vietnam War,* Vol. I: *Revolution versus Containment, 1955–1961* (New York, 1983), 224.

21. *Ibid.,* 257.

22. Arthur Krock, "Conversation Memo with President Kennedy," October 11, 1961, Box 1, Arthur Krock Papers, Princeton University Library, Princeton, NJ. I am grateful to Thomas G. Paterson for sharing this memorandum with me.

23. McGeorge Bundy, "Memorandum of Discussion on Southeast Asia July 28, 1961, 11 A.M.," July 31, 1961, Box 231a, NSF, JFKL.

24. Robert H. Ferrell, ed., *The Eisenhower Diaries* (New York, 1981), 387; Schlesinger, *Robert Kennedy,* 735; U. Alexis Johnson, with Jef Olivarius McAllister, *The Right Hand of Power* (Englewood Cliffs, NJ, 1984), 324–325.

25. Walt W. Rostow, Memorandum to the President, "Southeast Asia," August 4, 1961; Robert H. Johnson, "Memorandum for Mr. Bundy, Southeast Asia," August 25, 1961; Maxwell D. Taylor, Memorandum for the President, "Meeting on Southeast Asia Planning," August 29, 1961, all Box 231a, NSF, JFKL.

26. Dean Rusk, Memorandum for the President, "Gromyko Talks—Southeast Asia," October 6, 1961, *ibid.*

27. Ambrose, *Eisenhower,* 210; George C. Herring, *America's Longest War: The United States and Vietnam, 1950–1975* (New York, 1986, 2nd ed.), 70.

28. Walt W. Rostow to McGeorge Bundy, Memorandum, "Meeting, Saturday Morning, January 28, 1961 in the President's Office on Vietnam," Box 193, NSF, JFKL; Parmet, *JFK,* 139, 154; Frederick Nolting to Secretary of State, May 15, 1961, Box 242–252, NSF, JFKL.

29. Communiqué of the SEATO Council Meeting, Bangkok, March 30, 1961, extracted in *Documents on International Affairs, 1961,* D. C. Watt, et

al., eds. (London, 1965), 567; Memorandum from Deputy Secretary of Defense (Gilpatric) to the President, "A Program of Action to Prevent Communist Domination of South Vietnam," May 1, 1961, DS, *Foreign Relations of the United States, 1961–1963,* Vol. I: *Vietnam* (Washington, DC, 1988), 93 (hereafter cited as *FRUS*).

30. N. A. Veliotes to L. D. Battle, for W. W. Rostow through McG. Bundy, Memorandum, "Talking Points on the Vienna Conversations," June 12, 1961, Box 300, Chester Bowles Papers, Yale University Library, New Haven, CT.

31. Smith, *International History,* I, pp. 224–225.

32. *Ibid.,* 258ff; R. B. Smith, *An International History of the Vietnam War,* Vol. II: *The Kennedy Strategy* (New York, 1985), 107–112, 117, 207–221.

33. Smith, *International History,* I, 226–231.

34. Kahin, *Intervention,* 96–101.

35. Amembassy Saigon to DS, "Estimate of (a) DRV Courses of Action re SVN and (b) DRV Reaction to Escalation of US Military Measures in SVN," Box 195, NSF, JFKL.

36. Race, *War Comes;* William R. Andrews, *The Village War: Vietnamese Communist Revolutionary Activities in Dinh Tuong Province, 1960–1964* (Columbia, MO, 1973); James Walker Trullinger, Jr., *Village at War: An Account of Revolution in Vietnam* (New York, 1980); Smith, *International History,* I, 235. On the Delta, see William J. Duiker, *The Communist Road to Power in Vietnam* (Boulder, CO, 1981), 198–199, 211.

37. W. W. Rostow, *The Diffusion of Power* (New York, 1972), 273–274; Roger Hilsman, *To Move a Nation* (New York, 1967), 459–461.

38. *Pentagon Papers (Gravel),* II, 96, 108–109; Telegrams from Embassy in Vietnam to DS, October 16, 18, 1961, *FRUS, 1961–1963,* I, 383, 391–392; Larry E. Cable, *Conflict of Myths: The Development of American Counterinsurgency Doctrine and the Vietnam War* (New York, 1986), 5–6, 177–179; Andrew F. Krepinevich, *The Army and Vietnam* (Baltimore, MD, 1986), 36; Maxwell D. Taylor, Memorandum for the President, "Southeast Asia Planning," September 26, 1961, Box 231a, NSF, JFKL; L. L. Lemnitzer, Memorandum for the Secretary of Defense, "The Strategic Importance of the Southeast Asia Mainland," January 13, 1962, U.S. Congress, House, Committee on Armed Services, *United States-Vietnam Relations, 1945–1967: A Study Prepared by the Department of Defense* (Washington, DC, 1971), V.B.4, pp. 448–454—hereafter cited as *Pentagon Papers (House Committee);* Memorandum from the Secretary of Defense (McNamara) to the President, November 8, 1961, *FRUS, 1961–1963,* I, 559–561.

39. Maxwell D. Taylor to J. F. Kennedy, Taylor Mission Report, November 3, 1961, Box 195, NSF, JFKL; *Pentagon Papers (Gravel),* II, pp. 84–102; W. W. Rostow, Memorandum to the President, November 11, 1961, Box 195, NSF, JFKL; Telegram from President's Military Representative (Taylor) to DS, October 25, 1961, *FRUS, 1961–1963,* I, 427–428.

40. McGeorge Bundy, Memorandum for the President, November 15, 1961, Boxes 55–56, Theodore Sorensen Papers, JFKL.

41. General Edward G. Lansdale, Unconventional Warfare appendix to Taylor Mission Report, November 3, 1961, Box 195, NSF, JFKL.

42. Russell F. Weigley, *The American Way of War* (Bloomington, IN, 1973), 460.

43. "Notes of a Meeting, Department of State, Washington, November 9, 1961, 4:36 p.m.," *FRUS, 1961–1963,* I, 572–573; McGeorge Bundy, Memorandum for the President, "Notes for Talk with Secretary Rusk—Nov. 15," November 15, 1961, Box 195, NSF, JFKL.

44. Dean Rusk to (Acting) Secretary of State, Telegram, November 1, 1961, Box 194, NSF, JFKL.

45. Sterling Cottrell, Political-Social Appendix to Taylor Mission Report, November 3, 1961, Box 195, NSF, JFKL; John Kenneth Galbraith to J. F. Kennedy, Memorandum, "Neglected Parts of General Taylor's Report on South Vietnam," November 13, 1961, Box 195, NSF, JFKL.

46. George C. McGhee (DS), Memorandum for Dr. Walt Rostow, "Security in Southeast Asia," July 28, 1961, Box 223–231, NSF, JFKL.

47. U.S. Senator Mike Mansfield to J. F. Kennedy, Memorandum, "The Vietnamese and Southeast Asian Situation," November 2, 1961, Box 194, NSF, JFKL.

48. Theodore C. Sorensen, Memorandum for the President, "A TV Report on Viet Nam and Southeast Asia," November 24, 1961, Box 55-56, Sorensen Papers.

49. Averell Harriman to J. F. Kennedy, Memorandum and covering letter, November 11, 1961, Box 195, NSF, JFKL.

50. J. K. Galbraith to J. F. Kennedy, letter and memorandum, "A Plan for South Vietnam," n.d., Box 128a, POF, JFKL; C. Bowles to Adlai Stevenson, October 7, 1961, Box 301, Bowles Papers.

51. Pentagon Papers (*Gravel*), II, 110–111.

52. Montague Kern, Patricia W. Levering, and Ralph B. Levering, *The Kennedy Crises: The Press, the Presidency, and Foreign Policy* (Chapel Hill, NC, 1983), 3, 47, 60, 65, 75–84; *PPP, JFK, 1961,* p. 668.

53. *Pentagon Papers* (*Gravel*), II, 82; Memorandum for the Record, November 6, 1961, W. H. B[agley], *FRUS, 1961–1963,* I, 532; William Conrad Gibbons, *The U.S. Government and the Vietnam War,* Part II: *1961–1964* (Princeton, NJ, 1986), 86, 89.

54. Memorandum from the Chairman of the Joint Chiefs of Staff's Special Assistant (Parker) to the Chairman (Lemnitzer), December 18, 1961, *FRUS, 1961–1963,* I, 740; Gibbons, *U.S. Government,* II, 73–74, 79–80.

55. J. F. Kennedy, Memorandum for Secretary of State, Secretary of Defense, "used by President as talking paper Nov. 14 PM—before NSC," Box 195, NSF, JFKL.

56. McGeorge Bundy to Secretary of State, "First Phase of Viet-Nam Program," National Security Action Memorandum 111, November 22, 1961, *Pentagon Papers* (*House Committee*), V.B.4, pp. 419–421.

57. Gibbons, *U.S. Government,* II, 99.

58. "Notes of a Meeting, the White House, Washington, November 11, 1961, 12:10 p.m.," Lemnitzer, n.d., *FRUS, 1961–1963,* I, 577–578; "Notes on National Security Council Meeting 15 November 1961," Box 4, VPSF, LBJL.

59. *Pentagon Papers* (*Gravel*), II, 650–651, 662–666.

60. Frederick Nolting to Secretary of State, Telegram, November 18, 1961, Box 195, NSF, JFKL.

61. Letter from Ambassador in Vietnam (Nolting) to President Diem, December 5, 1961, Enclosure, Memorandum of Understanding, December 4, 1961, *FRUS, 1961–1963*, I, 713–716; Saigon to Secretary of State, Telegram, December 4, 1961, Box 195, NSF, JFKL; Edward G. Lansdale to Chairman, JCS, Memorandum, "Vietnamese Command Problem," *Pentagon Papers (House Committee)*, V.B.4, p. 427.

62. Saigon to Secretary of State, Telegram, November 24, 1961, Box 195, NSF, JFKL.

63. Gibbons, *U.S. Government*, II, 110.

64. Roger Hilsman (SD) to Maxwell D. Taylor, Memorandum, "A Strategic Concept for South Vietnam," February 2, 1962, Box 195, NSF, JFKL.

65. Herring, *America's Longest War*, 86–91.

66. Duiker, *Communist Road*, 206–208; Douglas Pike, *Viet Cong* (Cambridge, MA, 1966), 350–351; Allen E. Goodman, *The Lost Peace: America's Search for a Negotiated Settlement of the Vietnam War* (Stanford, CA, 1978), 12–14.

67. Herring, *America's Longest War*, 86–87; Kahin, *Intervention*, 140.

68. Hilsman, *To Move*, 438.

69. Krepinevich, *The Army and Vietnam*, 29–63, 113–157; Cable, *Conflict of Myths*, 27–33, 113–157, 177–179.

70. Ronald H. Spector, *Advice and Support: The Early Years 1941–1960, Center of Military History, United States Army in Vietnam* (Washington, DC, 1983), 241, 280, 301, 344–348; Douglas Kinnard, *The War Managers* (Hanover, NH, 1977), 165–166; Robert W. Komer, *Bureaucracy at War: U.S. Performance in the Vietnam Conflict* (Boulder, CO, 1986), 61; Krepinevich, *The Army and Vietnam*, 75–76.

71. Commander, U.S. Military Advisory Command, Saigon (Harkins) to JCS, "Province Rehabilitation Program," September 2, 1962, Box 196, NSF, JFKL; Race, *War Comes*, 132–134; *Pentagon Papers (Gravel)* II, 150–159; Komer, *Bureaucracy at War*, 46–48, 63–64, 138; Duiker, *Communist Road*, 214; Hilsman to Rusk, Research Memorandum, "The Situation and Short-Term Prospects in South Vietnam," December 3, 1962, *Pentagon Papers (House Committee)*, V.B.4, pp. 487–489; Timothy J. Lomperis, *The War Everyone Lost—And Won* (Baton Rouge, LA, 1984), 58.

72. Krepinevich, *The Army and Vietnam*, 36–37, 71–73; Cable, *Conflict of Myths*, 188, 191–195; Douglas S. Blaufarb, *The Counterinsurgency Era* (New York, 1977), 119.

73. Richard Tanner Johnson, *Managing the White House: An Intimate Study of the Presidency* (New York, 1974), 130–134; Stephen E. Pelz, ed., " 'When Do I Have Time to Think?' John F. Kennedy, Roger Hilsman, and the Laotian Crisis of 1962," *Diplomatic History* III (Spring 1979), 215–229; James C. Thomson, Jr., "How Could Vietnam Happen? An Autopsy," *Atlantic Monthly* CCXXI (April 1968), 47–53.

74. Kenneth W. Thompson, ed., *The Kennedy Presidency* (New York, 1985), 298–300.

75. *PPP, JFK, 1963*, p. 11.

76. Kenneth P. O'Donnell and David F. Powers, *"Johnny, We Hardly Knew Ye": Memories of John Fitzgerald Kennedy* (Boston, MA, 1972), 15; for Mansfield's views, see U.S. Senate, "Report of Senators Mike Mansfield, J. Caleb Boggs, Claiborne Pell, and Benjamin A. Smith," *Viet Nam and Southeast Asia*, 88th Cong., 1st Sess. (Washington, DC, 1963).

77. Kahin, *Intervention*, 142–143.

78. General C. V. Clifton to General Godfrey T. McHugh, January 7, 1963, Box 197, NSF, JFKL.

79. Michael V. Forrestal, Memorandum for the President, "Eyes Only Annex: Performance of the U.S. Mission," January 28, 1963, Box 197, NSF, JFKL.

80. Gibbons, *U.S. Government*, II, 138; Commander in Chief (Pacific) to JCS, February 14, 1963, Box 3, Roger Hilsman Papers, JFKL.

81. William A. Buckingham, Jr., *Operation Ranch Hand: The Air Force and Herbicides in Southeast Asia, 1961–1967* (Washington, DC, 1982), 16–17, 20–22, 82–87; Smith, *International History*, II, 144–145; Mieczyslaw Maneli, *War of the Vanquished*, Maria de Görgey, trans. (New York, 1971), 83–111.

82. Herring, *America's Longest War*, 96; Kahin, *Intervention*, 149–150.

83. Daniel C. Hallin, *The "Uncensored" War: The Media and Vietnam* (New York, 1986), 26–43; Kern, Levering, and Levering, *Kennedy Crises*, 199–200.

84. George Ball to Saigon, May 21, 1963, Box 196–197, NSF, JFKL; John Mecklin, *Mission in Torment: An Intimate Account of the U.S. Role in Vietnam* (New York, 1965), 99–151; Hallin, *"Uncensored War,"* 43–48.

85. David Halberstam, *The Making of a Quagmire* (New York, 1964), 268; Kennedy quoted in McGeorge Bundy, Memorandum for the Record, "Meeting on McNamara/Taylor Mission to South Vietnam," September 23, 1963, Box 200, NSF, JFKL.

86. Terry Dietz, *Republicans and Vietnam, 1961–1968* (New York, 1986), 55–56; Russell quoted in *Time* LXXXI (April 12, 1963), 34.

87. Parmet, *JFK*, 272.

88. Lewis J. Paper, *The Promise and the Performance: The Leadership of John F. Kennedy* (New York, 1975), 245–246; Parmet, *JFK*, 49–60, 272; Pool, *Candidates, Issues, Strategies*, 82–94; Theodore C. Sorensen, *Kennedy* (New York, 1965), 505.

89. Lou Harris to J. F. Kennedy, Memorandum, "Analysis of the 1962 Elections," November 19, 1962, Box 320, POF, JFKL; B. Brawley to J. Bailey, July 31, 1963, Box 99, POF, JFKL.

90. Pool, *Candidates, Issues, Strategies*, 90.

91. James L. Sundquist, *Politics and Policy: The Eisenhower, Kennedy, and Johnson Years* (Washington, DC, 1968), 456, 466–468.

92. William L. Lunch and Peter W. Sperlich, "American Political Opinion and the War in Vietnam," *Western Political Quarterly* XXXII (March 1979), 22.

93. Matusow, *Unraveling*, 134–135.

94. Geoffrey Warner, "The United States and the Fall of Diem" Part I: "The Coup That Never Was," *Australian Outlook* XXVIII (December 1974),

245; Kahin, *Intervention,* 143–145; CIA Information Report, "Indications of Government of Vietnam Plan to Request Reduction of American Personnel in Vietnam," April 22, 1963, Box 198–199, NSF, JFKL.

95. *PPP, JFK, 1963,* p. 421.

96. *Pentagon Papers (Gravel),* II, 160–190.

97. Thomas L. Hughes to Secretary of State, "Implications of the Buddhist Crisis in Vietnam," June 21, 1963, Box 197, NSF, JFKL; Special National Intelligence Estimate, 53-2-62, "The Situation in South Vietnam," July 10, 1963, *Pentagon Papers (House Committee)* V.B.4, p. 535.

98. *Pentagon Papers (Gravel),* II, 228–229; CIA, "Possible Change in Government of Vietnam Foreign Policy in Light of Appointment of Ambassador Lodge," July 17, 1963, Box 198, NSF, JFKL.

99. *Time* LXXXII (July 5, 1963), 22.

100. Herring, *America's Longest War,* 97.

101. Gibbons, *U.S. Government,* II, 146–147; *Pentagon Papers (Gravel),* II, 232–234; Kahin, *Intervention,* 152–158.

102. *Time* LXXXII (October 4, 1963), 33; Michael V. Forrestal, Memorandum for the President, August 24, 1963, Box 198, NSF, JFKL.

103. *Pentagon Papers (Gravel),* II, 734.

104. J. F. Kennedy to H. C. Lodge, Personal for the Ambassador from the President, August 29, 1963, Box 198, NSF, JFKL; *Pentagon Papers (Gravel),* II, 736.

105. *PPP, JFK, 1963,* p. 652.

106. *Ibid.,* 759–760, 828; Kahin, *Intervention,* 170–173.

107. U.S. Senate, Select Committee to Study Governmental Operations with Respect to Intelligence Activities, *Alleged Assassination Plots Involving Foreign Leaders: An Interim Report* (Washington, DC, 1975), 220–221.

108. H. C. Lodge to McG. Bundy, October 25, 1963, Box 201, NSF, JFKL.

109. *Pentagon Papers (Gravel),* II, 782–793.

110. Ellen J. Hammer, *A Death in November: America in Vietnam, 1963* (New York, 1987), 284–285; *Pentagon Papers (Gravel),* II, 268–269; Tran Van Don, *Our Endless War: Inside Vietnam* (San Raphael, CA, 1978), 110–113.

111. Dean Rusk to U.S. Embassy Saigon, November 13, 1963, Box 202, NSF, JFKL.

112. Robert Thompson, *Defeating Communist Insurgency: Experiences from Malaya and Vietnam* (London, 1966), 59, quoted in Hammer, *Death,* 129.

113. Hammer, *Death,* 314.

114. *PPP, JFK, 1963,* pp. 892, 894–898.

115. Sorensen, *Kennedy,* 651–652.

116. Sino-Soviet Task Force, CIA, "The Sino-Soviet Dispute and Its Significance," Boxes 21–27, China, General, NSF, JFKL.

117. Thomas G. Paterson, "Bearing the Burden: A Critical Look at JFK's Foreign Policy," *Virginia Quarterly Review* LIV (Spring 1978), 207–210; Ernest R. May, *"Lessons" of the Past* (New York, 1973), 94–99.

118. Johnson, *Managing,* 124ff; Alexander L. George, *Presidential Deci-*

sionmaking in Foreign Policy: The Effective Use of Information and Advice (Boulder, CO, 1987), 146–149.

119. O'Donnell and Powers, *"Johnny,"* 16–17.

Chapter 10. Africa

1. William Attwood OH Interview, JFKL; DS, "Briefing Paper for the President: Mali," July 12, 1961, Box 140, NSF, JFKL.

2. DS, "Memorandum of Conversation Between the President and Jean-Marie Kone of the Republic of Mali," July 12, 1961, Box 140, NSF: Mali.

3. John Foster Dulles, "The Cost of Peace," *DSB* XXXIV (June 18, 1956), 1000.

4. Dwight D. Eisenhower, *Waging Peace, 1956–1961* (Garden City, NY, 1965), 572–73.

5. George Allen, "United States' Foreign Policy in Africa," *DSB* XXXIV (April 30, 1956), 716–18.

6. "The Vice-President's Report to the President on His Trip to Africa," undated, Box 594, OF 116, WHCF, DDEL.

7. Thomas J. Noer, *Cold War and Black Liberation: The United States and White Rule in Africa, 1948–1968* (Columbia, MO, 1985), 58–60.

8. John F. Kennedy, *The Strategy of Peace*, Allan Nevins, ed. (New York, 1960), 131.

9. *New York Times,* July 6, 1957.

10. *PPP, JFK, 1962*, p. 10. See also Bruce Miroff, *Pragmatic Illusions: The Presidential Politics of John F. Kennedy* (New York, 1976), 110–11.

11. G. Mennen Williams, *Africa for the Africans* (Grand Rapids, MI, 1969), 172.

12. "Report to the Honorable John F. Kennedy by the Task Force on Africa," December 31, 1960, Box 1073, Transition Files, Pre-PP, JFKL.

13. DS, "Guidelines of U.S. Policy and Operations Concerning Africa," September 22, 1961, Box 2a, NSF: Africa.

14. William Hance, ed., *Southern Africa and the United States* (New York, 1968), 32–35.

15. Christopher Stevens, *The Soviet Union and Black Africa* (New York, 1976), 192–93, and Bruce D. Larkin, *China and Africa 1948–1970* (Berkeley, 1971), 167–92.

16. G. Mennen Williams OH Interview, JFKL.

17. Tom Mboya OH Interview, JFKL. See also Arthur M. Schlesinger, Jr., *A Thousand Days: John F. Kennedy in the White House* (Boston, 1965), 557–60.

18. Roger Hilsman, *To Move a Nation: The Politics of Foreign Policy in the Administration of John F. Kennedy* (Garden City, NY, 1967), 233.

19. "Analytical Chronology of the Congo Crisis," January 25, 1961, Box 27, NSF: Congo.

20. Richard D. Mahoney, *JFK: Ordeal in Africa* (New York, 1983), 38–40.

21. For American attempts to assassinate Lumumba, see U.S. Congress, Senate, Select Committee to Study Governmental Operations with Respect to Intelligence Activities, *Alleged Assassination Plots Involving Foreign Leaders* (Washington, DC, 1975), 20–32, 49–57. See also Madeleine Kalb, *The Congo Cables* (New York, 1982), 128–96.

22. Theodore Sorensen, *Kennedy* (New York, 1965), 636.

23. Dean Rusk to John Kennedy, "Suggested New United States Policy on the Congo," February 1, 1961, Box 25, NSF: Congo.

24. "Briefing on the Situation in the Congo," February 6, 1961, Box 1, G. Mennen Williams Papers, NA.

25. "Analytical Chronology of the Congo Crisis: Supplement," March 9, 1961, Box 27, NSF: Congo. See also Mahoney, *JFK,* 69–71.

26. "Analytical Chronology of the Congo Crisis: Supplement."

27. Rusk to Kennedy, "The Congo," August 3, 1961, Box 28, NSF: Congo.

28. DS, "Record of Understanding of the Meeting with the President," July 25, 1961, *ibid.;* U. Alexis Johnson to G. McMurtrie Godley, July 29, 1961, Box 30, *ibid.*

29. Mahoney, *JFK,* 86–87.

30. Rusk to Kennedy, "The Congo," August 3, 1961; Rostow to Kennedy, August 4, 1961, Box 28, NSF: Congo.

31. Hilsman, *To Move,* 251–54.

32. Ball to Kennedy, "New Policy on the Congo," September 23, 1961, Box 28, NSF: Congo. See also George W. Ball, *The Past Has Another Pattern* (New York, 1982), 228–34.

33. DS, Memorandum for Mr. Bundy, "Status Report on the Congo," November 2, 1961, Box 28, NSF: Congo.

34. Edmund Guillon OH Interview, JFKL; Rusk to Kennedy, "Next Steps on the Congo," November 11, 1961, Box 28, NSF: Congo.

35. Tshombe to Kennedy, December 14, 1961; Kennedy to Tshombe, December 15, 1961, Box 28, NSF: Congo. For the Kitona Conference see Kalb, *Congo Cables,* 317–23.

36. Quoted in Mahoney, *JFK,* 123.

37. *Ibid.,* 124.

38. DS, "Proposed Action Program for the Congo," February 9, 1962; Ralph Dungan to Bundy, February 9, 1962, Box 314, NSF: Meetings and Memorandum; Bowles to Kennedy, "Report on Mission to Africa," Box 3, NSF: Africa. See also Mahoney, *JFK,* 144–45.

39. McGhee to Kennedy, "Mission to the Congo, September 25–October 19, 1962," October 22, 1962, Box 28, NSF: Congo; *New York Times,* October 22, 1962.

40. *New York Times,* November 28, 1962; Sorensen, *Kennedy,* 725.

41. Hilsman to Kennedy, "The Congo: An Appraisal of Alternatives," December 11, 1962, Box 1, Roger Hilsman Papers, JFKL: Ball to Bundy, December 12, 1962, quoted in Mahoney, *JFK,* 152.

42. Hilsman to Rusk, "Congo Chronology—A Supplement," undated, Box 1, Hilsman Papers; DS, "Operating Plans for the Congo," December 17, 1962, Box 28, NSF: Congo.

43. John Bartlow Martin, *Adlai Stevenson and the World* (Garden City, NY, 1977), 750–51.

46. Kennedy to McGhee, January 17, 1963, Box 29, NSF: Congo.

45. Stephen Weissman, *American Foreign Policy in the Congo, 1960–1964* (Ithaca, NY, 1974), 194.

46. Rusk to C. Burke Elbrick, March 4, 1961, Box 154, NSF: Portugal.

47. *New York Times,* March 21, 1961.

48. Noer, *Cold War,* 70–71.

49. U.S. Congress, Senate Committee on Foreign Relations, Subcommittee on African Affairs, *Angola* (Washington, DC, 1976), 174.

50. Noer, *Cold War,* 72–78.

51. Bahram Farzanegan, "United States Response and Reaction to the Emergence of Arab and African States in International Politics" (Ph.D. dissertation, American University, 1966), 241–42.

52. Department of State Policy and Planning Council to Bundy, "Status Report on Portuguese Africa," May 25, 1961, Box 154, NSF: Portugal.

53. Schlesinger, *A Thousand Days,* 352–53; DS, "Talking Points on the Vienna Conversations," undated, Box 300, Chester Bowles Papers, Yale University Library, New Haven, CT.

54. "Report of the Task Force on the Portuguese Territories in Africa," undated; Sam Belk to Bundy, June 29, 1961, Box 5, NSF: Angola.

55. NSC, "Action Memorandum," July 14, 1961, *ibid.*

56. Paul Sakwa, letter to the author, September 24, 1979; Paul Sakwa, "U.S. Policy Towards Portugal," January 17, 1962, Box 154, NSF: Portugal.

57. NSC, "Financial Assistance to Portugal," March 23, 1962, Box 154, NSF: Portugal.

58. William Attwood OH Interview, JFKL.

59. CIA Memorandum, "Significance of Portuguese and Spanish Colonial Problems for the U.S.," July 11, 1963; "Memorandum for the Record: Meeting with the President on Portuguese Africa," July 18, 1963, Box 154a, NSF: Portugal; Martin, *Adlai Stevenson,* 767–68.

60. Elbrick to Rusk, August 13, 1963, Box 154a, NSF: Portugal.

61. Thomas J. Noer, "Truman, Eisenhower, and South Africa: The Middle Road and Apartheid," *The Journal of Ethnic Studies* XI (Spring 1983), 75–104.

62. U.S. Congress, House Committee on Foreign Affairs, *Hearings on U.S.-South African Relations* (Washington, DC, 1966), pt. 1, pp. 44–45.

63. Bowles to Kennedy, undated, Box 297, Bowles Papers.

64. William Brubeck to Bundy, undated, Box 159, NSF: South Africa; Joseph Satterthwaite, OH Interview, JFKL.

65. DS, "Republic of South Africa; Guidelines for Policy and Operations," May 2, 1961; Rusk to Satterthwaite, August 25, 1961, Box 2, NSF, Africa.

66. Noer, *Cold War,* 136–44.

67. David Garrow, *Bearing the Cross: Martin Luther King, Jr., and the Southern Christian Leadership Conference* (New York, 1986), 224; Rusk to Kennedy, June 21, 1963, Box 159, NSF: Africa. See also Williams to Kennedy, "Civil Rights," June 15, 1963, Box 3, Williams Papers.

68. Wiliams to Rusk and Kennedy, "U.S. Policy Towards South Africa," June 12, 1963, Box 3, NSF: Africa.

69. Dungan to Kennedy, "Background of the South African Problem," July 9, 1963, Box 1, Arthur M. Schlesinger, Jr. Papers, JFKL; Ball to Kennedy, "Next Steps with South Africa," July 16, 1963, Box 159, NSF: South Africa.

70. Rusk to Stevenson, August 1, 1963; DS, "Memorandum for the President," August 2, 1963, Box 159, NSF: South Africa.

71. *DSB* XLIX (August 17, 1963), 7.

72. Williams OH Interview.

73. *DSB* L (January 20, 1964), 96.

74. Hance, *Southern Africa,* 36–37; Edmond Hutchinson OH Interview, JFKL.

75. Attwood to Ball, May 12, 1961, Box 100, NSF: Ghana. See also William Attwood, *The Reds and the Blacks: A Personal Adventure* (New York, 1967).

76. Shriver to Kennedy, June 20, 1961, Box 284, NSF: Departments and Agencies.

77. DS, "Memorandum of Conversation: Guinea," May 16, 1963, Box 102, NSF: Guinea.

78. *New York Times,* September 26, 1960.

79. Thomas J. Noer, "The New Frontier and African Neutralism: Kennedy, Nkrumah, and the Volta River Project," *Diplomatic History* VIII (Winter 1984), 61–80.

80. F. H. Russell to Rusk, January 20, 1961, Box 99, NSF: Ghana.

81. DS, "Briefing Paper for President Kennedy: Ghana-U.S. Relations," March 6, 1961, *ibid.;* CIA, "Kwame Nkrumah," March 1961, Box 117a, POF, JFKL.

82. DS, "Memorandum of Conversation," March 8, 1961, Box 117a, POF.

83. Kennedy to Nkrumah, June 29, 1961, Box 99, NSF: Ghana.

84. Williams to Ball, September 12, 1961, Box 99a, NSF: Ghana; Rusk to Kennedy, September 11, 1961, Box 330, NSF: Meetings and Memorandum.

85. Arthur M. Schlesinger, Jr., *Robert Kennedy and His Times* (Boston, 1978), 560–61; Schlesinger, *A Thousand Days,* 573.

86. *New York Times,* September 23, 1961; NSC, "Summary of Volta Project Documents," undated; DS, Legal Affairs Division, to African Bureau, September 26, 1961, Box 99a, NSF: Ghana.

87. Nkrumah to Kennedy, September 29, 1961; CIA, "Likely Consequences of Various U.S. Courses of Action on the Volta Dam," November 16, 1961, Box 99a, NSF: Ghana.

88. "Notes for the Record: National Security Council Meeting on the Volta Dam," December 5, 1961, *ibid.*

89. Carl Kaysen to Kennedy, October 29, 1962, Box 100, *ibid.*

Chapter 11. Peace Corps

1. *PPF, JFK, 1962,* pp. 608–609.

2. Author's interview with Linda Bergthold, August 25, 1982.

3. Author's interview with Harris Wofford, September 3, 1987.

4. For Reuss's account of his role as a founding father of the Peace Corps, see Henry Reuss, "A Foreign Aid Program That Went Astray," manuscript, Henry Reuss Papers, Marquette University, Milwaukee, WI; for Humphrey, see *CR*, CVI (June 15, 1960), 12634–12638.

5. "Kennedy at Union," October 13, 1960, audio tape, University of Michigan Library, Ann Arbor.

6. Harris Wofford, *Of Kennedys and Kings* (New York, 1980), 247–248.

7. Quoted in *Michigan Daily,* November 3, 1960.

8. For student response to the Peace Corps at the University of Michigan, see *ibid.,* October 14, November 2, 3, 4, 5, 1960.

9. Wofford, *Of Kennedys,* 251.

10. Sargent Shriver, *Point of the Lance* (New York, 1964), 12–13; Wofford, *Of Kennedys,* 252–253; Gerard T. Rice, *The Bold Experiment* (South Bend, IN, 1985), 37–39.

11. Author's interview with William Josephson, September 18, 1987. For the views of the Peace Corps General Counsel during the Kennedy years, see William Josephson OH Interview, JFKL. See also Wofford, *Of Kennedys,* 253–262, and Rice, *Bold Experiment,* 39–47.

12. Shriver's report is quoted in Wofford, *Of Kennedys,* 259.

13. Roy Hoopes, *The Complete Peace Corps Guide* (New York, 1966), 79.

14. Wofford, *Of Kennedys,* 261–262.

15. Rice, *Bold Experiment,* 60; Wofford, *Of Kennedys,* 262–263.

16. Shriver is quoted in "Interviews," pp. 20–21, Harris Wofford Papers, Bryn Mawr, PA. See also Rice, *Bold Experiment,* 64.

17. The official—William Josephson—is quoted in Rice, *Bold Experiment,* 65.

18. Quoted in *ibid.,* 65–66.

19. Quoted in Wofford, *Of Kennedys,* 266. Author's interview with William Josephson.

20. Gerard T. Rice, *Twenty Years of Peace Corps* (Washington, DC, 1981), 24; David Hapgood and Meridian Bennett, *Agents of Change* (Boston, 1968), 44.

21. Harris Wofford, "Report on the Peace Corps in Ethiopia," May 25, 1963, p. 2, Peace Corps, FOIA (hereafter cited PC-FOIA); Kennett Love and Richard Elwell, "Ethiopia Overseas Evaluation: 1963," pp. 4, 7, PC-FOIA.

22. Meridan Bennett and Maureen J. Carroll, "Ethiopia Overseas Evaluation: 1967," pp. 25, 46, PC-FOIA.

23. *Who's Who in the Peace Corps Overseas Administration* (Washington, DC, n.d.), 56, PC-FOIA.

24. Wofford, "Report," 2.

25. Quoted in *The New Yorker* XXXVIII (June 30, 1962), 27.

26. Quoted in "Peace Corpsmen Trek West," *Washington Evening Star,* July 9, 1962, Peace Corps, 1961–1963, Box 1, Georgetown University Archives, Washington, DC.

27. *Washington Standard,* July 20, 1962, *ibid.;* Beulah Bartlett and Blythe Monroe, "Project Ethiopia I," p. 3, manuscript, John Coyne Papers, New York.

28. Neil Boyer, ed., "Ethiopia I—Ten Years Later," p. 1, PC-FOIA.
29. George H. Dunne, S.J., "Evaluation of the Afghanistan and Ethiopia Projects at Georgetown University," pp. 1, 16, Georgetown University Archives; Love and Elwell, "Ethiopia Overseas Evaluation," 38, 39, 40; Paul E. Tsongas, "Address to the National Congress of Former Peace Corps Volunteers," September 1981, p. 1.
30. Dunne, "Evaluation," 3–4. For a discussion of the "Numbers Game," see Kevin Lowther and C. P. Lucas, *Keeping Kennedy's Promse* (Boulder, CO, 1978), 21–48. For Wofford and Africa, see Wofford, Memorandum to the President, March 7, 1962, Wofford Papers.
31. Author's interview with Carol Miller Reynolds, August 9, 1987; Bergthold interview. See also Love and Elwell, "Ethiopia Overseas Evaluation," 92.
32. Bergthold interview.
33. J. L. Manuell, M.D., to Rev. George H. Dunne, January 31, 1963, p. 1, Georgetown University Archives.
34. Quoted in Love and Elwell, "Ethiopia Overseas Evaluation," 103.
35. Dunne, "Evaluation," 14–15.
36. Quoted in *The New Yorker* XXXVIII (June 30, 1962), 26.
37. Harris Wofford, "Report on a New Frontier," March 11, 1961, pp. 2, 3, Box 298, Chester Bowles Papers, Yale University, New Haven, CT.
38. Bergthold Interview. For Wofford's world view, see Harris Wofford, *It's Up to Us* (New York, 1946); Clare and Harris Wofford, *India Afire* (New York, 1951); Wofford, "The World as Our Question," February 1, 1962, Box 298, Bowles Papers; Harris Wofford OH Interview, JFKL; and Wofford, *Of Kennedys and Kings*.
39. George H. Dunne, "Letter," in Boyer, ed., "Ethiopia I," p. 173, PC-FOIA.
40. Addis Ababa to Secretary of State, September 7, 1962, PC-FOIA.
41. John Coyne, "A Cool Breeze for Evening," manuscript, n.d., p. 13, Coyne Papers; Tsongas, "Address," 1.
42. Coyne, "A Cool Breeze," *ibid.*, author's interviews with John Coyne, August 15, 1987 and Anne Martin, August 8, 1987; "Anne Martin" is a pseudonym; this volunteer wished to remain anonymous; Bergthold interview.
43. Tsongas, "Address," 2. For more on volunteer activities, see American Embassy, Addis Ababa, to DS, September 26, 1962, PC-FOIA; John Rex to family, September 12, 1962, John Rex Papers, Williamsville, NY.
44. Martin, Bergthold, and Coyne interviews.
45. Selassie and Wofford are quoted in *Ethiopia Herald,* September 21, 1962, Martha Stonequist Papers, Saratoga, NY.
46. Wofford, "Report," 4.
47. For biographical information on the Ethiopia volunteers, see "The Funny Book," Georgetown University Archives.
48. John Rex, "Why Stay?: A Point of View," March 12, 1964, pp. 1–2.
49. Martin interview.
50. Reynolds interview.
51. Author's interview with Lynn and Mary Lou Linman, August 10, 1987. See also Mary Lou Linman, "How About Ethiopia?" manuscript,

Linman Papers, Visalia, CA; author's interview with Ron Kazarian, August 12, 1987.

52. Author's interviews with Coyne and Reynolds.

53. John Rex, "Report on Debre Berhan," October 5, 1962, p. 2; author's interviews with Coyne and Reynolds.

54. Reynolds interview.

55. Ron Kazarian to family, October 3, 1962, Ron Kazarian Papers, Fowler, CA.

56. Mary Lou Linman, "Haile Mariam Mammo," manuscript.

57. John Rex to family, October 1, 1962; see also Lynn and Mary Lou Linman to Friends, January 4, 1963.

58. Mary Lou Linman, "Teaching in Ethiopia," manuscript, p. 2.

59. Bob Savage to family, October 5, 1962, Robert Savage Papers, Cebu, Puerto Rico.

60. Rex to family, October 1, 1962.

61. Martin interview; see also Mary Lou Linman, "Peace Corps Teacher," manuscript, p. 1.

62. John Rex to family, October 12, 1962.

63. *Ibid.*

64. John Rex to family, October 14, 1962.

65. Ron Kazarian to family, October 3, 1962.

66. John Rex to family, October 30, 1962.

67. Rice, *Bold Experiment,* 167–170.

68. Rex to family, October 22, 1962; "Funny Book" entries on Debre Berhan volunteers; Martin and Mary Lou Linman interviews.

69. John Rex to family, October 24, 1962; Bob Savage to family, October 26, 1962.

70. Savage to family, *ibid.;* Ron Kazarian to family, October 24, 1962; Lynn and Mary Lou Linman to Vold family, October 25, 1962; Linman to Friends, January 4, 1963.

71. Reynolds interview.

72. Martin and Reynolds interviews; author's interview with Marian Haley Beil, August 12, 1987.

73. Reynolds and Martin interviews; Mary Lou Linman to Wylda Vold, n.d. (but 1962).

74. Linman to Vold, *ibid.;* John Rex to family, October 31, 1962.

75. Coates Redmon, *Come as You Are* (New York, 1986), 160; see also John Coyne, "A View from the Rear of the Room," *Volunteer* magazine.

76. Martha Stonequist to family, November 3, 1962.

77. Bergthold interview.

78. Stonequist to family, November 3, 1962.

79. John Rex to family, November 3, 1962.

80. *Ibid.*

81. John Rex to family, November 9, 1962; John Rex to family, December 3, 1962; Ron Kazarain to Joyce, November 14, 1962.

82. Ron Kazarian to family, November 7, 1962; interview with Robert Savage, August 11, 1987.

83. Ron Kazarian to family, November 29, 1962.

84. On activities: Linmans, Martin, Reynolds, Savage, and Rex interviews; author's interview with Ron Kazarian, August 12, 1987; John Rex to family, November 22, 1962.

85. John Rex to family, December 3, 1962.

86. *Ibid.*

87. Ron Kazarian to family, December 15, 1962.

88. John Rex to family, December 11, 1962.

89. Lynn and Mary Lou Linman to Linman family, December 18, 1962; Lynn and Mary Lou Linman to Vold family, December 21, 1962; Rex to family, December 27, 1962; Ron Kazarian to family, December 28, 1962.

90. Kazarian to family, December 28, 1962.

91. Rex to family, December 27, 1962; Kazarian to family, December 28, 1962.

92. Quoted in Warren Wiggins to Peace Corps Representatives, January 17, 1963, PC-FOIA.

93. Wofford, "Report," 23.

94. John Rex to family, January 17, 1963.

95. "Anonymous," Ethiopia I, #16, Harar, March 6, 1963 in *PCVs Report, Volume 1, Letters from East Africa,* Peter Gessell Papers, Cambridge, MA; Wofford, "Report," 18.

96. Martha Stonequist to Mother and Dad, January 17, 1963.

97. Malcom Donald to Minister of Education, January 28, 1963, enclosure with Harris Wofford to Ato Gebre-Meskal Keflezi, January 22, 1963, PC-FOIA; see also volunteer comments on "methodology," in "Condensation of Subject Group Reports," 6–11, enclosure Wofford to Keflezi.

98. "Condensation of Subject Group Report," 17–18; see also Wofford, "Report," 20–21.

99. Rex to family, January 17, 1963; Lynn and Mary Lou Linman to Linman family, January 20, 1963.

100. Rex to Gammy, January 29, 1963; Rex to family, January 31, 1963; Rex to family, February 16, 1963; Rex to family, February 26, 1963; Rex to family, March 7, 1963; Lynn and Mary Lou Linman to Friends, July 15, 1963.

101. Ron Kazarian to family, May 6, 1963; Kazarian interview.

102. Kazarian to family, May 6, 1963; Kazarian, Rex, Reynolds, Martin, Beil, Savage, and Linmans interviews.

103. Martin interview; Linman to friends, July 15, 1963.

104. Ron Kazarian to family, May 15, 1963; John Rex to family, May 9, 1963; Linman to friends, July 15, 1963; Rex, "Why Stay?," 3; Beil, Reynolds, Martin, Rex, Savage, Linmans, and Kazarian interviews.

105. Kazarian to family, May 15, 1963; Kazarian and Savage interviews.

106. Rex to family, May 9, 1963.

107. Linman to friends, July 15, 1963; Kazarian to family, May 16, 1963; Kazarian to family, May 21, 1963; Rex, "Why Stay?," 3.

108. Reynolds, Savage, Rex, Martin, Beil, and Linman interviews.

109. John Rex to family, May 22, 1963; Kazarian to family, May 21, 1963; Linman to friends, July 15, 1963; Martin, Reynolds, Savage, Kazarian, Linmans, and Beil interviews.

110. Martin and Kazarian interviews.

111. Kazarian to family, May 16, 1963; Kazarian interview.

112. Rex, "Why Stay?," 4.

113. Kazarian, Savage, Reynolds, and Martin interviews.

114. Rex, "Why Stay?," 3; John Rex to Stephanie Rex, June 3, 1963; Linman to friends, July 15, 1963.

115. Reynolds interview.

116. John Rex to family, May 30, 1963.

117. Kazarian to family, June 2, 1963; Rex, "Why Stay?," 3; Kazarian interview.

118. Martin and Kazarian interviews; Rex, "Why Stay?," 3, 4.

119. John Rex to family, September 22, 1963; Martin and Beil interviews.

120. John Rex to Gammy, September 30, 1963; Savage and Kazarian interviews.

121. Lynn and Mary Lou Linman to Vold family, October 20, 1963.

122. John Rex to family, October 21, 1963.

123. Lynn and Mary Lou Linman to Vold family, December 1, 1963.

124. Lynn and Mary Lou Linman to friends, General Letter #4, May 1964.

125. John Rex to family, November 26, 1963.

126. Linda and Gary Bergthold to family, November 25, 1963; Carolyn Wood to Mother, November 23, 1963, Carolyn Wood Kneedler Papers, Palo Alto, CA. For reactions of Peace Corps volunteers worldwide to the death of President Kennedy, see "Small Staff Meeting," November 26, 1963, Files of Bill Moyers, LBJL; Redmon, *Come,* 391–394.

127. Bergthold, *ibid.;* Rex to family, November 26, 1963; Linman to Linman family, November 25, 1963.

128. John Rex to family, January 30, 1964; John Rex to family, May 14, 1964.

129. John Rex to family, April 23, 1964; Rex to family, January 30, 1964.

130. Mary Lou Linman, "Termination of Service Conference," 2.

131. *Ibid.,* 5.

132. Jane Campbell, "Completion of Service Conference Report— Ethiopia 1," p. 6, PC-FOIA.

133. *Ibid.,* 17, 11–12.

134. *Ibid.,* 1–2.

135. *Ibid.,* 19–20; Linman, "Termination," 9–10.

136. John Rex to family, June 5, 1964.

137. John Rex to family, March 9, 1964.

138. *Ibid.*

139. John Rex to family, July 14, 1964; Rex to family, July 11, 1964.

140. Rex to family, July 11, 1964.

141. *Ibid.*

142. Quoted in Kenneth W. Thompson, ed., *The Kennedy Presidency* (Lanham, MD, 1985), 23.

143. Wofford, "Report," 30.

144. Reynolds interview.

145. Paul Koprowski, letter, May 1964, Paul Koprowski Papers, La Jolla, CA.

146. Bennett and Carroll, "Ethiopia Overseas Evaluation Report," 6, 10.

147. Savage interview.

148. Arthur M. Schlesinger, Jr., *Robert Kennedy and His Times* (Boston, MA, 1978), 440, 441.

149. Wofford, "Report," 15.

150. Reynolds, Kazarian, Linmans, Martin, and Savage interviews. For details on the post-Peace Corps lives of the volunteers, see Boyer, ed., "Ethiopia I—Ten Years After."

151. "1987 Peace Corps Ethiopia Reunion," audio tape.

Selected Bibliography

Manuscript Sources, Oral Histories, and Government Reports

See the notes in this book for references to collections in the John F. Kennedy Library (Boston, MA), Dwight D. Eisenhower Library (Abilene, KS), and the Lyndon B. Johnson Library (Austin, TX), as well as for papers and oral histories in other archives and depositories. Also see the notes for government reports and publications.

Bibliographies

Burns, Richard D., ed. *A Guide to American Foreign Relations Since 1700* (1982).
Crown, James T. *The Kennedy Literature* (1968).
Newcomb, Joan I. *John F. Kennedy* (1977).
U.S. Library of Congress, *John Fitzgerald Kennedy, 1917–1963* (1964).

Books and Articles Attributed to John F. Kennedy as Author

Why England Slept (1940).
"Foreign Policy Is the People's Business," *New York Times Magazine,* August 8, 1954, pp. 5ff.
Profiles in Courage (1956).
"A Democrat Looks at Foreign Policy," *Foreign Affairs* XXXVI (October 1957), 44–59.
"If India Falls," *The Progressive* XXII (January 1958), 8–11.
The Strategy of Peace (1960) (Allan Nevins, ed.).
"Disarmament Can Be Won," *Bulletin of the Atomic Scientists* XVI (June 1960), 217–219.
"If the Soviets Control Space—They Can Control Earth," *Missiles and Rockets* VII (October 10, 1960), 12–13.

President John F. Kennedy's Public Statements

Public Papers of the Presidents, John F. Kennedy, 1961–1963 (1962–1964).

Memoirs, Diaries, and Studies by Kennedy Friends and 1960s Decisionmakers:

Attwood, William. *The Reds and the Blacks* (1967).
———. *The Twilight Struggle* (1987).
Ball, George W. *The Past Has Another Pattern* (1982).
Beam, Jacob D. *Multiple Exposure* (1978).
Berle, Adolf A. *Navigating the Rapids, 1918–1971* (1973).
Bohlen, Charles E. *Witness to History, 1929–1969* (1973).
Bowles, Chester. *Promises to Keep* (1971).
Bradlee, Benjamin C. *Conversations with Kennedy* (1975).
Bundy, McGeorge. "The History-Maker," *Massachusetts Historical Society: Proceedings* XC (1978), 75–88.
———. "The Presidency and the Peace," *Foreign Affairs* XLII (April 1964), 353–365.
Burns, James MacGregor. *John F. Kennedy: A Political Profile* (1960).
Cline, Raymond S. *Secrets, Spies, and Scholars* (1976).
Exner, Judith. *My Story* (1977).
Fay, Paul B., Jr. *The Pleasure of His Company* (1966).
Galbraith, John Kenneth. *A Life in Our Times* (1981).
———. *Ambassador's Journal* (1969).
Goodwin, Richard. *Remembering America: A Voice from the Sixties* (1988).
———. "Reflections," *The New Yorker* XLIV (January 4, 1969), 38–58.
Guthman, Edwin. *We Band of Brothers* (1971).
Guthman, Edwin, and Jeffrey Schulman, eds., *Robert Kennedy in His Own Words* (1988).
Hilsman, Roger. *To Move a Nation* (1967).
Kennan, George F. *Memoirs, 1950–1963* (1972).
Kennedy, Robert F. *Thirteen Days* (1969).
Lincoln, Evelyn. *My Twelve Years with John F. Kennedy* (1965).
Lodge, Henry Cabot. *As It Was* (1976).
Manchester, William. *Portrait of a President* (1967).
McNamara, Robert S. *The Essence of Security* (1968).
O'Brien, Lawrence. *No Final Victories* (1974).
O'Donnell, Kenneth P., and David F. Powers. *"Johnny, We Hardly Knew Ye"* (1972).
Rostow, Walt W. *Eisenhower, Kennedy, and Foreign Aid* (1985).
———. *The Diffusion of Power* (1972).
———. *View from the Seventh Floor* (1964).
Salinger, Pierre. *With Kennedy* (1966).
Schlesinger, Arthur M., Jr. *A Thousand Days* (1965).
———. "The Alliance for Progress: A Retrospective," in Ronald G. Hellman and H. Jon Rosenbaum, eds., *Latin America: A Search for a New International Role* (1975), 57–92.
———. *The Cycles of American History* (1986).
———. *Robert Kennedy and His Times* (1978).
Seaborg, Glenn T., and Benjamin S. Loeb. *Kennedy, Khrushchev, and the Test Ban* (1981).

Sorensen, Theodore C. *Decision-Making in the White House* (1964).
————. *Kennedy* (1965).
————. *The Kennedy Legacy* (1969).
Taylor, Maxwell D. *Swords and Plowshares* (1972).
Thompson, Kenneth W., ed. *The Kennedy Presidency* (1985).
Williams, G. Mennen. *Africa for the Africans* (1969).
Wofford, Harris. *Of Kennedys and Kings* (1980).

Other Autobiographical Works, United States and Foreign

Adenauer, Konrad. *Erinnerungen 1959–1963* (1978).
Ayub Khan, Mohammed. *Friends Not Masters* (1967).
Brandt, Willy. *People and Politics* (1978).
Bhutto, Zulfikar Ali. *The Myth of Independence* (1969).
de Gaulle, Charles. *Memoirs of Hope: Renewal and Endeavor* (1971).
Diefenbaker, John G. *One Canada* (1975–1977).
Donovan, Hedley. *Roosevelt to Reagan* (1985).
Dulles, Allen. *The Craft of Intelligence* (1963).
Eisenhower, Milton S. *The Wine Is Bitter* (1963).
Fleming, Donald M. *So Very Near* (1985).
Franqui, Carlos. *Family Portrait with Fidel* (1984).
Humphrey, Hubert. *The Education of a Public Man* (1976).
Johnson, Lyndon. *The Vantage Point* (1971).
Kirkpatrick, Lyman. *The Real CIA* (1968).
Khrushchev, Nikita. *Khrushchev Remembers* (1970).
Krock, Arthur. *Memoirs* (1968).
Macmillan, Harold. *At the End of the Day, 1961–1963* (1973).
Martin, Paul. *A Very Public Life* (1983–1985).
Morrison, Delesseps S. *Latin American Mission* (1965).
Pearson, Lester B. *Mike* (1972–1977).
Rovere, Richard H. *Arrivals and Departures* (1976).
Smith, Joseph B. *Portrait of a Cold Warrior* (1976).
Sulzberger, Cyrus L. *The Last of the Giants* (1970).
White, Theodore H. *In Search of History* (1978).

The Kennedys, the Kennedy Presidency, and Their Times: General

Barber, James D. *The Presidential Character* (1977).
Beck, Kent M. "The Kennedy Image: Politics, Camelot, and Vietnam," *Wisconsin Magazine of History* LVIII (Autumn 1974), 45–55.
Brauer, Carl M. *Presidential Transitions* (1986).
Burner, David. *John F. Kennedy and a New Generation* (1988).
Burner, David, and Thomas R. West. *The Torch Is Passed* (1984).
Carleton, William C. "Kennedy in History: An Early Appraisal," *Antioch Review* XXIV (Fall 1964), 277–299.
Chafe, William H. *The Unfinished Journey* (1986).
Clinch, Nancy G. *The Kennedy Neurosis* (1973).
Cohen, Warren I. *Dean Rusk* (1980).
Collier, Peter, and David Horowitz. *The Kennedys* (1984).

Davis, John H. *The Kennedys* (1984).
Decter, Midge. "Kennedyism,' *Commentary* XLIX (January 1970), 19–27.
Fairlie, Henry. *The Kennedy Promise* (1973).
Goodwin, Doris Kearns. *The Fitzgeralds and the Kennedys* (1987).
Halberstam, David. *The Best and the Brightest* (1972).
Heath, Jim E. *Decade of Disillusionment* (1975).
Lasky, Victor. *J.F.K.: The Man and the Myth* (1963).
Leuchtenburg, William E. *In the Shadow of FDR* (1983).
Lichtenstein, Nelson, ed. *Political Profiles: The Kennedy Years* (1976).
Martin, Ralph G. *A Hero for Our Time* (1983).
Matusow, Allen J. *The Unraveling of America* (1984).
"The Meaning of the Life and Death of John F. Kennedy," *Current*, No. 45
    (January 1964), 6–42.
Miroff, Bruce. *Pragmatic Illusions* (1976).
Neustadt, Richard E. *Presidential Power* (1976).
Paper, Lewis J. *The Promise and the Performance* (1975).
Parmet, Herbert. *Jack: The Struggles of John F. Kennedy* (1983).
———. *JFK: The Presidency of John F. Kennedy* (1983).
Schoenbaum, Thomas J., *Waging Peace and War: Dean Rusk in the Truman,
    Kennedy, and Johnson Years* (1988).
Sidey, Hugh. *John F. Kennedy, President* (1964).
Snyder, J. Richard, ed. *John F. Kennedy: Person, Policy, Presidency* (1988).
Solberg, Carl. *Hubert Humphrey* (1984).
Whalen, Richard J. *The Founding Father: The Story of Joseph P. Kennedy*
    (1964).
Wicker, Tom. *JFK and LBJ* (1968).
Wills, Garry. *The Kennedy Imprisonment* (1981).

John F. Kennedy's Foreign Policy: General

Ambrose, Stephen A. *Rise to Globalism* (1985).
Barnet, Richard J. *Intervention and Revolution* (1968).
———. *Roots of War* (1972).
Betts, Richard K. *Soldiers, Statesmen, and Cold War Crises* (1977).
Blaufarb, Douglas S. *The Counterinsurgency Era* (1977).
Divine, Robert A. "The Education of John F. Kennedy," in Frank Merli and
    Theodore A. Wilson, eds., *Makers of American Diplomacy* (1974).
Eckhardt, William, and Ralph K. White. "A Test of Mirror-Image Hypothe-
    sis: Kennedy and Khrushchev," *Journal of Conflict Resolution* XI (Sep-
    tember 1967), 325–332.
FitzSimons, Louise. *The Kennedy Doctrine* (1972).
Gaddis, John Lewis. *Strategies of Containment* (1982).
Gromyko, Anatolii A. *Through Russian Eyes: President Kennedy's 1036
    Days* (1973).
Gurtov, Melvin. *The United States Against the Third World* (1974).
Hartley, Anthony. "John Kennedy's Foreign Policy," *Foreign Policy*, No. 4
    (Fall 1971), 77–87.
Henry, John B., and William Espinosa. "The Tragedy of Dean Rusk," *For-
    eign Policy*, No. 7 (Fall 1972), 166–189.

Kateb, George. "Kennedy as Statesman." *Commentary* XLI (June 1966), 54–60.
Kern, Montague, Patricia W. Levering, and Ralph B. Levering. *The Kennedy Crises: The Press, the Presidency, and Foreign Policy* (1983).
LaFeber, Walter. *America, Russia, and the Cold War, 1945–1984* (1985).
Mahajani, Usha. "Kennedy and the Strategy of Aid: The Clay Report and After," *Western Political Quarterly* XVIII (December 1965), 656–668.
Martin, John B. *Adlai Stevenson and the World* (1977).
Packenham, Robert A. *Liberal America and the Third World* (1973).
Ranelagh, John. *The Agency: The Rise and Decline of the CIA* (1986).
Paterson, Thomas G. "Bearing the Burden: A Critical Look at JFK's Foreign Policy," *Virginia Quarterly Review* LIV (Spring 1978), 193–212.
Prados, John. *Presidents' Secret Wars: CIA and Pentagon Covert Operations Since World War II* (1986).
Walton, Richard J. *Cold War and Counterrevolution* (1972).
Wiegele, Thomas C., et al. *Leaders Under Stress* (1985).

Nuclear Arms Race and Defense

Art, Robert J. *The TFX Decision: McNamara and the Military* (1968).
Ball, Desmond. *Politics and Force Levels: The Strategic Missile Program of the Kennedy Administration* (1980).
Dean, Arthur. *The Test Ban and Disarmament* (1969).
Dick, James C. "The Strategic Arms Race, 1957–1961: Who Opened a Missile Gap?," *Journal of Politics* XXXIV (November 1972), 1062–1110.
Enthoven, Alain C., and K. Wayne Smith. *How Much Is Enough?* (1971).
Firestone, Bernard J. *The Quest for Nuclear Stability: John F. Kennedy and the Soviet Union* (1982).
Halperin, Morton H. *Nuclear Fallacy* (1987).
Herkin, Gregg. *Counsels of War* (1985).
Kahan, Jerome. *Security in the Nuclear Age* (1975).
Kaplan, Fred. *The Wizards of Armageddon* (1983).
Kaufman, William. *The McNamara Strategy* (1964).
Licklider, Roy E. "The Missile Gap Controversy," *Political Science Quarterly* LXXXV (December 1970), 600–615.
Mandelbaum, Michael. *The Nuclear Question* (1979).
Powaski, Ronald A. *March to Armageddon* (1987).
Rosenberg, David A. "Power and Responsibility: Power and Process in the Making of United States Nuclear Strategy, 1945–68," *Journal of Strategic Studies* IX (March 1986), 43–50.
Steinbruner, John D. *The Cybernetic Theory of Decision* (1974).
Yanarella, Ernest J. *The Missile Defense Controversy* (1977).

Economic Foreign Policy

Block, Fred. *The Origins of International Economic Disorder* (1977).
Boswell, Terry, and Albert Bergesen, eds. *America's Changing Role in the World-System* (1987).

Calleo, David P. *The Imperious Economy* (1982).
Calleo, David P., and Benjamin Rowland. *America and the World Political Economy* (1973).
Cohen, Benjamin, ed. *American Foreign Economic Policy* (1968).
Evans, John W. *The Kennedy Round in American Trade Policy* (1971).
Harris, Seymour E. *Economics of the Kennedy Years and a Look Ahead* (1964).
McCormick, Thomas. " 'Every System Needs a Center Sometime': An Essay on Hegemony and Modern American Foreign Policy," in Lloyd C. Gardner, ed., *Redefining the Past* (1986), 195–220.
Preeg, Ernest. *Traders and Diplomats* (1970).
Roosa, Robert. *The Dollar and World Liquidity* (1968).
Rowen, Hobart. *The Free Enterprisers* (1964).
Triffin, Robert. *The World Money Maze* (1966).
Wallerstein, Immanuel. *The Politics of the World-Economy* (1984).

Europe and Berlin Crisis

Calleo, David P. *Beyond American Hegemony* (1987).
Catudal, Honoré. *Kennedy and the Berlin Wall Crisis* (1980).
Cate, Curtis. *The Ides of August: The Berlin Wall Crisis, 1961* (1978).
Costigliola, Frank. "The Failed Design: Kennedy, de Gaulle, and the Struggle for Europe," *Diplomatic History* VIII (Summer 1984), 227–251.
———. " 'Like Children in the Darkness': The Impact on Europe of the Assassination of John F. Kennedy," *Journal of Popular Culture* XX (Winter 1987), 115–124.
Harrison, Michael M. *The Reluctant Ally: France and Atlantic Security* (1981).
Hoffmann, Stanley. *Decline or Renewal?* (1974).
Kissinger, Henry A. *The Troubled Partnership* (1965).
Kleiman, Robert. *Atlantic Crisis* (1964).
Kraft, Joseph. *The Grand Design* (1962).
Kubricht, A. Paul. "Politics and Foreign Policy: A Brief Look at the Kennedy Administration's Eastern European Diplomacy," *Diplomatic History* XI (Winter 1987), 55–65.
Lacouture, Jean. *De Gaulle* (1986).
Newhouse, John. *De Gaulle and the Anglo-Saxons* (1970).
Nunnerly, David. *President Kennedy and Britain* (1972).
Schick, Jack M. *The Berlin Crisis, 1958–1962* (1971).
Slusser, Robert. *The Berlin Crisis of 1961* (1973).
Smith, Jean Edward. *The Defense of Berlin* (1963).
Taber, George M. *John F. Kennedy and a Uniting Europe* (1969).

Canada

Bothwell, Robert, et al. *Canada Since 1945* (1981).
Ghent, Jocelyn. "Canada, the United States, and the Cuban Missile Crisis," *Pacific Historical Review* XVIII (May 1979), 159–184.

————. "Did He Fall or Was He Pushed? The Kennedy Administration and the Fall of the Diefenbaker Government," *International History Review* I (April 1979), 246–270.

Granatstein, J. L. *A Man of Influence: Norman A. Robertson and Canadian Statecraft, 1929–68* (1981).

————. *Canada 1957–1967* (1986).

Lyon, Peyton. *Canada in World Affairs, 1961–63* (1968).

McLin, Jon B. *Canada's Changing Defense Policy, 1957–1963* (1967).

Newman, Peter C. *Renegade in Power: The Diefenbaker Years* (1963).

Latin America and the Alliance for Progress

Alba, Víctor. *Alliance Without Allies: The Mythology of Progress in Latin America* (1965).

Hanson, Simon G. *Dollar Diplomacy Modern Style* (1970).

LaFeber, Walter. *Inevitable Revolutions: The United States in Central America* (1983).

Langley, Lester D. *The United States and the Caribbean in the Twentieth Century* (1985).

Leacock, Ruth. "JFK, Business, and Brazil," *Hispanic American Historical Review* LIX (November 1979), 636–673.

Levinson, Jerome, and Juan de Onís. *The Alliance That Lost Its Way* (1970).

Lieuwen, Edwin. *Generals vs. Presidents: Neo-Militarism in Latin America* (1964).

Lowenthal, Abraham F. "United States Policy Toward Latin America: 'Liberal,' 'Radical,' and 'Bureaucratic' Perspectives," *Latin American Research Review* VIII (Spring 1974), 3–25.

Rabe, Stephen G. *Eisenhower and Latin America: The Foreign Policy of Anticommunism* (1988).

Roett, Riordan. *The Politics of Foreign Aid in the Brazilian Northeast* (1972).

Schoultz, Lars. *Human Rights and United States Policy Toward Latin America* (1981).

Van Cleve, Jonathan V. "The Latin American Policy of President Kennedy: A Reexamination Case: Peru," *Inter-American Economic Affairs* XXX (Spring 1977), 29–44.

Cuba: Bay of Pigs, Missile Crisis, and Covert War

Allison, Graham. *Essence of Decision* (1971).

Bernstein, Barton J. "The Cuban Missile Crisis: Trading the Jupiters in Turkey," *Political Science Quarterly* XCV (Spring 1980), 97–125.

Blasier, Cole. *The Hovering Giant* (1976).

Detzer, David. *The Brink* (1979).

Dinerstein, Herbert. *The Making of a Missile Crisis: October 1962* (1976).

Domínguez, Jorge. *Cuba: Order and Revolution* (1978).

Draper, Theodore. *Castroism* (1965).

Garthoff, Raymond L. *Reflections on the Cuban Missile Crisis* (1987).
Gromyko, A. A. "The Caribbean Crisis." *Soviet Law and Government* XI (No. 1, 1972), 3–53.
Halperin, Maurice. *The Rise and Decline of Fidel Castro* (1972).
———. *The Taming of Fidel Castro* (1981).
Higgins, Trumbull. *The Perfect Failure* (1987).
Morley, Morris. *Imperial State and Revolution: The United States and Cuba, 1952–1987* (1987).
Nathan, James. "The Missile Crisis," *World Politics* XXVII (January 1975), 256–281.
Paterson, Thomas G., and William J. Brophy. "October Missiles and November Elections: The Cuban Missile Crisis and American Politics, 1962," *Journal of American History* LXXIII (June 1986), 87–119.
Pérez, Louis A., Jr. *Cuba: Between Reform and Revolution* (1988).
Powers, Thomas. *The Man Who Kept the Secrets* (1979).
Sagan, Scott D. "Nuclear Alerts and Crisis Management," *International Security* IX (Spring 1985), 106–122.
Schulz, Donald E. "Kennedy and the Cuban Connection," *Foreign Policy,* No. 26 (Spring 1977), 57–139.
Szulc, Tad. *Fidel* (1986).
Vandenbroucke, Lucien S. "Anatomy of a Failure: The Decision to Land at the Bay of Pigs," *Political Science Quarterly* XCIX (Fall 1984), 471–491.
Welch, Richard E., Jr. *Response to Revolution* (1985).
Wyden, Peter. *Bay of Pigs* (1979).

The Middle East

Ajami, Fouad. "The End of the Affair: An American Tragedy in the Arab World," *Harper's* CCLXVIII (June 1984), 253–263.
Badeau, John S. *The American Approach to the Arab World* (1968).
Burns, William J. *Economic Aid and American Policy Toward Egypt, 1955–1981* (1985).
Engler, Robert. *The Brotherhood of Oil* (1976).
Gazit, Mordechai. *President Kennedy's Policies Toward the Arab States and Israel* (1983).
Glassman, Jon. *Arms and the Arabs: The Soviet Union and War in the Middle East* (1975).
Kenen, Isaiah L. *Israel's Defense Line: Her Friends and Foes in Washington* (1981).
Kerr, Malcolm. *The Arab Cold War: Abd-al Nasir and His Rivals 1958–1970* (1971).
Kuniholm, Bruce. "Retrospect and Prospects: Forty Years of U.S. Middle East Policy," *Middle East Journal* XLI (Winter 1987), 7–25.
Little, Douglas. "New Frontier on the Nile: Kennedy, Nasser, and Arab Nationalism," *Journal of American History* (1988).
O'Ballance, Edgar. *The War in the Yemen* (1971).

Polk, William. *The United States and the Arab World* (1975).
Rubenberg, Cheryl. *Israel and the American National Interest* (1986).
Rubin, Barry. *Paved with Good Intentions: The American Experience and Iran* (1980).
Safran, Nadav. *Saudi Arabia: The Ceaseless Search for Security* (1985).
Spiegel, Steven. *The Other Arab-Israeli Conflict: Making America's Middle East Policy, from Truman to Reagan* (1985).
Stivers, William. *America's Confrontation with Revolutionary Change in the Middle East, 1948–83* (1986).
Stookey, Robert. *America and the Arab States* (1975).

China

Bachrack, Stanley. *The Committee of One Million* (1976).
Chang, Gordon. "JFK, China, and the Bomb," *Journal of American History* LXXIV (March 1988), 1287–1310.
Cohen, Warren I. *America's Response to China* (1980).
Dulles, Foster Rhea. *American Policy Toward Communist China, 1949–1969* (1972).
Gittings, John. *The World and China, 1922–1972* (1974).
MacFarquhar, Roderick ed. *Sino-American Relations, 1949–1971* (1972).
Thomson, James C., Jr. "On the Making of U.S. China Policy, 1961–1969: A Study in Bureaucratic Politics," *China Quarterly* L (April/June 1972), 220–243.
Van Ness, Peter. *Revolution and Chinese Foreign Policy* (1971).

South Asia

Barnds, William J. *India, Pakistan, and the Great Powers* (1972).
Brecher, Michael. "Non-Alignment Under Stress: The West and the India-China Border War," *Pacific Affairs* LII (Winter 1979–80), 612–630.
Burke, S. M. *Pakistan's Foreign Policy: An Historical Analysis* (1973).
Choudhury, G. W. *India, Pakistan, Bangladesh, and the Major Powers* (1975).
Gopal, Sarvepalli. *Jawaharlal Nehru: A Biography*, III: *1956–1964* (1984).
Graham, Ian C. C. "The Indo-Soviet MIG Deal and Its International Repercussions," *Asian Survey* IV (May 1964), 823–832.
Hitchman, James H. "Parry and Thrust: Eisenhower, the Soviet Union, and India, 1953–1961," *World Review* XXIV (April 1985), 11–24.
Irshad Khan, Shaheen. *Rejection Alliance: A Case Study of U.S. Pakistan Relations* (1972).
Jain, Rajendra K. *U.S.-South Asian Relations, 1947–1982* (1983).
Maxwell, Neville. *India's China War* (1970).
Singh, Mahendra. *Indo-U.S. Relations, 1961–64* (1982).
Tahir-Kheli, Shirn. *The United States and Pakistan* (1982).
Venkataramani, M. S. *The American Role in Pakistan, 1947–1958* (1982).
Wolpert, Stanley. *Roots of Confrontation in South Asia* (1982).

Vietnam

Duiker, William J. *The Communist Road to Power in Vietnam* (1981).
Gibbons, William C. *The U.S. Government and the Vietnam War* (1986).
Gelb, Leslie H., and Betts, Richard K. *The Irony of Vietnam* (1979).
Hammer, Ellen J. *A Death in November: America in Vietnam, 1963* (1987).
Herring, George C. *America's Longest War* (1986).
Kahin, George McT. *Intervention: How America Became Involved in Vietnam* (1986).
Kolko, Gabriel. *Anatomy of a War* (1985).
Pelz, Stephen. "John F. Kennedy's 1961 Vietnam War Decisions," *Journal of Strategic Studies* IV (December 1981), 356–385.
Race, Jeffrey. *War Comes to Long An: Revolutionarry Conflict in a Vietnamese Province* (1972).
Rust, William J. *Kennedy in Vietnam* (1985).
Selden, Mark. "People's War and the Transformation of Peasant Society: China and Vietnam," in Edward Friedman and Mark Selden, eds., *America's Asia* (1971), 357–392.
Smith, R. B. *An International History of the Vietnam War* (1983–1985).
Warner, Geoffrey. "The United States and the Fall of Diem," Part I: "The Coup That Never Was," *Australian Outlook* XXIX (December 1974), 245–258.
———. "The United States and the Fall of Diem," Part II: "The Death of Diem," *Australian Outlook* XXIX (March 1975), 3–17.

Africa

Brzezinski, Zbigniew, ed. *Africa and the Communist World* (1963).
Chester, Edward. *Clash of Titans* (1974).
Cotman, John W. "South African Strategic Minerals and U.S. Foreign Policy, 1961–1968," *Review of Black Political Economy* VIII (Spring 1978), 277–300.
Davidson, Nicol. "Africa and the U.S.A. in the United Nations," *Journal of Modern African Studies* XVI (September 1978), 365–395.
Davis, John. "Black Americans and United States Policy Toward Africa," *Journal of International Affairs* XXIII (No. 2, 1969), 236–249.
El Khawas, Mohamed A., and Francis A. Kornegay, eds. *American-Southern African Relations: Bibliographical Essays* (1975).
Howe, Russell. *Along the Afric Shore* (1975).
Howe, Russell W., and Sarah Hays Trott. *The Power Peddlers: How Lobbyists Mold American Foreign Policy* (1977).
Isaacman, Allen, and Jennifer Davis. "United States Policy Toward Mozambique Since 1945," *Africa Today* XXV (January–March 1978), 29–55.
Jackson, Henry F. *From the Congo to Soweto: U.S. Foreign Policy Toward Africa Since 1960* (1982).
Kalb, Madeleine. *The Congo Cables: The Cold War in Africa from Eisenhower to Kennedy* (1982).

Lefever, Ernest. *Uncertain Mandate: Politics in the UN Congo Operation* (1967).
Lamarchand, Rene, ed. *American Policy in Southern Africa* (1978).
Mahoney, Richard D. *JFK: Ordeal in Africa* (1983).
Marcum, John. "Lessons of Angola," *Foreign Affairs* LIV (April 1976), 407–425.
McKay, Vernon. *Africa in World Politics* (1963).
Nielsen, Waldemar. *The Great Powers and Africa* (1969).
Noer, Thomas J. *Cold War and Black Liberation: The United States and White Rule in Africa, 1948–1968* (1985).
———. "The New Frontier and African Neutralism: Kennedy, Nkrumah, and the Volta River Project," *Diplomatic History* VIII (Winter 1984), 61–80.
Shepherd, George W., ed. *Racial Influences on American Foreign Policy* (1970).
Weissman, Stephen. *American Foreign Policy in the Congo, 1960–1964* (1974).

The Peace Corps

Ashabranner, Brent A. *A Moment in History: The First Ten Years of the Peace Corps* (1971).
Hapgood, David, and Meridan Bennett. *Agents of Change* (1968).
Lowther, Kevin, and C. Payne Lucas. *Keeping Kennedy's Promise* (1979).
"The Peace Corps," *The Annals* CCCLX (May 1966), 1–146.
Redmon, Coates. *Come as You Are: The Peace Corps Story* (1986).
Rice, Gerard T. *The Bold Experiment: JFK's Peace Corps* (1986).
Textor, Robert B., ed. *Cultural Frontiers of the Peace Corps* (1966).
Viorst, Milton, ed. *Making a Difference: The Peace Corps at Twenty-five* (1986).

Index